709.02 P61

Comparative criticism

24

Fantastic currencies in comparative literature:
gothic to postmodern

Comparative criticism

An annual journal

Fantastic currencies in comparative literature: gothic to postmodern

with an Index to volumes 1–24

24

Edited by

E. S. SHAFFER

SCHOOL OF ADVANCED STUDY,
UNIVERSITY OF LONDON

CAMBRIDGE
UNIVERSITY PRESS

PUBLISHED BY THE PRESS SYNDICATE OF THE UNIVERSITY OF CAMBRIDGE
The Pitt Building, Trumpington Street, Cambridge, United Kingdom

CAMBRIDGE UNIVERSITY PRESS
The Edinburgh Building, Cambridge CB2 2RU, UK
40 West 20th Street, New York, NY 10011–4211, USA
477 Williamstown Road, Port Melbourne, VIC 3207, Australia
Ruiz de Alarcón 13, 28014 Madrid, Spain
Dock House, The Waterfront, Cape Town 8001, South Africa

http://www.cambridge.org

First published 2002

Printed in the United Kingdom at the University Press, Cambridge

A catalogue record of this book is available from the British Library

ISBN 0 521 81869 9
ISSN 0144 7564

SUBSCRIPTIONS *Comparative Criticism* (ISSN 0144-7564) is an annual journal. The subscription price (excluding VAT) to volume 24, 2002, which includes postage, is £75.00 (US $115.00 in USA, Canada and Mexico) for institutions, £36.00 (US $61.00 in USA, Canada and Mexico) for individuals ordering direct from the Press and certifying that the annual is for their personal use. EU subscribers (outside the UK) who are not registered for VAT should add VAT at their country's rate. VAT registered subscribers should provide their VAT registration number. Orders, which must be accompanied by payment, may be sent to a bookseller, subscription agent, or direct to the publishers: Cambridge University Press, The Edinburgh Building, Shaftesbury Road, Cambridge CB2 2RU, UK. Payment may be made by any of the following methods: cheque (payable to Cambridge University Press), UK postal order, bank draft, Post Office Giro (account no. 571 6055 – advise CUP of payment), international money order, UNESCO coupons, or any credit card bearing the Interbank symbol. Orders from the USA, Canada and Mexico should be sent to Cambridge University Press, Journals Fulfillment Department, 110 Midland Avenue, Port Chester, NY 10573–4930, USA. Japanese prices for institutions are available from Kinokuniya Company Ltd. P.O. Box 55, Chitose, Tokyo 156, Japan. Prices include delivery by air.

BACK VOLUMES Volumes 1–23 (1979–2001) are available from the publisher at £75.00 (US $115.00 in the USA, Canada and Mexico). Back volumes are available to individuals, paying direct to Cambridge and stating that the volume is for their personal use only, at the current individual rate. Postage and packing charges will be made for orders outside the UK.

CONTENTS

ILLUSTRATIONS

CONTRIBUTORS

DAME GILLIAN BEER is King Edward VII Professor of English Literature at the University of Cambridge. Her most recent books are *Open Fields: Science and Cultural Encounter* (1996), *Virginia Woolf: the Common Ground* (1996) and the second edition of *Darwin's Plots* (2000). She is at present finishing a study of Lewis Carroll's Alice books in the context of Victorian intellectual controversies.

ZBIGNIEW BIAŁAS is Professor of English and Head of the Colonial and Postcolonial Studies Centre at the University of Silesia, Poland; he is also Privatdozent at Essen University, Germany. From 1995 to 1997 he was Alexander von Humboldt Research Fellow in Germany and in 2001 he was Fulbright Senior Fellow in the USA. He is the author of three books: *Post-Tribal Ethos in African Literature* (Essen 1993), *Mapping Wild Gardens* (Essen 1997) and *The Body Wall* (forthcoming in 2002), editor/co-editor of five other volumes, and translator of English, American and African fiction into Polish.

FANFAN (FENG FANG) CHEN is Assistant Professor of English at the National Dong Hwa University in Taiwan. She specializes in Chinese and Western fantastic literature narratology. 'French Modernity and the Transformation of Fantastic Discourse' will be published in *Chung Wai Literary Monthly* (Chinese and Foreign Literature). She is also engaged in a research project on 'The Metamorphosis of Fantastic Fiction', sponsored by the National Scientific Council of Taiwan.

IAN CHRISTIE is Professor of Film and Media History at Birkbeck College and previously taught film at Oxford and the University of Kent. He has published mainly on Russian and British cinema, and has contributed to a number of major exhibitions. As former head of distribution at the British Film Institute, he has a continuing interest in the vicissitudes of European cinema. He is currently preparing a study of the British moving picture pioneer Robert Paul.

YVES CITTON is Associate Professor in French at the University of Pittsburg, Pennsylvania. He has published *Portrait de l'économiste en physiocrate: critique littéraire de l'économie politique* (Paris: L'Harmattan, 2000), *Impuissances: défaillances masculines et pouvoir politique de Montaigne à Stendhal* (Paris: Aubier, 1994) and *Les doctrines orthographiques du XVIe siècle en France*, with André Wyss (Geneva: Droz, 1989). He has also published articles on Rousseau, Condillac, Charrière and the Physiocrats. He is currently working on the neo-Spinozist tradition from Diderot to Deleuze.

PAUL COATES is Reader in Film Studies in the School of English and Film Studies of the University of Aberdeen, Scotland. His books include *The Story of the Lost Reflection: the Alienation of the Image in Western and Polish Cinema* (Verso, 1985), *The Double and the Other* (Macmillan, 1988), *The Gorgon's Gaze: German Cinema, Expressionism and the Image of Horror* (Cambridge University Press, 1991) and *Film at the Intersection of High and Mass Culture* (Cambridge University Press, 1994). He edited *Lucid Dreams*, a collection of essays on Kieslowski, for Flick Books (1999), and his *Through a Glass Darkly: Cinema, Religion and Spirituality* is forthcoming from Ashgate in 2002.

BRIAN COLE studied French and German at Oxford, and worked as a senior executive in three multinational groups. After retirement he started Brindin Press. His translation of Pablo Neruda's *The Captain's Verses* was published by Anvil Press in 1994. In 2000 Arc Publications published *Anthracite*, a selection of translations from the Italian of Bartolo Cattafi, and in 2001 Brindin Press published his translations of Circe Maia, *Yesterday a Eucalyptus*. The latter two works were Poetry Book Society Recommended Translations.

NEIL CORNWELL, Professor of Russian and Comparative Literature, University of Bristol, is editor of the *Reference Guide to Russian Literature* (Fitzroy Dearborn, 1998) and the author of two books on Vladimir Odoevsky, as well as translator of Odoevsky's *The Salamander and Other Gothic Tales* (Bristol Classical Press and Northwestern University Press, 1992). Among his other books are *The Literary Fantastic* (Harvester, 1990) and, most recently, *Vladimir Nabokov* (Writers and Their Works Series, Northcote House, 1999). He is currently editing *The Routledge Introduction to Russian Literature* and researching a general study of the absurd.

MARGARET ANNE DOODY is John and Barbara Glynn Family Professor of Literature at the University of Notre Dame, where she is currently

Director of the PhD Program in Literature. She has written a number of books, including *Frances Burney: the Life in the Works* (1988) and *The True Story of the Novel* (1996). The second novel in her 'Aristotle Detective' series, *Aristotle and Poetic Justice*, will be published in England in May. She is working on another 'Aristotle' detective novel as well as on a book about Venice, and a study of Apuleius.

ANNE GUÉRIN-CASTELL, director and film editor, teaches film at the University of Paris VIII and at the University François Rabelais in Tours, and is an instructor at the National Audiovisual Institute. In January 1998 she submitted a doctoral thesis in Aesthetics, Sciences and Art Technologies (specializing in cinema) at Paris VIII, on 'The Place of the *Saragossa Manuscript* in the Cinematic Œuvre of Wojciech Jerzy Has'.

CHARLIE LOUTH is Fellow in German at the Queen's College, Oxford, and has published *Hölderlin and the Dynamics of Translation* (1998). He is currently translating Hölderlin's letters.

CIRCE MAIA is a Uruguayan poet, born in 1932, widely known in South America but little known in Europe. She has been a teacher of philosophy and languages and has written and published several volumes of poetry. Her latest collection is *de lo invisible* (Montevideo, 1998).

SILVESTER MAZZARELLA taught English at Helsinki University in Finland, and translates prose, verse and drama into English from Italian and Swedish. His latest book, edited and translated from Finland-Swedish, is *The Poet Who Created Herself: Selected Letters of Edith Södergran* (Norvik Press, 2001). At present, he is translating contemporary Italian plays and researching and writing a life of his great-uncle, the author and journalist Filson Young.

A. D. NUTTALL taught for many years at the University of Sussex, where he was Professor of English and Pro-Vice-Chancellor. He is now a Fellow of New College and Professor of English Literature in the University of Oxford. His books include *Overheard by God* (1980), *A New Mimesis* (1983), *Why does Tragedy Give Pleasure?* (1996), and *The Alternative Trinity* (1998).

AGNETA PLEIJEL was born in Stockholm in 1940 and is a full-time writer. Her first novel was published in 1987. *Lord Nevermore*, her fifth novel, came out in 2000 and has so far won four awards in Sweden.

FRANÇOIS ROSSET, is Director of Studies and Research at the University of Lausanne. He is the author of many publications on eighteenth-century French literature and the Enlightenment in French-speaking Switzerland. His latest books are *L'Arbre de Cracovie. Le mythe polonais dans la littérature française* (Paris: Imago, 1996), *De Varsovie à Saragosse: Jean Potocki et son Œuvre* with Dominique Triaire (Louvain and Paris, Peeters, 2000); *Ecrire à Coppet: nous, moi et le monde* (Geneva: Slatkine, 2001); with Dominique Triaire he is editor of the complete French edition of Jan Potocki's works.

NINA TAYLOR-TERLECKA lectures on Polish Literature at the University of Oxford and at the Polish University Abroad. She specializes in Polish Romantic Drama, Polish writers from the former Grand Duchy of Lithuania, and Gulag and émigré literature. Most recent publications include an anthology of Polish Gulag poetry *Gulag polskich poetów. Od Komi do Kōymy. Wiersze* (London: PFK, 2001), a survey of literary doppelgangers ('Des Dioscures à Medardus – Goliadkine – Medrado et Martin Guerre – une typologie est-elle possible?' in *Figures du double dans les littératures européennes*, Paris: L'Age d'Homme, 2001) and a study of Polish Heimat literature ('Le Mythe de la petite patrie' in *Mythes et symboles en Europe Centrale*, Presses Universitaires de France, 2002); her book translations include works by Jarosław Rymkiewicz and Janusz Anderman.

DOMINIQUE TRIAIRE is Professor at the University of Montpellier III. He works on French cultural relations with eastern Europe in the eighteenth century. His many publications on Jan Potocki include an edition of his complete works, which he is editing with François Rosset.

ACKNOWLEDGEMENTS

Thanks are due to Eric Liknaitzky and Contemporary Films for access to the original publicity stills from *The Saragossa Manuscript* which appear in this volume.

Thanks are due to the Museo del Prado, Madrid, for permission to reproduce the engraving by Francisco de Goya, *El sueño de la razon produce monstruos*, for the frontispiece to the volume, and to the Muzeum Narodowc, Warsaw, for the portrait of Count Stanislas Potocki by Jacques-Louis David. We are grateful to the Cambridge University Library for supplying prints of these images.

Any permissions relating to Agneta Pleijel's *Lord Nevermore* and Circe Maia's poems have been obtained by their respective translators.

Francisco de Goya, 'The sleep of reason produces monsters'

Comparative Criticism 24, pp. xv–xxv. © 2002 Cambridge University Press
DOI: 10.1017/S0144756402005632   Printed in the United Kingdom

EDITOR'S INTRODUCTION

Fantastic currencies in comparative literature: gothic to postmodern

Comparative literary studies just after the millennium deal, as does the world, in fantastic currencies, past and present, and in possible futures. Gillian Beer's thoughtful meditation on 'currency' opens the proceedings, and together with Margaret Anne Doody's comprehensive overview of fiction, from *Daphnis and Chloe* to *Roger Ackroyd*, in its reflections on the multifarious forms of 'possession' that characterize the novel as genre, and A. D. Nuttall's essay on 'gold and iron', successfully set the stage not only for the conference on 'Money' held in 2001 but also for our special issue on the rediscovered European masterpiece, Jan Potocki's novel, *The Manuscript Found in Saragossa* (1797–1815), published in full in French only in 1989. The novel is a time-traveller which unlike most finds its own time.

It is fitting that the twenty-fourth volume of this journal, whose first volume appeared in 1979, should raise the curtain in English on this masterpiece of comparative European fiction, written in French in the Revolutionary period between 1797 and 1815 by a cosmopolitan Polish writer who combined the Enlightenment and the nascent Romantic modes, and enacted the struggle of reason and passion, of scepticism and strange undercurrents of belief that geometrical thinking could not after all stamp out. His own life seemed to participate in the change of sensibility, for he began as an enlightened aristocrat, who served as an army officer, fought bandits in Sicily, wrote court plays, carried on private research into the history and chronology of the early Slav peoples (in which he is a recognized pioneer), and played a considerable role in the government of the Polish nation, until in 1802 it lost its independence and its name under Russian domination; then, after working for the Russians for a time, he returned to his estate and wrote on his extraordinary novel, fell prey to fantasies, and finally died by his own hand like a young Romantic poet. The story of his death is operatic, combining both styles: he melted down a piece of household silver (variously described as a samovar and a handle), made it into a silver bullet, had it blessed by the priest, and then used it to commit an act not countenanced by the Church. It is a story worthy of his own fiction. Nina Taylor-Terlecka here gives us a full account of Potocki's illustrious family and his roots in the Polish and European Enlightenment.

Potocki published in his lifetime the first section, in St Petersburg in 1805, and other fragments (*Dix Journées de la vie d'Alphonse van Worden*) in 1813 in Paris, as well as leaving several versions (including one for the censors) at his death. A Polish translator made a version from one of these in 1847, while the French fragments were exploited by imitators. There is a long and complex history of the translations in whole and in part from the various extant versions. Rediscovered by the notable French critic Roger Caillois, who edited a short version (about a quarter of the whole) in 1958, with an excellent introduction to the second edition of 1967, the *Manuscript* began a new and circuitous route to full publication in French via a translation from a German version based on the Polish translation (1989), followed by a new French version based on manuscripts extant in Poland; the best edition is now the 1995 edition in Livre de Poche. The fantastical history of the manuscript of the *Manuscript* seems to parallel the novel, which opens with the discovery of the manuscript, written and buried seventy years earlier, by a young Napoleonic soldier during the Spanish campaign of 1808–9.

A *roman philosophique* in picaresque mode, full of argument and witty disputation, but also a gothic novel carrying the seeds of Romanticism, it has a large cast of characters centring round the young, inexperienced *Bildungsroman* hero Alphonse van Worden. Goethe's *Wilhelm Meister* (1795), the acclaimed model of what later became known as the *Bildungsroman* or novel of education, was undoubtedly one of the starting-points for the novel. The large cast includes a *philosophe* (Velásquez, a sympathetic figure whose geometrical reasoning is nevertheless always stymied, to both comic and tragic effect), van Worden's father, an aristocrat fanatical about points of honour that culminate in disastrous duels; a gypsy king, Zoto, who has some of the best stories; a subtle cabbalist and his daughter; the Wandering Jew (who as an eye-witness, condemned never to die, gives a pungent running commentary on European history since Rome ruled Palestine); and an Islamic equivalent to Goethe's *Turmgesellschaft*, or Brotherhood of the Tower, the group who secretly guide the hero's education; and in addition, from the realm of the undead, vampires, hanged bandits, the Inquisition, ghosts and houris or succubi who haunt the living.

Since the landmark publication of 1989 the novel has been translated into Italian, German, Spanish and English. In 1995 came the breakthrough into English, with Ian Maclean's translation (Viking) and publication in Penguin Classics the next year. A number of appreciative reviews appeared, recognizing the book as a lost masterpiece, and Maclean's translation was also widely praised. Maclean, a Renaissance French specialist at All Souls College, Oxford, was given credit for making the intricate book and its complex discourses available in lucid, flexible and well-shaped English prose. The most substantial reviews were by P. N. Furbank in the *London Review of Books* ('Nesting Time', 26 Jan. 1995) and John Weightman in the *New York Review of Books* ('Extravaganza in Progress', 30 Nov. 1995). Both gave searching attention to the work as a major rediscovery of European fiction, and between the two of them they suggested an impressive set of antecedents and influences and by implication placed Potocki in their ranks: Voltaire, Diderot, especially *Jacques le Fataliste*, published in 1798, itself an offspring of Sterne, and Le Sage (author of both *Gil Blas* and *Le Diable boîteux*). While they of course see the *Arabian Nights*, translated into French in 1700 and used as a model for a variety of *contes morales* (and *immorales*) through the century, often presented as emanating from distant, often oriental sources, as essential to the form of successive spell-binding stories, they strangely omit to mention *Don Quixote*, whose unfolding stories within stories told by different characters are closer to Potocki. *Don Quixote*, now voted the greatest of all novels by writers and critics, is the right comparison; for Potocki does for his era what Cervantes did for his, combining the major genres and playing off the opposed tendencies of the age, in Cervantes's case the idealist Romance and the realist picaresque, in Potocki's the claim to enlightened reason and the resurgence of the irrational, against each other. Several critics mention Potocki's interest in the style of Mrs Radcliffe, well-known in Europe since 1790, but seek comparisons with bigger game in the pantheon of established authors.

Other reviews were by Jonathan Coe, Salman Rushdie, Valentine Cunningham and David Coward; all the major dailies and literary weeklies carried at least a short notice. A number pointed to the 'modern' and indeed 'postmodern' quality of Potocki's work: it had finally found its own time. Cunningham, calling the novel a 'striptease machine', compared it with contemporaries as weighty as the professors of French had found in the past: Eco, Joyce, Calvino 'or even' Borges, and said it finds a 'happy niche in our post-modernist sensibility'

(Valentine Cunningham, 'Stories to stimulate desire', *Observer*, 5 Feb. 1995). James Woodfall (a Borges specialist) goes even further in ensconcing it in a twentieth-century theoretical framework, praising it as 'a truly useless book, a book of Barthesian *"jouissance"* if ever there was one'. If only Barthes had come across it, and left an interpretation, he suggests, it would long ago have achieved 'cult status' ('A Polish Casanova', *The Times*, 2 Feb. 1995). Whatever historical vantage point the critic adopts, Potocki's novel has both impressive traditional credentials and a powerful appeal to our own time. It is noteworthy that the critics stressed the most elevated predecessors and most intellectually ambitious of contemporaries, playing down the undoubted debt of Potocki also to the Gothic vogue of the 1790s, reflected in the subplot of 'a group of Moors' and the corrupt Spanish Inquisition drawn from Lewis's *The Monk*, and a number of allusions to Mrs Radcliffe, especially *The Sicilian Romance*, which began her vogue, and *The Romance of the Forest*. It is part of Potocki's achievement that he incorporated the extremes of eighteenth-century thought and feeling, from rational conceptualizing of abstract ideas to the wild rebellion of feeling and emotion, and melded the genres of the 'high' and the 'low'. In fact, this rich novel acts as a kind of compendium and summing up of the major tendencies in the history and fiction of the century.

In May 1998 I organized a Colloquium on 'Jan Potocki, *Le Manuscrit trouvé à Saragosse*: Novel and Film' at the School of Advanced Study, University of London. The film of the novel had preceded the novel on the European circuit, becoming known in the 1960s through a considerably cut and dubbed French version of the Polish original. Salman Rushdie, among others, including myself, remembers seeing it in Cambridge in the 1960s, and hails the rediscovery of the original fiction, which he had been intrigued by at the time. On the occasion of the London Colloquium we held the first showing of the full Polish version of the noted director Wojciech Has's film, with a simultaneous translation from the original. In this volume we bring the revised and extended versions of the papers given on that occasion, together with a number of newly commissioned or translated papers.

Nina Taylor-Terlecka's fascinating account of Potocki's life in the context of his Polish milieu places him in the Enlightenment tradition of his aristocratic eighteenth-century education (largely in Switzerland and in French), against the background of major Polish writers too little known in English. She explores his complex relation to the French *philosophes* (his early and inescapable mentors) and to Napoleon, in the fraught context of the Polish struggle to assert its own nationhood, a struggle which ended in 1802 with the hegemony of Russia.

Neil Cornwell places Potocki in the context of the powerful German and Eastern European tradition of 'the Nuits', or Nights. Here he stresses not the Enlightenment but the Romantic associations of Potocki, with the important German Romantics such as Novalis, and the strange, anonymous novella *Die Nachtwachen des Bonaventura*, Nightwatches of Bonaventura, as well as with the less familiar Russian Romantic Vladimir Odoevski, whose 'Nights' formed a significant link to later writers such as Dostoevski and Mann. Potocki's ability to command the styles both of the Enlightenment reasoners, sceptics and ironists and of the Romantic sense for the complex, dark and irrational, give him a unique pivotal place in the European novel, and create the powerful intellectual and emotional tensions represented in his fiction.

François Rosset, one of Potocki's major critics and advocates in Europe, gives a deft treatment of an essential theme of the novel, the manuscript or book itself. Zbigniew Białas traces the erotic intricacies of the narrative of the *Manuscript*.

Dominique Triaire, whose knowledge of Potocki is unrivalled, his critical works among the most insightful and subtle, supplies a fine analysis of the forms of humour in Potocki, including the whole gamut from theatrical comedy of manners and character (Potocki also wrote plays), to philosophical dialogues in the ironic mode of Diderot, the black gallows humour of his own country, and the romantic irony of Schlegel. His insight is so acute that we are given the movement of thought in Potocki's intertwined episodes, his grasp of the comic possibilities inhering in genres not intended to be comic, as well as overtly comic incident or witty sallies. The subtleties of his analysis of Potocki's rhetoric can be fully grasped only by the reader already intimately acquainted with the novel, and are not easily translated; but we are grateful to Charlotte Pattison for her gallant effort. (A French version of this essay may be found in François Rosset and Dominique Triaire, 'L'Effet comique dans le *Manuscrit trouvé à Saragosse*', *De Varsovie à Saragosse: Jean Potocki et son œuvre* (Louvain, Paris, Sterling, Virginia: Editions Peeters, 2000), pp. 235–52.)

A substantial new paper by Yves Citton explores the 'postmodern' aspects of Potocki's fiction in theoretical and generical detail. This is a contribution to the literature on 'postmodern fiction' as well as to Potocki studies, and gives some solid grounding to the immediate instinct of today's reviewers to place the new 'find' in a current context.

Fanfan Chen, comparing the French and the Chinese definitions and practice of the 'fantastic', and more broadly their respective modes of presenting the supernatural, goes further afield, and in so doing sheds light on Potocki's early nineteenth-century practice and that of his imitators. Charles Nodier, one of the major practitioners of the mode of the fantastic in its heyday in France, was a major and unacknowledged admirer and plagiarist from Potocki, whose work thus had an unacknowledged presence in major writings in this vein throughout the century. Roger Caillois, the French critic who made Potocki's reputation in France in the twentieth century, republishing him in part in 1958, setting in motion his complete recovery, pointed out that Potocki had long lived a subterranean life in the nineteenth-century French classics through Nodier's borrowings. Chen traces the 'aesthetics of the fantastic' through Nodier, Balzac, Gautier and Merimée. The American writer Washington Irving was also a notable borrower from Potocki. It is Nodier, though, who in employing Potocki's mode of construction, whereby one fantastic story prepares the reader to credit its amplification and heightening in another and another, draws closest to the Chinese practice of opening the door to the supernatural world with one impossible event and then moving on without explanation to another on the same higher plane.

The film of the *Manuscript Found in Saragossa* has led an independent life, and an exciting one, which three papers chart for us. It gained recognition and circulation in art houses in the 1960s in a shortened, French-dubbed, version, at a time when the complete novel was not available. When we set out in 1997 to hold a Colloquium on Potocki in London it cost us a great deal of effort to locate the complete Polish version of the film (some 80 minutes longer than the French) and a translation of it. The film version was sent on a video taken from a recent television broadcast in Poland (thanks to Zbigniew Białas and Alexandra Podgorniak of the University of Silesia); a translation of it was found neglected and only after repeated inquiry deep in the archives of the British Film Institute. The BFI had hoped to release a new version of the film to cinemas, but had not received the funding to do so. The translation, originally supplied by the Polish Film Bureau, was unidiomatic and clumsy. For the showing of the entire film in Polish at the British Film Institute Studio, which formed the second day of the Colloquium, we had the good fortune to find a simultaneous translator of long experience, Natalie van Svolkien, Russian by birth but a long-time resident in Poland, who was able to interpret the material persuasively. Later, just after the Colloquium, we located an American company that had reissued the film on video; on receiving it we discovered that the same clumsy translation had been transferred word for word onto the film as subtitles, where they were often overlong, interfered with the images, and were incomprehensible, sometimes running off the screen. This brilliant film deserves and, it must be hoped, will still obtain a new release in a full-length English-language version, as well as in other languages.

Ian Christie's discussion of the historical or 'costume' drama in the European film contemporary with Has's film sets the wider stage. Paul Coates, a specialist in Polish and German literature, as well as film, examines the political framework in which Has had to work in the Poland of the 1960s. Anne Guérin-Castell, who in her French dissertation has given the most extended and detailed treatment of the complex history of the film versions of the *Manuscript*, here gives us a succinct account of the full-length version as related to the novel and its subsequent cut versions. Guérin-Castell makes a strong if still controversial case for there having been not one but two different cut versions at the hands of the Polish censors.

Although the text of the novel is now widely available, and it has been selling very well, nearly all the critical work on Potocki has been in French, whether in France, Switzerland, or in Poland, where the French departments of Polish universities led the way. This volume of *Comparative Criticism* marks the critical breakthrough into English, seven years after Maclean's translation. To give an overview of the complex history of the editions and translations, and of the critical work to date, we are particularly pleased to be able to publish a comprehensive bibliography of Jan Potocki's work, the first in English, contributed by the leading French-language specialist in Potocki's critical reception and his French bibliographer, François Rosset (Lausanne). We are also indebted to others who have helped make the bibliography still more comprehensive: to Teresa Iribarren and Adelaida Martin-Valverde for the Spanish and Catalan editions and critical reception; and to Viking books, who made available the early reviews of Ian Maclean's translation into English. We hope this volume will be only the first of a number of publications on Potocki in English. The current vogue for work on the gothic should alone ensure attention to Potocki's novel, an encyclopedia of gothic modes current in the eighteenth and early nineteenth centuries. But beyond any current vogue it merits a place among the significant European novels of the last three centuries.

* * *

Our Translation section celebrates another complex and fantastical feat of translation. Charlie Louth's essay describes the extraordinary eighteenth-century German Biblical translator, Johann Jacob Junckherrott, whose translation of the New Testament (1732) went against all the prevailing canons of translation to try to capture the supra-human 'style of the Holy Spirit'. Ignored in his time, he nevertheless anticipated the shift in translation theory and practice that brought forward the practice of the 'difficult' reading that made manifest the foreign origin of the language rather than domesticating it. Only in this way, the poet Hölderlin and the theorist Schleiermacher would argue in the early nineteenth century, could the quality of the original be suggested and the target language enriched and extended. We have previously been concerned with this vital shift in translation theory and practice, in the Editor's introduction to volume 6, Jeremy Adler's translation of Hölderlin's essays on Greek tragedy (in volume 7), David Constantine's translation into English of Hölderlin's brilliant version of Sophocles's *Oedipus* (in volume 20) and Charlie Louth's translation in volume 21 of the twentieth-century Viennese sound-poet Ernst Jandl's essay on translation (together with Michael Hamburger's translations of Jandl's virtually untranslatable sound-poems matching his earlier translation of the sound-poet's radio play, in volume 9). The bibliography on literary translation by Louis Kelly in volume 6, contrasted to his bibliography on technical translation in volume 13, marks the awareness of a different set of translation problems and solutions in the new scientific age.

The BCLA/BCLT Annual Translation Competition winners for this year are also announced in this volume. They were first publicly announced in September 2001 at the annual two-day event held by the BCLT at the South Bank Centre where the Translators' Association prizes are also announced and the St Jerome Lecture on Translation is given. We are delighted to announce in print and to publish the winner of the First Prize, Silvester Mazzarella, for a chapter of Agneta Pleijel's novel *Lord Nevermore*, translated from the Swedish. Agneta Pleijel is well known for her poetry, some of which has been translated into English, and this beautifully nuanced opening chapter has many of the characteristics of poetry, making the translator's feat in rendering its subtleties of tone all the more impressive.

The Second Prize went to Brian Cole, who translated poems by Circe Maia from the Spanish, of which we publish a small selection here. Circe Maia is a well-known figure in Latin America, and her evocative poetic glimpses into the midst of the everyday are finely rendered by the translation.

The winning entries will also be published on the BCLA website from 2002. Inquiries and entries should be addressed to the British Centre for Literary Translation (BCLT), School of Languages and Linguistics, University of East Anglia, Norwich NR4 7TJ.

The Comparative Literature series of the LEGENDA imprint of the EHRC (European Humanities Research Centre, Oxford) continues to flourish. Two new volumes have appeared: Adam Czerniawski's translations of the Polish Renaissance poet Jan Kochanowski's *Treni*(*Laments*) (2001) (of which *Comparative Criticism* published Laments 5 and 14 in volume 19 from the translation of the *Laments* by Seamus Heaney and Stanislaw Baranczak, together with a review by George Gömöri); and Richard Serrano, *Neither a Borrower: Forging Traditions in French, Chinese and Arabic Poetry* (2002). Proposals for shorter critical studies, editions, or translations, as well as for theses and monographs, are welcome. Please write to any member of the Publications Committee: Professor Stephen Bann (Department of the History of Art, University of Bristol, Woodland Road, Bristol BS8 1TE), Professor Peter France (Department of French, University of Edinburgh, George Square, Edinburgh EH8 9JX), or Dr Elinor Shaffer (School of Advanced Study, University of London, Senate House, Malet Street, London WC1E 7HU). Orders for books may be placed with Mrs Kareni Bannister, at the European Humanities Research Centre, St Hugh's College, Oxford OX2 6LE or through its website, www.ehrc.ox.ac.uk.

It is an appropriate moment to recall the founding of this journal as the organ of the newly formed British Comparative Literature Association, which held its founding conference in 1975 at the University of East Anglia. In looking back over it the major fields of our concern are evident: to record and encourage the development of Comparative Literary studies in the UK, both institutional and scholarly; and to place it within the developing framework of international theoretical and critical studies, in a period of rapid change and intense debate. It has regularly published the plenary papers from the triennial Conference of the BCLA. Translation studies is one branch of comparative literature that has come to the fore over the period of our publication, and the translations themselves have provided readers with the possibility of extending their awareness of literary potentialities beyond the field of their first, second or third languages. Many of these have been winning entries in the annual British Comparative Literature Association Translation Competition, which only in the last five years joined hands with the BCLT (British Centre for Literary Translation) founded by the late Max Sebald to form the BCLA–BCLT Translation Competition. But many of the translations we have published were commissioned or submitted without reference to the competition. While Cambridge University Press does not normally publish creative writing as such, this journal has been concerned to provide the stuff of new perceptions as well as commentary on them. This journal also pioneered the Bibliography of Comparative Literature in Britain and Ireland, in order to highlight the scholarly and critical contribution of the United Kingdom to the international comparative literary community. Special bibliographies either of special subject areas or of the work of individuals (of which this volume adds an important example) have also been a feature of the journal.

It is also an occasion to express our thanks to the members of the Editorial Board, both the founder members, and the more recent additions, who have lent their names and their advice over many years. Some of the founders are among the departed: Northrop Frye, René Wellek, Peter Stern, J. W. McFarlane and Malcolm Bradbury; but their signal contributions to our subject live after them.

Thanks are owing to the Syndics of Cambridge University Press for their sustained support for this journal and to the staff of Journals. Successive production controllers, first Jill Walden, then Gwenda Edwards, have kept us on track in the nicest possible way. Special thanks are owing to our excellent sub-editors, and in particular Kay McKechnie, who has been a keen reader and tireless worker in the vintage fields of *Comparative Criticism*. Her level-headed good sense, her accuracy and her enthusiasm have been an unfailing resource. We are grateful to her also for compiling the Index of the first twenty-four volumes of the journal, which is included in this volume. I also thank my past Assistants, all of them Cambridge research students, many of them now eminent in their own right, and my current Assistant, Andrea Brady, who has also kindly agreed to help to assemble materials for the archiving of this journal after the appearance of volume 25.

We are pleased to announce that volume 25 of *Comparative Criticism* will be published by Edinburgh University Press in the autumn of 2004. Volume 25 will be on the theme of 'Lives of the Disciplines: comparative biography'. It will explore the art of biography in different, evolving disciplines, and address the challenges posed by writing biographies of individuals whose contributions are internal to their subject, whether that subject be mathematics, medicine, poetry, or music.

We are further pleased to announce that a new, successor journal will be published from 2005 by Edinburgh University Press which will absorb both BCLA journals, *Comparative Criticism* and the house journal *New Comparison*. The new journal, *Comparative Literary and Cultural Criticism*, appearing three times a year, will continue to feature themed issues, translation studies and translations, and will offer an expanded reviews section; one issue a year will feature Comparative Reception Studies, in conjunction with the multi-volume series on 'Critical Traditions: the Reception of British Authors in Europe' (Continuum Books), of which Elinor Shaffer is the General Editor. Association news, the full texts of prize-winners and commended entries in the annual BCLA–BCLT Translation Competition, and the Bibliography of Comparative Literary Studies in Britain and Ireland, will appear on the BCLA website at http://www.bcla.org. Further information and order forms are enclosed with the current volume. While we look back with gratitude and affection on our long association with Cambridge, we look forward with pleasure to our new association with Edinburgh University Press.

Elinor Shaffer

PART I

Fantastic currencies: money, modes, media

Comparative Criticism 24, pp. 3–13. © 2002 Cambridge University Press
DOI: 10.1017/S0144756402005425 Printed in the United Kingdom

Credit limit: fiction and the surplus of belief

GILLIAN BEER

Language is ever needing to be recalled, minted and issued anew, cast into novel forms.
(R. C. Trench, *The Use of Words*, 1858)

Money: an attractive topic, but there is a problem for the essayist. The essay is confined but money is everywhere, within literature and outside it.[1] Some writers have been direct about it: Bulwer Lytton wrote a play called *Money*, Philip Larkin a poem 'Money', Martin Amis a novel, *Money*. Some writers seemingly evade the topic until the crash comes, usually as a plotting deus ex machina: for example, Elizabeth Gaskell's *Cranford* with its serene and frugal surface suddenly collapsed by the breaking of the bank that brings about Miss Matty's ruin. Some writers concentrate money in the form of marriageability. Many sharpen its presence through its lack. And money manifests in life and in literature across a spectrum from the material to the entirely mental, from the small change of coins, with their weight often in inverse proportion to their power, through notes, bills, credit cards, to the increasingly invisible forms of IOUs: guarantees, mortgages, markets and futures.

My first defensive thought when considering this essay was to seek out a topic where money is not: money and solitude, perhaps. In complete solitude money has no function of exchange, nor – on the face of it – any useful function. First, find a location where money has no past, no material presence – no buildings, roads, mines, forests for felling – in fact, find a desert island. Take away all the electronic media and your bunch of credit cards, and even these most etherialized versions of money may lapse. The famous passage in *Robinson Crusoe* where the solitary castaway Crusoe returns to the shipwreck and removes all that can be of use to him – tools, clothes, a bible – reaches a laconic climax when he surveys the money left on board and addresses the coins in high and scornful style:

3

I found about thirty-six pounds value in money, some European coin, some Brazil, some pieces of eight, some gold, some silver.

I smiled to myself at the sight of this money. 'O drug!' said I aloud, 'what art thou good for? Thou art no worth to me, no, not the taking off of the ground; one of these knives is worth all this heap. I have no manner of use for thee; even remain where thou art, and go to the bottom as a creature whose life is not worth saving.' However, on second thoughts I took it away. (p. 72)[2]

Imperturbable in recording his contradictory impulses, as ever, Crusoe after his formal renunciation claims the money. By apostrophizing it – and scorning it 'as a creature whose life is not worth saving' – he in fact recognizes the life in it. The money will lie in wait. It is part of one possible future – that future for which overwhelmingly he hopes, in which he will return to human society and its need of coin. Coin is future life to Crusoe.

And moreover, the ship – even foundered – is a repository of the goods of the culture from which he has come, goods bought with the money of that culture: the past of exchange is locked in to objects and forms capital for his survival. Bare money may seem barren on such an island, but it still ingratiates a future.

That alliance of money with the future – multiple futures – is what I want to concentrate on in this argument. In the sober present, the power of money is limited:

> What riches give us let us then enquire:
> Meat, Fire, and Cloaths. What more? Meat, Clothes, and Fire.
> Is this too little? Would you more than live?[3]

'Yes', is the more or less universal answer to Alexander Pope's question 'Would you more than live?' The connection of money with desire, with surplus, and with what might be called a lateral immortality or the imagining of several possible future lives now, is what gives lustre and ferocity to the merely humdrum business of money. Or is that a description of its meaning for those secure in their finances? Meat, fire and clothes may well be the desperate matter of desire if you do not have enough of them. The link is in the longing, whether experienced through surplus or poverty. Wholesome contentment with a sufficiency is rarely the matter of fiction, indeed is perhaps even rarer in fiction than in ordinary life.

So imbalances, rather than equable exchange, provide the subjects of fiction, and the question of futures is as integral to the terminology of narrative as of the market.[4] Indeed, finance and fiction share a remarkable number of terms, many of them having to do with assessment and belief. 'Credit' is one powerfully generative shared term and for that reason I have chosen the close-to-home phrase 'credit limit' for my title. The Latin origin means to trust or believe and has sparked divergent adjunct words such as creditable (worthy) and credible (believable). Credit becomes immediately involved in questions of worthiness, and hence in circulatory systems such as conversation and gossip (I have written about those interactions elsewhere).[5]

The droll written disclaimer in small shops 'Please do not ask for credit as a refusal may cause offence' itself catches in a contingent future (the scene imagined and repudiated), which adds insistence to the request for a completed transaction: money safely exchanged, here and now. Credit is an exchange that includes a promise of performance from one side and a willingness to delay receipt from the other. It both brings the future into the present (purchase now) and wards off the present (payment) into the future. And the purchase of futures is one of the most active parts of the current financial market world-wide. In H. G. Wells's comic masterpiece *Tono-Bungay*, the first hint of his uncle's creative attitude to finance comes to the young narrator when he visits his uncle's chemist's shop:

a very ordinary chemist's window except that there was a frictional electrical machine, an air-pump and two or three tripods and retorts replacing the customary blue, yellow, and red bottles above. There was a plaster of Paris horse to indicate veterinary medicines among these breakables, and below were scent packets and diffusers and sponges and soda-water syphons and such-like things. Only in the middle there was a rubricated card, very neatly painted by hand, with these words

    Buy Ponderovo's Cough Linctus *Now*
    Now!
    Why?
    Twopence cheaper than in Winter.
    You store Apples! Why not the Medicine
    You are Bound to Need?[6]

The appeal to nature (You store Apples!) is a master-stroke, as is the fell assurance of your inevitable future winter cough. Ponderovo has already learnt the crucial move of the financier and the fiction-writer alike: guarantee future events whether or not they come to pass.

So far and no further: how far does your credit extend, in amount and in time? Something of the same question is implicit in the initial relation of reader to text: how far can we trust this writer? How fully do we believe? Isn't this taxing our credulity too far? Does this detail tell? Is the writer coining new words? Retailing or recounting improbable events? Is this character stamped sufficiently clearly? What does this episode lead us to speculate? Do we credit this account?

With greater or less vividness all the terms I have just cited are shared by finance and fiction (taxing, telling, coining, retailing, stamping, speculating, crediting, accounting). Moreover, in the Jewish and the Christian tradition we have become habituated to crucial concepts like redemption, a kind of inverse credit where the object must first be presented at the pawn-shop in exchange for cash and then may at a later date be redeemed for rather less cash. In theological usage reference to this somewhat graceless negotiation concentrates purely on the act of release: on grace. The process of release from debt – 'jubilee' in its biblical sense – is at the heart, for example, of Dickens's *Little Dorrit*, which merges the terms of the market and of grace at its conclusion.

So futures inhere in the way we think about money and about fiction. Near the end of *Middlemarch* Dorothea, seeking to break out of the prison of her wealth which is tied to an embargo on her marrying the man she loves, cries out to Will, offering herself: 'I will learn what everything costs.' This is a promise not only of domestic economy but of profound commitment, a willingness to search out and bear all the consequences of her desire. It carries the reader through and past the ending of the novel, offering an assurance that is not disappointed.

The actuarial skills of the reader are sometimes in conflict with those of the writer. Like an actuary, we measure probabilities and come to our own conclusions, sometimes rashly forgetting the final power of the writer to determine what will come. We speculate. We propose other futures, we hypothesize diverse possibilities as we read, not all of which are encompassed by the finished work. That, of course, is one of the generative pleasures of reading and one stimulated by skilled writers, who offer us hints, clues and forecasts that imply several different outcomes. Readers delight at once in believing and disbelieving: fraudulence and the surplus of belief are engaged at the level of both plot and reading process. The necessary creative disappointment of the ending of a fiction is that it enacts only one of the multiple futures it has conjured in the course of the story.

Fiction is fascinated by transformation and exchange. It is fascinated in particular by the irremediable incongruities in exchange: how rarely a full equivalent can be found in human bargains. The importunity of desire, the insufficiency of occasion, furnish many of the fundamental materials of story from Apuleius's *The Golden Ass* to Zola's *La Terre* with its horrific recognition that greed for land is a more physical form of greed for wealth and may drive to yet more ruthless crimes (the old man burnt alive). Barter is sometimes represented as an innocent form of exchange compared to coin, as being closer to produce and need; its innocence may be doubtful but what it certainly does do is acknowledge the inevitable *unlikeness* of what each receives from the other. Precisely the satisfaction of barter is that the exchange is between (say) cow and timber, and that the *difference* between needs is fully visible. This highlights the variety of individual and group identities and the futures they bring to the bargain.

Defoe is the English writer who most fully understands the psychic and social implications of money, in possession and in lack, for individual identity. He recognizes how identity depends not only on hand-to-mouth survival but on imagined futures for the self. He is matched in English only by a quite different writer, Henry James, beneath whose velleities the brute force of money curtails and controls human relations: excess of riches, lack of cash, each equally leads to foreclosed futures in *Portrait of a Lady*, *Wings of a Dove*, *The Golden Bowl*. James writes within the rhythms of privilege though he regards privilege exactingly. In each novel we watch the desperate ingenuity of characters who attempt to make futures that outwit the regime of the market. His characters' need for money seeps out of his sentences rather than appearing openly: the characters only hint lack, and they concentrate on other transformed states and objects – pictures, travel, houses – as the traffic through which they can express wealth and dearth.

Defoe, looking through his first-person characters from beneath, from the underworld of privation, observes how people produce justificatory fantasies that buoy up their right to money, equally with their right to identity. Moll Flanders is one of the great fabulators, endlessly inventing futures, personages, an entire theatre of blameworthy others:

I walked frequently out into the villages round the town to see if nothing would fall in my way there; and going by a house near Stepney, I saw on the window-board two rings, one a small diamond ring, and the other a plain gold ring, to be sure laid there by some thoughtless lady, that had more money than forecast, perhaps only till she washed her hands.

I walked several times by the window to observe if I could see whether there was anybody in the room or no, and I could see nobody, but still I was not sure. It came presently in my thoughts to rap at the glass, as if I wanted to speak with somebody, and if anybody was there they would be sure to come to the window, and then I would tell them to remove those rings, for that I had seen two suspicious fellows take notice of them. This was a ready thought. I rapped once or twice, and nobody came, when I thrust hard against the square of glass, and broke it with little noise, and took out the two rings, and walked away; the diamond ring was worth about £3, and the other about 9s.

Moll gains hard-denominated cash, but she conjures also a group of bit players so convincing that it is hard for the reader to disentangle these evoked presences from the bald facts of Moll stealing the rings: 'the thoughtless lady, that had more money than forecast' (i.e. foresight), and the 'two suspicious fellows' spring to life. The invention of the lady produces these further contingent beings, the supposed suspicious fellows who will come in handy only if someone comes to the window, which they do not. Time contracts and stretches in the fantasy of the passage even while it presses hard in, moment by moment, on Moll's predicament. The fictive personages secure Moll both from the reader's disapproval and from her own. They are forms of propitiation. They leave her intact, indeed justified, even a beneficent presence ready to save the invented lady from the consequences of her own slackness. The fantasy justification (which in the end she does not need since no one comes) leaves us ready to delight and to believe in Moll. Moll's own fictional status becomes invisible. The contingent unacted futures confirm the authenticity of the central event and objects: the diamond ring worth about £3 and the other about 9s become material under the aegis of these fantasies.

Defoe delights in the circumstantial, as in the list of the young pickpocket's trophies from Bartholomew Fair in *Colonel Jack*. What gives the objects their glamour for the reader is the fragments of snatched lives and moments they carry with them, for example:

1. 1. A white handkerchief from a country wench as she was staring up at a Jack-pudding; there was 3s 6d and a row of pins tied up in one end of it.
2. 2. A coloured handkerchief out of a young country-fellow's purse as he was buying a china orange.
   ...
3. 4. A knife and fork that a couple of boys had just bought and were going home with; the young rogue that took it, got it within the minute after the boy had put it in his pocket. (pp. 14–15)[7]

In this novel Defoe gives an account of the world through a child's eyes that is comic and touching at once. Jack has no parentage, no home; he lives by pickpocketing, which he thinks of as a trade, under the instruction of older and wilier men.

The authenticity of the telling of his story is indirectly vouched for – within the story – by the fact that he cannot 'tell' money. He cannot count, nor can he recognize guineas. This imputed circumstance makes him seem a credible and untarnished witness to his own life (though of course the whole is told through the pen of the adult Jack looking back on his young self, let alone the presence of the invisible author). The novel has an extraordinary sequence in which for the first time Jack is lumbered with a great deal of valuable cash that he doesn't know what to do with. He first holds it in his hand, but it is too unwieldy to carry far. He then puts it in his shoe 'but after I had gone awhile my shoe hurt me so, I could not go … then I found a dirty linen rag in the street, and I took that up, and wrapped it all together'. He dare not go back to the glasshouse where he sleeps with the other boys, lest they rob him, or suffocate him in the ashes, and he moralizes on the change that the possession of money has brought into his careless life. At last he finds a great hollow tree and drops the money in there for security. Secure indeed, since it plunges down into the body of the tree and cannot be reached. To our relief, it later emerges among the roots on the other side of the bank. And now Jack goes and for the first time in his life buys trousers for himself. The shop woman is kind to him. The sauntering progress of the negotiations described beautifully conjures his anxiety and eagerness for the breeches.

'Here is a good warm pair of breeches. I dare say,' says she, 'they will fit you, and they are very tight and good; and,' says she, 'if you should ever come to have so much money that you don't know what to do with it, here are excellent good pockets,' says she, 'and a little fob to put your gold in, or watch in, when you get it.'

It struck me with a strange kind of joy that I should have a place to put my money in, and need not go to hide it again in a hollow tree, that I was ready to snatch the breeches out of her hand.

And when at last they are Jack's, Defoe conjures the final example in the sequence of enclosures that Jack has discovered for his money: hand, shoe, rag, tree, pocket. And last, expanded in fantasy, coach:

So, in a word, I gave her two shillings for the breeches, and went over into the Church-yard and put them on, put money into my new pockets, and was as pleased as a prince is with his coach and six horses.

I was but a boy, 'tis true, but I thought myself a man now I had got a pocket to put my money in. (pp. 30–1)

The making and justifying of identity is a core concern in Defoe's fiction. The homeless child with two pockets in his breeches offers a charged image of security and possession, discovering surplus in poverty through the first experience of autonomy. The discovery of autonomy involves also the conjuring of futures, of fairytale and of excess: 'if you should ever come to have so much money that you don't know what to do with it, here are excellent good pockets,' says she, 'and a little fob to put your gold in, or your watch in, when you get it'.

Defoe delights in the process of transformation by which money gained and lost becomes goods and their vanishing. And since the whole of this circumstantial material world is expressed as words on the page he gains many of his effects by mental play: the setting of two possible sequences side by side; listing, with its euphoric endlessness; machinations, with their promise of indirect outcome; the making of the physical object out of language. Occasionally, he offers the reader absolute aesthetic pleasure, as the process of transformation from coin to object is performed. This he does once in *Captain Singleton* through the medium of gold. Heartsick at last with slaughter, Captain Singleton (Defoe's most pathologically debonair hero) and his companions in Africa find gold through the labour of the indigenous people they meet. The gold will in the future perhaps 'buy provisions' or 'even buy friendship, and the like'. They leave seven or eight pounds of it with the artificer to be worked and give 'about a pound to our black prince':

which he hammered and worked by his own indefatigable hand and some tools our artificer lent him, into little round bits as round almost as beads, though not exact in shape, and drilling holes through them, put them all upon a string, and wore them about his black neck, and they looked very well there, I assure you; but he was many months a-doing it. (p. 87)

Gold becomes work, becomes coin, becomes decoration, and – retaining all its states at once – is laid around the prince's dark neck.

Stealing, bartering, inveigling, persuading, Defoe's characters on the edge of society and just outside the law re-perform their tricks with us, making the reader collude and rejoice, and credit their adventures. Although they commit many frauds, fraud is not a term that surfaces in these novels because it is not a word the first-person narrators ever apply to themselves. This makes for a stable composition, unpersuaded of its own fictionality, drawing on a surplus of belief.

In contrast, H. G. Wells lets the reader delight in the instability of the fraudulent and the ruthlessness of the fraudulent imagination:

'there's Corners!'
'They're rather big things, aren't they?' I ventured.
'Oh, if you go in for wheat or steel – yes. But suppose you tackled a little thing, George. Just some leetle thing that only needed a few thousands. Drugs for example.

…. ,

'Lord! There's no end of things – no end of *little* things. Dill-water – all the suff'ring babes yowling for it. Eucalyptus again – cascara – witch hazel – menthol – all the toothache things. Then there's antiseptics, and curare, cocaine …'

'Rather a nuisance to the doctors,' I reflected.

'They got to look out for themselves. By Jove, yes. They'll do you if they can, and you do them. Like brigands. That makes it romantic. That's the Romance of Commerce, George. (p. 66)

The narrator and his uncle imagine cornering quinine and end up almost cornering a more sinister substance, remarkably up-to-date for the moment of the novel's publication and prophetic of much that was to come in the twentieth century: Wells's invented mineral 'quap' is radioactive (only three years after radioactivity was discovered):

So it was quap came into our affairs, came in as a fairy-tale and became real. More and more real it grew until at last it was real, until at last I saw with my eyes the heaps my imagination had seen for so long and felt between my fingers again the half-gritty, half-soft texture of quap, like sanded moist-sugar mixed with clay in which there stirs something –

One must feel it to understand. (p. 218)

The reader is promised understanding and excluded from understanding at once. Again, that disconcerting impression of something alive, not fully to be controlled, which here expresses the relation of the market to the characters, as well as the substance itself that they have uncovered on a remote island. The future market (and futures market) they have imagined at the outset of the novel moves in to crush them before its end. Wells allows the book to play on the edge of fantasy without grounded commitment from the reader, despite its social realist surface. The belief he here invites is in the stupendous oddity of the financial order of the world where wealth can make any absurd thing happen:

So much came to us that it seemed to me at times as though the whole world of human affairs was ready to prostitute itself to our real and imaginary millions. As I look back, I am still dazzled and incredulous to think of the quality of our opportunities. We did the most extraordinary things; things that it seems absurd to me to leave to any casual man of wealth and enterprise who cares to do them. I had some amazing perceptions of just how modern thought and the supply of fact to the general mind may be controlled by money. (p. 218)

The phantasmal futures imagined and briefly put in place by his main characters make for vertigo rather than full credence. But they also seem alarmingly, after nearly a century has passed, in line with the market events of the twentieth century. The story stretches credit. It outgoes its limit.

Popular songs give mixed messages about money: 'Money is the root of all evil', 'What do you want if you don't want money', 'Money can't buy you love.' Money has magical properties: it can transform itself into buildings or bombs, scholarship or sensuality. Can it transform itself into love? That is one question to which literature repeatedly returns. Can it transform itself into belief? That is another. Is there a radical asymmetry between money and such human drives? Establishing that asymmetry seems indeed often to be the hoped-for outcome, suggesting as it does a de-limiting of money's supremacy. Keats counters that assuaging thought with asperity at the opening of *Lamia*:

> Love in a hut, with water and a crust,
> Is – Love, forgive us! – cinders, ashes, dust.

The works I have cited offer a chilling possibility: that money does make belief and is at the very least the necessary condition for love's continuance into the future.

Perhaps I should end with a common experience that most will recognize, which simply recalls how closely money is bound to fantasies of the future and of identity: as I got on the train from Cambridge to London recently, with *Colonel Jack* in my bag and thinking about this essay, I discovered that my credit cards and bank cards were not in my purse. Instantly both the immediate past and the immediate and slightly longer future became disagreeably vivid. Where had I left the cards and how could I manage an overnight stay in London without them? – a hotel to pay, no access to cash, a lecture to give. Had I met pickpocketing Colonel Jack unawares? Unlikely. Worse, how was I to explain myself? Was I indeed still entirely me? – vitiated, light-headed, shrivelled, incapacitated, with a humiliating flurry of explanations and excuses forming themselves for the hotel, I had a bad quarter of an hour (and an uneasy twenty-four hours). Most striking to me was the unwilled rush of alternative stories, outcomes and possibilities that crowded my mind. And this episode was just the result of a foolish oversight, the cards left behind, not a continuing condition of dearth. The heroic self-belief of Defoe's unsupported characters came home fully to me, and the grandiose self-invention of Ponderovo. Both Defoe and Wells were interested in the human capacity for survival, not simply physical endurance but survival on our own terms, as worthy, as creditable: worthy of being believed in. That accounts for the celebratory temper of their books as well as for the credit we are inclined to give their first-person storytellers, always speculators in a difficult futures market.

NOTES

1 Jonathan Williams (ed.), *Money: a History* (London: British Museum Press, 1997).

2 Daniel Defoe, *The Life and Adventures of Robinson Crusoe* (Oxford: World's Classics, 1950), p. 72; first published 1719.

3 Alexander Pope, 'Moral Essays: Epistle to Bathurst', *The Poems of Alexander Pope*, ed. John Butt (London: Methuen, 1963) p. 575; first published 1733.

4 I pursue this in relation to narrative in 'Storytime and its Futures', in Katinka Ridderbos (ed.), *Time* (Cambridge: Cambridge University Press, 2002), pp. 126–42.

5 Gillian Beer, 'Circulatory Systems: Money, Gossip, and Blood in *Middlemarch*', *Arguing with the Past: Essays in Narrative From Woolf to Sidney* (London: Routledge, 1989), pp. 99–116.

6 H. G. Wells, *Tono-Bungay* (London: Penguin, 1946), p. 52; first published 1909.

7 Daniel Defoe, *The History and Remarkable Life of the Truly Honourable Colonel Jack* (London: Hamish Hamilton, 1947); first published 1722.

Comparative Criticism 24, pp. 15–36. Cambridge University Press 2002
DOI: 10.1017/S0144756402005437 Printed in the United Kingdom

In possession: person, money and exchange from *Daphnis and Chloe* to *Roger Ackroyd*

MARGARET ANNE DOODY

Prose fiction is intimately related to money. I don't mean that authors get money for their productions – though that has been a subject at times of contention and disapproval. Without 'the commodification of culture', the literary marketplace, there might never have been anything that we recognize as a novel, ancient or modern. Certainly, without the commodification, women authors would have had no access to the public, and have made no contribution. I cannot be sorry, speaking personally, for this 'commodification'. We know that the book which we enjoy, which we may think entertaining – or even a 'classic' – has been purchased. Even if we think of the book as a kind of friend or companion, it is still an object that is a product, and has been bought with money. Henry Fielding's narrator in the very first sentences of *Tom Jones* makes a frank joke about this exchange that lies at the heart of the reader's enjoyment. A novel is a consumable commodity, not very different from a dinner at a restaurant. It is not a dinner given by a private host to friends:

An Author ought to consider himself, not as a Gentleman who gives a private or eleemosynary Treat, but rather as one who keeps a public Ordinary, at which all Persons are welcome for their Money. In the former Case ... the Entertainer provides what Fare he pleases, and tho' this should be very indifferent, and utterly disagreeable to the Taste of his Company, they must not find any Fault; nay, on the contrary, good-Breeding forces them outwardly to approve and to commend whatever is set before them. Now the contrary of this happens to the Master of an ordinary. Men who pay for what they eat, will insist on gratifying their Palats ... and if every Thing is not agreeable to their Taste, will challenge a right to censure, to abuse, and to d—n their Dinner without Controul.[1]

Money is all very well, so we each secretly think. Those of us who get paid for writing are not antipathetic to the remuneration. The only thing wrong with money is that it is in the wrong hands. Prose fiction itself deals with money in 'the wrong hands'. Novels trace with considerable fascination (sometimes carrying on their inspection from generation even unto generation) the various ways in which persons not only acquire money but become money. The desire to escape poverty is well understood by writers of prose fiction, who constantly entertain us with prose narratives of beings not unlike ourselves. In these characters, the sense of self is related to a sense of possession, and 'being a person' means having means of some sort. Such observations and considerations link fictions of pre-capitalist eras with stories of the early modern or later modern periods.

In one of our earliest novels, the 'pastoral romance' (as it is sometimes known) *Daphnis and Chloe*, the question of wealth is raised first in connection with absolute innocence of wealth – even lack of need for it.

In this farming region a goatherd, Lamon by name, found a little boy-child being suckled by one of his goats. The place was in the oak grove, at the bottom of a little dip wreathed about with ivy and with fine grass on which lay the baby ... And presently at midday he saw the goat standing over the child, careful not to hurt it, and the child took milk as from a mother's breast. Marveling, he came closer and found a boy-child, of good size and wrapped in more beautiful clothes than you would expect on an exposed child. His purple mantle was fastened by a gold pin, and he had a little dagger with a handle of ivory.[2]

Lamon and his wife adopt this baby boy and call him Daphnis. In a counterpart to their find, two years later a neighbouring shepherd, Dryas, finds a little girl baby in the cave of the Nymphs, being nourished by one of his own ewes.

And beside her there were tokens (*gnorismata*): a sash (*mitra*) embroidered with gold, slippers gold-embroidered and gold ankle bands. (I, cap. 5)

Dryas takes the baby girl home to his wife Nape, and they adopt the child. Nape takes special care of her, trying to be more motherly than the ewe, lest the ewe should be better spoken of. And they call her by the bucolic name of Chloe ('green shoot'). She seems to come from Nature, given by the beneficence of the natural world like the grass.

The hero is nurtured by a female goat, the girl child by a female sheep, in a harmony of nature in which Nature seems to supply all that is wanted. The little girl-baby's face even shines because the ewe licks it clean. The idea of shining cleanness, a child and milk are connected later in the image of Eros, the boy-child 'white as milk and hair shining like fire, shining as if just washed': *leukos hosper gala*, *xanthos hosper pyr*, *stilpnos hos arti leloumenos* (ii, cap. 4). The babies are erotic in their first appearance. Nature seems both erotic and loving, with infinite resources and capable of almost infinite care. The relation between animal and baby in these two parallel early scenes is an image of love which asks for nothing but gives everything.

Both of the babies thrive under this odd but effective care; the world is sufficiently nourishing and trustworthy to give without asking for repayment. This is as the author and the narrator both know an idyll paramount – a world without payment and without possessions. Yet these 'foundling' children have come from a world of payment and possessions, and as soon as they are adopted they are thrust back into that world, even though they give a country reading in their youth to their environment. They are really in a world in which wealth is related to status, and everything is referred back to wealth and status. When found, each is surrounded by valuable tokens, *gnorismata*, materials by which he or she might become *known*. Anonymous and folded into nature, in their 'original state' we might say, the babies also have signs of their other original state – their social status and status at birth in the world of man. They were not allowed to stay born in the world of man, in the status and wealth which they would claim by custom and 'right' – if the law of the father which creates such rights didn't allow the father to thrust them out of cognizance of the law, out of identity, status and ownership.

Having been taken away, ejected from the world of wealth and possession, the nameless infants yet in a sense are – or are potentially – their associative possessions, which are both symbolic and real. Nor does the narrative ignore at all the exchange value of this wealth that they have about them. The goatherd Lamon spots the fine things that this boy-baby has and knows their value:

> At first he thought to himself that he would take away only the gnorismata and leave the baby behind. Then he was ashamed that he could not imitate the philanthropy (*philanthropian*) of a goat ... . (i, cap. 3)

The temptation to commit theft has already come into this pagan Eden early in the narrative; the goatherd (unlike Nature in the she-goat and the ewe) experiences the desire to take the possessions and let the person go. He is unlike the benevolent she-goat and the ewe who express Nature and yet seem to pertain to a moral world that they could not possibly understand – hence the shock of paradox in 'philanthropy', the teasing idea that a goat, who is conceptually precluded from philanthropy (a love of human beings), might have a benevolent and thoughtful charity towards the human. Of course, if the goatherd stole the baby's tokens, these possessions would be altered once separated from the baby – they would no longer be *gnorismata*, signs by which he could be known, but simply *objects*.

Daphnis the baby would seem to have little claim to our own attention without the wealth of his *gnorismata*, which hint at a story and a *telos*. It is these possessions, or rather potential possessions, that make him known as a person (or potential person). But with story or *telos* the animals were no more concerned than with gold. The infant child is totally without possessions – and does not need them to gain the goat's assistance; yet he is defined to us and to all other humans inside and outside the novel by his 'tokens', his potential possessions. Body and token fuse to become the unique identity, the 'self' which is to be covered by the name 'Daphnis' – though that is merely a name donated to him by his finder.

As the story progresses, and the hero and heroine inevitably fall in love, difficulties cloud their prospects. For the idyll in which we think we have been living while reading *Daphnis and Chloe* – more truly, the charming pastoral in which we readers would like to live – is perpetually broken into by reminders of status and the import of money in the outside world. Readers and personified narrator are trying to collude in escape into a sweet idyll, while the story itself perpetually refuses us this gratification.[3] The orchard has to be tidied up and rearranged so when the master and his family and friends come they can have a good time playing at being in the country. It turns out – to our shock – that Lamon and Myrtale are slaves – and thus Daphnis is a *slave* too.

First associated with his possessions, and apparently surviving in natural freedom, Daphnis in the middle of the story finds he has no possessions – not even his own body. He is the possession of someone else. In the end, the truth comes to light (as we the readers always knew it must) and Daphnis' real identity is revealed. He is the son of the owner of this very estate – a man named Dionysophanes who had the child exposed for purely financial reasons. Having had three other children (two sons and a daughter) Dionysophanes thought he had children enough, and exposed his fourth child (IV, cap. 24). He deposited those valuables with the baby *not* as *gnorismata* by which he could be identified, but as funeral offerings (or funeral adornments) (*ou gnorismata tauta synektheis*; IV cap. 24). Daphnis the baby was 'rich' because he was dead already – or treated as one already dead. Daphnis can be resurrected in the social world and reclaimed because of the tokens of wealth and status that accompanied him into that liminal, carefree natural state. Matters have changed in his family since he was exposed. Now that Dionysophanes has lost two of his older children he is quite pleased to get his son Daphnis back. Similarly, Chloe is reunited with her parent once the whole group go to the city. A wealthy man, Megakles, upon seeing her *gnorismata* exclaims his recognition. And then Megakles, the 'deadbeat dad' paramount, goes into an explanation of what prompted him to expose this child:

'A few years ago my life was very constricted. For I spent what I had in trierarchies and choruses. Things were thus, when I begot a daughter. Unable to nurture her fittingly because of penury, I exposed her with these handsome tokens (*gnorismasi kosmesas*), with the idea that many men are happy to be made fathers in that way.' (IV, cap. 35)

The sanguine spendthrift is rewarded for his sanguine callousness by a reunion of this mega-show-off Megakles (the Big Man) with his lovely young daughter, who is now of high enough station to marry Daphnis. Actually Daphnis and Chloe themselves wished to marry whatever the social condition of either. But both when they were poor and when they are rich, the families concerned will allow only the 'suitable' matching of wealth and status. Earlier, when Daphnis was a slave he had hoped that finding a bag of gold would assist him in achieving his unlikely objective, for then Chloe had been of higher station as the daughter of free though poor peasants. Novels keep emphasizing things found – money, foundlings. Things found are free gifts from the universe (apparently) which can be rapidly digested, assimilated into the game of possessions.

Longus' novel never escapes its economic underpinning – though the reader and the narrator may keep willing the narrative so to escape. Daphnis is his possessions – and he is *like* a possession, something lost and then revalued and happily found.

It seems that in order to be noted as a person, to be or have a character, one must both be possessed and have possessions. This seems to me always true in novels – in the Novel. Money is an inescapable motive, and love is not stronger than the drive – even if it rises from imagination and fantasy – for greater means, more possessions. 'We must have more money' is said by 'bad' characters (or deluded obsessed characters) in a D. H. Lawrence short story ('The Rocking-Horse Winner'). But it could be said by most characters in any novel. Most characters in novels can or do say or imply that at some point. The sense of pressing need for access to greater means can be acute, even though it entails a fantasized order of value. Chloe's father Megakles could have kept his daughter and enjoyed her companionship all along; she wasn't reft from him by shipwreck, or iniquitous plots, like a Marina. But Megakles was spending his money as a really wealthy citizen, fitting up galleys for the navy and also paying for the production of plays – both of these things being *liturgies*, public services publicly performed by the most important citizens of a Greek city. A man gained in civic importance and power by such expenditure. Megakles outstripped his real means, in order to show off. But Megakles himself never expresses any regret that his desire to show off and gain honour has injured his child, nearly resulting in her death as a baby. Even at the time, he comforted himself with the idea that she would not die but just become someone else's problem.

The goat and the ewe take on extra responsibilities out of their substance; the human beings will not use their substance to nurture and foster life in their own species, even their own children. Animals – comically enough – exhibit the *philanthropia* – the love of humankind – that humankind so strikingly seems to lack here. So great is the power of wealth evidently to warp what we wish to consider basic values. *Daphnis and Chloe* (a novel arriving very early in our European novel tradition) shows us that love, affection, familial attachment – all these emotional activities – are subordinated to other desires. The children want desire in itself, wish to find a pure and perfect Eros, away from the prying eyes of others, and outside the cultural value system. But the young hero and heroine never succeed in reinventing a sex without guilt, without responsibility, without caste, culture and money.

The narrative is dealing with the questions by investigating why it is not possible to find pure affection (aside from goats or ewes) or pure sexuality (aside from goats and ewes again). Human beings are marked by some other fantastic desires not easy to define or satisfy. The children must cease being infants, unspeaking, like lambs and kids. They become 'characters'. The children are 'characters' only because they are marked by their possessions, or tokens – something between money in the bank and tattoos. They can have real identities only by being recognized within a structure in which money is a primary determining factor.

'Person', Longus tells us, is almost impossible to imagine without wealth, money and possessions. This seems to be the stance taken by the

Novel in general – if never without some irony, and customarily with a great deal. But 'personality' and 'personal possessions' are intimately linked. The medieval Latin word *personalitas* means 'personal goods, personal estate'. Without some goods that identify the person – without *things* – there exists only the creature like an ewe or a nanny-goat, or else a personifications like Eros or a Nymph. ('Nymphs' never exist in the singular in Longus at all – they are functional only as a plural, and we hear only of 'the Nymphs'.) One of the deeper ironies is that of course the ewes and goats are part of an economy – the animals themselves just don't *know* that is so. As they grow up the adolescent children care for the goats and sheep (for which they feel an affinity), but this is not reciprocity. After all, the ewe and she-goat nurtured the young without expecting to kill and eat them later – the *animals themselves* are always outside the economy that makes shepherds and shepherdesses exist. When the children grow they can claim their identity through the wealth of the tokens which supply identity. The *gnorismata* are the showy means by which personhood is really made. Yet the young people are not fully happy with the new identity that is supplied and 'known' by the tokens – the signs by which something is known, and slotted into the social world. Possessions tie one to the past.

Longus' story may seem closer than one might like to a Lockean fable, a Whig story in which possession is the necessary activity of the individual, property the primary imaginative structure and goal. Persons in novels – even idylls, fables, or non-realistic stories – are closely associated with the character of their money. Without this, they are colorless, lacking in personhood, identity. Cheats, frauds and mad consumerists abound in prose fiction. Think, for example, of Lady Clonbrony in *The Absentee*, or Dickens's Mr and Mrs Merdle in *Our Mutual Friend*. But it is evidently hard for us to believe in someone who has *no* money – or rather no relation to money. Poverty itself can be one form of truth to the reality of possessions, vouching for the reality of the person who is strongly related by need to the social and economic world. A 'person' in a fictional narrative appears to us always dressed, a character in his or her characteristic money – garb. Possessions of numerous variable kinds, and chiefly the lovely fungible money, or gold which is so swiftly exchangeable – these are the guarantors that someone is a person. A 'character' in a novel, in order to convince the reader (or even other characters) that s/he is a person, must have possessions – and, I would add, more startlingly, must potentially be – or be seen as – a possession of some kind.

In Defoe's famous fable, Robinson Crusoe in an indefatigable lust for possessions swims out again and again to his dying ship, loading himself with the potential for the multiple crafts of civilization, potentially more civilized each time he takes a raft out. He debates whether to take the little hoard of gold and silver coins:

I smil'd to my self at the Sight of this Money, O Drug! said I aloud, what art thou good for? Thou art not worth to me, no not the taking off of the Ground; one of these Knives is worth all this Heap; I have no Manner of use of thee, e'en remain where thou art, and go to the Bottom as a Creature whose Life is not worth saving.[4]

But despite this moralizing (of which Rousseau was later to approve so highly) Robinson then decides not to do without the money: 'However, upon Second Thoughts, I took it away.' The 'Life' in the money may be worth saving after all. Although Robinson recognizes the money is but an inane symbol now, while he is on a desert island, if he ever rejoins the European social world these coins will be the most important of *gnorismata*.

Robinson often appears to be possessed by his things. When he is a man dressed in skins he seems like a possession of the wilderness and even of his pitying parrot. But he knows that he has resources in reserve. In *Gulliver's Travels*, Swift's hero Gulliver, an ironic version of Robinson in some respects, after his shipwreck becomes something of a 'person' to the Lilliputians when they catalogue his possessions, however strange and even bizarre these may appear to them. The Lilliputians are in turn real to Gulliver because they have not only beautiful clothes but also fine carriages, and miniature money: '*Sprugs* (their greatest Gold coin, about the bigness of a Spangle).' He soon feels connected to them indeed, precisely through their high-class possessions, and adjusts Swift-ly to their markers of status and success: 'And I have often had four Coaches and Horses at once on my Table full of Company'.[5] Gulliver loves to keep carriage company, and begins to forget the implications of the miniature. (To an imagined external onlooker, a viewer with a 'normal' human view, he would look like a man playing with toys.)

Most of the time, during the last 2000 years, the society being represented in novels – and in any novel – is unlikely to express itself 'purely' through the exertion of direct and visible forms of power. It can do that, it is true. A novel can deal with a battle, or with Hanging Day at Tyburn. But that episode of purer power gets tied up with, for instance, the story of Prince Andrei Bolkonsky, or with the story of

Jonathan Wild picking pockets and so on. The moment of direct power becomes alchemically transformed or sublimated into saleable stories. Society is most most likely to find expression and reveal the nature of its truest power through the intervening, softening and malleable medium of money. All novels of whatever kind – and of whatever period – seem designed to express some comprehension of the ways in which a person is treated as fungible, as a commodity, as something to be identified by something else, a mode of living in a continuum, a medium. There may be revolts against this categorization – revolts enacted *within* the novel. One mode of protest is the emphasis on or examination of an adherence to some other and 'older' form of value, something that is prior to money. Some wealth has transcendental power, is a treasure surpassing treasure, a meaning, an object with no fungibility. So it is with the sacred objects of the Incas, in Françoise de Graffigny's powerful and witty novel *Lettres d'une Péruvienne*, first published in 1747.

In this novel, the heroine, Zilia, an Inca princess and Virgin of the Sun, is kidnapped first by Spaniards and then by a benevolent Frenchman when her city – and with it her world – is attacked and destroyed by the Spanish conquistadors. Thus rescued by the benevolent Déterville – who falls in love with her – Zilia has to construct a new identity for her new self. To the French this is an improved self, more civilized, but to her it is a fallen or imperfect self, reft from the society that gave her meaning. Towards the end of this ironic novel, the conventional 'hero' Déterville restores to Zilia some of the objects of the Incas' religious veneration. In her convent cell, she stubbornly resists the new religion urged upon her and as an Inca venerates the great golden image of the Sun, captured from the Inca temple of the Sun and restored to her:

La grande figure du Soleil ... excite ma vénération, je me prosterne devant elle, mon esprit l'adore ... [6]

Later, Déterville 'gives' Zilia what is the object of so much desire in eighteenth-century life and fiction – a country estate. Zilia is taken around this estate, all furnished in delightful taste. The hangings are adorned with 'figures extrêmement bien dessinées, imitaient une partie des jeux et des cérémonies de la ville du Soleil ... On y voyait nos Vièrges représentées en mille endroits avec le même habilement que je portais en arrivant en France' (Lettre xxxv, pp. 350–1). The temple ornaments are now supported by 'pyramides dorées'. Zilia's new decorated house rejoices in a clutter of symbols: gilded pyramids recollecting Egypt with attractive natives of South America and their costumes. These images all serve to adorn a precious but stunning room, 'ce magnifique cabinet', made brilliant and spectacular also with the mirrors that the Incas did not know (and that Zilia herself found so puzzling at first) as well as with specially made wall-covering in fashionable Western style and material. As for the great and venerable image of the deity, the figure of the Sun:

> la figure du Soleil, suspendue au milieu d'un plafond peint des plus belles couleurs du ciel, achevait par son éclat d'embellir cette charmante solitude; et des meubles commodes assortis aux peintures la rendaient délicieuse (p. 351)

The sun has now become a partner object in this pretty mock-magnificence, suspended from a ceiling painted in lovely sky colours and serving with its brilliance to illuminate and embellish the rest of the objects; it is subordinated, contributing to a striking and picturesque impression of the space. The luxurious and charming French country house proves to have been purchased through the sale of some of the Inca objects. Déterville gazes at Zilia gazing at 'her' new house, and explains why the Inca golden throne is no longer one of the items on display:

> Vous pourrez vous apercevoir, belle Zilia, que la chaise d'or ne se trouve point dans ce nouveau temple du Soleil: un pouvoir magique l'a transformée en maison, en jardin, en terres ... il a fallu respecter votre délicatesse. Voici, me dit-il en ouvrant une petite armoire pratiquée adroitement dans le mur, voici le débris de l'opération magique. En même temps il me fit voir une cassette remplie de pièces d'or à l'usage de France.[7]

A magical operation has transformed everything that once had a primary significance into exchangeable value. The residual value of the golden throne is the 'debris' of gold pieces hidden in the prudently hidden wall cupboard. In accepting this gift, of the liquidation of the wealth of her people, Zilia herself becomes the latest conquistador of the Inca nation, and the destroyer of its culture. It is not the least of the novel's many ironies that its story colludes in this fashion with what destroys the heroine's world, and almost destroys her. Her culture and religion are now 'history' – worse, they are materials for new variants on the 'oriental', charming exotic figures of occidental Indian maidens. The house is an elegant jumble of elaborate décor: Virgins of the Sun, religious objects, depictions, and Western objects and materials like the mirrors. It is one of the tenets of décor that one culture makes an insufficient source. The Sun, the emblem of the primary object of worship, has become a charming Enlightenment home decoration. We too can share in a sense of its attractions: one could imagine Zilia's house featuring in one of the many magazines that cater to such tastes, reading matter (of a sort of which I become fonder with advancing age), magazines which might collectively be termed 'house pornography'.

Objects of religious value once – and at the beginning of this story – acted as transcendent absolute objects shared and venerated by all, outside of the exchange system. These have become nothing more than individual booty. This 'treasure' which was 'lost' and then 'found' (restolen from the Spanish thieves who sacked the city) has been transformed in two directions. It becomes (a) money, the medium by which an estate can be bought and maintained; (b) décor. A whole culture is colonized, ravaged, ruined and privatized. Zilia is now what all Frenchwomen and men desire to be – rich and blessed with an elegant estate, a lovely house complete with individual decorative touches – and of course a good library. All this has been wrought, Déterville says truly, by the magical power which transforms all. Nothing can be said to be above or outside of exchange value.

The heroine Zilia is at the end imagined by the author of a series of changes wrought upon the treasure. She herself is the end-point of a reconstruction and reinterpretation. The treasure is feebly recharged with a new and illicit function as a love gift. Zilia, victim and heroine, in the end is also the conqueror. She agrees to privatizing the wealth that belongs neither to herself nor her lover. In a colonial move of great perfection, because rendered as unconscious to himself, the lover Déterville – illegitimately but most successfully – makes the treasure of a people, the Inca gold, into Zilia's personal property. When these objects becomes possessions, they lose meaning, at least to the degree that they are possessions merely. The golden sun becomes just an agreeable curiosity, an aesthetic object. Zilia is more important than the objects, though her original identity has become an object, a style, a motif – the Virgin of the Sun is now turned into wall hangings. Her story has become a wallpaper design of pleasing exoticism, not unlike the wallpaper derived from *Télémaque* that graces the walls of Andrew Jackson's home, the Hermitage, in Nashville. The fact that Zilia is now surrounded by such objects yields her the kind of importance and significance that Déterville wants her to have – as a woman of the privileged class in France. And Zilia, not the objects she owns, commands our interest. Having experienced a mournful fading, a pining away of self and significance and world structure, she is now, having gained possessions, in command of a structure, at the centre of a pattern of significance that she can grasp, and able to assert her identity as a self. Indeed, at the very end she says that is the only thing she can rely on: 'Le plaisir d'être ... *je suis, je vis, j'existe*' (Lettre XLI, p. 362).

Walter Scott, who was I think influenced by Françoise de Graffigny's novel (among many others) repeats this transforming 'magic' very effectively in his first novel, *Waverley* (1814). In almost all of Scott's novels, some characters are shown adhering to value systems other than those associated with the direct measure of money. They highly esteem the idea of *power* as a direct and unmediated force and entity. Command over persons equals direct power. But that is always presented as nostalgic or idyllic thinking, a somewhat fake desire, like that of Werther at the beginning of *The Sorrows of Young Werther*, to return to some imaginary patriarchal antiquity of great simplicity and concomitant aesthetic beauty. In novels of any era, the return to a serene and fulfilling non-money culture is always presented as idyllic thinking and almost always mocked. Perhaps that is because such a desire is felt to reflect a wish to return to a life without individuation, 'personality' – or at least a wish to return to a time when the Others had beauty but no vexing personality. In *Waverley*, Fergus MacIvor, really in part a Continental by upbringing, is living a tribal life in Scotland, where his Scottish clansmen admire him because of his great 'tail', his entourage of followers. Evan Dhu is most disappointed when Fergus betrays his expectations by not turning up with a great entourage:

... he said, with an appearance of mortification, 'And it is even he, sure enough; and he has not his tail on after all ... '

In fact, Fergus MacIvor 'had no idea of raising himself in the eyes of an English young man of fortune, by appearing with a retinue of idle Highlanders disproportioned to the occasion'.[8]

Fergus knows not only that a train of 'idle' followers is expensive, requiring feeding and upkeep, but also that they do not meet with approval according to modern practices. Evan could think neither of these thoughts. Fergus is well aware of money, and of image presentation, even advertising of a kind. As he is planning the Stewart uprising for Bonnie Prince Charlie, he must look about him for means. Only at first glance can Fergus seem like the original or 'pure' being, the tribal chieftain in an economy unmediated, of power without need of money. The more obtuse of his followers can give voice to that apprehension of being, although actually the poor clansmen know the value of money very well, as they have suffered under the taxation imposed by the English and the need to give something to their secret rulers or representatives the chiefs.

Baron Bradwardine is living between highlands and lowlands, creating and perpetuating the life of a Renaissance baron, a man of power in a domain which reflects an original wildness. There is a sense of frontier life (likely also to remind Americans of regions like Kentucky in the nineteenth century) in Bradwardine's proud motto, 'Bewar the Ba'ar' (ch. 8, p. 79). The baron's rough Renaissance house and estate is ravaged by war. In the end, the old-fashioned wealth of Tully Veolan becomes smartened – one is tempted to say 'tarted up – by the power of money. After the damage of war, it is affectionately restored by those to whom it is a curio rather than a living entity: felled trees are cleared away, and the stumps grubbed up, and all is tidied:

> ... the heavy stables, which had been burnt down, were replaced by buildings of a lighter and more picturesque appearance ... the pigeon-house was replenished; the fountain played with its usual activity; and not only the Bear who presided over its basin, but all the other Bears whatsoever, were replaced on their several stations ... the house itself had been thoroughly repaired, as well as the gardens, with the strictest attention to maintain the original character of both, and to remove as far as possible, all appearance of the ravage they had sustained. (p. 484)

It is the money of wealthy Colonel Talbot, the Englishman, that has done all this. This metamorphosed house, transformed, as Déterville says to Zilia by the magical power of money – this magically tidy house is not the home Bradwardine knew. It has lost its organic character, and is a simulacrum – it has been 'restored'. It is now a décor, a style in which things must be in keeping – the new stables are not only more convenient but also more 'picturesque'. The language that hangs about this description of Tully Veolan reminds us of nothing so much as a modern hotel. Tully Veolan which had once seemed to its owner to express himself, his family and his power in a fitting and complete way, is now detached from that significance. It has lost a primary meaning in becoming more completely possession. Rendered merely pretty and merely sign, it is incapable of pointing beyond money to some other significance. Its claim to power now seems *quaint*. Possessions which cannot become 'personality' become décor and serve to act as a background to personality – or as 'filler' for it.

The novel as a form tends to offer us a glimpse of what I call 'Treasure'. Or rather, it shows the quest for treasure. This comes to the fore in an adventure story like *Treasure Island*. Incidentally, what a wonderful title that is! – expressing the whole idea of personality within its intriguing geographically seductive trope. For the individual, *pace* John Donne, *is* an island and the individual is also an island which is associated with treasure and in which treasure is to be found. Treasure haunts the pages of all novels. A possession of any kind can become a curious treasure. Without having possessions, the person is nowhere – not quite a personality without personal property. Yet, having possessions is dangerous. And lest I sound too much as if my theme were a praise and parable of capitalism, I should point out that the Novel knows truly and deeply how dangerous possession is. The body can become property – the most literal and terrible case being enslavement, a fate frequently befalling both male and female central characters in ancient novels. But there is also the treatment of the body as property in prostitution and in forms of work, and the extraction of property from the body – as Jo March does in selling her hair in *Little Women*. Jo is understandably proud to think she is her own possession – that one is that. In the Lockean sense the body may be assumed to be the primary property of the individual, though this right has yet to be fully acknowledged in the case of females, which makes Jo's secret decision so bold an action.

Characters, manifesting themselves real by having possessions, may of course be possessed by possessions, undone by goods that may or may not be good. Possessions in novels tend to be sneaky, tending to round on the possessor. There is a certain impurity about all these 'good goods' (to borrow Pepys's phrase), even when they proclaim purity. The emerald is a signal of chastity and transcendental yearning. In *Middlemarch*, in the comic jewels scene Dorothea Brooke divides her mother's jewels between herself and her younger sister, and gives herself the emeralds, exclaiming at their symbolic significance. While she thus emphasizes the symbolism and the transcendental otherworldly value, she is acquiring goods which are of much greater financial worth than the amethysts which she allots to her sister Celia. The scene displays Dorothea's mixture of idealism and self-deception, and assures us that we would be wrong if we think of her as incapable of egotism. Dorothea's ego reaches out to possess the emeralds – with a feeling that they 'suit her'. Such are the feelings that advertisers play on, over and over again. Every character in *Middlemarch* is good at covetousness and at hiding real value even from the self. It is partly their devotion to this hidden activity that makes us so comfortably certain that these are characters, and worth attending to.

That possessions possess is worked out in numerous ways in Victorian novels. Wilkie Collins's *The Moonstone* brilliantly focuses our attention on the magical object of mystery and desire, the gem that represents and is great wealth, as existing simultaneously in the world of the transcendent and of fluctuating values. For it is an object of absolute and unexchangeable value to the Indians (like the Inca religious objects in their original site). But it becomes (briefly) an object of personal property and association (Rachel suits the moonstone); and it moves (downwards, one is tempted to say) to the world of commerce and exchange for Godfrey Ablewhite, whose profession is significantly 'charity', who sees the gem clearly as – and only as – an object fungible in the mobile world, convertible into money. *The Moonstone* has put a small community into a state of desire, into a state of possession, whose equivalent is the opium dream. So, Collins indicates, the dream of empire and fantasies of the wealth of India has possessed the English people.

The delirium of possessions, of possessions associated intimately with the body on the one hand, and on the other with the disembodied world of calculation and the abstraction of money, can be richly illustrated. But what of the opposite case? What about the representation in novels of objects that are disgusting or distasteful to the possessor or to the person in strongest association with these objects? This one might call the 'anti-possession'. Of course, numerous dirty and disgusting objects can be found. But sometimes, interestingly, an object that would disgust the reader (or the author) does not disgust the character associated with it. In *Cranford*, Mrs Forrester's fine lace is a mark of her gentility: 'I treasure up my lace very much' (ch. 8, p. 157). She is proud of her own recipe for washing her convent-made lace in milk. But the lace, because it is in the little bowl of milk, meets with an untoward accident – it is swallowed by her cat. She tells Lady Glenmire at the genteel tea party about the accident in thorough self-engrossed detail, explaining how the cat had to be worked on with the administration of currant jelly mixed with 'tartar emetic':

'I shall never forget how anxious I was for the next half hour ... I could have kissed her when she returned the lace to sight, very much as it had gone down. Jenny had boiling water ready, and we soaked it and soaked it, and spread it on a lavender-bush in the sun, before I could touch it again, even to put it in milk. But now, your ladyship would never guess that it had been in pussy's inside.'[9]

To Mrs Forrester, the lace is too defining a possession, too great a symbol of value – a treasure – to lose its glamour because of its association with a cat's guts. Her hearer may feel repulsed, and may look askance at the lace, but its owner gazes on it with pleasure, confident that it is an essentially radiant material and social object of value that can be totally rescued and restored because ultimately not susceptible to contamination by animal or mundane accidental associations.

At other times, things that would not, or would not necessarily disgust the reader are disgusting as possessions and environment to the character. This trope of the unwanted or 'filthy' possession can be found in works of fiction other than novels: for instance in Euripides' *Elektra*, where his heroine bearing water from the well and working at housekeeping very evidently hates the lowly work into which she has been thrust by the usurper of her father's place. Her whole marriage is a sham, a degradation, and her house is something for which she has perfect contempt. To take another example, from an ancient novel rather than an ancient play, the heap of grains that Venus gives the dismayed Psyche to sort is a massive object of sustaining food, a possession and an obstinate thing that glares at her and weighs upon her as a dismal task and a conundrum. We may be our things without liking our things. The heap 'possesses' Psyche in a way. Of course she never chose this as a possession. Unwanted possessions can be thrust upon one, even more intimately. In *Anne of Green Gables*, Anne's terrible dress, the skimpy dull thing made of the ugly-sounding 'wincey', is an intimate personal possession which is detested. It offers an ugly definition which the human entity, the living person put in contact with and defined by it, must defiantly insist on rejecting.

Environments can also work like possessions – as active centres of defining the person, surrounding and touching the personality at numerous points. To express disgust at surroundings is thus a sign of spiritual freedom – the ability to cast off false possession by things. Some novelists really excel at describing the ugly or distasteful – Balzac and Zola are leaders in this field.

The description of the boarding house, 'la maison Vauquer', near the beginning of *Père Goriot* is a fascinated elaboration of the mildly but incessantly unpleasant. It displays at length the lower-middle-class world of things – bad things which are proud and glaring and pathetic and absurd affectations. This *pension* is full of reiterated and tired reproductions:

> This salon, badly enough floored, is covered with wainscot to a high point in the wall, and the upper wall is covered by a varnished paper representing the principal scenes of *Télémaque*, in which the classical characters have all been colored in ... The chimney-

piece in stone, whose hearth, always so clean, attests that there is no fire there except on great occasions, is ornamented with two vases full of artificial flowers, old and encaged, which keep company with a clock in bluish marble of the worst taste. This first room exhales an odour without a name in our language, which should be called 'odour of pension' ...

Everything reflects the bad taste and pretensions of the landlady, and we are urged to share the shudder at the ugly surrounding and possessions inflicted on the inhabitants of the boarding house. Yet the kind of snobbery aroused in the reader by this vision of lower-class life is exactly the same as the two terrible daughters of Goriot feel in their repulsion from him – in an ironic twist of the novel, the reader's 'taste' makes him or her a reflection of the Goneril and Regan of the tale.

Such a boarding house proclaims that the resident is poor, lacking in money to spend, though it has its own layers of pretension. The way out is the claim of the individual to a proud and transcendental 'taste' which relieves him or her (at least inwardly) of the burden of these low-class objects. Balzac understands that such 'taste' is a necessity and can be a trap. Similar taste or feeling is exhibited in Proust's Marcel when strolling through the bourgeois garden of the place his friend the painter has rented – he despises the little statue, the big gazing ball. Taste, however, is limited – it sometimes mocks the possessor, and it is constantly assumed by crass, greedy and ignorant people. 'Taste' can be mimicked, and it can be purchased. It is the subject of discourse, so public, so closely connected to advertising that it is 'always already' in collusion with the cheapness it must pretend to despise. Money buys us; others can play upon our comic self-consciousness, our determination not to be possessed by possessions that don't reflect the way we would like to see ourselves – or the way in which we currently have learned to imagine ourselves, a mode the world would not condemn. Money leads to repetition of effects. Constant dives into the marketplace are undertaken in order to find that which will express what is supposedly unique, the spiritual and inward content of the personality. Personality gets spilled outward and outward into fashion. 'Taste' is supposed to free one from lowly covetousness, but it offers instead pretentiousness, affectation, and a stimulus to unease. Lockwood in his visit to *Wuthering Heights* sees the place as crude, lacking in taste – and displays his second-rate watering-place mentality and preferences to our amused pleasure not unmixed with scorn. Yet, the kitchen of Wuthering Heights as described by Lockwood comes off as attractive, with its dresser holding silver objects, and its simplicities and weightiness:

The floor was of smooth, white stone: the chairs, high-backed primitive structures, painted green: one or two heavy black ones lurked in the shade.[10]

Lockwood seeks to gratify us and himself by playing with a decorator-magazine kind of love for idyllic old-fashioned charm.[11]

Lockwood's own money is not scorned by Wuthering Heights, be it noted, nor theirs by him. Lockwood tellingly calls Heathcliff 'A capital fellow!' (p. 1). Heathcliff has acquired respect for capital, and cash values; Lockwood presumably is not wrong when he thinks that Heathcliff becomes more civil to him after the dog-attack because he is 'probably swayed by prudential considerations of the folly of offending a good tenant' (p. 13). Heathcliff would not seem real to us at all if he didn't have some money string attaching him to the world of personality. Even so, Heathcliff works hardest of all the characters at turning objects of market value into psychological-spiritual property, making matter into spirit to borrow the Hegelian formula.

Lockwood has taste; but he is Heathcliff's prey. Or rather, he reflects the 'tasteful' Lintons, who are Heathcliff's rightful prey. Some characters are always likely to be seen as prey, or as possessions. Women are the characters most likely to be seen as pure possessions meant for others; women perpetually fulfill this role. As characters are or represent their possessions, they can be sought after and used as possessions, especially by characters who are obsessed with the idea of possession. If our possessions may possess us, another's idea about our possessions can make them the target object of mad possessiveness. The 'innocent' possessor then becomes the victim.

The genre we call 'the murder mystery' perpetually plays around the edges of all these definitions of personalty/personality, and the variety of possessions which can be identified with a human being – who is easily through the act of murder turned into an object. Dull possessions may harbour a hidden secret treasure, as in the case of Agatha Christie's *After the Funeral*. In the novel, the murderess, a most harmless-looking ladylike companion to a rather silly lady, knows that the silly Cora's daubs hide paintings of real market value. Cora's assertions of personality were insufficient to hide the fact that her real value lay in someone else's expression. The murderess also adopted the self-expression of 'someone else', murdering her employer in such a ghastly axe-murder that suspicion could not possibly fall on one so feebly genteel. This murderess of course has a kind of 'dual personality' forced upon her by the economic and social subservience in which she lives. But her own desire, her ultimate objective, is of the most banal – she commits a violent axe-murder but her ultimate objective is to be able to open a tea-room.

In *The Woman in White*, possession covers and colours the character in the very title. Anne Catherick *is* her whiteness – the white dress which expresses her mania, her relationships and her innocence. She is filed away as a thing in an asylum by Percival Glyde, and would make an ideal murder victim if her poor health and her likeness to her counterpart Laura Fairlie did not make an even fairer target for a complex theft of identity. Laura has money, especially that tempting £120,000 in ready cash which her husband could obtain at once in full on her demise. Laura is an object, and a possession, in a novel in which almost everyone is fixated on possessing someone or something. Even the most indolent character in the story is a full player in that game. Mr Frederick Fairlie is first encountered delicately brushing the coins in his valuable collection:

Placed amid the other rare and beautiful objects ... was a dwarf cabinet in ebony and silver, containing coins of all shapes and sizes, set out in little drawers lined with dark purple velvet. One of these drawers lay on the small table attached to his chair; as near it were some tiny jewellers' brushes, a washleather 'stump', and a tiny bottle of liquid, all waiting to be used in various ways for the removal of any accidental impurities which might be discovered on the coins.[12]

In cleaning the money, Mr Fairlie tries to give the lie to the old image of 'filthy lucre'. Money itself, he insists, through an odd magic, can be turned from its vulgar common meaning, rescued from exchange of the ordinary sort and turned into even more valuable art objects through the magic of transformative value. Mr Fairlie speaks to Mr Hartright, the drawing master (himself involved in the circulation of taste as value), in tones of drawling aestheticism, showing off his capacity to appreciate things on the aesthetic plane. He asks the comic if slightly insulting (perhaps deliberately insulting) question 'Do you like coins? Yes. So glad we have another taste in common beside our taste for Art. Now about the pecuniary arrangements between us – do tell me – are they satisfactory?' (p. 41). Mr Fairlie's refusal to connect coins with salary reflects his insolence as a self-supposed maker of value. At the end of the conversation he says, 'So glad to *possess you* at Limmeridge, Mr Hartright' (p. 44, italics mine). As an appurtenance of taste the drawing master must be his possession. Hartright's own lack of possessions – no money, few prospects – blocks him from Laura, while his beloved is to be the possession of another. Sinister Count Fosco, whose live possessions already include his canaries and his frightened wife, and whose appetite for possession is indicated by his obese body, tries to take possession of Marian. The Novel harps on possessions and possessiveness, and the demonic possession brought upon us by our own possessions; we find in the 'sensation novel' simply renewed attention to these aspects of narrative.

Love so often plays with the beloved as possession that cases of enslavement or murder do not totally surprise us, even in novels. (They are real enough in life.) The desire for possession gives rise to plot – to guile and misreading. The desire to get away from an unwanted possession can lead also to guile, misreading, delusion and deceit. Personality is a dangerous demented game. So Agatha Christie shows in *The Murder of Roger Ackroyd* in which the narrator, the apparently harmless village doctor – a sort of Watson as we expect him to be – proves to be the ingenious murderer. He was after the treasure of others (as a blackmailer) – but most people in the novel are after someone else's treasure, or treat someone else as treasure. So this un-idyllic blackmailer and murderer is not singular. Murder was the second crime, to cover the simple desire for more money. The character is James Shepherd, and he too is a would-be 'shepherd'. He looks like a village innocent, a healer leading the simple life, and part of him likes that role and responds to the village idyll – and makes us respond, with good natured slightly scornful benevolence. This idyllic wish is parodied by Poirot's (temporary) determination to retire and grow vegetable marrows. Of course, Shepherd has found that nowadays one must have more money. Idyllic thinking about the world in which money is not needed, in which possessions are few and simple, plays behind the absurdity not only of Shepherd's mentality but the minds of the other game-playing characters.

Most (but not all) murder mysteries take the desire for possession as a source of 'possession' in the demonic or psychological sense. To have a firm desire, to be overtaken by an Eros, is to be possessed, and in that state the lives and fortunes of others are alike targets of opportunity. That we as readers acquiesce in this view is shown by the popularity of the genre. But part of the fascination of the genre is related to its close attention to the manner in which 'personality' (both narrative and social) is constructed, mimicked, formed or enacted. We look at the ways in which things that are merely personal signs, or 'trademark' objects and gestures – like the necklace of pearls constantly worn by one handsome elderly lady – may have a significance outside the normal range. We never know when the significance of objects is going to turn and bite us. The objects loved by advertisers can become sources of hostility and dread.

We cannot have personality without *personalty* – and we reckon on the novel characters (at least, the ones we are fond of) having personally significant 'things'. But the significance can alter. No possession is stable and not even the motive to possess can be purely or simply ascertained (as in the case of Heathcliff, for instance). The interest in possession turns upon the reader in the end – as in A. S. Byatt's comic novel *Possession*. For the desire to read is itself a form of *Possession*, yielding to somebody else and being possessed by author or character – and if we go further and try to ferret out more about the 'author' our desire to possess the author may lead to our being possessed. The state in which one reads fiction – especially novels – is, I would think, a perfect elemental state of possession. Or perhaps just 'elementary'.

NOTES

1 *The History of Tom Jones, a Foundling*, Book I, chapter 1: taken from *Tom Jones*, ed. Sheridan Baker (New York: W. W. Norton, 1995), p. 25.
2 *Daphnis and Chloe*, Book I; my translation is based on the Greek text of Longus given in the Budé edition (Paris: Belles Lettres, 1987); although I am indebted to the work of other translators my own version is not identical with theirs.
3 I am indebted to the very fine reading offered by Professor John Morgan in his paper on *Daphnis and Chloe* delivered at the International Conference on the Ancient Novel in Groningen, July 2000.
4 Defoe, *The Life and Adventures of Robinson Crusoe*, in Michael Shinagel (ed.), *Robinson Crusoe* (New York: W. W. Norton, 1975), p. 47.
5 Swift, *Gulliver's Travels*, Book I, chapter 6 (Oxford: World's Classics), p. 53.
6 *Lettres d'une péruvienne*, in *Lettres Portugaises, Lettres d'une péruvienne et d'autres romans d'amour par lettres* (Paris: Flammarion, 1983), Letter XXVII, p. 325. Mme de Graffigny obtained these images and ideas about Inca culture and objects from a reading of Garcilaso the Inca.
7 'You can see, beautiful Zilia, that the golden chair is not to be bound in this new Temple of the Sun: a magic power has transformed it into a house, into a garden, into lands ... It was necessary to respect your delicacy. Here, he said to me, opening a little cabinet cunningly set into the wall—here is the debris of the magical operation. And he showed me a box filled with gold pieces current in France.'
8 Scott, *Waverley* (Harmondsworth: Penguin Books, 1976), p. 153.
9 *Cranford* (London: Chapman and Hall, 1853), pp. 157–160. 'Pussy's inside' sounds sexually suggestive to us, though not to Mrs Forrester.
10 *Wuthering Heights* (London: Thomas Newby, 1847), p. 6.

11 Wuthering Heights' kitchen can supply a magazine-attentive kind of speculation, a desire to reproduce the effect. I myself rather covet the green chairs. Characters' surroundings are perversely susceptible to being reappropriated as décor. I have recently seen a magazine in which the 'Red Room' described early in *Jane Eyre* as a scene of terror for little Jane, is cited admiringly and in detail offering an example of pleasingly Victorian style.

12 Collins, *The Woman in White* (Oxford: World's Classics, 1974), p. 40.

Comparative Criticism 24, pp. 37–51.   © 2002 Cambridge University Press
DOI: 10.1017/S0144756402005449   Printed in the United Kingdom

Christopher Marlowe: iron and gold

A. D. NUTTALL

'Reduction' and 'reductionism' are commonly terms of abuse, in literary circles. This is much less clearly the case among scientists. The whole history of the rise of science in the modern world is the story of a gradual progression from description or mere mapping of the territory to explanation. A. N. Whitehead believed[1] that Aristotle, for all his subtlety was a repressive influence on the earlier time, because he had said to the scientist, 'Classify!' and not 'Measure!' These endless Linnaean taxonomies were strangely fruitless. But controlled experiment, designed to isolate what caused what, was suddenly spectacularly successful. If nature is not a random heap of unstable particulars but is in fact organized according to certain underlying principles, the demonstration that a whole mass of phenomena may be the intelligible effect of a certain cause becomes exciting, and earns trust. In 1687 Newton in his *Principia* showed how innumerable, seemingly unrelated movements of physical objects, from water swirling in a bucket to the sun as it rises in the eastern sky, were all susceptible of explanation in terms of an underlying law which could be stated mathematically. This, if you like, was a great act of successful reduction. And so we can begin to think that those who oppose reduction are opposing explanation, and are relegating themselves to a kind of infantilism of the mind, to a world of essentially inert, piecemeal description.

The grand reduction of the *Principia*, however, is not any clear way a reduction from one level to another which had previously been felt to be different in kind. Human language and thought has evolved different orders of discourse, implying different orders of reality. There is, so to speak, one language for physical objects, another for logical relations, another for number, another for human beings, another for morality, another for religion and so on. Now hackles rise when it is suggested that one of these orders of discourse can be reduced to – collapse into – another (for example, when it is suggested that everything we say

37

about thought can be re-expressed in chemical terms). As long as we put
the difficulty in terms of discourse it may be thought that we are dealing
only with what may be called 'formal reduction', that is, the mere
translation of one set of terms into another. But it is part of my point
that such shifts are seldom felt as simple problem-free translations.
Where the translation is from one order to another, the formal reduction
is always felt to imply an ontological reduction, is felt to have an impact
on the real world. '*Equus* means "horse"' changes nothing. 'Morality
is disguised economics' changes everything. Newton had some impact
(wholly undesigned) on religious belief. For example, he showed that a
moving object would continue to move unless something else, such as
friction, stopped it, while Aristotle thought that any moving object must
either be moved by a living force or else be alive itself. This meant that
people looking at the stars on a clear frosty night gradually ceased to
assume that they were looking at a spectacle of living movement but
began to think that they were instead gazing at a huge machine. But the
main achievement of Newton was seen as happening within the order of
the physical; by and large the perception was that Newton had reduced
physical multiplicity to – Physics.

There remains a heroic glamour about the successful reductive
explanation – which is indeed at its most macho when it is applied
across different orders of discourse. It is notable that the towering
prophets of the modern world offer exactly this. Marx said economics
determined consciousness[2]. Freud said that early libidinal experiences
determined mental character (including, presumably, the economic
theories we form). It is quite fun, in a *New Statesman* competition sort
of way, to try to imagine what happens when one such reductive prophet
meets another (rather like the book about putting together a number of
mental patients each of whom claimed to be Jesus). Freud says to Marx,
'You only think that because of your potty-training'; Marx says to
Freud, 'You only think that because you are an economically
marginalized nineteenth-century Jew.' Each tries to edge under the
body of theory presented by the other, to prove *his* explanation the more
fundamental.

Where rival reductions, across orders of discourse, co-exist, mistrust
can begin to creep in. We begin to think, 'Each must be simplifying to
attain his end; the initial complexity of things needs after all to be
accorded a more careful respect.' And so powerful thinkers begin to
launch counter-reductive theories. G. E. Moore fought the idea that
ethical judgements say nothing about the object but merely record a

sentiment of approval in the subject: 'This is good' really means 'I like this'. Anyone can see, he drily observed, that someone who asks himself if pleasure is good is not merely asking himself if pleasure is pleasant[3]. Ethics cannot be reduced to psychological sentiment without ceasing to be ethics. Moore's argument works by ascribing primary authority to the internal logic of ethical statements. But it remained open to the reductionist to argue, as A. J. Ayer did,[4] that ethical statements have exactly the meaning Moore ascribed to them, but those who mean thus are simply deluded. 'Good' names a property, but it is a 'pseudo-property'. Here people react variously. Some say, with gritted teeth, 'Of course Ayer is right'; others do not see why they should tamely submit to the elimination of the ethical and denounce Ayer's relegation of ethical contents to the sphere of delusion as mere unwarranted destruction. Gilbert Ryle once observed that he had been taught to respect the conception, 'economic man', where the basic idea was that human beings are motivated by economic self-interest. 'Fine,' said Ryle, in effect, 'But it just doesn't seem to fit anyone I actually know – when I think of Jane consumingly interested in ornithology, unconcerned and ill-informed about her own bank balance ... ?'[5] Suddenly, in the field of human beings especially, the need to remain open to a possible plurality of motivations comes flooding back. It was this that led me many years ago to describe the work of Shakespeare as 'Ockham's beard, luxuriant, not yet subdued (happily) by the famous razor'.[6] Ockham's razor, 'Entities are not to be multiplied beyond necessity', is the principle of maximum economy in explanation, and it has served scientists well. Not all the great minds, however, are on Ockham's side. For every thinker who says 'Dammit, it all comes down to x' we need another thinker to say 'but could it not also be y and z (and v and w ...)?' This is what Shakespeare does all the time. We have not, note, reverted to mere, inert taxonomy. Shakespeare is into explanations, but they are empathically that; explanations (plural) rather than *the* unitary explanation.

After deciding that Shakespeare was Ockham's beard, I began to wonder if literature as a whole could have an anti-reductive, cognitive force. The Novel, say, then becomes a body of truly respectable psychology; not a unified reductive theory like Adler's, but a just appraisal of the real field of possible motivation. But now I hesitate. Not all the artists are on Shakespeare's side.

Shakespeare was not the only literary genius to be born in England in 1564. Christopher Marlowe is Shakespeare's anti-type, and Marlowe is a great reductionist.

On a winter day in 1607 Francis Bacon addressed the House of Commons. He posed the question, which is fundamental to power, iron or gold (or, as we might say, military strength or economic wealth)?[7] He tells the story of rich King Croesus who tried to impress his might upon Solon by showing him a great quantity of gold. But Solon answered, 'Why, Sir, if another come that hath better iron than you, he will be lord of all your gold.' In other words 'Iron is more fundamental, because with my iron sword I can take all your gold away.' It is a little like the *New Statesman* competition we imagined between Marx and Freud, but here we seem to have a clear winner.

We are in the field of early modern reductive theory, in the world of Machiavelli (to whom Bacon refers in the very next sentence). Marlowe, like Bacon, loves to ask, 'What does it all come down to?' This shows that it is not only the scientists and philosophers – think of David Hume with his notorious 'nothing-buttery' – but poets also who can mine this vein. There is a poetry of reductionism. To be sure, Shakespeare, who could do everything, occasionally did this too. Fine reductive poetry is given to Edmund in *King Lear*, but the difference is that Shakespeare confines these harshly reduced intensities to a manifestly limited character, who exists within a world evidently richer than his own consciousness; in Marlowe the poetry of reduction becomes the language of the play itself.

So which horse does Marlowe back? Iron or gold? In *Tamburlaine* he backed iron; in *The Jew of Malta*, gold. Once more, let's play our silly game. What happens if Tamburlaine encounters the Jew of Malta? The answer (on Solon's lines) may seem obvious. The roaring warrior would simply blast his way through the Jew, with all his money bags. With his iron sword Tamburlaine would take (and throw away) the purse of Barabas. But can we be sure of this? Can we be certain that Barabas would not, with his 'policy', have bribed the soldiers of Tamburlaine before the battle, which, in consequence, fails to unfold? We are asking here not 'Who commands the moral high ground?' But 'Who commands the infrastructure, the low, causally primary level?'

Where other major innovative poets work by making the simple more complex, by introducing irony, reflexive consciousness and the like, Marlowe made his mark at once by being simpler. Outside his dramatic writing, the cast of mind can be seen in what he did with and to the Latin poet, Ovid. By the late sixteenth century Ovid was effectively buried in the allegorizing moral commentary which had accumulated round his writings. Marlowe had the wit to say, 'But it's all about sex'.

Tamburlaine, Part One, was written without any sense, it seems, that it would be followed in due course by *Tamburlaine*, Part Two (in which the hero dies). In Part One we have the story of a big-talking warrior who gets bigger and stronger. After getting bigger and stronger, he then gets bigger and stronger. After that he gets bigger and stronger still. And then the play ends. It is a slow unbroken crescendo. This weird simplicity is of course played against an audience expectation with which it is at odds. The audience, used to the *De Casibus Principum* tradition, are all waiting for this proud man, carried high on Fortune's wheel, to be brought down at last through some vicious mole of nature. Pride is supposed to be followed by a fall, sin to be punished. Zenocrate, the Soldan's daughter captured by Tamburlaine, says to him near the beginning of the play, 'The gods, defenders of the innocent, will never prosper your intended drifts' (1.ii.68–9). Hearing these words the first-time audience must have nodded sagely, only to learn slowly that Zenocrate is completely wrong. Tamburlaine prospers. It is a deep convention of drama that predictions are fulfilled, but not in this play. The Soldan says, 'Tamburlaine shall rue the day, the hour / Wherein he wrought such ignominious wrong / Upon the hallowed person of a prince'; but this never comes to pass: the expected moral structure is simply flattened by the juggernaut advance of the hero. In a manner, Tamburlaine dares not only the armies of the world but the natural form of the drama in which he moves and breathes, when he says, 'I glory in the curses of my foes' (1 *Tamburlaine*, IV.iv.29). When the virgins of Damascus plead for Tamburlaine to spare their city, even modern audiences can hardly believe their ears and eyes when Tamburlaine simply kills them all (see v.i.326f). There is nothing chivalrous about him, he will kill a child as easily as a heroic antagonist. Even within the category of heroism, we can distinguish, perhaps, ethical and non-ethical heroism. Ethical heroism is, for example, fighting bravely, against overwhelming odds. This stirs the moral imagination. Since Tamburlaine rises from obscurity we might expect to find a good deal of this species of heroism, as the humble Scythian shepherd confronts the armies of kings. But Marlowe plays it differently. In Part One, II.ii, when Tamburlaine engages Mycetes, already his forces are more numerous that those of the enemy; Mycetes' scout reports, 'An hundred horsemen of my company / Scouting abroad upon these champion plains, / Have viewed the army of Scythians, / Which make report it far exceed the King's (II.ii.39–42). Conversely, at III.iii when Tamburlaine confronts the Turkish Emperor, he is outnumbered, but then in Part Two when Tamburlaine faces Callapine, the son of Bajazeth, Tamburlaine's army has become innumerable as the 'quivering leaves of the forest' (III.v.5) and Callapine's – it turns out – is similarly innumerable (III.v.10). Once more it is as if Marlowe toys with our expectation of a noble courage exercised against the odds and then deliberately bombards us with a confusion of numbers which finally become meaningless. The result is that we have no sense of David slaying Goliath. Rather, Goliath slays Goliath.

In Part Two, Tamburlaine, once more, gets stronger and stronger, and then, with an odd abruptness, falls ill and dies. At the very end the audience is given what it was straining for but, because the death is not integrated morally with the preceding sequence of events, it is somehow wholly empty. It is as if one's opponent in a wrestling match deliberately stopped resisting, causing one to fall on one's nose.

How can so simple a structure engage continuous interest, how can it avoid being boring, how can it succeed as art? Part of the answer no doubt lies in the continuous excited fencing – behind the action of the play – with the structured expectations of the audience. This means that we have here not unison but a kind of latent counterpart. At the same time Marlowe does permit complexity of a sort, within the drama. For example he gives Tamburlaine three sons, two warlike, one (Calyphas) cowardly and self-indulgent. Tamburlaine in a hideous sequence, parodic of Christ before doubting Thomas, wounds himself (woundless till now) and invites his children to search the wound (Part Two, III.ii.126). All this to teach them valour. The two warlike sons, like little children clamouring for sweeties, cry out 'Give me a wound father! ... And me another!' (III.ii.132–3). But Calyphas says 'tis a pitiful sight' (III.ii.131). Here for a moment the 'noble' sons sound almost idiotic, and the despised Calyphas merely sane. We sense the beginning of a paradox: the cowardly son is the only one of the three brave enough to stand out against the dominating father. But Marlowe, having allowed this brief counter-movement, crushes it. At IV.i.27 Calyphas, taunted with his absence from the fight, says,

> I know, Sir, what it is to kill a man –
> It works remorse of conscience in me.
> I take no pleasure to be murderous –

So far, so strong; but then Marlowe brings him down on the last line. 'Nor care for blood when wine will quench my thirst' (i.30). Before the scene is over his tone changes entirely, from Christian morality to his own brand of non-violent Machiavellian policy

Take you the honour, I will take my ease;
My wisdom shall excuse my cowardice   (2 *Tamburlaine*, IV.i.49–50)

The moral counter-note is there but it is there to be elided.

Similarly, when Zenocrate pleads weeping for the city, Tamburlaine is moved and we scent, again, the chance of human moral conflict.

There angels in their crystal armours fight,
A doubtful battle with my tempted thoughts
For Egypt's freedom and the Soldan's life
His life that so consumes Zenocrate,
Whose sorrows lay more siege unto my soul
Than all my armies to Damascus walls   (1 *Tamburlaine*, v.ii.88–94)

But this huge speech, full of splendour, wholly without warmth, ends by telling us that it is beauty, not the imperative to mercy, which shakes Tamburlaine. The language, golden, opaque, aestheticizes all, and finally answers womanish beauty with male resolution.

This Marlovian simplicity is not the unproblematic effect of a simple mind. It is won with difficulty. Thus Marlowe thematizes his own central act of dramaturgy when he has Zenocrate plead with her terrible husband, that he will allow her to be weak, will, of his love, allow her to die:

But let me die, my love, yet let me die,
With love and patience let your true love die;
Your grief and fury hurts my second life.   (2 *Tamburlaine*, II.iv.65)

The drama, *Tamburlaine*, Part One, in its inhuman hardness, will not let its hero die, as such a proud man should die.

Yet at the very end of Part Two, Tamburlaine burns a Holy Book, crows of his invulnerability and then falls into sickness and dies. Here, it may be said the moral scheme is utterly clear and this comes at the formally significant point, the conclusion of the tragedy. Yes, except for one thing. Tamburlaine burns the wrong holy book, not the Bible but the Koran. This alone is enough to produce a strange evacuation of morality, at the heart of the concession to conventional imperatives.

The favourite reduction of the British Empiricists, reaching a chilling climax in the philosophy of Hume, is psychologistic. We have, finally, nothing but ideas confronting the mind, imprisoned in the skull. The favourite reduction of literary theorists in recent years has been to language or to text ('Il n'y a pas de hors-texte'). Marlowe, the connoisseur of reduction, seems to play with our favourite reduction, harshly cancelling it with his own. Thus we can feel at first that Tamburlaine is a mere tissue of rhetoric, of what Ben Jonson called 'furious vociferation'.[8] Part One opens with the foolish King Mycetes. His line 'yet live, yea live, Mycetes wills it so', if taken in isolation, looks, with its grand *illeism* – referring to oneself in the third person – like aesthetic high style. But the context turns it into inadvertent mock-heroic. Thus the first thing Marlowe does is to alert us to the possible hollowness, the emptily formal character of high language. In the second scene Theridamas comments explicitly on the rhetorical brilliance of Tamburlaine:

Not Hermes, prolocutor to the gods,
Could use persuasions more pathetical.   (1 *Tamburlaine*, 1.i.209–10)

But Tamburlaine answers

Thou shalt find my vaunts substantial ...   (1.ii.212)

At 11.iii.25–6 Theridamas speaks of the working words of Tamburlaine, but then adds that the actions top the speech. What we at first take for ranting sets like concrete, hardens into fact. In Part One, act IV, Tamburlaine says he will refute 'geographers' who exclude certain territories which he will trace. 'With this pen', he will reduce them all to a map. By this time we have seen enough of Tamburlaine to understand that he is not in this speech transposing action into text.

We understand that 'with this pen' means 'with my sword'. The force of the joke is materialist, cancelling the writerly metaphor. Marlowe's *Tamburlaine* is not an exercise in windy rhetoric. It is the single most sustained example in English Literature of authentic high style. This wholly successful exaltation is, eerily, the product of the accompanying brutalist reduction. There is a Latin tag which seems to have fascinated Marlowe: *Oderint dum metuant*, 'Let them hate me, as long as they are afraid of me.' Suetonius puts it in the mouth of the megalomaniac emperor Caligula.[9] In *Edward II* the younger Mortimer says, 'feared am I more than loved; let me be feared' (v.iv.52). In *The Jew of Malta* Barabas says, 'rather had I, a Jew, be hated thus, than pitied in a Christian poverty' (i.i.13–14). It is a question which haunts Machiavelli, the genius of reduction who stands behind Christopher Marlowe. Famously, in *The Jew of Malta* Marlowe brought Machiavelli onto the stage as Prologue. He makes him say 'Admired am I of them that hate me most' (line 10). This tag catches very exactly a certain eeriness at the heart of Machiavellian reductionism. It has the accent of realism – everything comes down to power in the end – and at the same time it is humanly crazy; it affirms, entirely unrealistically, that human beings do not need or want to be loved. As the philosopher Ansell says in Forster's *The Longest Journey*, 'How impractical! They live together without love.'[10] The final dramatic effect is a new species of alienation. Wilbur Sanders caught it well with the phrase, 'realist's sentimentality'[11] and linked the thought to Bertolt Brecht. Marlowe is not a simple uncomprehending victim of this strange error of the would-be realist. He knows that men like Tamburlaine and Barabas are unnatural in their very naturalism, that a queer effort of will is needed to produce so violent a reduction of the human. There is speech in Shakespeare's *Henry V* (iii.i.9f) where the king tells the soldiers before battle to turn their human faces into rocky precipices. Marlowe catches the paradox of a physicalism which is strangely unreal, when he makes Tamburlaine taunt the virgins of Damascus with their poor eyesight. Can't you see, he says, death on the point of my sword? (v.i.108–10). At this point, we might feel substance draining away from his utterance. But we know that he will, as philosophers say, make it true, just as earlier we saw the metaphor of the pen resolve itself into hard steel. This sword will indeed kill the virgins. These men who do not need love are unreal, and as palpable as steel itself.

When Machiavelli considers this proposition in *The Prince*, he decides that 'it is much safer to be feared than loved'.[12] And then adds the advice to escape hatred if possible. There is hesitation here but it is not morally prompted. Machiavelli is only unsure about what does and does not pay, in terms of power. It used to be said that Machiavelli was absurdly demonized by the Elizabethans, that they misread a neutral treatise on political power relations as diabolical immoralism. I was indoctrinated with this view before I read *The Prince*, but nevertheless found the text quite horrifying.

Federico Chabod, writing in the 1950s, may serve to represent what may be thought of as the orthodoxy: 'Nothing is further from Machiavelli's mind than to undermine morality – the truth is that Machiavelli leaves the moral ideal intact, and he does so because it need not concern him.'[13] But things seem to be changing. Harvey C. Mansfield in his recent translation of *The Prince* (1998) points out that Machiavelli clearly engages, in a destructive manner, with ethics; when he says there are no moral rules other than those made by men, he implies that these are freely alterable fictions. Mansfield roundly describes the book as 'a fundamental assault on all morality'.[14] Of course as Machiavelli was gradually transformed into the wicked 'Machiavel' of the Jacobean stage, extraneous elements crept in. Basically immoralism is supplemented by Italianate intricate aestheticism. The killings in *The Prince* are simple – rather like those in the Godfather films – but the murders done by the Machiavels are, increasingly, brilliantly complex, elegant, artistic. But the basic proposition 'Machiavelli is an immoralist, to whom power is all-important' – this is simply correct.

I have said that in *Tamburlaine* Marlowe backs iron as fundamental, and, in *The Jew of Malta*, gold. In both plays, however, he thinks about both possibilities. At the beginning of *Tamburlaine*, Part One, Cosroe speaks of 'prowess' and 'policies' ('prowess' belongs naturally to Tamburlaine, and 'policy' to Barabas, for whom it is a favourite word). In act II Meander tells his men to fling heaps of gold about the battlefield so that the 'greedy minded slaves' who fight in Tamburlaine's army will be distracted. This is rather like my idea earlier that the Jew of Malta might have bought Tamburlaine's army ahead of time. For the record, Meander's plan fails completely, here.

In *The Jew of Malta* the power of wealth and policy is played off against warlike action. Ferneze, the Christian Governor of Malta, unable to meet a demand for tribute made by the Emperor of Turkey, applies to the Jew for help. Barabas answers, affecting not to understand,

> Alas, my Lord, we are no soldiers;
> And what's our aid against so great a prince?

The 'First Knight' replies,

> Tut, Jew we know thou art no soldier;
> Thou art a merchant, and a monied man,
> And 'tis thy money, Barabas, we seek.   (I.ii.49–53)

Tamburlaine is all about kingship, about the toppling of kings by a rising super-king. Barabas says at the outset,

> I must confess we come not to be kings.

But it doesn't follow that he is uninterested in power. He speaks gleefully of the enormous wealth of the Jews, far greater than any Christian can command. He can afford to scorn war.

At one fascinating point, however, he appropriates the language of war. After he has been deprived of his wealth he says,

> But give him liberty at least to mourn,
> That in the field amidst his enemies
> Doth see his soldiers slain, himself disarmed,
> And knows no means of his recovery   (I.ii.203–6)

Remember the speech in which Tamburlaine appropriated the language of writing, referring to his sword as a pen. There, I said, the force and direction of the speech were to back the notion that, really, the sword would do the work. He we have a converse effect. The audience knows well that the Jew is not – will never be – an endangered military hero. The lines depend for their peculiar effect on a strong sense of the underlying reality of money. It is the use of consciously thin metaphor which brings both speeches close to humour.

Once the idea is put about that morals are made up by societies, cultural relativism can begin to take hold of the imagination. It is a doctrine which can take either of two basic forms. One is to suggest that ethical systems vary intractably, across societies, and that it is clearly futile for us to judge another society adversely because, had we grown up there, we would think as they do. The other form is to stress not so much variety as an unlooked-for likeness. Thus, where traditionally Christendom was the illuminated area and all beyond, infidels, Jews, etc., existed in a hellish darkness, one can suddenly surmise that we are in fact no different from our supposed antitype. For a while Marlowe plays quite lightly with simple transpositions, as Wilbur Sanders has shown.[15] When Barabas makes a great business of not wishing to be downwind of a Christian (II.iii.46–7) he blandly mirrors the Christian idea of *foetor Judaicus* 'Jewish stink', allegedly caused by menstruation in Jewish males (for this see Sir Thomas Browne, *Vulgar Errors*, IV.x). 'It's no sin to deceive a Christian', looks like a parallel case. J. S. Cunningham has pointed out in his edition of *Tamburlaine*[16] (p. 17) that Marlowe may have known Antonius Bonfinius' account in his *General Historie of the Turks* (published in Latin in 1543, translated by Knolles in 1603) of the Battle of Varna, where Cardinal Julian persuaded the Christian Vladislaus that it was right to break faith with his pagan antagonist, Amurath: 'Against a perfidious enemy it is lawful to us all cunning force and deceit ... deluding fraud with fraud. *Fides non est servanda haereticis.*'[17] In V.iii Barabas says that only he who will confer some advantage on me shall be called my friend. Remember Al Dunlap,[18] the source of the most Marlovian line to appear since Marlowe himself died: 'If you want somebody to like you, get a dog.' Incidentally, the runner up in this category is Liberace's 'Oh dear, yes, I cried all the way to the bank.' Barabas lightly adds five words of incalculable effect, 'for Christians do the like'. It is perhaps deeply characteristic of Marlowe that his essay on cultural relativism should take the form of a levelling down rather than of an explosion of bewildering moral variety.

But, that said, there is nevertheless a play of inversive wit in Marlowe's tragifarce of money. Before he levels all, he turns the conventional account upside down by making the Christians (supposedly the party of love and forgiveness) into the obvious exemplars of iron, of the military way. Thus Christian Ferneze says, 'Honour is bought with blood, and not with gold' (II.ii.56). The implication here is not that all are the same but rather, 'If the essence of Christianity is peace-making, the Jews are more Christian than the Christians.' There is a delicious moment near the end of *The Jew of Malta* where Barabas has Malta at his mercy. The governor assumes that they will be killed and publicly grits his teeth. Barabas answers,

> As for Malta's ruin, think you not
> 'Twere slender policy for Barabas
> To dispossess himself of such a place?
> For sith, as once you said, within this isle
> In Malta here, that I have got my goods,
> And in this city still have had success,

And now at length am grown your Governor,
Yourselves shall see it shall not be forgot:
For as a friend not known but in distress,
I'll rear up Malta, now remediless.   (v.ii.64–73)

In other words, 'Don't be silly. Why should I destroy a going concern?
I can make money here'.

Of course the half-thought that Marlowe will show that it is the Jews
who are more truly Christian – more genuinely merciful – than the
Christians does not survive for long. Barabas does not melt in pity for
his fellow creatures. One mode of egotism – the economic – meets
another – the militaristic – and outflanks it. The sparing of life is a lucky
by-product. I am reminded of E. R. Dodds lecturing, many years ago,
on Aeschylus. He explained how by the logic of vendetta, the logic of
iron, blood begets blood, one killing produces another, in a seemingly
interminable process. But then, said Dodds, came the invention of
money: the Saxon *Wergeld*, Greek blood money, broke the chain.
Instead of waiting to be killed in your turn, you could pay. A formal
system of fiduciary tokens, socially agreed, can save human flesh from
being cut. It isn't the human beings who have suddenly turned merciful.
Instead, as Marxists used to say, 'It's the system.' I think here of Karl
Popper's observation about the human faculty of forming testable
hypotheses, which are either falsified, or survive. We send them ahead
like expendable troops. As Popper said, 'They die in our stead.'[19] It
begins to look as if the real difference between Tamburlaine and Barabas
is that Tamburlaine is pre-social, while Barabas is social. The old
reductionist jibe, 'Aren't they silly? They think bits of shiny metal are
of huge importance',[20] is in a way foolish (we have returned to the
paradox of the unrealistic realist), for a piece of shiny metal will buy
bread which will feed a starving child. But this, indeed, depends on a
preliminary conceptual *fiat* – 'let this gold equal value X' which all
accept. And they do accept it, and so it works. But Popper thought
Barabas and Karl Marx were wrong, and that Francis Bacon was right.
He wrote, 'Marx discovered the significance of economic power; and it
is understandable that he exaggerated its status … The argument runs,
he who has the money has the power; for, if necessary, he can buy guns
and even gangsters. But this is a roundabout argument. In fact, it
contains an admission that the man who has the gun has the power. And
if he who has the gun becomes aware of this, then it may not be long
until he has the gun and the money.'[21] He then goes on to say that

wealth and ownership are strong only as long as they are protected by a state machine, by law, and offers Russell's examples: Caesar was raised to power by his creditors who bet on his success, but, having attained power, was able to defy them. Charles V borrowed to become emperor and then snapped his fingers at the Fuggers, who had bank-rolled his success. So iron wins.

And Shakespeare answers, 'You think you are kings of infinite space but you are bounded in a nutshell. Your down-to-earth theory is just one more dream of false control.'

NOTES

1 See his *Science and the Modern World* (Cambridge: Cambridge University Press, 1927), p. 57.
2 Strictly, he said, 'Social being determines this consciousness' (Preface to *A Critique of Political Economy*). But he has just said, before this, that 'the mode of production' determines social being.
3 *Principia Ethica*, I.xiii, (1st edition, 1903; Cambridge: Cambridge University Press, 1962), p.16.
4 *Language, Truth and Logic* (London: Gollancz, 1936), chapter 6.
5 See his *Dilemmas* (Cambridge: Cambridge University Press, 1960), p. 69.
6 *A New Mimesis* (London: Methuen, 1983), p. 181.
7 See Hiram Haydn (ed.), *The Portable Elizabethan Reader* (New York: Viking Press), pp. 221–2.
8 *Discoveries*, 960; printed as Appendix One in Ben Jonson, *The Complete Poems*, ed. George Parfitt (Harmondsworth: Penguin Books, 1975), p. 398.
9 *Caligula*, xxx. Curiously, Caligula thought he ruled the world – and *did*. His megalomania, like the vaunts of Tamburlaine, was 'substantial'.
10 Chapter 26 (Harmondsworth: Penguin Books, 1960), p. 212.
11 *The Dramatist and the Received Idea: Studies in the Plays of Marlowe and Shakespeare* (Cambridge: Cambridge University Press, 1968), p. 58.
12 Translated with a commentary by Harvey C. Mansfield (Chicago and London: University of Chicago Press, 1998), p. 66.
13 *Machiavelli and the Renaissance* (London: Bowes and Bowes, 1958), p. 142.
14 *The Prince*, intro., p.x.
15 *The Dramatist and the Received Idea*, pp. 42–3.
16 Manchester: Manchester University Press, 1981.
17 See e.g. Thomas Lupton, *A Persuasion from Papistrie* (London: 1581), p. 47 (where, however, the doctrine is seen as wicked!).
18 Al Dunlap sacked 11,000 people at Scott Joyce. See *Forbes*, 28 August 1995. This could be described (spanning the worlds of Barabas and Tamburlaine) – as 'economic carnage'.
19 See 'Of Clouds and Clocks' in his *Objective Knowledge: An Evolutionary Approach* (Oxford: Clarendon Press, 1979), pp. 206–55, at p. 244.

20 See e.g. Thomas More, *Utopia*, ed. E. Surtz and J. H. Hexter (New Haven and London: Yale University Press, 1965), p. 152.

21 *The Open Society and its Enemies*, 2 vols. (London: Routledge and Kegan Paul, 1966), vol. II, p. 127.

PART II

Literature and translation
Jan Potocki and *The Manuscript Found in Saragossa*: novel and film

Jacques-Louis David, *Count Stanislas Potocki* (1781)

Comparative Criticism 24, pp. 55–77. Cambridge University Press 2002
DOI: 10.1017/S0144756402005450 Printed in the United Kingdom

Jan Potocki and his Polish milieu: the cultural context

NINA TAYLOR-TERLECKA

The biography of Jan Potocki – the historian, archaeologist, traveller, ethnographer, orientalist, pioneer in Slavonic archaeology, collector, political activist and publicist, publisher, printer, aeronaut, novelist and dramatist – begins in Pikow, near Tarnopol on the Seret river, proceeds via Warsaw, Geneva and Lausanne, Bavaria, Italy, Austria, Tunis, Malta, Spain, Hungary, Serbia, Turkey, Egypt, Paris, the Orkneys, Morocco, Berlin, Lower Saxony, Denmark, St Petersburg, the Caucasus and Mongolia, and terminates on his estate of Uładówka in the Ukraine. To honour his memory, the German scholar J. Klaproth suggested naming some islands in the Yellow Sea Potocki Archipelago;[1] but the idea was never implemented.

Books of heraldry trace the Potocki pedigree back to 1236 in Potok (Torrent, or Brook) in the Palatinate of Kielce, not far from the Hills of the Holy Cross, Łysogóry or Bald Hills and their summit Łysica (Bald Pate). Over the centuries the family multiplied and prospered, married into the best circles, and manned many of the most prestigious and lucrative appointments within the administration and military hierarchy of the Polish–Lithuanian Commonwealth. By the early 1600s they belonged to the magnate class. By the eighteenth century, their joint fortune matched the income of the Polish state; and notable signs of degeneracy had set in.[2] Franciszek Salezy (1700–72) accumulated a vast fortune and, when his second wife brought him a dowry of forty villages and several townships, he became virtually the richest man in the entire Commonwealth, the proprietor of some 2 million hectares of land and over 130,000 peasant serf families in the palatinates of Sandomierz, Cracow, Ruthenia, Podolia and Bracław. With an annual income of 3 million Polish zlotys, he was known as the *Mały królik Rusi* – the little king of Ruthenia.

Jan Potocki was born in 1761 in the twilight years of Saxon rule. After

55

sixty years of anarchy and apathy under the Wetting dynasty, Polish culture was at its lowest ebb. Spiritually stagnant, internally paralysed, the Polish–Lithuanian Commonwealth was drained by wars and totally dependent on powerful neighbours who posed a permanent threat to its territorial integrity. Stifled by outmoded notions of nobility, the Polish gentry of the day was a notoriously unproductive class, a venal prop of the corrupt magnate oligarchy, easily manipulated by foreign powers. Educated within the now obsolete Jesuit system, the squirearchy clung to its *złota wolność* or golden freedom, the dogma of free elections, which allowed a non-Pole to be elected to the Polish throne, and the prerogative of *liberum veto*, whereby the vote of one muddle-minded landowner in the pay of a magnate or alien government (usually Russia) could suspend parliament and effectively block any attempt at reform. The burghers were disabled by outdated legislation (Parliamentary Statutes of Piotrków 1496). The magnates, by virtue of their wealth, remained a law unto themselves.

When Jan Potocki was three years old, Stanisław August Poniatowski was hoisted to the Polish throne on Russian bayonets (1764). The new king had to address an urgent need for reform in every realm of public life – economic, political, constitutional, social, legal, religious, military, demographic. Though impeded on every side by society and the system, he evolved a complex and far-ranging programme for modernizing Poland and restructuring the state. His aim was to transform traditionalistic Poles into enlightened Europeans, and the obsolete, anachronistic, malfunctioning gentry republic into a constitutional parliamentary monarchy. Ever his own minister of culture and propaganda, the king took charge of the nation's spiritual life, his court playing the role of central office of arts and education. Culture was not an end in itself but a means.

Early on in the reign the king's private chaplain, Ignacy Krasicki, drafted a plan for a periodical named *Monitor*, largely modelled on the French edition of the *Spectator*. In the service of reform, the first professional theatre opened in 1765. Modelled on the Comédie Française, but conceived primarily as an educational aid in the propagation of modern ideas, it was financed from the king's privy purse. Dramatic repertoire had to be created *ab initio*. Stanisław August hand-picked his authors, and probably edited their manuscripts. For most of the reign, the theatre served as tribune and soap-box, voicing new postulates and programmes. In the words of the playwright Franciszek Zabłocki 'Ambona grała sceny, teatr – katechizm' (The pulpit staged theatricals, the theatre enacted the catechism). There was also a private court theatre, where 'the intriguing fantast Jan Potocki' and young prince Józef Poniatowski acted 'without overmuch talent, but with temperament'.[3]

Some of the ideas enunciated in *Monitor* must have struck its readers as being radical in the extreme – as when it asserted that loom, plough and hard toil were nobility's best credentials. In harnessing stage productions to editorial directives, the strategists at the Royal Castle resorted to diversionary tactics, but in the main Stanisław August's cultural campaign was uncompromising, and made little allowance for the ignorant and impoverished ranks of the middle and lower nobility. It was symptomatic that the gentry protested *en masse* at the proposal to legalize freedom of religious practice. The bulk of the nation was unable to assimilate reform, and in the political arena the king encountered opposition at every step. In 1767 the aristocratic Confederates of Radom appealed to Catherine II of Russia to overthrow Stanisław August. As one of their leaders, Jan Potocki's father Józef was partly responsible for the 'Russian guarantee'. In 1768–72 the Confederates of Bar, an armed union of reactionary magnates, struck out against the king, the dissenters and the Russian empire in a desperate attempt to preserve religious intolerance, reactionary forms of government, and the old prerogatives of the landowning class. After four years of partisan fighting, they were suppressed by the combined forces of the Russian and Polish armies. The upshot was the first partition of Poland (1772).

Prior to the reign of the last king, Polish interest in West European narrative fiction was restricted by normative poetics and cultural backwardness, aggravated by the inarticulacy of the Tiers Etat (the bourgeoisie).[4] At the time of Jan Potocki's birth, the favourite reading stock of the 'unenlightened' comprised such hardy perennials as Pseudo-Kallistenes' *The History of Alexander the Great*,[5] the *Gesta romanorum*, and tales of *Till Eulenspiegel*, now condemned as crude, tasteless, and lacking rhyme or reason. Provincial wives and daughters indulged in medieval and baroque romances: *La belle Maguellone*, the story of the noble and beautiful Melusina from Jean d'Arras's *Chronique de la Princesse*, Wacław Potocki's adaptation of John Barclay's *Argenis* (1621), Giovanni Ambrogio Marini's tale of baroque chivalry *Il Calloandro fedele* (1652), and Mme d'Aulnay's *Histoire d'Hippolyte*. These staunch favourites had to endure the gibes of the Enlightened critics when, in the 1760s, *Monitor* launched a campaign against the romance: disseminating an outmoded ideology, it was seen to be remote from life's real problems and detrimental to morality. *Mélusine* was labelled a soporific, and *Maguellone* pilloried as a supreme example of corrupt taste: it was fit reading only for the fashionable, and in the *bibliomachia* of Wegierski's mock heroic *Organy* (*The Organ*, 1784), it is used as a heavy ballistic missile. Yet both fair heroines weathered the onslaught for another quarter of a century, making their last appearance in print in 1787. Meanwhile romance-baiting generated some of the stock jokes of the period; and there may be a distant echo of the polemic in the story of Lopez Suarez (Days 32 and 33 of the *Manuscript*), when the travellers set out in a coach packed full with romances.

Meanwhile positive models were needed. Pending the production of native fiction that would serve as a weapon in the struggle for social change, translation policy was targeted at a wide reading audience (the 'enlightened' read French as a matter of course, though only the hyper-enlightened read English in the original). *Monitor* set the tone by printing excerpts of Rousseau's *Emile* in 1765 and Montesquieu's *L'Esprit des lois* in 1768. The first major book translations included Antoine Galland's *Thousand and One Nights*, Daniel Defoe's *Robinson Crusoe*, Lesage's *Gil Blas*, praised by Krasicki as a 'romance of manners', and l'abbé Prévert's *Manon Lescaut*. As 'Prince of Poets' and leading cultural policy-maker of the reign, Krasicki provides a convenient measure of official taste and aspirations. He had his own copies of *Robinson Crusoe* (Feutry's version), *Manon Lescaut*, and the bowdlerised French edition of *Gulliver's Travels* (1765) by l'abbé Desfontaines, on the basis of which he considered Swift to be a first-rate, though sometimes intemperate satirist. He quoted most often from *Candide*, preferred *Don Quixote* to almost any other book, highly commended Lesage and Goldsmith, but had reservations about Richardson. In mooting that Polish reality and Polish problems provided a worthy novelistic theme, he first and foremost promoted the message of Fénelon's *Télémaque* (1699) (curiously enough, the only serious work of literature to have been translated in the cultural doldrums of the Saxon kings[6]), valuing 'that immortal work' less for its epic dimension than for its didactic usefulness. Fénelon's work, immensely popular across Europe, was a sequel to the *Odyssey* following the education of Telemachus, son of Odysseus. 'Telemachomania' may have been a major contributory factor to the birth of modern Polish fiction.

The European reading list of a progressive Pole was thus largely defined by the time Jan Potocki reached his ninth birthday. Yet, if we are to judge by philosopher, mathematician and Jesuit professor Jan

Bohomolec's *Diabeł w swojej postaci z okazji pytania 'Jeśli są upiory'* (*The Devil in His Own Shape with reference to the debate on the existence of vampires*, 1772),[7] superstition was rife in rural districts; and the 1789 edition appealed directly to parish clerks and estate managers to stamp out such reprehensible practices among the peasantry.[8] Bohomolec defines the natural and the supernatural from the position of an enlightened theologian, and in stating the case for sacred history and reason, he distinguishes between belief in magic, witchcraft, vampires and the devil, which he condemns, and God-sent visions and dreams, likewise visitations of souls from heaven and purgatory, and the ability of a possessed soul to 'foretell a distant future and perform deeds that surpass the common powers of man' – all of which may be trusted. In a rationalist age, Bohomolec reinstated the tenets of faith and defined the limits of criticism within a Polish margin of tolerance.

Two points here deserve the attention of readers of *The Manuscript Found in Saragossa*. Bohomolec defines the Cabbala as 'a secret theology or ability raising the human mind to consider heavenly matters and commune with the spirit through the discovery of divine nature and perfection, the hierarchy and offices of angels, number of heavens, the proportions among the elements, the efficacy of herbs and stones, animal instincts and the most secret human thoughts' (p. 227). Yet 'although the Cabbala appears to have God Himself as its aim, it is free neither of superstitions nor of godlessness'. As an example of naïve superstition, he adduces the tale of an enchanted tower in Spain, taken from the Arab manuscript of one Abulacim Tristaberig. After his lawless conquest of the Spanish kingdom, the hero Rodrigez has no money to raise an army and decides 'to seek for treasure in a magic tower that no one had hitherto dared enter. That tower stood between two precipitous rocks half a mile to the East of the city of Toledo' (Part II, p. 270). In the vast subterranean hall he encounters a statue of Time, inscribed with prophecies of doom, which hurls its mace to the ground. Following a great crash, fearful screams and the roar of thunder, the tower collapses and vanishes. Zdzisław Libera comments that the tale of the magic tower has little in common with Jan Potocki save for its Spanish scenery, the motif of treasure hidden in a rocky underground, and the mysterious awe of the underground chamber.[9] Rather, Bohomolec's anecdotal use of this motif reminds us that somewhere on the fault-line Otranto–Udolpho the nucleus of a Gothic chronotope contained in an old Arab tale had been customized for a Polish readership, and awaited further exploitation.

Bohomolec's book appeared in 1772, the year of the First Partition. Having focused on targets and programmes, the first decade of the new reign – coinciding with Potocki's childhood – ended in political shock, destabilization, and considerable loss of territory. In view of 'the troubles that disrupted Poland from the very beginning of the reign' Jan and his brother Seweryn were sent to school 'in a country sheltered from so many upheavals' (of which Potocki père had once been a major instigator). Jan, for his part, 'always remembered the pleasure he derived from the bustle of their precipitous flight when the Bar Confederates approached the parental estate in Podolia'.[10] By taking their sons to Switzerland, Count and Countess Potocki rejected the option of Warsaw's élitist Szkoła Rycerska, or Cadet Corps, founded in 1765, which inculcated Enlightenment ideas and educated boys in a spirit of public-mindedness and civic loyalty. Its pupils imbibed patriotism through the poetic medium, declaiming each morning Krasicki's 'Hymn do Miłości Ojczyzny' (Hymn to Our Love of Our Country, 1774).[11] The school's alumni came to include national heroes such as Tadeusz Kościuszko (1746–1817) and, among Jan Potocki's peers, politicians and poets such as Julian Ursyn Niemcewicz (1758–1841), and Napoleonic generals, such as Karol Kniaziewicz (1762–1842).

On the banks of Lake Geneva the brothers received private and public tuition in languages and history for four years,[12] though Jan claimed to his second wife Konstancja that he had reached his sixteenth year without acquiring any knowledge.[13] In the wake of catastrophe, the dissolution of the Jesuit Order by the Pope in 1773 created the opportunity and provided the funds to devise a modern, secular educational system in Poland under state control, and centrally supervised by the Komisja Edukacji Narodowej (Commission for National Education), to which a whole bevy of erstwhile Jesuits were co-opted. This ministry of education adopted the French system, inviting Condillac among others to write a text-book in logic.

The programme of the 1760s came partly to fruition in the 1770s. Jan Potocki's years of absence in Geneva and Lausanne coincided with the first flowering of imaginative literature in Poland. Krasicki, the literary legislator of the 1760s, now entered a spate of intense creativity, publishing works that were instantly recognized as canonical texts of the Polish Enlightenment and unsurpassed models in their respective genres. His poetry and novels became bywords, to be quoted and emulated. In 1775 he gave the Stanislavian era its first poetic masterpiece,

Myszeidos pieśni dziesięć (*The Mousiad in Ten Cantos*), a mock heroic hybrid in the mould of Ariosto, Boileau and Pope, in consummate *ottava rima*. His burlesque epic of Cats and Mice at war is a send-up of primitive historiography, a satire against medieval credulity, and a political allegory all in one; and the king of the Mice's flight on a magic broomstick to the Witch's Bald Mountain harks parodistically back to the dark sciences of a superstitious age.

The following year, 1776, saw the abolition by the Polish Sejm of torture and the death penalty for witches, and the birth of the modern Polish novel. Krasicki wrote *Mikołaja Doświadczyńskiego przypadki* (*The Adventures of Mikołaj Doświadczyński*, 1776)[14] in an atmosphere of sharp ideological debate because he was convinced of the utility of the novelistic form; and he wrote according to the rules he had laid down in *Monitor*. In the event, it proved to be an early instance of *Bildungsroman*.[15] As artistic incarnation of the Enlightenment manifesto in politics, culture and morality, *Doświadczyński* also provides a true encyclopedia of the genre. A tripartite educational romance that quashes and supersedes Baroque romances, the hero's fictional autobiography emerges in Part I from the matrix of a satirically-tinged domestic novel, critical of contemporary education. It evolves into a 'novel of manners' of provincial and metropolitan life, then incorporates fragments of travelogue to assume the garb of the picaresque. The central panel combines a Robinsoniad on the island of Nipu and Utopia (or rather *eutopia*) largely inspired by the ideas of Rousseau's *Emile*. Then *Lehrjahre* give way to more *Wanderjahre*, and stories of pirates and slavery in the vineyards of South America turn Part III unashamedly into a *roman d'aventure*. Condemnation of contemporary Polish society and the Polish nobility in the closing chapters extends the work into a civic novel, or correlate of the *conte philosophique*. Like Voltaire's Candide, Doświadczyński resolves to cultivate his garden, not as a hermit in self-sufficient seclusion, but as a Benevolent Squire, philosopher philanthropist or 'Polish physiocrat', who aspires to enhance the well-being of his subjects and transform his estate into a Polish Nipu. A panoply, or picture-gallery of fictional genres, *Doświadczyński* spelled the rise of the novel in Poland. Systematically inverting the despised romance into a framework for didacticism, Krasicki deploys all the devices of his time in a thoroughly integrated though unpatterned, temporal and linear sequence.

While Potocki studied in Switzerland, the literary scene in Poland was enriched by further translations: Marmontel's *Contes moraux*

(1776–8), Lesage's *Le Diable boiteux* (1777), the full text of *L'Esprit des lois* (by Czarnek, 1777) and the *Lettres persanes* (1778). Aged sixteen, Potocki left for Vienna and took part in the war of the Bavarian succession as a sub-lieutenant in the Austrian army (1778), only to have his dreams of military fame shattered by the peace treaty of Techen in the same year. If we accept his words at face value, it was the boredom he experienced in the Hungarian hinterland, in a remote garrison near the city of Buda, that turned him almost overnight into a voracious reader. Books were scarce, but 'a few works of Voltaire's fell into his hands. He read them with relish, he read everything he could procure.' A new world now opened, and with it a passionate interest in travel, history, ancient chronology and scientific progress.[16]

Even as Potocki discovered Voltaire in a Hungarian garrison, Krasicki earned the sobriquet of 'le Voltaire de la Pologne' for his most extreme articulation of Enlightenment ideas. Although he never attacked religion *per se*, he provoked a scandal by publishing the mock heroic *Monachomachia czyli wojna mnichów* (*Monachomachia or the War of the Monks*, 1778), a virtuoso satire on the gluttony, ignorance and bibacity of the monastic orders, whose theological dispute deteriorates into a brawl resolved by the *deus ex machina* of a famous drinking bowl; though the work is ultimately an indictment of manners rather than of religion. In the same year, he summarized the Polish enlightened ideal and the social, economic and political programme of the royal reformist camp in *Pan Podstoli* (*The Pantler of the King's Household*), a carefully welded, unashamedly utilitarian, discursive novel, without plot, psychological evolution or internal dynamics. Krasicki's most popular book, and arguably his most influential, *Pan Podstoli* is a fictionalized manual of estate management and a treatise on the humanitarian treatment of serfs. Set in an ideal Polish countryside and ideal Polish manor house, the eponymous hero of this everyday utopia is an average gentleman-farmer and advocate of the golden mean, representing the kind of model paternalism Krasicki wishes to promote nationwide. Some radical asides may be fortuitous (Znałem wiele dusz chłopskich w panach, wielu chłopów, którym by jaśnie wielmożnymi, jaśnie oświeconymi być przystało'– I found many of the lords had a peasant soul, and many peasants could have been right honourables), and Krasicki proposes no fundamental legal reforms, but recommends a humane approach, including better housing and health care and increased productivity. Whether the *War of the Monks* or *The Pantler* reached the provincial waters of Buda is a moot point, but Potocki's personal acquaintance with Krasicki is documented in the latter's correspondence.[17] Potocki may yet have been intrigued by *Historia na dwie księgi podzielona* (*History Divided in Two Books*, 1779),[18] in which Krasicki resorts to a hoax preface and the fiction of a manuscript found under a feeding trough in the stable of a woodland inn between Biłgoraj and Tarnogród.[19] This was followed in the space of just a few months by a rich spate of comedies, satires, translations of Ossian, the epic *Wojna Chocimska* (*The Chocim War*), a compendium *Zbiór potrzebniejszych wiadomości, porządkiem alfabetu ułożonych* (*Collection of Most Essential Information, Alphabetically Arranged*, Warsaw, 1781), and fables. His works invariably set new standards and provided a blueprint for aspiring poets.

Untempted by Krasicki's didactic elegy of the landed estate, Potocki then visited Italy, Sicily (1778–9) and Tunis, served with the Knights of Malta in their expeditions against the pirates in the Mediterranean (1779–80), and probably visited Spain (1781). By the time Potocki reappeared in Warsaw and was appointed royal chamberlain (1782),[20] Krasicki had created most of the literary masterpieces of the Stanislavian era. In other areas, Enlightenment was at risk. The Zamoyski Code of Law had been rejected (1780), signifying the failure of four years of reform work in the Polish Parliament. The industrial developments of Antoni Tyzenhauz had crashed, the porcelain factory of Belvedere had closed. Alchemy was popular. Two French chemists had died from the poisonous fumes of a broken retort.[21] During a brief sojourn in Warsaw the charlatan Cagliostro had promised to raise ghosts from the dead, rejuvenate mature ladies and manufacture gold, and had consequently fleeced more than one gullible nobleman of his fortune.[22] Magnate opposition was triumphant, and following the Sołtyk affair at the Sejm (1782) the nobility was sinking into apathy. More and more the theatre was becoming an arena of conflict between different ideologies. No longer the exclusive stamping-ground of the titled and landed, it attracted an audience of intelligentsia, burghers, and in due course the plebs. In the spirit of Diderot, the stage began to present scenes of everyday family life and heroes from the Tiers Etat – merchants, lawyers and craftsmen – and money played an increasingly important role in the motivation of comic plots. Warsaw audiences saw Friedrich Schiller's rebellious *Die Räuber* for the first time (1781).

At this juncture Jan and Seweryn inherited a fortune of 2 million zlotys from their unmarried uncle Piotr, to redeem which their kinsman Stanisław Felix gave them gratis the sum of 300,000 zlotys.[23] Potocki now began research into the antiquities of Hungary and Serbia (1783), then travelled east through Oczaków to Constantinople, where he spent six weeks and was decorated with the Order of Saint Stanisław (1784). He also started writing short tales in which he sought 'to imitate faithfully the expressions and figures' of Eastern writers. After visiting Egypt, he sailed from Alexandria to Venice, travelling on to Florence to see the Borgia archives and collection of Coptic manuscripts in Velletri, which further fired his interest in ancient chronology. The travel descriptions contained in his letters to his mother provided the basis of his first published book, *Voyage en Turquie et en Egypte* (1788).

In Warsaw in 1785 Potocki married Julia Lubomirska, one of the four daughters of Stanisław Lubomirski,[24] who was estimated to own thirty-one towns and 738 villages,[25] and of Elżbieta née Czartoryska, a first cousin of the king. In the process, he became the brother-in-law of two of his Potocki kinsmen, Ignacy (1750–1809) and Stanisław Kostka (1755–1821), sons of Eustachy.[26] Julia's dowry included the palace of Łańcut and Krzeszowice. Known in the drawing-rooms of Warsaw as *Giuletta la bella*, her charm and grace were universally held to be beyond compare,[27] though Princess Lubomirska later commented that her daughter lacked any notion of duty or constraint.[28] No sooner wed, the young Potockis left for Paris, where they lived with Julia's mother in her apartments at the Palais-Royal and where their sons Alfred and Artur were born (in 1786 and 1787 respectively).

It was during Jan Potocki's Parisian sojourn that the main novelistic output of the Polish Enlightenment appeared. Satirical, tendentious, political, educational, didactic, it all bears the hallmark of Krasicki. Dymitr Michał Krajewski's (1747–1817) bestselling *Podolanka, wychowana w stanie natury, życie i przypadki swoje opisująca* (*The Maiden of Podolia, reared in the natural state, describing her life and adventures,* 1784)[29] is often polemical with regard to Rousseau. But his *Wojciech Zdarzyński, życie i przypadki swoje opisujący* (*Wojciech Zdarzyński, describing his life and adventures,* 1785) is an overt tribute to Krasicki, and the hero's journey by air balloon to an ideal lunar land, whose rational human order is contrasted to the feudal realities of Poland, resorts to devices of the grotesque familiar from the world of Cyrano de Bergerac.[30] Brought up according to the principles of *Emile*, the heroine of Krajewski's *Pani Podczaszyna* (1786) might be styled a 'nouvelle Héloïse' in the Polish manner. In his *Ksiądz Pleban* (*The Parish Priest,* 1786) Józef Kazimierz Korwin Kossakowski offers an unimpeachable model for the conscientious clergy, not inspired by utopian models, but replicated from the real-life republic of Pawłów (Merecz) near Wilno, a village whose peasants had prospered after the reforms of Paweł Ksawery Brzostowski in 1769. In *Obywatel* (*The Citizen*, 1788), Kossakowski presents a discussion on legal and parliamentary issues between a critical son, recently returned from abroad, and his father, who favours compromise. As his legacy was thus exploited, Krasicki turned to writing oriental tales.

In Paris, meanwhile, Potocki appears to have been sympathetic to the social and political aspirations of the French bourgeoisie. He was acquainted with Helvetius's widow and with Constantin, comte de Volnay, whose ideas on the relativity of religions he would have found congenial. Volnay's *Voyage en Syrie et en Egypte* (1787) and *Les Ruines ou Méditations sur les révolutions des empires* (1791) would likewise have provided congenial reading. From Paris Potocki visited Italy and Holland (his month's stay during the civil war resulted in *Voyage en Hollande*, 1789) and England, leaving London for Paris on 20 December, 1787. It was presumably on this occasion that, much to the chagrin of Stanisław August, 'instead of studying England's system of government for what we would be well-advised to imitate', Potocki set out for the Orkneys in search of Ossianic remains.[31] Earlier that year Princess Lubomirska had travelled to England with Jan's cousin and brother-in-law Stanisław Kostka and the scientist Lamotte, one of Mesmer's first pupils. An afficionada of Mesmer's art, the princess had her thinning hair threaded to 'magnetic bushes' in vases on bedside tables to ensure an abundant new crop of curls. Lamotte tried out his experiments in the carriage, and on the cross-channel vessel attempted to magnetize the elements, much to the anger of the superstitious captain, who threatened to have him thrown overboard. According to Niemcewicz (who translated Jan Potocki's *Voyage en Turquie* and *Voyage en Hollande* into Polish), 'Each time the princess, Mr Potocki, the abbot Piattoli, Lamotte, young prince Henryk Lubomirski and I held hands and created a magnetic chain at Lamotte's behest, everyone experienced diverse emotions. I alone was recognized as *rebelle au magnétisme*.'[32] In England Stanisław Kostka met Horace Walpole.[33]

In January 1788 Potocki and his wife left for Vienna. On hearing rumours that the king of Prussia was planning to invade Poland, he returned post-haste to Warsaw in April, his head a-whirl with pre-Revolutionary events and seemingly outlandish projects. As an outward sign of patriotic commitment, he now donned the traditional costume of the Polish nobleman, a return to which was advocated by the king's cousins, Prince and Princess Adam Kazimierz Czartoryski. Indeed the *kontusz*, as it was known, played an essential if symbolic role in the current renaissance of patriotism and reforming tendencies. Potocki's appearance at court in hybrid Cossack and Circassian garb, complete with sabre and shaven head 'in the manner of fifteenth-century engravings'[34] caused a sensation in Warsaw, eliciting an endless flow of gossip, the rumour being spread that 'the entire Potocki household would dress up in the Polish fashion'.[35] In the year of his first book publication, his sartorial patriotism made him the hero of a series of jokes, epigrams and satirical verses that circulated in manuscript form.[36]

Fashion apart, Potocki's views constituted a strange political cocktail. He entered civic life as distinct opponent of Prussia, disseminating anti-Prussian leaflets. His political brochure entitled *Essai de Logique* touched dangerously on Polish–Russian relations, alluding to the passage of foreign armies and their stationing on Polish territory in peacetime; its publication would inevitably create difficulties for Stanisław August in his attempt to secure an alliance with Russia.[37] On 13 May 1788, he offered one-fifth of his private annual income to increase the corps of engineers, in which he was appointed to the rank of captain, and was elected deputy for Poznań in time for the opening on 6 October 1788 of the four-year Sejm. A last struggle to save Poland's independence, the Long Parliament's campaign for renewal and reform was a moral crusade that – if succesful – would result in a bloodless revolution.

For the next four years parliamentary sessions were stormy, sensational and dramatic. While his cousins Ignacy and Stanisław Kostka took an active part in political debates, Jan was unfamiliar with matters of administration and legislation, and ill-prepared by his Swiss education for making speeches in Polish. Instead, having founded a free printing-press beyond the censor's reach in the parental palace on Rymarska Street, he published the *Journal hebdomadaire de la Diète de Varsovie* (Weekly Journal of the Warsaw Parliament) (9 November 1788–6 June 1792) for a mainly foreign readership, contributing some twenty unsigned articles, often in the form of letters to the editor. His press also printed political brochures, parliamentary speeches chiefly of the *Stronnictwo Patriotyczne* (Patriotic Party), and numerous literary works.[38] He moreover converted three large rooms in a side wing of his palace into a public reading-room, which he furnished with chairs, tables, writing materials, and a good supply of Polish and foreign newspapers and brochures.[39] He also helped launch a political debating club in the Borch Palace in Miodowa Street. One hundred and fifty subscribers contributed to its opening, and their payments covered maintenance costs.[40]

It was in this period of heightened patriotic fervour that Potocki published one of his most valid historical works, the five-volume *Essay sur l'histoire universelle et Recherches sur celle de la Sarmatie* (Warsaw, 1789–92). Meanwhile, literature was becoming politicized to an unprecedented degree. Tendentious to a fault, though still concerned to entertain its public, theatre reflected the burning issues of the day, and focused on inculcating the correct message. For the sake of the patriotic cause, novels of the period break the commandments of modern scholarly historiography. Krajewski inaugurates a line in heroic ancestral history with *Historia Stefana na Czarncy Czarnieckiego, wojewody kijowskiego, hetmana polnego koronnego* (*The Story of Stefan Squire of Czarnca, Palatine of Kiev, Field Hetman of the Crown*, 1787), then reactivates the myth of honest forebears in *Leszek Biały, książę polski, syn Kazimierza Sprawiedliwego* (*Leszek the White, Prince of Poland, Son of Casimir the Just*, 1789), a highly publicistic and topical prose poem in twelve books modelled on *Télémaque*. In *Goworek herbu Rawicz, wojewoda sandomirski* (*Goworek, coat-of-arms Rawicz, Palatine of Sandomierz*, 1789) the radical political publicist Franciszek Salezy Jezierski (1740–91) resorts to transparent allusiveness, and the internecine feuds related by a thirteenth-century palatine in a village scenery of Youngian tombstones unambiguously reflect magnate intrigues at the Polish court. Describing treason and skulduggery at the court of a legendary Leszek VIII, Jezierski's *Wypis z Kroniki Witykinda* (*Extract from the Chronicle of Wtykind*) is merely a polemical pamphlet in historical costume; while his *Rzepicha, matka królów* (*Rzepicha, Mother of Kings*, 1790) revives the national legend of how the peasant Piast became a Polish prince and, in Aesopic language, highlights the perennial problems of the peasantry and constitutional reform, contrasting the depraved and parasitical ways of the nobility with the wisdom and modesty of industrious country-folk.

Taking off from the fairyland of Krasicki's *Mousiad*, the airborne theme weaves its way through the literature of the Polish Enlightenment, reappearing in science fiction guise in Krajewski's *Wojciech Zdarzyński*. After the Montgolfier breakthrough in 1783, ballooning became the obsession of the Polish magnate class.[41] Even as the future of the nation was being debated at sittings of the Long Parliament, Potocki designed at his own expense with the help of Jean-Pierre Blanchard[42] the construction of a balloon equipped with a huge tin furnace and two side cabinets for carrying out experiments in mid-air. It was stitched over a period of several months by eighteen journeymen tailors from 13,000 ells of rainbow-coloured Chinese silk imported from foreign manufactories, and filled three large halls of his palace in Rymarska Street. In May 1790 he ascended above the garden of the former Mniszech palace in Mysia Street with his poodle and his favourite Turk Ibrahim, who weighed 230 pounds, on board. According to Blanchard, 'The enthusiastic Turk could not recognize the town of Warsaw which he now saw in miniature below and exclaimed "Captain, do you know to whom this English-style garden just below belongs? To the Republic, I replied"'.[43] When, according to other accounts, Ibrahim panicked at the sight of the blazing furnace and nearly wrecked the enterprise by trying to jump from aloft, Potocki held him at pistol-point, and the stove was jettisoned instead.[44] The first Polish aeronaut to return safely to land (the balloon launched by the young Czartoryski princes in Puławy in February–March 1784 with their favourite cat on board burst into flames),[45] Potocki spent half-an-hour in the air and descended in time for an important parliamentary debate. There are unfortunately no extant copies of his *Relation d'un voyage aérostatique*, published the same year.

The period 1791–4 saw an unprecedented flowering of the Warsaw theatre. It became a kind of second national assembly, and witty didacticism gave way to overt political propaganda in the battle to win the nation's soul and a vote for reform. By October 1790, however, Potocki was in Paris, attending meetings of the Club des Jacobins. He was still abroad in 1791 when the Sejm proclaimed the Constitution of 3 May, which he always defended in public with conviction and gusto. He then travelled through Spain and Morocco, then back to Paris via Cadiz, Lisbon and England. His return to Warsaw via Dresden coincided with the news that parliament had stripped his cousin Stanisław Felix Potocki and his wife's brother-in-law Seweryn Rzewuski of their functions (27 January 1792). Weeks after he relinquished his army commission (10 April 1792), the Targowica Confederates' conspiracy to overthrow the Constitution (14 May) and the invasion of Poland by Russian troops caused him to re-engage in political life (29 May 1792) and revert to his old project of organizing a corps of Kurpian fusiliers. In June, with his brother Seweryn, he enlisted as a volunteer in the Lithuanian army under the command of General Michał Zabiełło, warning Stanisław August after the latter's accession to Targowica (24

July) that Poland would become the communal property of three powers.

Thereafter Jan Potocki withdrew from public life to devote his days to scholarship and writing. In August, his *Parades* in the manner of *commedia dell'arte* and the French *théâtre de la foire* were perfomed on the stage of the Lubomirski Palace at Łańcut.[46] Publications proliferated. After *Voyage dans l'Empire de Maroc... Suivi du Voyage de Hafez, récit oriental* (Warsaw 1792) his *Chroniques, mémoires et recherches pour servir à l'histoire de tous les peuples slaves* appeared in the year of the Second Partition (1793), followed by *Fragments historiques et géographiques sur la Scythie, la Sarmatie et les Slaves* (Brunswick 1796). During the Kościuszko Insurrection (24 March–16 November 1794), which caused him to view his fellow-Poles as victims of their own ill-directed, unpragmatic patriotism,[47] Potocki saw his lachrymose comedy entitled *Les Bohémiens d'Andalousie. Comédie mêlée d'ariettes en 2 actes et en vers.* staged at Rheinsberg (20 April 1794). Then, as Julia lay dying of tuberculosis in Cracow, he travelled from Berlin through Lower Saxony to study Wendish antiquities; barely a month before her death, he wrote of 'personally having no cause for grief'. Princess Lubomirska commented laconically that although his wrongs were infinite, he was scrupulous in paying Julia's monthly allowance.[48] According to the social grapevine, Julia had been faithful to her husband, even though she enjoyed an ideal, reciprocated love for Eustachy Sanguszko, who after her demise came by night to raise the lid of her coffin, but failed to resurrect her with a kiss.[49] Potocki duly set out on a two-year journey to Hamburg, Denmark and Vienna (1794–6), and published his *Voyage dans quelques parties de la Basse-Saxe pour la recherche des antiquités slaves ou vendes* in the year of the third and last partition, when Poland was razed from the map of Europe, and her last king sent in exile to St Petersburg (1795).

Over the next decade and a half Potocki was outside the orbit of Polish public and cultural interests, being intermittently in Russian service. Delegated by the nobility of the government of Bracława to attend the coronation of Tsar Paul I in 1796, he was refused permission to travel to Siberia. Despite this initial rebuff, his subsequent travels (to the Caucasus and Outer Mongolia) and sundry political activities all pertain to the interests of the Russian empire. Wedded for a second time, to Konstancja Potocka, the erstwhile fiery patriot had no difficulty evolving a *modus vivendi* with his father-in-law Stanisław Felix, one of the instigators of Targowica and, in drafting the biographical sketch *Le*

Comte Stanislas Félix Potocki né en 1750, he came close to condoning past transgressions.

As Stanisław August once observed, perhaps not without irony, every Potocki distinguished himself in his own specific field;[50] and the microcosm of the clan provides yet another comparative context. As an agent of treason, Stanisław Felix has understandably received a bad press; but, though his verse may not rank with Krasicki's, he undoubtedly wrote Polish with more grace than his son-in-law Jan.[51] His significance for literature is, however, of a different nature. The murder of his first wife Gertruda Komorowska at his parents' behest provides the plot for one of the finest narrative poems of the Romantic age, Antoni Malczewski's *Maria*, dedicated to Niemcewicz (1825); while his latter-day horticultural follies on the estate at Tulczyn inspired one of the great poems of the Polish Rococo, Stanisław Trembecki's *Sofijówka* (first fragments published 1804).

Two of Jan Potocki's other cousins were serious authors in their own right. Ten years Jan's senior, a Freemason and long-serving member of the Commission for National Education, likewise an anti-monarchist who once travelled to St Petersburg to seek the help of Catherine II against the Polish king, Ignacy Potocki (1750–1809) was a renowned political orator whose public speeches acquired exemplary status as early as 1785.[52] The owner of a rich library and numismatic collection, he penned 'Remarks about Architecture', universals, occasional verse, a three-act comedy *Sekator* (*The Pruning Shears*, 1777), dramatic sketches, and a lyrical drama entitled *Pożar w Pałacu Rzeczypospolitej* (*A Fire in the Palace of the Republic*, after 12 December 1782). As one of the leaders of the Patriotic Party during the Long Parliament, he favoured the Polish–Prussian alliance and co-created the Constitution of 3 May. For his part in the preparations for the Kościuszko Insurrection, he was imprisoned in St Petersburg, and later interned by the Austrians.

As a young man, his brother Stanisław Kostka (1755–1821) wrote travel diaries (*Itinéraire de Glaciers de Chamonix*, 1774; *Voyage en Italie, contenant* ... 1779; *Voyage en Italie et en Allemagne*, 1783, 1795–7; *Voyage en Vésuve*, 1786), and translated Cicero, Ossian and Rousseau's *Discours sur les sciences et les arts*. Although their political profiles differ over some major issues, Stanisław Kostka and Jan shared many interests. An erudite collector of fine art, Stanisław Kostka filled his Warsaw and Wilanów palaces with canvases by Leonardo, Guido Reni, Annibale Carracci, Correggio, Carlo Dolci, Tintoretto and the latest Angelica Kauffman. A Freemason, he also collected prints, coins, medals, Etruscan vases, ancient gems and sculptures, manuscripts and books. Jan apparently gave him his own archaeological collection of Egyptian, Greek, Etruscan, Roman and Chinese objects.[53] From 1778 onwards Stanisław Kostka was a deputy at the Sejm, and during the Long Parliament was one of the best speakers from the Patriotic Bench. In the Polish–Russian war of 1792 he fought on the Lithuanian front at Mir; after Targowica he joined Ignacy in Leipzig, and then Dresden, and helped prepare the Kościuszko Insurrection, in which he was unable to participate, having been arrested and imprisoned by the Austrians. Following the demise of Poland, he remained passionately interested in problems of language, art, literature and architecture. He organised schooling (after 1815), designed the facade of St Anne's church in Warsaw, wrote about rural building (*O architekturze wiejskiej. Projekt dzieła* MS) and rhetoric (*O wymowie i stylu* 1815–16), became involved in theatrical polemics, compiled a Chinese chronology,[54] wrote operas,[55] and published a Polish version of the great German art historian Winckelmann, who moulded eighteenth-century neo-classicism (*O sztuce u dawnych, czyli Winkelman polski* Warsaw, 1815). He thus ranks as Poland's first art historian.

When Potocki began work on his *Manuscrit trouvé à Saragosse*, Polish literature had not yet produced its own 'Gothick'. As from the early 1770s, traces of the style were to be found in the sentimental gardens of the Czartoryskis at Powązki, at Princess Lubomirska's in Mokotów, at Kazimierz Poniatowski's in Solec and the Radziwiłłs in Nieborów, and the new vogue for Ossian created a congenial climate of mystery and gloom. There is a Gothic air to the otherwise southern landscape of Krasicki's *Chocim War*, and the manner permeates Cecylia Dembowska's illustrations to Adam Jerzy Czartoryski's *Bard polski* (*The Polish Bard*, 1803).[56] The first literary Gothic to reach Poland was, however, the translation of an unidentified German novel *Błaganie, scena z szrednich wieków* (*Implorings, a Scene from the Middle Ages* 1796).[57] Fashionable society read the troubadour romance *Les Chevaliers du Cygne* (1795) in the original French. Sundry feudal-chivalrous novels and brigand adventure romances could be perused in Polish versions,[58] but the English Gothic novels were available only in French translation. Ann Radcliffe's *Romance of the Forest* (1791) had to wait almost four decades to appear in Polish as *Puszcza, czyli Opactwo St Clair* (*The Wilderness, or the Abbey of St Clair*, 1829).

In the event, the published fragments of Potocki's *Manuscrit trouvé à Saragosse* in St Petersburg in 1804–5 precede the birth of the first 'original' Polish Gothic story by a year. Countess Anna Mostowska, née Princess Radziwiłł, followed her collection of Gothic tales entitled *Strach w zameczku* (*Ghost in the Little Castle*, 1806) with *Astolda księżniczka z krwi Palemona pierwszego księcia litewskiego czyli nieszczęśliwe skutki namiętności* (*Astolda, a Princess of the Blood of Palemon, the First Lithuanian Prince, or the Unfortunate Consequences of Passion*, 1807), a marriage of fiction and perfunctorily treated source material, interlaced with Gothic elements, sentimentalism and historicism. There is something cerebral about Mostowska, or at least an acute awareness that the fate of Clarissa and Pamela could no longer move a female audience, and that a romance 'in the taste of our century' must combine terrible apparitions, ghosts, earthquakes, ruined castles, devils and witches. In resorting to the stereotypic motifs and devices of the European models and dutifully replicating their melancholy landscape of mystery and dread, she wrote to please her public.

In the wake of Ossianism, Youngism and the Gothic, the Polish novel evolved through psychologism with Maria Wirtemberska's *Malwina, czyli domyślność serca* (*Malvina, or The Heart's Intuition*, 1816)[59] and the sentimental fiction of Feliks Bernatowicz *Nierozsądne śluby. Listy kochanków na brzegach Wisły mieszkających* (*Absurd Vows. Letters of Lovers Living on the Banks of the Vistula*, 1820) and Ludwik Kropiński *Julia i Adolf czyli nadzwyczajna miłość dwojga kochanków nad brzegami Dniestru* (*Julia and Adolph, or the Extraordinary Love of Two Lovers Living on the Shores of the Dniester*, 1824). Historical romance then paves the way to Romanticism.

Five years after Jan Potocki's death and a year before his own, Stanisław Kostka, who had devoted the latter part of his life to defending the achievements of the Enlightenment and propagating liberal ideas, published his most famous work, the novel entitled *Podróż do Ciemnogrodu* (*A Journey to the Obscure City*, Warsaw 1820) which was unfavourably received by conservative circles. In the guise of a travelogue it delivers a great diatribe against monks, astrologers and charlatan doctors, against clericalism and obscurantism, medievalism and sentimental or sensational literature, and the current fashion for ghosts, vampires and brigands. Small wonder that its author became, albeit posthumously, the bête noire of Polish romantics. Several years before the new literary school came of age in Poland with Adam Mickiewicz's *Ballady i romanse* (1822), Stanisław Kostka had derided a trend that he identified with a gratuitous return to the Middle Ages and mysticism, and the bad old ways of pre-Enlightenment Poland. The name Ciemnogród has earned a place of its own in the Polish language as a synonym for stupidity, fanaticism and superstition, and Potocki's relentless campaign on behalf of knowledge and reason was to cost him his post as Minister of Public Education only a few months before he died. A spokesman for neo-classicism (although he encouraged his daughter-in-law Anna Maria Tyszkiewicz to redesign her palace in the new pseudo-Gothic style), Stanisław Kostka remains the product of a rational age. His ideology would have been congenial to Jan who – as Tadeusz Sinko has pointed out – rather than offend his reader with the blasphemy of deriving Christian dogmas and sacraments from ancient pagan mysteries, preferred to hide behind the mask of the Cabbalist, Ahasverus, and Velasquez.[60]

Symbolically, perhaps, Stanisław Kostka dedicated his *Journey to the Obscure City* to Jan's widow Konstancja, relying on her 'doubly Polish nature' to accept his 'modest work', which he felt to be 'Polish', and in which she would find nothing 'borrowed from foreigners'. In later years, Konstancja proved to be an extreme pro-liberal and devoted Polish patriot. By yet another twist, her second husband, Edward Raczyński, a traveller who published works on the Orient and devoted much of the income from his Rogalin estate in western Poland to cultural or publicly useful causes, blew his brains out. Rumour later had it that Raczyński staged his own death by dressing the corpse of a Jew in his clothes and blowing off the man's head with cannon shot, then set off on a pilgrimage to the Holy Land; he was allegedly sighted in Rome in penitential garb.[61]

In conclusion, the components of Jan Potocki's prose were largely to be found in the common pool of Polish Enlightenment literature. At about the time of his birth, novelistic theory and form were imported, adapted and customised to meet the cultural and political agenda of the day. Long before he began writing *The Manuscript Found in Saragossa*, narrative genres from world literature were available in Polish translations. Ignacy Krasicki had created a stockpile of models and devices to be exploited by lesser talents. Their overriding, often mundane, duty was to educate, persuade and win over their readers to a new type of social and political thinking, so they harnessed fantasy, satire, pseudo-fiction and pseudo-history to the cause of national survival. Jan Potocki did not suffer these constrictions and, while his patriotic *engagement* (his battle with censorship, and his urgent plea to strengthen Poland's military power) cannot be overlooked, his shortcomings in his native tongue meant that in literary matters he was unlikely to resort to vernacular sources and models. Acclaimed as an architect of the French novel, he was prevented by an accident or oversight of education from contributing to the Polish-language fiction of his age.

NOTES

1 J. Klaproth, *Notice sur l'Archipel de Jean Potocki* (Paris, 1820).
2 Jerzy Łojek, *Potomkowie Szczęsnego. Dzieje fortuny Potockich z Tulczyna 1799–1921* (Lublin: Wydawnictwo Lubelskie, 1980), pp. 29–72.
3 Andrzej Zahorski, *Warszawa za Sasów i Stanisława Augusta* (Warsaw: Państwowy Instytut Wydawniczy, 1970), p. 135. Prince Józef Poniatowski (1763–1813), the king's nephew, was later Maréchal de France.
4 Aleksander Lipatov in *Istorya polskoy literatury*, edited by V. V. Witt, I. S. Miller, B. F. Stakheev and V. A. Chorev (Moscow: Izdatelstvo 'Nauka', 1968), vol. 1, p. 123.
5 *Wokół Doświadczyńskiego. Antologia romansu i powieści*, edited by J. Jackl (Warsaw: Państwowy Instytut Wydawniczy, 1969).
6 First Polish poetic version by Jan Stanisław Jabłonowski, Palatine of Ruthenia, Sandomierz 1726; prose translation by Michał Abraham Trotz (based on Rotterdam original of 1736), Leipzig Gröll, 1750. Reprinted in 1768 and 1775.
7 Praised by Krasicki in his satire 'Pochwała wieku' (Praise of Our Century), it went through several editions between 1772 and 1777.
8 Władysław Smoleński, *Przewrót umysłowy w Polsce wieku XVIII. Studia historyczne*, edited with an introduction by Andrzej Wierzbicki (Warsaw: Państwowy Instytut Wydawniczy, 1979), pp. 109, 110–12, 115, 117.
9 Zdzisław Libera, '*Rękopis znaleziony w Saragossie* Jana Potockiego na tle polskiej kultury literackiej XVIII wieku. (Uwagi i spostrzeżenia)', in Zdzisław Libera, *Wiek Oświecony. Studia i szkice z dziejów literatury i kultury polskiej XVIII i początków XIX wieku* (Warsaw: Państwowy Instytut Wydawniczy, 1986), pp. 203–12.
10 Maria E. Żółtowska, 'Jan Potocki w oczach żony: nie dokończony szkic biograficzny', *Wiek Oświecenia 3. Wokół problemów literatury i filozofii* (Warsaw: Wydawnictwo Uniwersytetu Warszawskiego, 1978), pp. 68–9.
11 Published in *Zabawy Przyjemne i Pożyteczne*, and reprinted the same year in Adam Kazimierz Czartoryski's *Katechizm moralny dla uczniów Korpusu Kadetów* (Moral Catechism for Pupils of the Cadet Corps). Krasicki twice recycled his poem in parodistic vein as a hymn to a liquor glass.
12 The dates given by Żółtowska in *Polski Słownik Biograficzny*.
13 Żółtowska, 'Jan Potocki w oczach'.
14 Ignacy Krasicki, *Mikołaja Doświadczyńskiego przypadki* (*The Adventures of Mikołaj Doświadczyński*, 1776) was reprinted four times in five years and translated into German. The English version is entitled *The Adventures of Mr Nicholas Widsom*, trans. Thomas H. Hoisington; with an introduction by Helena Goscilo (Evanston, Ill.: Northwestern University Press, 1992).
15 Yu. L. Bulakhovskaya and A. Lipatov have described *Doświadczyński* as one of the first attempts in European literature to show a hero in development, using elements

of psychological motivation and individualization of language of characters. Chapter 'Ignacy Krasicki' in *Istoriya polskoy literatury*, pp. 164–5.

16 Żółtowska, 'Jan Potocki w oczach'.

17 In a letter to Antoni Krasicki from Berlin dated 21 July 1794, Krasicki mentions that Jan Potocki visited him there earlier that month. Ignacy Krasicki, *Korespondencja*, edited by T. Mikulski, 2 vols. (Wrocław: Zakład Narodowy im. Ossolińskich, 1958), vol. II. p. 644. Other letters contain references to Julia Potocka. In 1793, Jan Potocki's sister Anna Maria (1767–1829) married Krasicki's nephew Jan.

18 It was subsequently translated into German (1784) and French (1817).

19 The device was imitated by Franciszek Salezy Jezierski in *Wypis z Kroniki Witykinda tłomaczony przez Grzegorza z Słupia, dekretorum doktora, opata świętokrzyskiego, który żył około roku 1375, z autografu w bibliotece na Łysej Górze najdującego się* (c. 1790) (*Excerpt from the Chronicle of Witykind, translated by Grzegorz of Słup, doctor of decrees, abbot of Holy Cross, who lived c. 1375, from the manuscript in the library situated on Bald Mountain*).

20 Antoni Magier, *Estetyka miasta stołecznego Warszawy*, with an introduction by Jan Morawiński (Wrocław and Warsaw: Zakład Narodowy im. Ossolińskich – Wydawnictwo, 1963), p. 438.

21 *Ibid.*, p. 130.

22 *Ibid.*, pp. 129, 226.

23 Teodor Ostrowski, *Poufne wieści z oświeconej Warszawy*, edited with an introduction by Roman Kaleta (Wrocław and Warsaw: Zakład Narodowy im. Ossolińskich – Wydawnictwo, 1972), p. 136.

24 The author of memoirs. Stanisław Lubomirski, *Pod władzą księcia Repnina. Ułamki pamiętników i dzienników historycznych (1764–1768)*, edited with an introduction by Jerzy Łojek (Warsaw: PAX, 1971).

25 In 1770. See Stanisław Zahorski, *Stanisław August polityk* (Warsaw, 1957).

26 Stanisław Felix, Ignacy and Stanisław Kostka and Jan's father Józef were all great-great-grandsons of Stanisław 'Rewera' Potocki (1579–1667), Grand Hetman of the Crown.

27 Fryderyk Schulz, *Podróże Inflantczyka z Rygi do Warszawy i po Polsce w latach 1791–1793*, trans. Józef Ignacy Kraszewski, edited with an introduction and notes by Wacław Zawadzki (Warsaw: Czytelnik, 1956), p. 169 and footnote p. 348.

28 Maria Ewelina Żółtowska, 'Stosunek Jana Potockiego do Insurekcji. Listy Jana Potockiego do Henryka Lubomirskiego z 1794 r.', *Wiek Oświecenia* 11. *W dwusetną rocznicę Powstania Kościuszkowskiego* (Warsaw: Wydawnictwo Uniwersytetu Warszawskiego, 1995), p. 32.

29 Michał Krajewski, *Podolanka, wychowana w stanie natury, życie i przypadki swoje opisująca* (1784). An adaptation of Henri Joseph Du Laurens's *Imirce ou la Fille de la nature* (1765), it went through seven editions in one year.

30 Jerzy Pietrkiewicz, 'Krajewski's Warsaw on the Moon', *The Slavonic and East European Review* (1962).

31 Zofia Libiszowska, *Życie polskie w Londynie w XVIII wieku* (Warsaw: Instytut Wydawniczy PAX, 1972), p. 223. See also Nina Taylor 'Ossian in Poland', in *Scotland and the Slavs. Selected Papers from the Glasgow-90 East-West Forum,*

edited by Peter Henry, Jim MacDonald and Halina Moss (Nottingham: Astra Press, 1993) pp. 1–14.

32 J. U. Niemcewicz, *Pamiętniki czasów moich*, 2 vols., edited by J. Dihm (Warsaw: Państwowy Instytut Wydawniczy, 1957), vol. 1, pp. 243–4.

33 Libiszowska, *Życie polskie*, p. 222.

34 Schulz writes that his costume was half-Polish, half-Eastern. Schulz, *Podróże*, p. 157.

35 Ostrowski, *Poufne wieści*, p. 256.

36 See Józef Szczepaniec, 'Jan Potocki w poezji z lat 1788–1789', *Wiek Oświecenia*. 10. *W kręgu nauki i sztuki* (Warsaw: Wydawnictwo Uniwersytetu Warszawskiego, 1994) pp. 51–88.

37 Jerzy Łojek, *Dziennikarze i prasa w Warszawie w XVIII w.* (Warsaw: Książka i Wiedza, 1960), p. 91.

38 Józef Szczepaniec, *Drukarnia Wolna Jana Potockiego w Warszawie 1788–1792* (Wrocław: Wydawnictwo Uniwersytetu Wrocławskiego, 1998).

39 Schulz, *Podróze*, p. 272.

40 Zdzisław Libera, *Życie literackie w Warszawie w czasach Stanisława Augusta*, (Warsaw: Państwowy Instytut Wydawniczy, 1971), p. 135.

41 In 1783, Stanisław Okraszewski, one of Moszyński's assistants in the Royal Collection, built a cardboard balloon seven feet high and six wide. Painted blue, and with a gold belt at the join of the two hemispheres, it was released by the king's sister, Ludwika Zamoyska, Madame de Podolie. August Fryderyk Moszyński, *Dziennik podróży do Francji i Włoch Augusta Moszyńskiego architekta JKM Stanisława Augusta Poniatowskiego 1784–1786*, translated from the French and edited by Bożena Zboinska-Daszyńska (Cracow: Wydawnictwo Literackie, 1970), p. 480 and footnote p. 649. Moszyński was architect to King Stanisław August.

42 Blanchard first came to Warsaw in 1788 and made a balloon ascent above Warsaw on 10 May 1789.

43 Jean-Pierre Blanchard *Analyse de la nouvelle machine aërostatique que j'ai inventée et exécutée a Varsovie pendant l'année 1789 et 1790* (Berlin: G. J. Decker et fils, no year), pp. 12–13; cited in Jean Potocki. *Ecrits politiques*, rassemblés, présentés et annotés par Dominique Triaire. Centre d'Etude du dix-huitième siècle de Montpellier (Geneva: Editions Slatkine, 1987), p. 15.

44 Magier, *Estetyka*, p. 131 and footnote p. 356.

45 See Nina Taylor, 'F. D. Kniaźnin and the Polish Balloon', in *Literature and Politics in Eastern Europe*. Selected Papers from the Fourth World Congress for Soviet and East European Studies, Harrogate, 1990, edited by Celia Hawkesworth (London: Macmillan and New York: St Martin's Press, 1992), pp. 125–48.

46 They include *Gile amoureux*, parade en 2 scènes et en prose; *Le Calendrier des vieillards*, parodie de la Cloison, comédie du Théâtre de Mme de Genlis; *Le Comédien bourgeois*, scène italienne; *Voyage de Cassandre aux Indes*, parade; *Cassandre homme de lettres*, parade en 1 acte et en prose; *Cassandre démocrate*, parade.

47 Żółtowska 'Stosunek Jana Potockiego'.

48 *Ibid.*, pp. 40, 32.

49 Roman Kaleta, *Anegdoty i sensacje obyczajowe wieku oświecenia w Polsce. Dokumenty. Wspomnienia. Facecje* (Warsaw: Czytelnik, 1958).

50 Magier, *Estetyka*, p. 131.

51 *Wiersze Józefa Koblańskiego i Stanisława Szczęsnego Potockiego – zapomnianych poetów Oświecenia*, edited with an introduction and commentaries by Elżbieta Aleksandrowska (Wrocław: Zakład Narodowy Imienia Ossolińskich, Wydawnictwo Polskiej Akademii Nauk, 1980).

52 He is one of the models recommended in Krajewski's *Wojciech Zdarzyński*.

53 Fortia de Piles and Boiseglin de Kerdu, *Voyage de deux Français en Allemagne, Danemarck, Suède, Russie et Pologne* (Paris, 1796).

54 *Rys chronologii, religii, języka, nauk, ludności, rządu, handlu, obyczajów, zwyczajów, sztuk, pomników i celniejszych wynalazków Chińczyków … Z źródłowych pisarzy zebrany* 1815. An outline of chronology, language, sciences, population, government, customs, arts, monuments and most outstanding discoveries of the Chinese … Collected from source authors.

55 *Umarły żyjący, czyli diabeł włoski. Komedioopera w 3 aktach* (*The living dead, or the Italian devil. A comic opera in three acts*) was staged in Warsaw on 27 April 1803 as *Diabeł włoski, czyli nieboszczyk żyjący. Zejście Bielawskiego do prewetu. Opera w 1 akcie* (*Bielawski's descent to the privy*, c. 1820–2) and *Cyrce i Ulisses, czyli bydlęta. Opera buffo.* (*Circe and Ulysses, alias the beasts. Opera buffo*) were published by Roman Kaleta in *Anegdoty*.

56 *Bard Polski. Pisany przez Xięcia Adama Czartoryskiego a przez siostrę jego Marię z Czartoryskich Xiężnę Wirtemberską w Świątyni pamięci złożony. Roku 1803* (*The Polish Bard. Written by Prince Adam Czartoryski and deposited by his sister Maria née Czartoryska Princess of Wirtemberg in the Temple of Memory in 1803*), is to be found in the Czartoryski Library in Cracow. See also L. Dembowski *Moje wspomnienia*, 2 vols. (St Petersburg, 1898).

57 Zofia Sinko, 'Gotycyzm', in *Słownik literatury polskiego Oświecenia*, edited by Teresa Kostkiewiczowa (Wrocław: Zakład Narodowy Imienia Ossolińskich, 1977), pp. 183–90.

58 *Ibid.*

59 There is an English version entitled *Malvina, or The Heart's Intuition*, trans. Ursula Phillips (London: Polish Cultural Foundation, 2001).

60 Tadeusz Sinko, *Historia religii i filozofia w romansie Jana Potockiego* (Cracow, 1920), p. 52; cited by Smoleński, *Przewrót*, p. 31.

61 In 1850. Natalia Kicka, *Pamiętniki*, with an introduction and notes by Józef Dutkiewicz (Warsaw: Instytut Wydawniczy PAX, 1972), p. 459. See also Edward Raczyński, *Rogalin i jego mieszkańcy* (London: The Polish Research Centre, 1964), pp. 93, 123, 144 ff.

Comparative Criticism 24, pp. 79–98.   © 2002 Cambridge University Press
DOI: 10.1017/S0144756402005462   Printed in the United Kingdom

The comic effect in *The Manuscript Found in Saragossa*

DOMINIQUE TRIAIRE

TRANSLATED BY CHARLOTTE PATTISON

It is curious to note that contemporary literary criticism is powerless when confronted with emotion: why does a book make us fearful? Why does it make us weep? Why is a licentious novel arousing? It is true that emotion cannot be understood independently of its context and that it has been carefully distanced by recent criticism. Any discussion of the subject will be controversial and as the comic is the topic of this paper, we know only too well that what is hilarious to one person is not necessarily so to another. Moreover, emotion is fragile and in this study, whilst looking, pursuing, analysing the comic, I have often found myself under the gibbet of Los Hermanos, before dried-out corpses, wondering indeed whether comic there has been.

Therefore, I shall cautiously talk of the comic *effect*, rather than the comic as such, which serves well to reintroduce the subject: at a given moment, something made me laugh and it is from this point that I departed, with the risk of sometimes (let us hope not too often) walking alone. Laughter impregnates *The Manuscript Found in Saragossa*; it is woven into the speech of the narrator, it bursts forth, breaks off and remains menacing at the heart of even the most pathetic of stories. If the effects of the comic are innumerable in the novel,[1] it seems that they appear at three different levels: at the level of the word through rhetoric, at the level of the proposition through the absurd and at the level of the sentence through action.

Comic effects produced by rhetoric are the most frequent. I shall pass rapidly over the standard effects such as accumulation: 'nous savions déjà l'hébreu, le chaldéen, le syro-chaldéen, le samaritain, le copte, l'abyssin, et plusieurs autres langues mortes ou mourantes'[2] (we already knew Hebrew, Chaldean, Syro-Chaldean, Samaritan, Coptic, Abyssinian, and several other dead or dying languages) or accumulation combined with alliteration: 'Ce souverain était un grand, gros, gras, blond, blanc, blafard' (p. 158) (This ruler was a fat, podgy, pale, fair-skinned, pasty-faced grandee, p. 152). Most of the effects of the comic through rhetoric rest on a duality and are divided into two categories: the first following a principle of contradiction, the second a principle of identity.

The antiphrasis, which combines two antithetical and explicit terms, serves as a good example of the first category; it is the rhetorical device which is used most often: 'des *pendus* plus *honnêtes*' (p. 72) (more obliging hanged men, p. 58), 'livre *lumineux*, appelé ainsi parce que *l'on n'y comprend rien du tout*' (p. 111) (a book of splendour, which is so called because nothing can be understood of it at all, p. 101), 'le *spectre lourdaud*' (p. 287) (the one who had helped, p. 289), 'un bas *noire* et un *blanc*, une pantoufle *rouge* et une *verte*, peut-être même une *culotte* sur sa *tête*' (p. 617) (a black and a white sock, a red and a green slipper, perhaps even breeches on his head [my translation]), 'l'on pourrait faire de vous un *très bel objectif de téléscope* [...] vous m'offrez là *une image tout à fait riante*' (p. 411) (you could be turned into a nice telescopic lens [...] what a very droll picture you are painting, p. 417). This last example shows how the second term may be superfluous; by disappearing, it gives rise to *irony*, which brings together two antithetical terms, however, in which one is explicit and the other implicit: 'on a par hasard trouvé mon poignard dans le corps d'un homme assassiné' (p. 73) (my dagger was by chance found in the body of a man, p. 60) – noting the fact that 'by chance' was a clear intention; 'Croyant sans doute que le mouvement était salutaire aux enfants' (p. 381) (Doubtless believing that to be active was good for children, p. 387) – Busqueros knows that his mother, who could not have read Rousseau, cared but little for his health. A further example dismantles the mechanism in the same way, but underlines its fragility:

Si Folencour eût su le sens que mon père attachait à ce qu'il venait de dire, il n'en eût pas été très flatté; mais il prit son compliment dans le sens le plus littéral et il en parut fort content. (p. 256) (If Folencour had known the meaning my father attached to what he had said, he would perhaps not have been very flattered by it. But he took my father's compliment quite literally and seemed very pleased by it, p. 256–7)

Without any implicit terms, no irony: it eludes Folencour, who fails to notice it. But who knows the implicit term, and with this the burst of laughter, if not the reader? Emotion restores the author–reader relation. In irony, the author leaves a kind of gap, which the reader has to fill in, which then releases the laughter.

However, the two terms do not necessarily have to be contradictory; a shift in meaning, however slight, may suffice and we find once again the two explicit terms on the side of the misunderstanding, the implicit and the explicit term on the side of the metaphor. *Misunderstanding* separates the point of view of Soarez and the Moro (p. 360); it is frequent with Busqueros who, ignoring the habitual silence of Avadoro senior, continues to speak to him when he has fainted and then wonders: 'Vous ne dites rien, Seigneur Avadoro [...] tout le monde vous parlera, apprêtez-vous à répondre' (p. 536) (You're not saying a word [...] Everyone will speak to you. Make sure you have an answer ready! p. 546). And what is more, the comic effect is accentuated by the fact that Busqueros, whilst misinterpreting what has been said to him, does, however, without wanting or knowing it, arrive at the truth: 'Seigneur don Lope, je conçois qu'à votre âge vous n'ayez pas envie de vous marier [...]' ('Señor Don Lope, I imagine that at your age you have no desire to get married ...); up to this point the confusion is simple because we know that Lope is in love with Ines, but he continues: 'alléguer à une fille le courroux de votre bisaïeul Iñigo Soarez [...] voilà véritablement une idée bizarre' (p. 378) (But to offer a girl as an excuse the anger of your great-grandfather Iñigo Soarez, [...] that's really eccentric, p. 384). A discovery which will not remain without philosophical consequences. The metaphor opposes the ordinary term, which remains implicit, to an explicit term with displaced meaning: Thibaut fears that he will 'effaroucher le *gibier*' (p. 124) (startle the quarry, p. 115), i.e. 'la pauvre dariolette' (the fair maiden); Velásquez thinks he has a right to the pâté 'qui d'ailleurs n'avait pas de *maître*' (p. 273) (which in any case had no owner, p. 273). Evidently, following the metaphor: 'cette fierté ne savait pas trop où elle en était et courait le risque de faire un fameux naufrage' (p. 554) (this same pride didn't quite know what was happening to it and ran the risk of suffering a notable shipwreck, pp. 565–6). Misunderstanding and metaphor display the limits of the rhetorical analysis: real or virtual bringing together of two terms does not suffice to incite the comic effect; one would have to study the choice of words – even for the antiphrasis, in language and even more so in literature, the contrary is never one. Therefore, when for Busqueros, a piece of 'monnaie' metaphorically become 'une pièce de collection' (p. 362; Maclean, p. 368), three phenomena enter into the comic effect:

metaphor, the object of the device and the term substituted or added in the case of the antiphrasis.

Potocki uses a very simple and in the long run very efficient comic procedure, which is situated between contradiction and identity; using adverbs, modal correctors, which slightly shift the meaning. The first: 'je me mis à manger, *un peu* goulûment à la vérité' (p. 32) (I began to eat, somewhat greedily, it is true, p. 13); the last: 'j'avoue que votre réponse ne me satisfait pas tout à fait' (p. 561) (I confess that your reply does not wholly satisfy me, p. 573) – I shall show you why other examples are not listed here above. But also: 'quelques passages du livre de ben Omri, dont nous n'avons pas *bien* saisi le sens' (p. 36) (explain to us some passages of ben Omri's book whose meaning was not clear to us, p. 18); 'le souper fut *assez* gai' (p. 76) (the supper was merry enough, p. 63); 'il y trouverait *peut-être* d'autres objets.' (p. 87) (it might contain [other] things, p. 77); 'Il me *parut* qu'en pareille occasion l'honneur me commandait le suicide' (p. 101) (it seemed to me that in such circumstances honour dictated that I should commit suicide, p. 91); 'sous un point de vue qui ne lui fasse pas *trop* de peine' (p. 109) (look on this affair in a way which will not cause him *too much* distress, p. 100); 'je puis dire que j'en suis aujourd'hui à *peu près* corrigé' (p. 270) (Today I am *more or less* cured, p. 272); 'Je crois en avoir eu quelques autres depuis.' (p. 296) (I think I have felt it on several occasions, p. 299); 'C'est *presque* lui faire entendre' (p. 384) (is *almost* to lead him to understand, p. 390) and to finish: 'un Napolitain aime à se venger plutôt *un peu* plus qu'*un peu* moin*s*' (p. 84) (Neapolitans prefer to take *a little more* than *a little less* revenge, p. 73).[3] Each adverb or locution is repeated several times in the text. The goal is to say what you want to say, but with a slight nuance which immediately introduces a distance: the thing no longer exists in itself, in the full truthfulness of its being, but through a perspective which places it in the relative. We understand that Alphonse, who is starving, eats like a boor in front of his cousins; the 'un peu' (a little) not only lightens the blame, but places a wink between the reader and the scene, a knowing look, which discreetly shows the reader that things are never so grave or so sad that they cannot be laughed at.

The second category of effects through rhetoric is grounded in a principle of identity; duality remains, but instead of opposing or distancing themselves, both terms merge so as to be confused. The simple form is *evidence*, when a definition is added to a word. From his political articles in 1792 on, Potocki takes pains, though not without

humour, to give 'de nouvelles définitions, faute des quelles, en pronon-
çant les mêmes mots, l'on se trouve ne pas dire les mêmes choses' (new
definitions, thanks to which, in pronouncing the same words, you find
yourself not saying the same things [my translation]).[4] The dissertation
on hazelwood sticks (p. 61) provides not only the directions of use, but
distinguishes between the different kinds. Evidence, too, in the pseudo-
naïve commentary: 'ils n'étaient occupés que de leur amour [...] ce qui
est un grand péché' (p. 59) (they could only think of their love [...]
which is a great sin, p. 43). Evidence again, when a word repeats what
a different word explains or implies: 'l'un était pas plus *incroyable* que
l'autre, ce que les plus *incrédules* lui accordaient *sans peine*' (p. 29) (that
one of them should be a vampire was no less *unbelievable* than that the
other should be: an argument that even the most *unbelieving* were forced
to agree was sound, p. 9); having trespassed, Valornez is not able to
'assister lui-même à l'ouverture de son propre corps' (p. 288) ([be
present] at the dissection of his own body, p. 289); 'Nous croissions
donc, non pas sous les yeux du bon Dellius qui n'en avait plus' (p. 357)
(So we grew up under the gaze of the good Dellius, who could no longer
see but guided us, p. 363). *Parody*, as an imitation of an implicit
discourse model, functions only on one term. Potocki, who until then
had been experimenting with oriental tales and 'théâtre de foire',[5] has
a remarkable ability in this domain. Clerical parody: 'Mon fils, [...] Se
peut-il que vous ayez été en *conjonction charnelle* [...] avouez votre
coulpe. La *clémence divine* [...] Seriez-vous tombé dans *l'endurcissement?*'
(p. 106) (My son [...] it is possible that you had *carnal knowledge* of two
demons. Come, confess your *sin*! [...] The *mercy of God* is infinite [...]
Has your heart become *hardened*? p. 96). There is parody of poetry in
the conversation of Agudez (p. 476), but above all there is parody of the
philosophico-mathematical language of Velásquez (pp. 228, 230 etc.).
Let us take a close look: is the vision which Velásquez gives of Torres
Rovellas' 'path of life' (p. 467) really comical? As a first stage, we can
look at it as a brutal mockery of scientific knowledge; however, on a
closer look, the discourse reminds us of the chronological calculations of
Potocki: the different readings show that the passage was worked upon
for a long time. Has he not, in a second instance, tried to present a
hypothesis, inspired by the works of the ideologues and the first
statisticians? Or even, which should not surprise us with Potocki, has he
not assembled theory and the ridiculous, knowledge and its criticism,
object and vision? Rovellas mocks, but Rebecca listens. As mentioned
already: there is nothing so sad that it could not provoke a smile; there

is nothing so cheerful as not to contain a certain amount of bitterness. Elvire and Lonzeto embrace sadly ... in a henhouse, and the parody of courtly love becomes burlesque (p. 190). The principle of identity can also bring together two terms so as to confuse them into unity: that is literal meaning. It appears clearly in the dialogue between Toledo and Aguilar (p. 349): Toledo keeps to *univocal* meaning, refusing the figurative and melancholic meaning of Aguilar, which shows that the principle of identity, and even that of unity, is grounded in two terms. Despite seeming to avoid misunderstanding, literal meaning does not protect against error and the naïve Velásquez covers himself in ridicule when understanding Antonia's question literally: 'la géométrie ne vous a-t-elle point appris comment l'on fait les enfants?' (p. 264) (hasn't geometry even shown you how babies are made? p. 265).

The effects of rhetoric that I have just analysed are clearly not the only ones to provoke laughter. We also find hyperbole: 'la nature [...] a produit en moi un véritable chef d'œuvre' (p. 142) (in me Nature has produced ... a veritable masterpiece, p. 135); comparison: 'comme les femmes quand elles promettent d'être fidèles à leur maris' (p. 343) (like wives when they promise to be faithful to their husbands, p. 348); the syllepsis on 'entendre' (p. 124) (the ellipsis 'la singulière intervention' (p. 126) is not described), but these devices are too rare (less than five occurrences in the novel) to be studied here.

The absurd, which I define as a logical anomaly, equally gives rise to numerous comic effects. Potocki is particularly sensitive to this type of effect and gives a superb example in the *Mémoire sur L'Ambassade en Chine*:

> Dans tout cet entretien l'Ambassadeur employa des formes logiques. Il argumenta, posa des principes, tira des conséquences. Et s'il faut le dire. C'est la première et la seule fois qu'il m'ait paru totalement manquer d'esprit. (In all of this discussion, the Ambassador deployed logical forms. He argued, posited principles, drew conclusions. And if we must comment, it is the one and only time that in my opinion he lacked all signs of intelligence [my translation])[6]

The absurd is created through a rupture or a particularity of the cause–effect chain. A first group assembles the different types of causes. The cause can at first remain unapprehended, the comic effect linked to the stupidity of the person who understands nothing; confronted with the tears of Mlle Cimiento, Avadoro senior is disconcerted: 'il n'en devinait la cause que confusément' (p. 533) (he only dimly understood their cause, p. 543). As for Busqueros, he has developed into a master of pretexts, or of the false cause (to be understood as the comic opposition between the suggested and the real cause). The audacity of the peaceful inhabitants of Salamanca who leave their windows open, which are 'twenty feet above' the heads of the students (p. 389), will authorize all of Busqueros's indiscretions; in order not to 'faire injure à la providence' (offend providence) (p. 616), he avoids feeding the young Avadoro; but he succeeds better in evading the cause: far from finding a pretext (even less an excuse) for sharing young Soarez's meal, he orders a second place-setting on the grounds that it would not be fitting that 'tous les deux mangeaient à la même assiette' (p. 362), ([both] eat off the same plate, p. 368); having attracted his interlocutor's attention to the elementary rules of *savoir-manger*, table manners, he avoids asking for a place at his table. The cause can be *assumed*.

Savez-vous que cette expression suppose la possibilité d'un démenti donné par vous à mon bisaïeul? [...] que le ciel vous préserve de faire des excuses, car elles supposeraient une offense. (p. 61) (Do you realise that such an expression presupposes that you call my great-grandfather's word into question? [...] heaven preserve you from excusing yourself, for to excuse yourself is to imply that you have given offence, p. 45)

A brutal and comic change in the language register: a heavy menace intrudes into an amicable conversation; comic too through the opposition between a flimsy supposition and a terrible consequence. The *hypothesis* is no less attractive: if Frasqueta ceased to be 'virtuous', she would comfortably have Arcos 'sous la main' (p. 397) (by her side, p. 399). Looking closer, the situation borders on nonsense: what does this hypothesis mean? How can Frasqueta at the same time combine conjugal faithfulness and the idea of breaking it? Only by being and not being ...

A second group of logical anomalies is composed of those where the consequence is so far *removed* from the cause, or so *unexpected*, that through this a comic effect is produced. The examples are numerous: 'Le toit de nos pères, privé de la présence de ses maîtres [cause], l'était aussi d'une partie de ses tuiles [conséquence]' (p. 56) (On being abandoned by its masters [cause], the ancestral roof had also been abandoned by a fair number of its tiles [consequence], p. 40). The surprise provoked by the causality chain is here reinforced by an analogy, the absence of the masters and of the tiles. A little further down the page, the surprise is due to a compression of time: 'Cet ouvrage fut achevé le jour même de notre arrivée au château, et je suis venu au monde neuf mois après, jour pour jour' (This construction was completed on the very day they arrived at the castle. Exactly nine months later to the day, I came into the world, p. 40). The revelation of the cause habitually destroys, whereas the revelation of the circumstances augments the comic effect.[7] The consequences can, however, be veiled by a modest metonymy, which does not reduce the surprise: 'Vous vous êtes donc mariés, et les suites en ont été que la duchesse a dû passer quelques mois dans ses terres' (pp. 554–5) (So you were married and the duchess had to spend some months in her country estate to avoid the eyes of the curious, p. 566). Despite cause and consequence being simultaneous, they are nonetheless well distanced; and so Marie de Torres notes: 'A mesure que ma soeur grandissait, notre rue se trouvait toujours plus encombrée de guitares' (p. 178) (As my sister grew older, the street below grew more and more congested with guitars, p. 174). The causal link can take on a hypothetical value without losing any of its comic quality: 'si j'eusse obtenu la main d'Elvire, les Assiniboins, les Apaches Chiricahuas n'eussent pas été convertis à la foi chrétienne' (p. 211) (if I had obtained Elvira's hand in marriage, the Assiniboins and the Chirichua Apaches would not have converted to Christianity, p. 209). Let us add that they were converted because *etc*, which is a nice example of distancing. More complicated finally, even syllogistic:

le jour du jugement dernier tous les Juifs seront métamorphosés en ânes et devront porter les croyants au paradis. Donc, si [un Juif devient Mahométan], nous risquons un jour de manquer de montures. (pp. 604–5) (on judgement day all the Jews will be transformed into donkeys and will have to carry believers to paradise. So if you adopt our faith [if a Jew becomes a Mohammedan] we will risk one day finding ourselves short of mounts, p. 621)

Or even: when the weather is nice, Agudez does not satirize, but the roof of Agudez does not arbitrate so 'je pense que les jours où vous faites des satires, lui dit Avadoro, il ne fait pas trop sec chez vous' (p. 621) (I think that the day you start satirizing, Avadoro comments, you'll no longer be dry).

A bizarrely elaborate cause, an unexpected logical sequence, the laws of causality, however, respected – minimum causality, it is true, causality according to Hume, but still causality. Potocki was able to pinpoint the nuances of Enlightenment Logic. Once again the comic comes to serve as a vector to his thinking. To Juan van Worden, who is annoyed at having been overtaken, the colonel d'Urfé replies: 'Il me semble que ce ne sont point mes postillons qui ont devancé les vôtres, mais que ce sont les vôtres qui [...] sont restés en arrière' (p. 57) (It seems to me that it was not my postilions who overtook yours but rather yours who by lingering fell behind mine, p. 38). Is there a better example of relativism? Let us remark that Potocki does not (at least not yet) destroy causality, he only underlines that each experience hides at least *two meanings*, and the strong assurance of the expert on honour cracks. The same embarrassment arises for Lope Soarez, who discovers that the wishes of Busqueros' father contradict those of his own father. Which path to follow? What moral to adopt? The Comic emanates from the situation of these two characters baffled by the shock: their comforting certainties abandon them, things are no less simple than words.

However, Potocki goes even further in the fourth group of anomalies and presents consequences which are contrary to what they should have been. This anomaly is, certainly, explained at times and Avadoro expands on why the young Alphonse van Worden duelled even if he did not want to, which incites Rebecca's irony: 'La crainte d'une querelle inutile l'incita à se battre quatre fois en duel le même jour' (p. 562) (The fear of a pointless quarrel incited him to fight four duels in one day, p. 574). The comic effect emerges from a contradictory and unexpected consequence. The lesson stresses the relativity and even the vanity of human efforts. The explanation is, however, not always that clear, and the contradiction becomes more coarse: Fraqueta knows that she should reject a gift, but she was persuaded to accept it by 'quelques réflexions [...] que je ne me rappelle pas dans cet instant' (p. 392) (considerations that I then had and which I cannot now recall, p. 394). No explanation on the next page, when Cornadez, made indignant by the presence of Frasqueta, 'se tourna tant et se retourna, qu'au bout de deux mois il [la] demanda en mariage' (p. 393) (turned away and returned so often that after two months had passed he asked for [her] hand in marriage, p. 395). The most striking case is that of the young Avadoro disguised as the 'amorous Lirias'; at the moment when there is a risk of Sanudo discovering his identity, he realises that he should flee, but 'je ne sais quel mauvais génie m'inspira d'ôter mon voile et de me jeter au cou du recteur' (p. 285) (an evil demon gave [him] the idea of taking off [his] veil, throwing [his] arms around the neck of Sanudo, p. 287). The expected consequence arises and Sanudo recognizes the young impostor. The laughter here is grating: Potocki does not contest the real cause and we know from recent editions of the *Manuscript* that the fantastic always resolves itself in rational explanations. No, the inconsistency is psychological: Frasqueta, Cornadez and Avadoro for reasons (should I be speaking of reasons?) that escape us, with the unconscious surely having its part to play too, turn causality on its head.

Opposed to the serene sense of immutability of the laws of nature, here we have man, who himself destroys the divine causality which exists in the world through his own conscience. More unsettling still, these characters refer the reader to his own instability, his impulses, his anguish.

After rhetoric and the absurd, let us examine the comic through action. This type is distinguished from the former two by the fact that it rises to representation: action presupposes a subject and a verb which make possible the mental image. The comic effect issues then from the action or from its consequences.

There are four main types of comic actions: the fall, body movement, disguise, and on the margin, satire, with each of these types capable of taking on different forms. I subsume under the emblem of the *fall* all brief, brutal, unexpected action as, for example, the large broken inkwell (p. 138) or the blow to Busqueros' nose (p. 367). The comic effect is not only due to the unexpected nature or the enormous flow of ink; the blow, seen a thousand times (and perhaps because it has been seen a thousand times) is funny too. In a surprising manner, memory – especially theatrical, as in this case – instead of using and toning down the procedure, seems on the contrary to guarantee the effect. There are, naturally, falls *stricto sensu*: Velásquez, who falls whilst dancing (p. 259), or Blas Hervas, whom Sparadoz cruelly sends to the river (p. 510). There is, however, a particular fall which should specifically interest us: the Principino faints (p. 86), Avadoro-Elvire faints (p. 235), Avadoro-senior faints (p. 546). The comic effect is linked first to the situation: the ostrich-character, incapable of confronting the experience, cuts off his relation to the world, disappears from the scene – a false and amusing coincidence between this psychological fall and a painful situation, what is more, memory reminds us that we no longer count the many heroines, who, pressured by their lovers, faint at the supreme moment in order to savour the pleasure without displeasure (the feeling of guilt). *Body movement* is opposed to the fall by its length, with most of the verbs in the imperfect tense. Just as theatrical as the fall, it becomes comical by the apparent absence of meaning which it obeys, by its grotesque allure. The Arabs, who collect Velásquez, do not expect to see him dancing the sarabande, nor does Velásquez, who recognizes that he is obeying 'without consciously wishing to do so' (p. 267). After learnedly having put life into equations, 'Velásquez se leva, agita ses bras d'un air terrible' (p. 463) (Velásquez rose to his feet, waved his arms with a terrible air, p. 469). The solemn Lope Soarez is

ridiculous when he attempts to climb up a tree to escape from Busqueros
(p. 386). The body movement is not necessarily extraordinary: poor
Sanudo 'allait, venait, sortait, questionnait' (p. 283) (went out, came
back, left again, made inquiries, p. 284), displaying in his behaviour,
with a moving, but funny naivity, the pangs of his conscience. Body
movement can ultimately be reduced to an attitude: 'Nous portons
nos nez très haut et ne craignons personne' (p. 557) (we carry our heads
high and fear no one, p. 569). The comic effect in the last example is
reduced here by Sanudo's suffering on the one hand (we must admit
that wickedness is a component of laughter), on the other hand by the
haughtiness of Busqueros who does not even fear the ridiculous. This
type of comic action unites all that proceeds from *deception*, including
self-deception in error. The field is vast and can be well defined by the
mechanism of the *quid pro quo*: to take one human being, one thing, one
phenomenon for another, with all the comic effects this confusion brings
with it. A classification can easily be established: let us distinguish
on the one hand active deception (disguise) from passive deception
(confusion) and on the other hand deception due to chance from deception due to artifice. Let us start with voluntary disguise: the lackey
husband (p. 61) proves that the intention to deceive does not necessarily
signify deception as such; in fact nobody falls for this new kind of lackey.
On the other hand, when Avadoro takes Elvire's place, he succeeds in
deceiving the viceroy through the care he gives to his make-up, letting
laughter burst forth, despite the gravity of the situation (p. 210).
Laughter is also occasioned when the viceroy, in love with the wrong
Elvire, wishes her to breast-feed his children (p. 204). It would be
imprudent, however, to look for a comic effect in all instances of
confusion; the doubts that Alphonse harbours on the identity of the
women with whom he spent his first night do not incite laughter. No
more do the *disguises* of the fair maiden or the Princess de Monte
Salerno. When deception is active and voluntary, it becomes error, as
with Velásquez ('trempa[nt] son crayon dans le chocolat', p. 214)
(plunging his pencil in the chocolate). It can, lastly, be passive and
accidental: when Zoto, black with soot, appears out of the chimney of
the Principino, he 's'avisa de [le] prendre pour le diable' (p. 68) (takes
him for the devil), a confusion which the vindictive chimney sweep
does not fail to exploit.

There remains a last type of action, different to the three preceding
ones, the comic effect of which is not always very clear. The action does
not present anything, or very much, that is comic, but indirectly attacks

a group of individuals: namely, *satire*. The French 'curtsey' and 'pirouette' (pp. 256, 572); the Spanish smoke cigars (p. 484). Satire against justice and religion is more severe and frequent; it is sometimes comic, sometimes less so. Zoto and his father never forget 'the part of the officers of the law' in their plundering (pp. 63, 68, 77) and the chief gypsy keeps 'ballots marqués en rouge [...] destinés à être saisis par les alguazils [...] qui n'en seront que plus attachés à nos intérêts' (p. 138) (the bales marked in red [...] to be seized by the *alguazils*, who [...] will be all the more devoted to our interests, p. 130). Hervas watches his inheritance being reduced to a tenth of its worth by 'a variety of circumstances' (p. 487). The ambiguous character of satire, which denounces through mocking, renders its comic effect uncertain, depending on whether the reader belongs to the category attacked or has been a victim of it. The same difficulty affects satire of religion: we can (or could) be scandalized by monks who divested a child of his inheritance (p. 79) or that a 'belle figure et des bas violets [soient] de puissantes recommandations auprès du beau sexe de Rome' (p. 436) (a handsome face and violet stockings were taken at that time in Rome to be strong recommendations by the fair sex, p. 441), but the scene does not lack bitterness when the monks, thinking that the devil has taken away the body of Valornez, 'arrivèrent armés de goupillons, aspergeant, exorcisant et braillant à tue-tête' (p. 288) (appeared, armed with aspergilla, and set about sprinkling hot water, exorcizing and braying at the tops of their voices, p. 291).

Apart from action, the circumstances or the conditions of its realization can create a comic effect; there are three kinds: repetition, contrast and excess. Some examples of *repetition*: on three occasions, Blas Hervas is pushed into the gutter (pp. 511, 513, 515); Avadoro senior opens his mouth and closes it again without saying a word nine times (pp. 538–45). The comic relies essentially on repetition, for taken alone, its actions are tiresome. Instead of repeating the same action, the contrast brings together two opposing actions. The comic effect is created through this bringing together, each action taken by itself not having a particular effect. Faced with an enemy who has drawn his sword, Zoto's father kills him with a shot of the pistol (p. 65)[8]: 'Lorsque [le viceroy] parlait aux hommes, il avait une voix de tonnerre, et lorsqu'il parlait aux femmes c'était une fausset flûté que l'on ne pouvait entendre sans rire' (p. 198) (When [the viceroy] addressed men, his voice was like thunder, when he spoke to women, it was a fluting falsetto you couldn't hear without laughing, p. 195). I have elsewhere[9] examined the interesting work on perspective in the narrative on the encounter of Velásquez and Antonia; here I add the comic in the opposition between the behaviour of Antonia, who 'complaining of the heat, took off the kerchief she wore on her breast' (p. 264), and that of Velasquez, who 'started musing about the nature of logorithms' (p. 264). A last example: we know how Toledo withdraws from the world, but Avadoro reveals to him Soarez's story:

Cela ne fit d'abord aucune impression; mais Tolède, se tournant vers moi, me dit aussi à l'oreille: 'Mon cher Avarito, crois-tu que la femme de *l'oidor* Uscariz m'aime encore et qu'elle me soit restée fidèle?' (pp. 400–1) (At first this had no effect on him but then Toledo turned to me and mouthed in my ear: 'My dear Avarito, do you think that the wife of the *oidor* Uscariz still loves me and has remained faithful to me?' p. 406)

The comic effect is due to the pious impassiveness of Toledo (he is praying, Avadoro's words will not divert him from salvation) which is in stark contrast to his question. The third circumstance is that of *excess*: tattooing is not especially funny, but becomes funny when the snake tattooed onto the body of the viceroy winds round 'sixteen times' (p. 211). Believing himself to have been deceived, Zoto, in less time than it would take to write it (around ten lines), stabs Sylvia, Antonino, Moro and Rocca Fiorita to death (p. 88). Pathetic is the arithmetic excess of the young Avadoro who fears, after having heard Giulio Romati, seeing 'at any moment [...] the princess's skeletons emerging' (p. 171) or who weeps with compassion on seeing Elvire and Lonzeto 'weeping piteously' (p. 172), which make his aunt laugh.

Two further remarks to complete this analysis: the comic effect can emerge not from an instance (at the level of the sentence), but from a continuity, by which I understand not an addition to the comic effect, but a whole which because of its unity creates a comic effect. The whole is constituted itself with the character, as the sum of actions and characteristics. The *Manuscript* presents a whole gallery of comic characters: Zoto, Avadoro senior, Rovellas, Carlos Velásquez, Busqueros or Santa Maura.[10] The most interesting is certainly Juan van Worden; the obsession which animates him, whatever its object may be, furnishes a long tradition of comic characters: we need only cite Cervantes or Molière. But laughter depends on a subtle equilibrium between the suffering of a character and that of others. Should it be pushed too far, the obsession becomes insupportable to those around it, if it is confined, the character is engulfed in hopelessness. In both cases the comic disappears. Thus, Busqueros in his insolence, through the troubles that it causes to Soarez, to Avadoro senior and the younger, incites the annoyance of the reader, menacing thus the comic effect. The inverse case: Avadoro senior, deprived in marriage of his dear tranquillity and forced to speak (p. 546); all his history bleakened *a posteriori* by the image of his last moments.

If the comic effect can be maintained continuously by a character, it can also be born in a single occurrence, from the combination of several techniques. Let us examine, for example, the extraordinary coincidence of the thirty-sixth day, one of the high points of the comic in the novel, when Soarez reveals himself to be the one whom Toledo had mistaken for the ghost of Aguilar on the thirty-first day. Six phenomena work towards the comic effect here: the *error* of Busqueros who gets the wrong window, the *confusion* of Toledo who mistakes Soarez for a ghost, the *fall* of Soarez at the bottom of his ladder, the *distancing* of the cause (Soarez's confusion) and the *consequence* (the fall of Soarez), the *contrast* between the dramatic and erroneous interpretation given to the episode by Toledo and its grotesque explanation, and finally the *temporal distortion* which put this five days after that (twelve days in the exposition). In itself, this last phenomenon does not contain anything comic, but the unexpectedness of the explanation increases the comic effect, which is temporally unexpected (nothing hinted at this moment) and logically unexpected (such an explanation in the dark night of Toledo was unthinkable).

The comic runs through the novel and does not spare anything. Let us start with the fantastic, of which one has long since wished to see the *Manuscript* as a flagship. Potocki discovered this new aesthetic through Ann Radcliffe, issuing from the Anglo-Saxon fogs and carried by the Illuminist movement, but it does not move him; he is but little sensitive to laden skies and sombre terrains. Invariably, from Morocco to Odessa, he turns towards the south, towards the light. And when he travels to England, it is to buy a compass;[11] when he travels to Holland, it is for politics; and when he travels to Lower Saxony, it is for 'antiquités slaves ou vende' (slavonic or *vende* antiquities). Potocki does not believe in the fantastic; it is for him the sign of strayed reason or of a diseased imagination:

les illusions ne manquent guères d'attaquer celui qui est seul de son avis, comme les illusions de satan ne manquoit jamais d'assaillir les hermites dans le désert. Et comme ceux-ci croyoient voir des lumies, des Empouses, des Egipans, et autres êtres imaginaires, les autres croyent voir [...] là où il n'y a en effet que leurs formes fantastiques, sous les quelles se cache le malin. (The illusions never failed to assail those who stand alone in their opinions, just as the illusions of Satan never fail to attack hermits in the desert. And as the former believe they are seeing phantasms and spectres, the latter believe they see [...] that which is in effect nothing but their fantastic forms, behind which lurks their own wickedness. [my translation])[12]

Potocki summarizes as: *melius est cum aliis errare quam sapere soli*. It is better to err with others than to know the truth alone.[13] The fantastic does not only arise from the solitude of a lofty reason, but the imagination is sometimes affected by

une maladie [...] qui consiste à se faire des idées fausses de son propre individu, et qui tient à celle que les anglois appellent fixation [...] les gens affligés de la fixation s'imaginent être, l'un une théière, l'autre un vase de terre, ou tel un meuble. (an illness [...] which consists in creating false images of one's own self, which is similar to what the English call a 'fixation' [...] people afflicted by fixation believe themselves to be, this one a tea pot, that one a earthenware vase or any other piece of furniture [my translation])[14]

The fantastic never has any source other than the subjective. The individual, or more precisely a mental malfunctioning of the individual, creates the fantastic, which is nothing else but the *fantasmic*. Potocki maintains the tranquil assurance of a world exactly marked out by Newton, Linnaeus or Buffon. He does not perceive that by accepting a deformation of perception (*le regard*), it is the whole of that which is perceived that risks moving; apart from the subject which is soon embodied and submerges in romanticism, apart from a language less transparent, the human being retains his dullness. So the fantastic, which is nothing but the dealings of a deranged mind, invites the criticism of platitudinous jokes. The diabolical torturer of Pacheco is a music-lover (p. 49), the nocturnal anguishes of Cornadez fade away before the tomfooleries of Busqueros (p. 384). The result is unique; among the contemporaries of Potocki, only Goya has mastered in such an accomplished manner this impossible mix of the fantastic and laughter.[15]

This should not lead us to believe that Potocki is a positivist, convinced of the almighty power of reason. If he maintains a humorous, albeit derisive, view of his century, he has renounced all absolutes. As for the rest, it is neither the French Revolution, nor the sinking of Poland, nor the Napoleonic upheavals which have deprived Potocki of his beliefs (supposing he had beliefs in the first place): these events would probably have plunged him into an absolute scepticism, which he loathes as much as absolute belief. I believe that his *floating* vision of things is derived from a certain indifference of a *grand seigneur* and from a fatalism contracted from oriental peoples. The optimism of the

Enlightenment, the belief in progress (let us parody Potocki himself): he does not entirely believe in it. Of course he considers it his task to discover the laws of causality which illumine History:

Leur utilité [des recherches historiques] *est de nous montrer le chemin que les choses ont fait pour arriver jusqu'à nous*, et par analogie de jeter une lumière quelconque sur les routes conjecturales de l'avenir; car Le passé a épuisé les combinaisons par rapport à nous, comme nous achevons de les épuiser par rapport à la postérité. (The utility [of historical research] *is to show us the path that things have taken in order to reach us*, and by analogy, to throw some light on the conjectural paths of the future, because the Past has used up the combinations in arriving at us, just as we have succeeded in using them up) with regard to posterity [my translation])[16]

There is, however, a playful aspect to the mechanism of logic;[17] through this crack, which astonishes and disturbs at the end of the century, the fantastic slips in, which does not settle it there for Potocki: for him, the limits of reason do not authorize a recourse to the old magical thinking, of which he underlines the ridiculous nature. When reason stumbles, Potocki prefers to laugh. A malicious fate overthrows the most solid of reasonings, the most assured conjectures – and Enrique Velásquez, future duke, future husband of Blanche, finds himself on the rock of Ceuta. For Potocki, exiled deep in the Ukraine after having hoped for a great political career in St Petersburg, still hoping for the success of his historical writings, this curious and pleasant destiny has nothing imaginary: it is where reality becomes the comic. It can be more painful: Busqueros, fickle image of stupidity, who understands nothing, tells the truth (p. 384). What use are arid and long studies, if the first clown arrives at the same results as the austere scholar? This is where the comic becomes true. Laughter not only translates a certain look or a distance; more than a part of life, it is a law of life which helps us to understand. The lesson is given in the forty-eighth day:

Mais c'est là la grande énigme du cœur humain, que personne ne fait ce qu'il doit faire. Tel ne voit de bonheur que dans le mariage, passe sa vie à faire un choix et meurt célibataire. Tel autre, qui jure de n'avoir jamais de femme, se marie et se remarie. (pp. 477–8) (But therein lies the great mystery of the human heart. No one does what he should do. One person may imagine there to be no happiness except in marriage, spends his life making a choice, and dies single; another swears never to take a wife, marries and remarries, p. 485)

Causality and failure of causality. It is vain to try and formulate everything in equations like Velásquez, but what means do we have to do differently? If experience convinces us sufficiently that it is pointless to reason endlessly, that our correct calculations are wrong, it also convinces us that we must reason, that each failure becomes a further reason to continue. And Potocki himself, endlessly recalculating his chronologies, illustrates well enough the tireless effort called for. Not that the world is insane, not that we should resolve to wait for the rats of Hervas (who, by the way, will not appear unless there is a *polymath* to devour), but it can always play the law of laughter which releases a *torro marrajo* (ferocious bull) on Rovellas and sends him tossing through the air (p. 178).

This philosophy, which mixes laughter with the rules of causality, which never judges *from*, but always *in relation to*, is found in Potocki's political texts as well as in his theatrical and travel writings. Thus it is that Potocki is an exception in the great contemporary literature of his time. At the moment when he is composing the *Manuscript Found in Saragossa*, German Romanticism, with Schiller, Hölderlin and Novalis, is in full swing; Mme de Staël, Benjamin Constant or Chateaubriand are no less sombre. Finally, England, the birthplace of the fantastic and the historical novel, has turned away from the humour of Swift or Sterne. Rousseau is victorious in these years of rupture and combat. The period was, however, not exactly favourable towards Potocki. Besides his domestic upsets – difficult relations with his mother-in-law, Princess Lubomirska, the failure of the marriage to his second wife, Constance – Potocki, instead of the brilliant political career that his name should have allowed him, instead of the scientific or literary success which his talents should have bestowed upon him, witnesses the disappearance of Poland, the closure of all doors to high administration, and has to endure the gibes of French scholars,[18] not to mention his financial difficulties. Despite all of this (and we should add the ups and downs of publication), the joyous novel is here. On 11 June 1788, Potocki wrote to the king of Poland: 'je crois que d'ennuyer est précisément la plus odieuse de toutes les manières dont on puisse manquer aux rois ...' (I believe that to occasion boredom is the most odious manner in which one can cause offence to kings [my translation]) or to the reader.[19] Potocki was a man of the Enlightenment, but also a man of the *ancien régime*, torn from old propriety: not only was it improper to flaunt his state of mind, but it could also have been very tedious subject matter. Even when addressing his close friends, his brother Séverin or his niece Maria, he remains reserved; just remember the tone in which he tells of the first infidelity of his wife, the not so constant Constance.[20] Far from being frosty, reservedness releases laughter or a smile which brings charm to a life in society, in those salons closed by the Revolution, where the aristocracy debate on reservedness in artists or philosophers.

The comic, nevertheless, reveals in an indirect manner some part of Potocki's feelings. Making a list as precise as possible of the comic effects in the *Manuscript*, it is easy to note that their frequency diminishes gradually.[21] The history of the composition of the novel is still largely incomplete; I believe that it started during the German years, following the *Bohémiens d'Andalousie*, in 1795 or 1796. The period that followed was a happy one for Potocki. The Polish page turned, he plunged himself into historical studies. He was held in good esteem by the Russian court and maintained amicable relations with Platon Zoubov. He attended the crowning of Paul I, then travelled in the Caucasus. From 1802, he moved closer to imperial power, thanks to Adam-Jerzy Czartoryski, Minister of Foreign Affairs, and shortly after entered the Asian Department. He felt supreme satisfaction when he was appointed scientific officer at the Russian Embassy in China in 1805. We know that at around this time the novel had proceeded as far as the thirteenth day. The next ten years of his life followed a downward slope. To start with, the Embassy in China did not reach beyond Mongolia. On returning from St Petersburg, Potocki solicited a post at the Ministry of Foreign Affairs which he would never obtain, and directed a governmental journal which was violently hostile to Napoleon ... in the year of Tilsit. He retired to Ukraine, disillusioned and ill; 'le coin du monde où nous vivons est à quelques égards un infame coin', he writes to Maria Potocka (the corner of the world that we inhabit is in some respects a despicable one [my translation]).[22] In 1808, he was divorced; in the following years, he was constantly tormented by the education of his children, who stayed at times with him, at times with their mother. We know his end. I think that the novel echoes this slow darkening. Laughter is the most beautiful manifestation of life, insolent and carefree, which mocks the reasoners severely, the vaporous wooer or the thrower of dice. It gradually left Potocki.

A word game composed by Potocki when he was writing his novel:

Le Comte de Laus	1
Fut élévé dans les principes d'E	1000
Si ce n'est sur l'article de la foi, où il se conformoit au concile de	30
Aussi entra t'il dans le monde avec un cœur tout	9
Mais avec un caractère un peu	20
Qui le fit tomber dans	2 1/4
C'est à dire dans deux écarts. Le prémier avec une dame de Ca	10

Ils avoient diné ensemble et il étoit pris de	20
Il quita avec elle le salon et	120
dans un autre, heureusement il survint	1/3
Le second écart fur avec une dame de Verd	1
Ils lisoient ensemble l'histoire du siège de	3
L'idée du beau Paris aluma son cœur et	700
le Comte voyant que son cœur n'étoit pas de br	11
lui dit Madame n'en prenez aucun sou	6
Ces choses se sont faites depuis le patriarche	7
Faisons de même ou encore	+
Et si vous ne le voulez pas cela m'est	=
Ce ton deplut à la dame qui lui répondit par	10
Impertinent sortez d'I	6
Le Comte sortit et trouva un pa	100
il eut avec lui une	r'x
Le passant lui dit je n'ai mis mes fonds	40
viagères, et si je meure le roi heritera	2
Le comte repondit Laissez là vos mais et vos	6
et degainez l'epée dont vous êtes	5
Le passant tira son epée et envoya le comte en para	10

NOTES

1 To be taken literally: two readers will never agree on the same effects, they will never share exactly the same emotions, and will therefore never count the same number of effects. We ought to accept the approximate nature of the subject matter.

2 Potocki, *Manuscrit trouvé à Saragosse* (Paris: Le livre de poche, [1992] 1995), p. 110. English quotations are taken from *The Manuscript Found in Saragossa*, translated by Ian Maclean (London: Penguin, 1996), p. 101. All references to subsequent quotations from these two works will be indicated in brackets in the text.

3 Given the limits of this study, I refer the reader to the various contexts to better appreciate the impact of the quoted examples.

4 *Ecrits politiques*, edited by Dominique Triaire (Paris: Champion, 1987), p. 97.

5 See *Voyages*, edited by D. Beauvois (Paris: Fayard, 1980), vol. 1, pp. 65, 68, 103 ff., and *Parades*, edited by D. Triaire (Arles: Actes Sud, 1989).

6 D. Beauvois, A. Stroev and D. Triaire, 'Jean Potocki rentre en Chine trop tôt ...', in *Dix-huitième siècle* 31 (1999), 364.

7 Consider Tristram Shandy, so precise on the circumstances of his birth, yet they themselves are so removed from their happy consequences.

8 Scenes shown time and again at cinemas.

9 D. Triaire, *Potocki* (Arles: Actes Sud, 1991), p. 206.

10 The comic nature of certain characters is more clearly perceived when compared to tragic characters: the wandering Jew, Lonzeto-Torres Rovellas, the Duke of Sidonia, Giralda etc.

11 *Ecrits politiques*, ed. Triaire, p. 27.

12 *Ibid.*, pp. 98–9.

13 *Ibid.*, pp. 119.

14 *Ibid*, p. 99.

15 A different Pole appears to have achieved the same result: Roman Polanski in his irresistible *Ball of the Vampires*.

16 *Histoire primitive des peuples de la Russie* (St Petersburg, 1802), p. 3.

17 Note that Potocki uses the word 'combinaisons', much more subtly, offering a multitude of possibilities to be played with.

18 See D. Triaire, 'Trois lettres de Jan Potocki à son frère Séverin', *Parole et révolutions* (Paris: Champion, 1992), p. 216.

19 *Ecrits politiques*, ed. Triaire, pp. 36–7.

20 D. Triaire, 'Treize lettres inédites de Jean Potocki', *Studies on Voltaire* 317 (1994), 131–2.

21 They disappear from the fifty-eighth day onwards; however, we are dealing with the text of Chojecki, who with as little compunction eliminated the comic, the erotic and the heretical.

22 Letter from the beginning of 1811 to Maria Potocka, Biblioteka Pan in Cracow, shelfmark 6183, 116/92.

Comparative Criticism 24, pp. 99–110. Cambridge University Press 2002
DOI: 10.1017/S0144756402005474 Printed in the United Kingdom

Quotation and intertextuality: the books in *The Manuscript Found in Saragossa*

FRANÇOIS ROSSET

TRANSLATED BY CATHERINE NICHOLSON

One of the strange and spectacular qualities of *The Manuscript Found in Saragossa* is the sort of mysterious aura radiating from this text, like that of a Pharaoh's sarcophagus, affecting its desecrators and their descendants. The striking similarities between the characters of the novel and their author have often been noted, and we can see a similar relationship between the tales of adventure in the text and those of the novel's manuscripts. The dramatic history of the various editions of the book itself could even be seen as an extension of this phenomenon. There is also a plurality on the part of readers in their relationship with the text seen in the diversity of their possible identities and also in their role of receivers or transmitters. In this sense, we can consider the example of the Gomelez family, whose members are scattered through time and space, but nonetheless united by a shared secret, jealously guarded. In addition, the themes of the occult and of the cabal developed in the novel and the motif of the secret society, recognizable in the rich Masonic imagery, mirror a phenomenon observed among the novel's readers: for many of them humanity is divided into two distinct and unequal groups. There are those who have read *The Manuscript Found in Saragossa* – the initiated – and those who have not. There are those who belong to the Gomelez clan and those who remain outsiders.

In the same way that a secret society recognizes its members by a murmured password, these readers recognize each other in allusions, in shorthand evocations or references which can become slogan-like, and also in varied literary associations, sometimes boldly construed but invariably influenced by the surrounding intellectual environment. So, in the midst of the post-modern fatality of today, it is almost as natural to suspect Jan Potocki of having read Jorge-Luis Borges, Italo Calvino, John Barth or Salman Rushdie[1] as it is to find in his work echoes of Shakespeare, Cervantes, Sterne or Voltaire. Thus, whatever the direction taken to follow the invisible threads which link texts like so many tangled roots in the fertile soils of world literature, it is always to the notions of total-text, of body of work or even of encyclopaedia, of receptacle and of intersection that we return to qualify this novel. If one has a heightened sense of history, the book can be considered as both a rendering of a dying world and the sketch of a new one named modern. Associations, we see, are found not only inside the work, but equally outside, in the types of interpretation that it inspires.

Since the first Polish critiques, from 1830 onwards, right up until the most recent critical works,[2] we can assess the effects of a literary temptation which inspires in readers a contradictory movement: in seeking to uncover the mystery of meaning in the text, they are consistently forced to go out, in order to create connections with other works. Whether it is in the context of a traditional hunt for sources, which can go as far as to seek to faithfully reconstruct the library of the author; or in freer approaches, based on the postulate of reading autonomy, we quickly realize that both the sources of the novel and the associations of the reader must inevitably disappear into the bottomless depths of the Danaids' barrel, so endless is the possible list of associations. When it comes to justifying the critical approach, it is undoubtedly the classic notion of *filiatio*, or the more modern and complex notion of *intertextuality*, which is the most relevant.

Since the coining of the term by Julia Kristeva in 1967,[3] there have been countless attempts to answer the question: 'What is inter-textuality?' There have been equally as many responses, and this diversity of opinion is certainly one of the reasons new studies continue to appear. It is certainly not my intention to enlarge this already rich critical body of work by examining the notion of intertextuality exhaustively, but it seems nonetheless necessary to treat the question of how it applies to a reading of Poctocki's novel.

If we consider it, for instance, in the terms of Roland Barthes or those – clearly quite different – of Mikhail Bakhtin, intertextuality must be considered as one of the most relevant notions to *literariness* in general. However, it must also be considered that choosing it as an interpretative tool for a particular text implies nothing in terms of the specificity of the work, nor of the originality of the reading proposed. In this sense, intertextuality becomes self-defining as soon as we treat a text which is recognized as *literary*, and which is in turn recognized as literary exactly because signs of intertextuality are visible in it. There is a danger of tautology if these concepts are employed superficially or simplistically;[4] it is not on such a basis that a valid approach to a particular text can be founded, even if that text is recognized as a *paragon* of intertextuality.

With this in mind, I hope you will excuse me if I avoid a general theoretical discussion of the subject, in order to begin my analysis in the present moment, when after thirty years of consideration and debate, certain forms or manifestations of intertextuality are accepted and recognized. They can generally number six,[5] and I would like to briefly consider each of them from the perspective of *The Manuscript Found in Saragossa*.

1. Within the text we can bring to light and analyse the relationships between different parts, different layers and different properties of the work. From this perspective, we may then both look at the principles which have led to the division of the text and examine what it is that links the text's different parts. Certain idiolects belonging to individual characters may also be isolated and the oppositions between them exposed. Links between text and metatext can also be examined, or even more concretely (for the notion of intertextuality), between text and paratexts. In our case, all of the approaches above are both relevant and fruitful. In the global sense of intertextuality, it is interesting:
– to reconsider the division of the narrative into sixty-six days. Representing the infinitely recurring, this seemingly neat dissection is constantly undermined by the narrative complexity which emphasizes the variety and the changeability of the narrative voice, or rather, voices;
– to analyse the relationship between the hero's adventures and the commentaries attached to them, or even to go as far as to consider the doubling of certain scenes in different stories as glosses with a meta-narrative dimension;
– to examine the journal of Alphonse van Worden in the discursive framework established by the Foreword and the Epilogue, not to mention the significance of the novel's title, which was the object of long and careful consideration on the part of the author. This fact seems to impose an equally careful examination of the writing process.

This gives a number of starting points for a revealing study of the self-quotation omnipresent in this novel.[6]

2. In a text, or in certain parts of that text, we can identify imitations
of characteristic discursive forms such as sociolects, dialects, historically
marked and identifiable styles, and many kinds of stylization; that is, of
mimesis or parody. In Potocki's novel these elements are multiple and
varied. They give a kind of 'colour' visible in the speech of different
characters and which aids us in identifying cabalistic jargon, a Masonic
setting or the code of honour pushed to its limits. The italianisms and
hispanisms can also be considered in this light, as can the splendours
of the court of Louis XIV, grotesquely depicted by Don Carlos de
Velasquez. There is also the sober pride of the ancient Aztecs,
represented by the Princess Tlascala and the archaisms in the story of
the Commander of Toralva. The list could go on, but we can also
regroup all these examples under the collective sign of a motif which
recurs throughout the stories and which is emblematic: the motif of
disguise.

3. It is here that we come to the notion of intertextuality in the strictest
sense, which is that of the copresence[7] of two or more texts. Using the
devices of quotation, of paraphrasing, of cross-reference or of allusion,
a text can incorporate within itself other texts which are known and
recognizable. In *The Manuscript Found in Saragossa*, these relations are
numerous and are linked in different ways:
– There are explicit quotations in the text, indicated by the name of an
author and a title, which allow for verification procedures. These show
a large variation in the degree of accuracy, to the point where one
wonders if the references are false. An example is the case of the famous
story of Thibaud de la Jacquière which is supposedly read in Happelius'
Relationes Curiosae (1647), although the narrative gives another possible
source, namely the *Histoires tragiques de notre temps* by François de
Rosset (1614). In such cases, admitting the act of quotation focuses the
attention far less on the reference texts than on the discursive procedure
of quotation itself. In this manner the act of quotation becomes a
defining characteristic of the narrative. This trait takes on many
different forms in the novel, as it is not only books which are cited, but
letters, maxims, proverbs and so on. The tale which encapsulates all the
others is also a quotation, the story being presented to the reader as
merely as improvised translation, as we learn in the Foreword.
– In other situations we find implicit references, many of which have
been identified, convincingly or not; but there are surely many more yet
to be brought to light. Surnames and place names, motifs and *topoi*,

narrative sequences, various idioms: all of these are possible triggers for the comparing and combining reflexes of the erudite reader. The character of Velasquez the geometer, for example, makes one think of the life of Blaise Pascal as told by his sister Marguerite Périer, or of Montesquieu's *Lettres persanes* (precisely, letter 128), or of the confidences of the narrator of Diderot's *Jacques le Fataliste*; or again of the significant amount of theatre produced after 1750 in which we find the almost obligatory figure of the geometer. Whether valorized or ridiculed, this figure there clearly represents Jean d'Alembert.

Here as well, we can summarize the multiplicity of these phenomena in the image of the novel within the novel, as we shall see shortly.

4. In a more general sense, we can also look at the novel as belonging to a certain group of works which share the same morphology, that is, the same literary genre. In this case, it is not a matter of an explicit or implicit copresence, but of an established taxonomic similarity. In the case of *The Manuscript Found in Saragossa* we cannot help but establish the connections between the novel and certain *types*[8] such as the baroque novel, the journal novel or the frame-tale; but also with certain *genres* defined by their dominant theme, such as travel writing, the picaresque novel, the gothic novel, the *Bildungsroman* and so on. As regards the *mode* or discursive category, *The Manuscript Found in Saragossa* declares its narrative structure in its title and in the sequence of stories. However, in many instances there are signs of something like dramatic imitation.

All of the above is already widely accepted, to the point that we have seen the novel considered as an *anthology*, as a *museum of literary genres* or as an *encyclopaedia of the novelesque*.[9] We need, however, to refocus attention on the essential point: it is not the generic relations themselves which are most significant, but precisely their abundance and extraordinary diversity, which refuses all simplistic categorization. What we see in the novel is not just the objects of reference but the method of imitation or of parody itself. The best example of this characteristic of the text is the episode of the gibbet of Los Hermanos, the story being retold five times by different narrators.

And all of this could be represented in shorthand by the image of the *olla podrida*, a mix of various meats and vegetables served to the hero by his two mysterious cousins. The metaphorical literary resonance of this meal is clear, as developed by Cervantes in the second part of *Don Quixote* (II, 47).

5. From a broader point of view, we can also examine the inter-semiotic relations which exist between a discourse based on the verbal signs of language and discourses based on other sign systems, such as music, art or cinema; that has been named by Marc Angelot *interdiscursivité*.[10] From the cabal to Ozymandias's labyrinth, from maps to mathematical and geometrical formulas, to the extraordinary collection of paintings and sculptures belonging to the Princess of Monte Salerno, the codes multiply, creating as many echoes or reflections as there are narrative voices. Just as the adventures and experiences of the hero are broken down into various symbolic units, the various dogma, as depicted in the text are relativized by the number of conflicting, seemingly incompatible religious references. At a first reading, this would seem to be a kind of ecumenical syncretism, encompassing not only religion but knowledge and culture as well. However, it would be more correct to focus critical attention on the points of interaction of the very different sign systems themselves.

And to go outside the text itself, we can see how the parallels between the critical reception of Potocki's book and its cinematic adaptation by Wojciech Has can be extremely instructive. A thesis by Anne (Guérin-Castell) (see her article in this volume) treats this subject and, in working through a rigorous analysis of filmic language, has disclosed structural configurations never before considered.[11]

Similar observations could be made in connection with the language of theatre of which there are many traces in the text. These have recently been evoked in an excellent production by Tadeusz Bradecki, entitled *Saragossa* and staged at the National Theatre of Warsaw.

6. Lastly, a little apart from the text itself, it is also relevant to examine the links which Potocki's novel has with other literary works. These include continuations of stories found in other novels, various readings of the novel and the critical commentaries it has provoked. This approach is particularly justified for *The Manuscript Found in Saragossa*, as it is for almost any work which has stimulated public opinion. There is not only its eventful publishing history – which is certainly not finished yet, the perfect edition is still to come – but also the phenomenon of plagiarism. Examples include Washington Irving, Cousin de Courchamps and Charles Nodier.[12] There are also the 'dialogues' opened with the text by authors inspired by Potocki, such as Rüdiger Kremer, Manuela Gretkowska, Tomasz Jurasz, Tadeusz Bradecki or Francisco Nieva.[13] Translations of Potocki's work also provide valuable

information on the state of reception of the original text. It is particularly interesting to follow the history of interpretations of this text, which is inevitably linked to its publishing history. This history is characterized by its mystery – there is much veiled, disguised or missing information – as much as it is by real discoveries or revelations. Today, though, a sudden flowering of Potocki studies is taking place. This interest, partly due to a greater availability of the text, is no doubt also due to the similarities that we find between Potocki's aesthetic project and our own contemporary sensibilities. As if to prove the point, I find myself here developing this theory ...

But whoever the reader and whatever the context of his/her reading, he/she will be able to identify with one of the interpreter-figures in the novel: whether the doctor in a clinical theatre, the cabbalist and geometer consulted on the smallest matter, the decoders of hieroglyphs or listeners and readers at work, receiving information.

Inside this text, which is thus permanently menaced by its own disintegration in the unlimited mass of other texts, the reader is still able to find points of reference. For example, the recurrent motifs whose symbolic value is reinforced as the 'days' go by; enriched by variation and interlaced through the sequence of stories, they finish by forming a solid framework. It is a framework through which the countless threads of the story wind, tangling and untangling themselves in the discourses made real by the novel's characters. I have noted in passing several of these motifs, such as doubling, disguise and the moment of reception. It would be simple, too, to recall the famous labyrinths, underground sites, gold mines or castles, or to interpret the geography in the novel, or treat a hundred other themes. To conclude though, and to illustrate these rapid and general remarks on the intertextuality in Potocki's novel, I would like to dwell a moment longer on a motif so loaded with meaning that we can consider it one of the *leitmotivs* of *The Manuscript Found in Saragossa*. It is the motif of the book itself; but what book?

A BOOK TO BE WRITTEN

The Foreword of the novel informs us of various military and literary mishaps and adventures. We learn, among other things, that a manuscript written long ago has been found, then read in a different form, translated from the Spanish and recopied as a dictation. A written text is thus rewritten. This text tells the story of an eventful journey in the form of a journal where the days follow each other in a regular and cumulative manner. There are always processes underway, everywhere things which are done only to be redone afterwards. The story which could encapsulate and draw together all the others would be one which told of the transformation of a Spanish manuscript which ends in the form of a printed book before a community of readers. It would be a story rich in possible mishaps, but always and necessarily beginning again, never finished.

This abstract and general lesson is illustrated by a succession of stories delivered to the reader, in which we can see a network of images dedicated to showing the process of creation, production and distribution of a book.

Many answers can be given to the primordial question: *why write?* On the basis of *The Manuscript Found in Saragossa* some of them may be: we write in order to spread a truth, or to give moral or religious lessons; we write to publish a new discovery or to contribute to a field of knowledge; we write in order to commit a precept to posterity, in the form of a will engraved on a tombstone; we write to communicate a lesson to our children, to pass on a secret without revealing it, to respond to an order, to satisfy the vanity of an author of academic; or quite simply, we write to tell a story. However, the multiplicity and variety of all these contrasting motivations tend to reduce their value: the reason for writing is unimportant, as long as one writes. Similarly, the form and the content of the text are no longer important, as long as it can be read.

In order to reach the stage of being read or 'received', however, certain conditions must be fulfilled. To begin with, a code must be chosen, considering the size of the intended audience. It is thus that the novel is overflowing with encoders and decoders, translators and transcribers, twinned symbolically with travellers, educators and smugglers who assure the transmissibility of messages, while incarnating the condition of communicability.

If we follow the elaboration of tales in the novel, it is evident that each one results from prior readings and experiences. The story of the Wandering Jew gives a new version, seen from another angle than that of a well-known Bible story (Jesus chasing the money-lenders from the temple); Don Enrique de Velasquez writes a treatise on the engineering corps where he positions himself in relation to the canonical works of Vauban and Coehorn; his son, the geometer Don Pedro, refers to Newton, Cassini or Huygens; the stories of cabbalists go back to their origin in the *Zohar* – to cite but a few. No one writes, no one speaks, no one tells a story without first having read or listened.

And when one is ready to write, there are still technical and material conditions to be fulfilled, which also manifest themselves in the novel. Materials used for writing are varied: a tombstone, the walls of underground chambers, papyrus, parchment and finally paper. To write on the latter, one needs ink, preferably the one produced by Don Felipe d'Avadoro, alias Don Felipe del Tintero Largo, father of the irrepressible talker chief of the Bohemians. The written pages are then taken to the printer's, then to the bookbinder's who will glue them together with a glue particularly appreciated by literary rats. If and when the book is lucky enough to be put on sale, it will be in the shop window of the famous Moreno bookshop in Madrid, remarked on by the customers or confiscated by zealous censors. In short, the whole production path of a book can be reconstituted if we take the trouble to gather the scattered fragments in the different stories. If we consider too the Foreword and the Epilogue, which tell us the story of this manuscript which had been hidden, then found again in Saragossa, we can see the self-thematization of the novel and of these stories of books to be written, which are created and destroyed, which disappear and reappear, which are produced then devoured by rats, and reproduced only to be burnt, like Diego Hervas's encyclopaedia.

A TOTAL-BOOK

All of these stories are included in a single book entitled *Manuscript Found* and which tells how a young man ends up by writing down, at the end of his journey, the events of sixty-six very adventurous days. However, in the midst of these adventures and the stories in which they are told, and among all the other books evoked, there are several which stand out as trying to reassemble the whole, or to tell us everything. I have just mentioned the encyclopaedia belonging to Diego Hervas, which seeks to reunite all forms of learning, but which can only be condemned to ruin as a blasphemous Tower of Babel. We could also mention the famous white book kept by the father of the hero, Don Juan van Worden, in which he chronicles the details of his duels, resulting in an obsessive sampler of the code of honour. The white book is inimitable: it is an incontestable reference in its area, to the point where we can find descriptions of episodes retold within the novel by other characters: it serves as a reference in the matter of justice but it is also a mirror-image of the larger book. However, the ridicule of the white book's authors as well as the absolute impossibility to seize and hold onto every single narrative incident, condemn to failure his ambitious project, which is to gather all the information, in order to explain everything.

Nonetheless, two objects represented in *The Manuscript Found in Saragossa* seem to escape this condemnation. One is the *Sepher ha-Zohar*, 'or book of splendour, which is so called because nothing can be understood of it at all, for it sheds so bright a light that it dazzles the eyes of the mind', the other, the *Siphra di-Zaniutha* 'or book of concealment, which at its most explicit might be thought to be written in riddles' (the ninth day). These key works of the cabbala are also supposed to be keys to understanding, but represent the highest degree of mystic synthesis, where the human faculties, paradoxically, seem to fail completely. At the opposite end of the spectrum is the geometer, the character in the novel who represents the mathematical dream of the universal formula. This formula would make possible a system which shows and explains all the facts of human existence and which would be the quintessence and synthesis of human intellectual capacity.

Shaped in structure by organization and calculation, yet pushing to the point of confusion all the configurations which this structure could represent, *The Manuscript Found in Saragossa* situates itself at the impossible intersection of the cabal and of geometry. A total-book, as we have said, it offers the reader the image of a book that, if it is not able to contain everything, at least seeks to represent the problematic idea of entirety.

NOTES

1 Salman Rushdie, 'Currently Reading', *Guardian*, 9 June 1995, p. 4.
2 M. E. Zoltowska, 'Un précurseur de la littérature fantastique: Jean Potocki, sa vie et son *Manuscrit trouvé à Saragosse*', thesis, Yale University, 1973, pp. 276–339.
3 Julia Kristeva, 'Bakhtine: le mot, le dialogue et le roman', *Critique* 239 (1967).
4 Roland Barthes, *Le plaisir du texte* (Paris: Seuil, 1973), p. 9; V. B. Leitch, *Deconstructive Criticism: an Advanced Introduction* (New York: Columbia University Press, 1983); H. Markiewicz, 'Odmiany intertextualnosci', *Ruch Literacki* 29: 4–5 (1988), 245–63.
5 Gerard Genette, *Palimpsestes. La littérature au second degré* (Paris: Seuil, 1982); M. Pfister, 'Konzepte der intertextualität', in U. Broich and M. Pfister, *Intertextualität: Formen, Funktionen, anglistische Fallstudien* (Tübingen: Max Niemeyer, 1985), pp. 1–30; J. Slawinski, 'Intertextualnosc', in M. Glowinski et al. (eds.), *Slownik terminow literackich* (Wroclaw: Ossolineum, 1988), p. 201; N. Piégay-Gros, *Introduction à l'intertextualité* (Paris: Dunod, 1996).
6 J. Ricardou, *Pour un nouveau roman* (Paris: Seuil, 1971); L. Dällenbach, 'Intertexte et autotexte', *Poétique* 27 (1976), 282–96.

7 Genette, *Palimpsestes*.

8 Gerard Genette, 'Genres, "Types", Modes', *Poétique* 39 (1977), 389–421.

9 Roger Caillois, 'Nouvelle préface' for the second edition of *Manuscrit trouvé à Saragosse* (partial edition by Caillois) (Paris: Gallimard, 1967); François Rosset, *Le Théâtre du romanesque*: Manuscrit trouvé à Saragosse, *entre construction et maçonnerie* (Lausanne: L'Age d'Homme, 1991); M. Delon and P. Malandain, *Littérature française du XVIIIe siècle* (Paris: PUF, 1996).

10 M. Angenot, 'Intertextualité: enquête sur l'émergence et la diffusion d'un champ notionnel', *Revue des Sciences Humaines* 189 (1983), 121–35.

11 A. Guérin-Castell, 'La place de *Manuscrit trouvé à Saragosse* dans l'œuvre cinématographique de Wojciech Jerzy Has', thesis, Université de Paris VIII, 1997.

12 Zoltowska, *Un précurseur de la littérature fantastique*.

13 Rüdiger Kremer, *Der Graswanderer*, a radio play produced in Bremen in 1980, published in Polish under the title *Wedrowiec wsrod traw* in *Dialog* 8 (1993), 21–33; Manuela Gretkowska, 'Czy Potocki Jan wampirem byl?', *Ex-Libris – Zycie Warszawy* 39 (Nov. 1993), 12–13; Tomasz Jurasz, *Rozkosze nocy, czyli ostatnia podroz Jana hr. Potockiego* (Warsaw: Iskry, 1997); Tadeusz Bradecki, 'Saragossa. Romans sceniczny na motywach zycia i powiesci Jana Potockiego', *Dialog* 1 (1998), 5–35; Francisco Nieva, *El manuscrito encontrado en Zaragoza*, in *Teatro completo*, vol. 2 (Servicio de Publicaciones de la Junta de Comunideales de Castilla-La Mancha, 1991), pp. 1005–51.

BIBLIOGRAPHY

Angenot, M., 'L'intertextualité: enquête sur l'émergence et la diffusion d'un champ notionnel', *Revue des Sciences Humaines* 189 (1983), 121–35.

Barthes, R., *Le Plaisir du texte* (Paris: Seuil, 1973).

'Texte (théorie du)' in *Encyclopaedia universalis* (Paris, 1973).

Bradecki, T., 'Saragossa. Romans sceniczny na motywach zycia i powiesci Jana Potockiego,' *Dialog* 1 (1998), 5–35.

Caillois, R., 'Nouvelle préface' for the second edition of *Manuscrit trouvé à Saragosse* (partial edition by R. Caillois) (Paris: Gallimard, 1967).

Dällenbach, L., 'Intertexte et autotexte', *Poétique* 27 (1976), 282–96.

Decottignies, J., 'Variations sur un succube: histoire de Thibaud de la Jaquière', *Revue des Sciences Humaines* 111 (1963), 329–40.

Delon, M. and Malandain, P., *Littérature française du XVIIIe siècle* (Paris: PUF, 1996).

Genette, G., *Palimpsestes. La littérature au second degré* (Paris: Seuil, 1982).

'Genres, "types", modes', *Poétique* 39 (1977), 389–421.

Gretkowska, M., 'Czy Potocki Jan wampirem byl?' *Ex-Libris – Zycie Warszawy* 39 (Nov. 1993), 12–13.

Guérin-Castell, A., 'La place de *Manuscrit trouvé à Saragosse* dans l'œuvre cinématographique de Wojciech Jerzy Has', thesis, Université de Paris VIII, 1997.

Herman, J., 'Tout est écrit ici-bas: le jeu du hasard et de la nécessité dans le *Manuscrit trouvé à Saragosse*', *Cahiers de l'Association Internationale des Etudes Françaises* 51 (1999), 137–54.

Jurasz, T., *Rozkosze nocy, czyli ostatnia podroz Jana hr. Potockiego* (Warsaw: Iskry, 1997).

Kostkiewiczowa, T., '"Comme une truite parmi les carpes": Jean Potocki dans le paysage intellectuel des Lumières européennes', *Cahiers de l'Association Internationale des Etudes Françaises* 51 (1999), 110–17.

Kremer, R., *Der Graswanderer*, a radio play produced in Bremen in 1980, published in Polish under the title *Wedrowiec wsród traw* in the *Dialog* 8 (1993), 21–33.

Kristeva, J., 'Bakhtine: le mot, le dialogue et le roman', *Critique* 239 (1967), and then in Σημειωτικη. *Recherches pour une sémanalyse* (Paris: Seuil, 1969).

Leitch, V. B., *Deconstructive Criticism: an Advanced Introduction* (New York: Columbia University Press, 1983).

Markiewicz, H., 'Odmiany intertekstualnosci', *Ruch Literacki* 29: 4–5 (1988), 245–63.

Nieva, F., *El Manuscrito encontrado en Zaragoza*, in *Teatro completo*, vol. 2 (Servicio de Publicaciones de la Junta de Comunideales de Castilla-La Mancha, 1991), pp. 1005–51.

Pfister, M., 'Konzepte der intertextualität', in U. Broich and M. Pfister (eds.), *Intertextualität: Formen, Funktionen, anglistische Fallstudien* (Tübingen: Max Niemeyer 1985), pp. 1–30.

Piégay-Gros, N., *Introduction à l'intertextualité* (Paris: Dunod, 1996).

Potocki, J., *The Manuscript Found in Saragossa*, translated by Ian Maclean (Harmondsworth: Penguin, 1996).

Ricardou, J., *Pour un nouveau roman* (Paris: Seuil, 1971).

Riffaterre, M., 'L'intertexte inconnu', *Littérature* 41 (1981), 5–6.

Rosset, F., 'W muzeum gatunków literackich: Jana Potockiego *Rekopis znaleziony w Saragossie*', *Pamietnik Literacki* 76: 1 (1985), 47–68.

— *Le Théâtre du romanesque*: Manuscrit trouvé à Saragosse, *entre construction et maçonnerie* (Lausanne: L'Age d'Homme, 1991).

Roudaut, J., *Les Dents de Bérénice. Essai sur la représentation et l'évocation des bibliothèques* (Paris: Deyrolle Editeur, 1996).

Rushdie, S., 'Currently Reading', *Guardian*, 9 June 1995, p. 4.

Ryba, J., 'Les aventures éditoriales de Jean Potocki', *Europe* 863 (March 2001), 10–23.

Slawinski, J., 'Intertekstualnosc', in M. Glowinski et al. (eds.), *Slownik terminów literackich* (Wroclaw: Ossolineum, 1988), p. 201.

Zoltowska, M. E., 'Un précurseur de la littérature fantastique: Jean Potocki, sa vie et son *Manuscrit trouvé à Saragosse*', thesis, Yale University, 1973.

— 'Le Manuscrit qui n'a pas été trouvé à Saragosse', in J. Herman and F. Hallyn (eds.), *Le Topos du manuscrit trouvé. Hommages à Christian Angelet* (Louvain and Paris: Peeters, 1999), pp. 267–76.

Comparative Criticism 24, pp. 111–120.   Cambridge University Press 2002
DOI: 10.1017/S0144756402005486   Printed in the United Kingdom

Fabula interrupta: on taking (textual) liberties

ZBIGNIEW BIAŁAS

I INTRODUCTION

Critics frequently maintain that Jan Potocki's *Manuscript Found in Saragossa* is, like so many Chinese tales, an example of nesting narratives, stories within stories. That, in itself, would not make the text so intriguing. Rather, as I would like to claim here, Potocki provides us with stories which happen beyond stories. Not only because the indeterminate 'real' is distanced from the narrativized 'given' and not only because in the text itself, the arrival of a stranger is always a promise of a new story, but also because there is no closure to the process of deferral.

The Polish classical translation by Chojecki (1847), which I will refer to in my essay, was undertaken from fugitive, unavailable manuscript versions of the *Manuscript* and – at least in Poland – it is popularly considered to be the only accessible version of the whole text. Obviously, this claim yields to immediate criticism, because the genuine manuscript is absent and it is a known fact that Chojecki made significant changes, some of which I shall scrutinize here. My belief, let me state in advance, is that Chojecki's text is censored on moral grounds; also, it is closer to Romantic Polish than French Enlightened libertarian mood. Moreover, it is, after all, only a translation and as such, cannot be faithful to the original, even if it existed.[1] In view of this, Kukulski's postwar edition of 1956 revises Chojecki's translation which, much as the ambition is to get closer to the original, problematizes the issue further and so does the subsequent edition of 1965.

Roger Caillois, referring to the standard Polish 1956 Chojecki/ Kukulski-revised translation proclaimed: 'De toute façço, fidèle ou non, la traduction de Chojecki, en l'absence du texte français disparu, fournit aujourd'hui la seule version integrale de l'œuvre.'² In other words, the palimpsestic version of the text, on the strength of its exclusive integrity, never mind its legitimacy, acquires almost the status of the original from which the French version is reconstructed in 1989, and then the English version in 1996. All that is accomplished with the knowledge that it is *not* Potocki's original text. In Poland, in fact, readers would readily reject the 'almost' and the 'liberal translation', remembering 'the original'. After all, some Polish critics still cannot forgive the 'traitorous' Joseph Conrad for choosing English as a medium of expression.³ I will, at the same time, problematize the English translation. One learns from Ian Maclean's 'Introduction' that in 1989 René Radrizzani published the complete story in French for the first time, 'cutting the Gordian knot of speculations'.⁴ But now, in the 'Translator's Note' Maclean explains that he translated the text from Radrizzani's French edition, although *not entirely accurately*.⁵ This re-ties the Gordian knot of speculations. The English version is then a version of the French version partly translated from the liberal Polish translation. Every arrival of the new version of Potocki's *Manuscript* is, necessarily and logically, a promise of a new story. In the case of Ian Maclean's translation this promise is fulfilled. But the Penguin Classics edition suggests that this is a classic. The palimpsestic English version of the text, on the strength of its exclusive integrity, the internationality of English and the politics of canonicity acquires almost the status of the original with the knowledge that it is not. In England, in fact, readers may readily wish to reject the 'almost' and the 'liberal translation' remembering 'the classic'.

A convoluted aristocratic simulacrum is, one might say, a time-honoured tradition in Polish culture and the futility of attempts at getting at the Potocki original may be understood by extension, if one considers the history of salvage of another eighteenth-century edifice. The Royal Castle in Warsaw, destroyed completely during the Second World War, was reconstructed in the 1970s according to the original eighteenth-century plans. But this reconstruction was, actually, an act of original construction because the castle, as it stood before the war, did not conform to the original plans, mostly for financial reasons at the time of its erection. Therefore, what was reconstructed is a copy of the original that never existed, though *the* Royal Castle, *a* Royal Castle did exist. I think the parallel is pretty obvious even if the conclusion sounds slightly too postmodern. In the absence of an original it is only signs of the real that matter. In Potocki's case it is always a copy, always a translation. I do not want to repeat what has been amply said so far. I will only concentrate on a handful of examples that reveal fascinating discrepancies, opening yet another dimension for the analysis of what happens beyond stories, and to the stories, not within them.

Bearing in mind the momentous episode of the erection of the Royal Castle in Warsaw, I will present ways in which Chojecki takes liberties with the French text. Examining several selected cases where the protagonists take liberties with each other I will, in turn, examine how the English text takes liberties with the text which is saturated with liberties.

2 ZUBEIDA, ZIBEDDÉ, ZIBELDA

At the close of the first day, when Alphonse is worried that Emina and Zubeida are spirits of darkness, he reasons with himself that they want to 'make [him] succumb to the temptation of lechery' (Potocki/Maclean, p. 21). In Polish, however, the women intend to *znęcić mnie rozkoszą* (Potocki/Chojecki, p. 36), 'to lure me with delight'. The word may also mean happiness, rapture and ecstasy, but not lechery, if the latter signifies inordinate indulgence in sexual activity. Later on, at the very end of that same First Day, Zubeida 'pressed her lips to [Alphonse's] in a seemingly unending kiss' (Potocki/Maclean, p. 22). That is almost in accordance with the French 'Zibeddé colla sa bouche sur la mienne et parut ne pouvoir l'en détacher' (Potocki, Folio Texte Intégral, p. 68). But the Polish translation, 'Zibelda złożyła na ustach moich czuły pocałunek' (Potocki/Chojecki, p. 37) has it that the kiss was not unending, simply 'tender'. A tender kiss by a cousin is a family matter.[6] An unending kiss between cousins is the domain of Marquis de Sade. Roland Barthes would explain such suspension of the embrace, the temporary motionlessness as the realm of sleep without sleeping, 'the voluptuous infantilism of *sleepiness*: this is the moment for telling stories', this is 'companionable incest where everything is suspended: time, law and prohibition: nothing is exhausted, nothing is wanted.'[7] The *continuous* implied by 'unending' will change into the *continual* implied by 'again and again' one paragraph later.

As a result of sleep without sleeping, of the moment for telling stories, of the companionable incest where time, law and prohibition are suspended while nothing is exhausted, Alphonse's subsequent narcotic dream carries him into new realms: 'my thoughts, transported on the wings of desire, carried me into the midst of African harems, where I contemplated the charms of those confined within their walls, rapturously enjoying them again and again in my imagination' (Potocki/Maclean, p. 22). The repetitive rapturous enjoyment 'again and again' may well be a pre-Viagra male dream but the French version is less crude: 'ma pensée, emportée sur l'aile des désirs, malgré moi, me plaçait au milieu des sérails de l'Afrique et s'emparait des charmes renfermés dans leurs enceintes pour en composer mes chimériques jouissances' (Folio Texte Intégral, p. 69). First, what is seen as 'into the midst of African harems' in Maclean's translation is in French 'au milieu des sérails de l'Afrique'. *Serai* is a Turkish and a Persian word for a mansion, a palace or an inn. It is used in English, if rarely, in the meaning of caravansery or seraglio in the latter's meaning of a palace of a sultan. The English word seraglio has, from the sixteenth century onwards, had two meanings: (a) harem, and a separate meaning (b) a palace of a sultan. It is the legacy of Orientalism to equate the two, because the East is not only a career, as Benjamin Disraeli famously proclaimed in *Tancred*, the Orient has always been a space where unrestrained sexual fantasies of the West could be, and indeed, were textually located. In Polish, *seraj* is only a sultan's palace, Moslem ruler's residence, and *harem* is a separate word. The Polish translation is rather close to the French text: 'Myśl moja, niesiona na skrzydłach żądzy, mimowolnie stawiała mnie śród afrykańskich serajów, odsłaniała wdzięki ukryte w ich zaklętych murach i pogrążała w toni nieopisanych rozkoszy' (Potocki/Chojecki, p. 37). Which in translation is: 'My thought, transported on the wings of desire carried me unawares into the midst of African seraglios, [my thought] unveiled the charms confined within their enchanted walls, in the depths of undescribable raptures'. In the language, where *seraj* is simply a sultan's palace, Alphonse 'contemplated the charms confined within enchanted walls' not 'the charms of *those* confined within their walls'. While in the Polish translation *seraj* with its charms is rather like Kubla Khan's Xanadu and the charms may be, say, architectural or horticultural, in choosing 'African harems' where the charms of those confined within their walls are rapturously enjoyed again and again, the English translator limits the possibilities of rapturous enjoyment, the *jouissances chimériques*, to an unending orgy, commensurate with an unending kiss.

3 REBECCA

At the close of Day Nine, Rebecca, the Cabbalistine, refers to the two heroines as 'two female demons called Emina and Zubeida' yet concedes that cabbalists do not know much about the nature of these 'demons' (Potocki/Maclean, p. 109). The French text also uses *démons* twice in this context (Folio Texte Intégral, p. 169, 170). But the Polish version has none of this. The word *demon* does exist in Polish but Emina and Zubeida are referred to as 'Dwa złe duchy niewieście' and 'szatany' (i.e. 'two evil female spirits' and 'satans' respectively). I cannot find a satisfactory linguistic explanation for such a change and no Romantic propensity justifies it. On the other hand, we do detect traces of Romanticism in Rebecca's reveries. Actually, the poetics of Rebecca's reveries begs to find its own Gaston Bachelard. She herself would happily renounce mysterious arts and would have been '*well satisfied* to rule over *the heart of a husband*' (Potocki/Maclean, p. 109). That is the English translation and the French version is equally unenthusiastic about bonds of matrimony: 'Je me serais *bien contentée* de régner sur *le coeur d'un époux*' (Folio Texte Intégral, p. 170). But the Polish translation is not satisfied with such matter-of-factness when it comes to marital bliss and ravishment, therefore Rebecca says: 'Wolałabym *stokroć* bardziej panować nad sercem *przywiązanego* małżonka' (Potocki/ Chojecki, p. 131). Thus: 'I would have been a hundred times more satisfied to rule over the heart of a devoted husband'. 'Well satisfied' gets changed into 'a hundred times more satisfied' and 'the heart of the husband' is 'the heart of an 'attached, affectionate, devoted' husband because that is part of the meaning of the word *przywiązany*. The other part, equally legitimate in the context of amorous regime, might have yet another meaning in Polish. *Przywiązany małżonek* also means 'tied down', for instance with a rope. The English expressions highlighting 'bondage' and 'being in harness' probably come closest to the ambiguous, somewhat power-freakish declaration. Therefore, in opposition to the French and the English unimpassioned Rebecca, the Polish Rebecca retains the potentiality of total ravishment in different variants: from the purely romantic to the purely sadistic.

4 ORLANDINE AND FACES IN THE MIRROR

Let us compare the following three versions:

– Orlandine, Orlandine ... que veut dire ceci?
– Je ne suis point Orlandine ... je suis **Belzébuth** (Folio Texte Intégral, p. 183)

And in English:

'Orlandine, Orlandine, what is the meaning of this?' ...
'I am not Orlandine [...] I am **Beelzebub**' (Potocki/Maclean, p. 120)

Finally, in Polish:

– Orlandyno, Orlandyno ... co to ma znaczyć? ...
– Jam nie Orlandyna [...] jam **Lucyfer** (Potocki/Chojecki, p. 144)

Why does she get promoted from Satan's Deputy (Beelzebub, the Lord of the Flies) to the very Prince of Darkness? The Morning Star? Satan himself? We are, as usual, in the realm of discursive speculation. Maybe because Thibaud sees in her and addresses her as his 'lovely wandering star' and then says that his 'star brought it about that [they] have met' that night (Potocki/Maclean, p. 115). The corresponding version in French describes Orlandine as *la belle étoile errante* (Folio Texte Intégral, p. 177). On the one hand, the lovely errant star is Venus, the bright morning star; in other words, the star of the *discursus*, of the running about, because that is what *dis-cursus* originally signifies; etymologically, it is an act of running about.[8] On the other hand, 'Lucifer' means the carrier of light and the morning star. The name may have been given to Satan because of multiplied misunderstandings (cf., for example, Milton's *Paradise Lost*, where Lucifer is Satan before the Fall). 'Bright morning star, you have fallen from heaven', we read in Isaiah (14:12) and 'I saw Satan fall like lightning from heaven' says Jesus (Luke 10:18).

This is neither the commencement nor the denouement of Orlandine-inspired predicament. Before she appears to be Lucifer/Beelzebub, she suggests to Thibaud they make use of the mirror. What in fact does she wish to do? In the English version she suggests: 'Here is a tall mirror. Let us play the game I played at the castle of Sombre. There I amused myself by seeing whether my governess was built differently from me. I'd like now to see whether I am differently built from you' (Potocki/Maclean, p. 120). What she proposes is interpreted as a game. In the French version Orlandine suggests: 'Voici un grand miroir. Alons y faire des mines, comme j'en faisais au châtel de Sombre' (Folio Texte Intégral, p. 183). In French, 'faire de petites mines' may be equivalent to 'being coquettish' or, less probably, to 'making faces'. Being coquettish obviously seems more logical in the depicted situation. Strangely enough, in the Polish version one finds the following: 'Widzisz to wielkie zwierciadło? Chodźmy stroić w nim miny ...' (Potocki/

Chojecki, p. 144), which literally means simply: 'Can you see the tall mirror? Let us go and make faces in it.'

Let us see in practice: does Orlandine want to play games (a childish English option), does she want to be coquettish and provocative in front of the mirror (a seductive French option) or does she want to make faces (a childish Polish option – incidentally, an obsession which will return to Polish literature with Gombrowicz in modernist times)? Orlandine places two chairs in front of the grand mirror, unlaces Thibaud's ruff, then makes him take off his belt, undo his doublet, take off the laces, then she compares their chests, makes comments on the newly acquired plumpness of her breasts and this is where the game? the coquetry? the making of faces? ends because Thibaud cannot control himself any more, he takes her to bed, finds her to be Lucifer/Beelzebub/*La Belle Dame Sans Merci*/Sister Helen/Queen of the Elves ..., you name it, and pays with his life for yielding to the game? the coquetry? or the making of faces?

5 SYLVIA

'So you see, my little Spaniard, that up to now you have been completely fooled. But you haven't the right to complain about what happened subsequently, and my mistress has no complaints about you. As for me, I found you charming when you sought my arm to support you in your weakness. Then I swore that I would have my turn.' That is how the soubrette expressed herself. (Potocki/Maclean, p. 447)

And the Polish version:

Widzisz więc, mój młody Hiszpanie, że wpadłeś w zastawioną siatkę, wszelako nie możesz się skarżyć, ani też moja pani, na koniec komedii. Nigdy nie zapomnę, jak byłeś piękny, gdy cały omdlewający wychodziłeś od Laury wspierając się na moim ramieniu. Odtad czuję, mój luby, że i ja kocham cię nad życie! (Potocki/Chojecki, p. 401)[9]
(So you see, my young Spaniard, that you fell into a trap. But you haven't the right to complain, and my mistress has no complaints about the end of the comedy. I will never forget how beautiful you were when all swooning you were leaving Laura and you sought my arm to support you. Since then I feel, my love, that I too love you more than my own life!)

The English translation, faithful to the French text, presents a soubrette directly from de Sade with her *blasé* expressions: 'my little Spaniard', 'completely fooled', 'my mistress has no complaints about you', 'I swore that I would have my turn'. The Polish version is incurably Romantic instead. The young Spaniard fell into a trap and that does not necessarily entail stupidity, and Laura, not a soubrette at all, feels that she too loves him more than her own life. This is hardly equivalent to the vulgar 'having her turn'.

In accordance with the above logic, this is what follows in the English version:

What can I say? I was astounded by what I had just heard. I had been stripped of my illusions. I didn't know where I was. Sylvia profited from my confusion to bring turmoil to my senses. She had no difficulty in succeeding. She even abused the advantages she had. At last, when she put me back in my carriage, I didn't know whether to feel fresh remorse or not to think any more about it. (Potocki/Maclean, p. 447)

While the Polish version consistently sticks to Romantic traditions:

Cóż mogę wam więcej powiedzieć? Wysłuchałem Sylwii pomieszany, ogłuszony i nie pojmując, jak można w jednej chwili rozwiać komuś wszystkie złudzenia. Ale Sylwia była tak piękna, czarne jej oczy błyskały tak przenikliwym ogniem, śnieżne łono tak rozkosznie wznosiło się, miotane gwałtownym uczuciem, że sam nie wiem, jak przepędziłem resztę czasu; dość, że gdy Sylwia odprowadzała mnie do powozu, nie wiedziałem, czy należy dręczyć się nowymi wyrzutami, czy też wcale o nich nie myśleć. (Potocki/Chojecki, p. 401)
(What else can I tell you? I listened to Sylvia confused and astounded. I didn't understand how in one moment one can be stripped of all illusions. But Sylvia was so beautiful, her black eyes blazed with such penetrating fire, her snowy bosom rose so delightfully, tossed by violent emotion that I do not know how I spent the remaining time. At last, when Sylvia saw me back to my carriage, I didn't know whether to feel fresh remorse or not to think any more about it.)

Sylvia of the English version, who profits from the confusion to bring turmoil to the senses and even abuses the advantages she has, is a different Sylvia from the one in the Polish version where she is beautiful, her black eyes ablaze with penetrating fire and her snowy bosom rises delightfully, tossed by violent emotions. In other words, Sylvia of the English Potocki is cunning, Sylvia of the Polish Potocki is only irresistible. In the English version she is plainly a seducer, in the Polish text she is gorgeous.

6 INTERRUPTION/CONCLUSION

We could continue our *discursus* but it is time to stop at this point of the story. In concluding I would like to abstract from biographism and from the fact that Jan Potocki was reputed to have had love affairs with his mother-in-law, his sister and his mother.[10] I would rather concentrate on the question of vulnerability to *discursus*.

One of the aspects of the interruption is the insistence on the juxtaposition of 'the peripatetic/the dynamic' and 'the still'. The Wandering Jew can only talk while walking. Furthermore, what the Gypsy Chief accomplishes by his constant comings and goings, by his running here and there, is making the book possible. Discourse, i.e. verbal interchange, conversation is only thinkable because of motion. Without movement there is no possibility to meet strangers, there is no potentiality to obtain stories. The protagonists of Potocki's novel travel mostly to proceed. Their telos is not a particular place, it consists in locating a suitable resting place where they can temporarily stop proceeding. The standstill is necessary to let the Wandering Jew (whether invented or not) rest from articulating his own *fabula interrupta*. There is an interesting, inverted symmetry of roles that could be analysed (but we shall refrain), where, for example, the Jew cannot talk when the company rest, while the Gypsy Chief speaks only in between acts of running about, i.e. in between his acts of *discursus*. In other words, somewhat paradoxically, his discourse is possible in the fissures and in the cracks of *discursus*.

Manuscripts usually tend to be found either in fissures and cracks (e.g. the Qumran scrolls) or in locked containers, bottles and tubs. There is no shortage of archaeological good luck, suffice it to recall Edgar Allan Poe's short story 'MS. Found in a Bottle' (1831), Franciszek Fenikowski's *Rękopis z gospody 'Pod Łososiem'* (1957), Stanislaw Lem's *A Manuscript Found in a Tub* (1961) and Cortázar's and Borges's short stories. If Jan Potocki's *Manuscript Found in Saragossa* is an edifice of the eighteenth century's technology of literary salvage, for the manuscript to be found in Saragossa not in a fissure, a crack, a container, but simply in the corner of a room, is highly symbolic: of its openness, dynamism, its vulnerability to *discursus*, understood as the act of running here and there. Let us additionally remember that although much is made here of the Polish, French and English versions, the Prefatory 'Avertissement' makes it clear that the original manuscript was written in Spanish. Is it gallows humour? Which reminds me: even the bodies of Zoto's hanged brothers are victims of *dis-cursus*, a curse, being continually embraced at the foot of a gibbet, continually travelling between the gallows and the gallows' footholds, forever accompanying the peripatetic strangers with their promises of stories, and stories of people who have stories to tell.

NOTES

1 See: Leszek Kukulski, 'Wstęp', in: Jan Potocki, *Rękopis znaleziony w Saragossie*, text based on Edward Chojecki's translation of 1847 (Warsaw: Czytelnik, 1956); also Roger Caillois's comment: '[M. Leszek Kukulski] en procura une édition critique en 1956, accompagnée d'etudes et de notes. [...] Il compare la version polonaise au texte français et donne des exemples des nombreux changements introduits par le traducteur qui semble avoir pris avec l'original d'assez grandes libertés.' *Jean Potocki et Le Manuscrit trouvé à Saragosse. Actes du Colloque organisé par le Centre de Civilisation Française de l'Université de Varsovie (Avril 1972), Les Cahiers de Varsovie* 3 (1981), 28.

2 Roger Caillois, *Jean Potocki et Le Manuscrit*, p. 28.

3 There are more correspondencies between Conrad and Potocki. See, for example, Laurence Davies, 'Conrad and Potocki: A Speculation', in Alex S. Kurczaba (ed.), *Conrad and Poland* (Boulder: East European Monographs/Lublin: Maria Curie-Skłodowska University, 1996), pp. 179–94.

4 Ian Maclean, 'Introduction', in Jan Potocki, *The Manuscript Found in Saragossa*, trans. Ian Maclean (Harmondsworth: Penguin, 1996), p. xiii.

5 Ian Maclean, 'Translator's Note', p. xix. See also: René Radrizzani, ed. *Manuscrit trouvé à Saragosse*. (Paris: José Corti, 1989.)

6 However, in the new translation based on the seventh Polish edition of 1965 (Lublin: Test, 1995) one reads: 'Zibelda przylgnęła do moich ust i długo nie mogła się od nich oderwać', which is exactly as in the French version: 'she could not get detached from my lips' (Potocki/Kukulski, p. 28).

7 Roland Barthes, *A Lover's Discourse: Fragments*, tr. Richard Howard (Harmondsworth: Penguin, 1990), p. 104.

8 Barthes, *A Lover's Discourse*, p. 4.

9 The translation revised by Kukulski (1965) corrects Chojecki's 'I feel, my love, that I too love you more than my own life' into 'Przysięgłam sobie wtedy, że i na mnie musi przyjść kolej' [I swore that I would have my turn' (Potocki/Kukulski, p. 105)].

10 Versions repeated both by some historians (see, for example, Janusz Tazbir's introduction to the 1998 Polish edition of *The Manuscript* (Wrocław: Wydawnictwo Siedmioróg) as well as novelists (see, for example, a novelistic account of Potocki's life in Tomasz Jurasz's *Rozkosze nocy, czyli ostatnia podróż Jana hr. Potockiego* [Nocturnal Delights or Count Jan Potocki's Last Journey], Warsaw: Iskry, 1997).

Comparative Criticism **24**, pp. 121–139.   Cambridge University Press 2002
DOI: 10.1017/S0144756402005498   Printed in the United Kingdom

The European 'nights' tradition: Potocki and Odoevsky's *Russian Nights*

NEIL CORNWELL

Odoevsky's *Russian Nights* (*Russkie nochi*, 1844) may be best described as a 'philosophical frame-tale' and it is sometimes termed a 'philosophical novel'.[1] It comprises a series of short stories of an assorted romantic nature (most of which had earlier been published separately), collected and embedded in a philosophical discussion on romantic aesthetics and the prospects of Russia as a force for the reinvigoration of the so-called 'dying west' (eighteen sections in all, within nine 'nights'). As such it is a formal curiosity, unique in Russian literature and perhaps even in European literature. None of the comparisons we can make with other comparably structured works (see the 'Tentative genealogy of the "frame-tale"': Appendix 1 which follows) would be valid in isolation, although many of these may have been contributory influences – as, in some cases too, on Potocki's *The Manuscript Found in Saragossa*. One thing that can be said is that *Russian Nights* is an illustration *par excellence* of the romantic principle, inspired by Schelling, Novalis and others, of the mixing of genres and the mixing of styles. Rather like Potocki's work (Potocki seems to have at first thought of his work as a Gothic novel '*à la* Radcliffe'),[2] it derives both from romanticism and from the antecedents of romanticism, including the Gothic, alchemical and esoteric traditions, as well as the all-important tradition of eastern story-telling. Odoevsky's compilation spreads far and wide in its settings, while Potocki settles largely for Moorish-influenced Spain and introduces an erotic element into his *mélange* of the fantastic. *Russian Nights* has been aptly termed (in the Soviet 1981 *History of Russian Literature*[3]) 'an encyclopedia of romanticism', while both Prince Vladimir Odoevsky and Count Jan Potocki were acknowledged 'encyclopedists'.

What sets *Russian Nights* apart from other models is the almost equal treatment accorded the philosophical and the 'fictional' components.

Frontispiece to the Russian edition of Potocki's *Manuscript Found in Saragossa*

Whereas in most instances of comparable cycles or frame-tales the 'frame' is somewhat perfunctory, in *Russian Nights* it occupies almost as much space as the fiction; indeed, its embedded stories could almost be said to be reduced to providing a background. It introduces the, at least apparently, authorial protagonist named Faust, who conducts lengthy discussions with several foils; and – therefore, and in addition – this frame constitutes the forum for many of the ideas of the work. This is especially the case in its lengthy epilogue, which provides ample coverage of the main strands of Russian thought of the 1820s and 1830s: a kind of proto-Westernizer/Slavophile debate in itself.

The stories comprising the fictional element had been written over a period of about fifteen years, nearly all being published along the way, and the entire project grew from a grandiose abandoned scheme, to have been called 'The House of Madmen' (*Dom sumasshedshikh*). This too had its roots in dialogues planned for a proposed 'Dictionary of the History of Philosophy' of the mid-1820s, which was to have been reduced to 'a huge drama ... enacted by all the Philosophers of the world, from the Eleatics to Schelling'.[4] Many of these stories enjoyed individual success during the 1830s; several, including those centring on such 'sublime eccentrics' (*vysokie bezumtsy*) as Piranesi, Beethoven and J. S. Bach, stand comparison with Odoevsky's best stories, and indeed with most of the romantic and society tales produced in the Russia of the 1830s; only obvious works of genius, such as Pushkin's *The Queen of Spades* (*Pikovaia dama*) and Gogol's *The Overcoat* (*Shinel'*), can claim a clear superiority. 'Sebastian Bach', in particular, is of itself a minor masterpiece: an alternative 'inner biography', it ironically depicts its arch-classical subject in ultra-romantic terms. Cycles within the main cycle, elaborative narrational distancing devices, social satire, and explorations of the ideas of such thinkers as Bentham and Malthus are further features of what is now generally seen as Odoevsky's *magnum opus*. Taken together, the links and themes connecting these stories with the material of their surrounding frame (the power of music, the quest for truth and communication, social responsibility, touches of the supernatural and anti-Utopian fantasy) only struck their author with their full significance (or so it would seem) with hindsight. Only in the last third of the twentieth century, moreover, has the hidden poetic scheme underlying *Russian Nights* as an integral work even begun to be fully appreciated in the critical literature.[5]

A key source-book for Russian romanticism and for the social and aesthetic thought of its epoch, *Russian Nights* represents the culmination of Russian romanticism and, in 1844, proved to be, to all intents and purposes, the valedictory work of Odoevsky's literary career.[6] Notwithstanding its many years of subsequent neglect, however, *Russian Nights* did not remain totally unnoticed in the world at large: even within its author's lifetime, one of the most striking of its stories, 'The Improvisor' (*Improvizzatore*), was plagiarized almost word for word, via its French translation, by the Irish-American writer Fitz-James O'Brien, who retitled it 'Seeing the World' in 1859 (and it still appears under his name in modern editions; moreover, O'Brien's best-known story, 'The Diamond Lens' bears a remarkably strong resemblance to Odoevsky's tale 'Sil'fida').[7] We know from Odoevsky's later remarks (in a 'Foreword' to a never completed second edition) that he was aware of the phenomenon of 'pilfering' and of consequent 'curious works wandering around the world'; whether he was aware of the particular efforts of O'Brien, we cannot say.[8]

There would seem to be no dispute that the frame-tale, comprising a group or groups of stories or novellas arranged in a cycle or within a frame (*Rahmen*),[9] and perhaps even the novella form itself, originated in the literature of the East. Harald Weinrich (as quoted by Martin Swales[10]) writes of the eastern idea that man comes to insight and understanding not so much by thought process as by telling and listening to stories. Walter Benjamin (in a view which closely coincides with Odoevsky's romantically expressed theory of legend – or 'epic' in its broadest sense, to include tale and folk-song) states that 'experience which is passed from mouth to mouth is the source from which all storytellers have drawn'; he emphasizes the role of travellers, the trade structure of the Middle Ages, and the vital importance of memory in the furtherance of this process.[11] These points would seem to be of equal importance, too, to the fictional universe of Potocki, whose extended narrative could well be termed the ultimate 'novel of frames'.[12] The novella, or the frame-tale, frequently assumes a didactic quality, the frame's function later being taken over by the broad panoramic social background customarily depicted in the realist novel. Frame-tales, indeed, can themselves assume the dimensions and many of the overall qualities of the novel. Certain frame-tales, at least, may justifiably be considered novels and are frequently referred to as such. *The Manuscript Found in Saragossa* and *Russian Nights* are two such instances, lurking in the margins of the novel, or on the threshold between story and novel; certain acknowledged novels, for that matter, can equally be seen as frame-tales (Maturin's *Melmoth the Wanderer* is as good an example as any). Romantic and Gothic literature, of course, also use framing devices, such as the 'manuscript' or oral retelling, in works of more limited scale.

Invariably cited as the most prominent early model for works of this type of construction is *The Thousand and One Nights*, which presents a vast compendium of stories, purportedly told or retold over that time scale by a single primary narrator under particularly constrained circumstances. The first European example usually cited is *The Decameron*, Boccaccio's fourteenth-century book of a hundred tales, supposedly told in ten days by 'an assembled company of raconteurs'. Chaucer's *The Canterbury Tales* soon followed in England. The French *nouvelle* took *The Decameron* as its formal model, but by the mid-sixteenth century the term had become virtually interchangeable with *conte* and formal requirements inherited from Boccaccio, such as the frame, were generally abandoned; as seventeenth- and eighteenth-century prose proliferated diversely in theme and form, the terms *roman*, *nouvelle* and *conte* seem to have retained few overtones of generic differentiation. At the close of the eighteenth century, however, the romantic practice, particularly in Germany, of reusing old literary forms in new ways brought a new spate of experimentation with the frame-tale genre.

During this period in particular (I quote here, and in the appended 'Tentative genealogy', a dozen or so examples from the half century separating Goethe's *Conversations with German Emigrants* and Odoevsky's *Russian Nights*), considerable variations take place: in the function of the frame; in the deployment of the narrative voice (or voices); and in the arrangement of the material narrated – not to mention the nature of this material and questions of overall authorial intent.

Martin Swales has pointed out that the frame can be used either 'as a pointless piece of narrative sophistication', or 'it can have profound implications for any understanding of the narrative technique of the novelle as such'; when any significant use of the frame device applies, 'the work as a whole operates within two kinds of narrative direction: there is a world of which the narrator tells, and also a world within which and to which he tells his story'.[13] The relationship between these two aspects of narrative reference is accordingly of the essence, setting up a tension within the work as a whole, and the whole process can, of course, be multiplied or extended.

Early examples, notably *The Thousand and One Nights*, tend to operate within a structure devised to exploit the motivating principle of 'narration under pressure', or, in Todorov's phrase, 'a story or your life!'[14] The process of narration is thereby used within the text, as a matter of life or death and, beyond the text, has implications for the relationship between, as Swales points out, 'the narrator and the world that receives his art'; this applies to the listener within the frame situation and, to an extent, the readers outside it; thus 'the aim and function of narrating (and of listening) becomes part of the overall import'.[15] This serves to feed the already mentioned essentially didactic quality of the frame-tale.

The role of the listener and the possibility, indeed the dire necessity, of his/her being influenced by the narration is obviously of vital importance in *The Thousand and One Nights*, where the process of narration is used continually (for 1,001 nights, excepting the twenty-night gap which Sheherezade takes off to give birth clandestinely to twins!) to put off and off the dreaded hour. Something of this duress remains in *The Decameron* in the motivation of a frame situation under the threat of plague, seen, in the light of the hundred stories told, to be both medical and moral. The stories themselves are presumed to be imaginary (indeed Boccaccio in the Author's Epilogue expressly denies being their inventor) and purport to adapt to the needs and nature of their particular audience (e.g. the presence within the ten of seven ladies!), whose reception of each story is (generally uniformly) commented upon.

The device of narration under pressure, or at a time of freak catastrophe, tends to fade somewhat in later examples, although it is still present in the background of Goethe's *Conversations of German Emigrants* (who have been displaced by the French Revolution), while it receives an ironic and perhaps parodic reversal in the motivating device of Heine's *Florentine Nights*, by which 'fantastic stuff enough' is narrated by one Maximilian for the nocturnal entertainment and edification of 'a languid girl moribund with consumption'.[16] The art of oral narrative is more commonly, however, replaced by the reading of literary works already composed (as in the examples by Tieck and Hoffmann) by the story-tellers themselves, or, in the cases of Wackenroder, Potocki and Odoevsky, of manuscripts purportedly written by, or memorized from, some third party (or parties), not present in the frame situation, who may be well removed in time and space and is often dead. Several layers of subsidiary narrators are, in some cases (such as Potocki and Odoevsky), involved. In the concept of the 'night', when retained, there may be preserved something of the flavour of its oriental origins, but it is now rather more a social occasion when friends foregather, or merely betokens a convenient breaking-off point.[17] Even when the 'day' replaces the 'night', as in *The Manuscript*, the storytelling mostly takes place in the evening.

The loss of one strong compositional ingredient from the foregoing 'novella tradition' of the frame-tale may be compensated for by the introduction of a more complex, abstract and plotless discussion, which can be seen to descend from the 'philosophical tradition' of Plato's dialogues. Goethe's *Conversations of German Emigrants*, 'a collection of novellas with a discursive dialogue framework', probably influenced by Diderot's *Jacques le Fataliste*, may well have been a key work in establishing this trend.[18] Thus the frame may take on the qualities of a symposium on art and aesthetics (as with Hoffmann) or a philosophical discussion of the future of Russia (*Russian Nights*). Alternatively, however, it may be considered to be merely 'an excuse' whose effect is to diminish the stories within it (as has been said of Tieck's *Phantasus*);[19] or be virtually non-existent, as exemplified by *The Night Watches of Bonaventura* (essentially a fictional biography in the first person, told out of chronological order, but including interpolated contributions by a variety of sub-narrators) – or even Potocki's *Manuscript* (the overall framing device of which work does not extend beyond the initial Foreword, although there is, of course, a very extensive secondary framework).

Of the near-contemporary works suggested as possible influences upon the form of *Russian Nights*, first mention must be given to those of Goethe. Although *Faust* and *Wilhelm Meister* had a considerable impact upon Odoevsky (as is evidenced by Odoevsky's adoption of the name Faust and by the second epigraph to *Russian Nights*, quite apart from any other points of contact), it would scarcely be arguable that these works could have had more than the most fleeting effect upon the structural design of *Russian Nights* (Goethe's *Faust* being in a sense a 'fragment' and *Wilhelm Meister* including interpolated novellas or narratives). *Conversations with German Emigrants* (generally considered a lesser work) merits closer comparison, given both the content and the attention paid by Goethe to the frame situation which, in the words of Swales, explores 'the full thematic implications of a particular kind of narrative constellation', involving questions (not far removed from Odoevsky's interests) of interpretation and understanding.[20] This apparently unfinished work includes six stories of a previous epoch (four of them narrated by a priest); the brief dialogues between stories explore moral and aesthetic issues.

Wackenroder's *Fantasies on Art* (*Confessions and Fantasies*), completed and published posthumously by Tieck in 1799, includes the novella of the fictional musician Joseph Berglinger and his purported associated writings. C. M. Wieland's *The Hexameron of Rosenhaim* (1805), a late and lesser work by a more minor writer, contains three prose fairy-tales and three novellas – the first group being of a wondrous nature and the second contemporary and prosaic, reflecting Wieland's view of the novella as taking place in the real world. The six stories issue from six narrators, the last of whom is a woman telling what purports to be her own story. The frame is of a contrived nature, involving superficial salon discussions.

Tieck, himself something of a theorist of the novella, combined in 1812 some of his published stories (such as 'The Fair-Haired Eckbert') with new material (such as 'The Elves'), added a framework (which he considered to be 'a novel on a small scale') and 'Boccaccio-like showed a group of friends reading and discussing the contributions' in rather 'prolix' conversations on literary and other aesthetic questions.[21] It was probably the compositional history of the finished product, known as *Phantasus*, which more than anything suggested the parallel with *Russian Nights* discerned by some Russian critics.

The most discussed work in this connection (by Russian critics from Belinsky onwards, not forgetting Odoevsky's own comments dating from the early 1860s and included in subsequent editions of *Russian Nights*) has been Hoffmann's *The Serapion Brothers*. This extensive work of approaching 1,000 pages (of which there is no English translation, other than of some of the individual tales) includes some twenty-eight stories, among which are a number of Hoffmann's best-known tales. Again the frame was constructed *a posteriori* and the form is considered to owe something to *Phantasus*; the frame is motivated as 'a reunion of young friends', six literati in all, who hold eight weekly evenings to read aloud their own compositions, which are designed to illustrate the literary, musical, aesthetic and supernatural questions arising in their animated and important between-story discussions, which comprise something like a quarter of the whole text. A 'remarkably professional' full translation into Russian of *The Serapion Brothers* was published (in eight volumes) in Moscow in 1836; this fact and the rather equivocal nature of Odoevsky's (much later) denial of any imitation of Hoffmann in *Russian Nights* leave the question open, quite apart from the extent of Hoffmann's overall impact upon Odoevsky.[22] Nevertheless, the structural parallel is perhaps no closer than in the cases of some of the other works mentioned and Odoevsky would not necessarily have had to be familiar with specifically *The Serapion Brothers* in its complete form to have been able to devise the structure of *Russian Nights*.

In the same year which saw the Russian translation of *The Serapion Brothers*, and in the following issue of the same journal in which Odoevsky's 'The First Night' was published, there appeared a translation of the 'First Night' of Heine's *Florentine Nights*. One Russian commentator perceives 'a direct contact' between Heine's work and Odoevsky's aesthetic preoccupations and even suggests that Odoevsky may have acted as Heine's translator.[23] There is, however, little structural similarity between the two works; Heine's 'novel', composed hurriedly as an uncontroversial pot-boiler, got no further than its second 'night' (though nevertheless was originally to include a further portion which the author had deemed it wiser to suppress), and the closest parallel with *Russian Nights* lies in the inclusion of romanticized depictions of musicians: in Heine's case, Bellini and Paganini.

A minor Russian work occasionally cited as a predecessor to *Russian Nights* is Pogorel'sky's *The Double, or My Evenings in Little Russia* (*Dvoinik, ili moi vechera v Malorossii*, 1828), a frame-story containing four tales and also (like Hoffmann and Tieck, its likely sources) employing the device of reading one's own stories (in this case those of the narrator and his double) from manuscript. Other contributory Russian works which may be described as frame-tales include the little-known P. L. Yakovlev's *Tales of the Luzhnitsky Elder* (*Rasskazy Luzhnitskogo startsa*, 1828) and Odoevsky's own cycle *Variegated Tales* (*Pestrye skazki*, 1833).[24]

Of at least equal relevance to *Russian Nights*, though, may be those other structural curiosities of the period: *The Night Watches of Bonaventura* and Potocki's *The Manuscript*. The former, the authorship of which has never been settled, was published anonymously in 1804; the first part of the latter was privately printed, though not commercially exploited, in St Petersburg almost simultaneously (the first thirteen 'days' of Potocki's work were printed there 1804–5). The extraordinary text of 'Bonaventura', although seeming to anticipate much in nineteenth-century Russian literature, seems to have been little known outside a small circle in Germany.[25]

Potocki's compendious work, however, may be a different matter: its original Petersburg printing, its known impact upon Pushkin and the poet and critic Prince Petr Viazemsky, and Potocki's masonic connections with Count M. Iu. Viel'gorsky[26] (later a close friend of Odoevsky) all make it unlikely that Odoevsky could have failed at least to be aware of *The Manuscript*. Potocki may also have had an impact on certain works of the period by the romantic writer Aleksandr Vel'tman and at least one of the early vampirical tales of A. K. Tolstoy.

Of particular interest is the Pushkin connection, in that Pushkin, who is thought to have come across *The Manuscript* in the south of Russia as early as 1821, still had Potocki's masterwork uppermost in his mind in a late poetic fragment (of forty-five lines), beginning 'Alphonse mounts his horse', of 1836 (written during the last months of his life: see Appendix 2).[27] In the intervening years, Pushkin had sought in vain to obtain his own copy of the St Petersburg publication of *The Manuscript* (as did Vel'tman) and eventually had to settle for one of the Paris printing of 1813–14.[28] Pushkin, in his travelogue *A Journey to Arzrum* (*Puteshestvie v Arzrum*, 1835), noted that Potocki's 'scientific researches are just as absorbing as his Spanish novels', while both Pushkin and Viazemsky were struck, in the light of the execution by hanging of the Decembrist leaders in 1826, by the image of the Los Hermanos gibbet of Zoto's brothers.[29]

Apart from the device of the manuscript itself, the motif of travel and a certain common northern Gothic fascination with some of the exotic manifestations of southern Europe, however, there is little enough immediately striking formal or thematic similarity with *Russian Nights*. Odoevsky does at times, though, almost match Potocki in levels of embedded narration; furthermore, his later admission that the greater part of his tales came to him by means of dreams would surely have struck a chord with Potocki.

The best-known structural eccentricity (or perhaps monstrosity) of the time was certainly Maturin's *Melmoth the Wanderer* (1820), which had no small impact in Russia; this work was originally planned as a frame-tale (a series of stories depicting encounters with the tempter Melmoth) or a cycle, but Maturin instead chose a system which has been described as 'Chinese-box perversity – story within story within story, a perpetual shift and distancing of narrator from reader which chills the latter's interest and belief', as Alethea Hayter perhaps contentiously opines.[30] As it is, Maturin's 'tale' (such is the subtitle) spans nearly 700 pages, a length similar to that of *The Manuscript Found in Saragossa*, and greatly exceeding that of *Russian Nights*. In tone, content and setting, such staples of the European Gothic-Fantastic tradition as Cazotte's *The Devil in Love* and Schiller's *The Ghost-Seer* would seem to have had their impact here – and no doubt on Potocki, in particular.[31]

Not to be ignored either are various other recognized influences upon Odoevsky's literary development: *The Pancatantra*, the ancient Indian collection of didactic stories; al-Hariri's *Maqamat* (partly translated into Russian in this period); the work of Cervantes, whose narrative techniques set the pattern for European literature thereafter (quoted or referred to by Odoevsky, along with Sterne, in his later additions to *Russian Nights*, and a lurking presence too in Potocki); La Bruyère's *Les Caractères* (1688), an important model for Odoevsky's apologues of the 1820s; the cabbalistic *Le Comte de Gabalis* (1670), by Monfaucon de Villars (a source too for Hoffmann); and the works of Jean Paul Richter, frequently cited by Belinsky and others as antecedents of narrational techniques in particular Odoevsky tales.

In the case of *Russian Nights*, the connection between form and content can be traced also in philosophical precursors: Odoevsky acknowledged that his interest in Plato was by no means solely philosophical; alongside the mystical ideas of John Pordage and Louis Claude de Saint-Martin may be set the dramatic dialogues of Giordano Bruno, the poetic theosophy of Jacob Boehme and the *Naturphilosophie* of Schelling. The most immediate philosophical work descended from the dialogical tradition of Plato, however, was Joseph de Maistre's *Les soirées de Saint-Pétersbourg* (1821), a series of eleven dialogues (or *entretiens*) dealing with human government and other political and philosophical problems conducted by three 'characters' (the Count, the Knight and the Senator). The work begins with a six-page description of St Petersburg, in the first-person narration of the Count (apparently de Maistre himself), and then breaks into a three-way dialogue; the setting device (it can scarcely be termed a frame) establishes time (July 1809) and place, then gives way to a '*symposie philosophique*'.[32] Copious notes follow each dialogue. In works of this tradition, of course, fictional tales as such are normally completely absent. Notwithstanding Odoevsky's later hostile comments on de Maistre's Catholic messianism, it seems likely that *Les soirées de Saint-Pétersbourg*, written by a pupil of Saint-Martin, at very least impelled Odoevsky towards his earlier intention of calling his main work (which was eventually to become '*Russian* nights') 'Petersburg Nights'.

Potocki clearly shared similar occult and cabbalistic interests to

Odoevsky, and Ian Maclean has mentioned 'affinities with the tarot pack' in the structure of *The Manuscript*.[33] Indeed, the hidden structural presence of occult systems may yet emerge from the manuscripts of both Potocki and Odoevsky. The Chevalier de Saint-Germain – a personage featuring in stories by both Pushkin (*The Queen of Spades*) and Odoevsky (*Letter IV* [*to Countess Ye. P. Rostopchina*]) – makes a fleeting appearance in *The Manuscript*, while Odoevsky's Piranesi takes on something of the aspect of the Wandering Jew.

Russian Nights represents a synthesis of the novella tradition of the frame-tale, stemming from *The Thousand and One Nights*, and the philosophical tradition descending from Plato. Odoevsky himself considered its form a 'higher synthesis' between the genres of drama and novel; he considered (in an earlier draft preface, only recently published) that: 'the novel separate from drama and drama separate from the novel are defective publications, that the one and the other can be combined in a single higher synthesis, that the contours of such a novellistic drama can be more spacious than the forms of normal drama and a normal novel, that the protagonist may be not one person but a thought, developing naturally in numerous and varied personages'.[34] The German romantics, like Odoevsky, conceived grandiose encyclopedic projects which often got no further than the fragmentary stage, or conceived of the romantic novel as a fragment. *Russian Nights*, Odoevsky's single completed major project, can essentially be seen as a collection of fragments; the romantic fragment itself is described as 'a new revolutionary and still only partly accepted form' created by Novalis and Schlegel.[35] According to Todorov, 'the romantics' favorite genres are specifically the dialogue and the fragment, the one for its unfinished character, the other for the way it stages the search for and the elaboration of ideas: both share in the same valorization of production with respect to the product'.[36] This statement could have been written as a virtual commentary on *Russian Nights* and it is by no means irrelevant either to the extensive chain of stories, and stories within stories, comprising Jan Potocki's fantastical narrative. The very philosophical import of Odoevsky's work and the view it presents of Russia preserve more than a vestige of the didactic function of the original eastern tales. *The Manuscript Found in Saragossa*, for its part, remains very much an eastern (as well as, by its authorship at least, an east European) tale in confrontation with the west, while synthesis, as a concept in itself, embodies one of the fundamental ideas of romantic philosophy and provides in these remarkable frame-tale novels two extraordinary illustrations of the romantic aesthetic of the mixing of genres, and the combination of innovation with archaism.

NOTES

1 V. F. Odoevskii, *Russkie nochi*, edited by B. F. Egorov, E. A. Maimin and M. I. Medovoi ('Literaturnye pamiatniki': Leningrad, Nauka, 1975); V. F. Odoevsky, *Russian Nights*, translated by Olga Koshansky-Olienikov and Ralph E. Matlaw, with a new Afterword by Neil Cornwell (Evanston, Ill.: Northwestern University Press, 1997; original publication 1965).

2 Jan Potocki, *The Manuscript Found in Saragossa*, translated by Ian Maclean (New York: Viking, 1995), p. xiv (Maclean's 'Introduction').

3 N. N. Petrunina, 'Proza vtoroi poloviny 1820-kh–1830-kh gg.', in *Istoriia russkoi literatury*, edited by N. I. Prutskov et al., vol. 2: *Ot sentimentalizma k romantizmu i realizmu*, edited by E. N. Kupreanova (Leningrad: Nauka, 1981), p. 519.

4 Odoevsky, *Russian Nights* (1997), p. 30.

5 See, for example: Iurii V. Mann, *Russkaia filosofskaia estetika (1820–30ye gody)* (Moscow, 1969), pp. 109–48 and 295–303; the apparatus to the 'Literaturnye pamiatniki' edition cited above; L. A. Levina, 'Avtorskii zamysel i khudozhestven-naia real'nost' (Filosofskii roman V. F. Odoevskogo "Russkie nochi")', *Izvestiia Akademii nauk SSSR. Seriia literatury i iazyka* 49, no. 1 (1990), 31–40; Olga Glówko, *Idee romantyzmu w 'Nocach rosyjskich' Wlodzimierza Odojewskiego* (Łódź, 1997); and Neil Cornwell, *Vladimir Odoevsky and Romantic Poetics* (Providence and Oxford: Berghahn Books, 1998), especially pp. 69–99 (from which some of the present material is excerpted).

6 For a full account of this, see Neil Cornwell, *The Life, Times and Milieu of V. F. Odoevsky* (London: Athlone, 1986); for an account of the ideas in *Russian Nights*, see *ibid.*, chapter 2 (*passim*).

7 See Cornwell, *Odoevsky and Romantic Poetics*, pp. 157–67.

8 Odoevsky, *Russian Nights* (1997), p. 22.

9 The term 'frame-tale' appears to derive from the German *Rahmenerzählung* and is used by Charles E. Passage in his book *The Russian Hoffmannists* (The Hague: Mouton, 1963).

10 See Martin Swales, *The German 'Novelle'* (Princeton: Princeton University Press, 1977), pp. 52–3.

11 Walter Benjamin, 'The Storyteller: Reflections on the Work of Nikolai Leskov', in his *Illuminations*, translated by Harry Zohn (London: Collins/Fontana, 1973), p. 84.

12 Ian Maclean uses the phrase 'a novel of frames' in his 'Introduction', p. xiv. The expressions utilized here may be compared with the French term 'roman "à tiroirs gigogne"', used by René Radrizzani, in his Preface to *Manuscrit trouvé à Saragosse* (Paris: Le Livre de Poche, 1992), p. 8. I. F. Belza's afterword essay to A. S. Golema's Russian translation (Ian Pototsky, *Rukopis' naidennaia v Saragose*, Moscow: Nauka, 1968, p. 590) uses the term '*shkatulochnyi roman*' ('box novel').

13 Swales, *The German 'Novelle'*, pp. 45–6.

14 Tzvetan Todorov, *Grammaire du Décaméron* (The Hague: Mouton, 1969), p. 94.

15 Swales, *The German 'Novelle'*, p. 46.

16 *The Works of Heinrich Heine*, translated by Charles Godfrey Leland, vol. 1 (London, 1891), p. 1.

17 On the concept of 'night' in *Russian Nights*, see the discussion in 'The Sixth Night' (Odoevsky, *Russian Nights*, 1997, pp. 120–3); and Mann's comments, in *Russkaia filosofskaia estetika*, pp. 137–40.

18 See Eric A. Blackall, *Goethe and the Novel* (Ithaca and London: Cornell University Press, 1976), pp. 88–90.

19 E. K. Bennett, *A History of the German 'Novelle'*, revised by H. M. Waidson (Cambridge: Cambridge University Press, 1961), pp. 56–7.

20 See Swales, *The German 'Novelle'*, pp. 49–51. Bennett (*A History of the German 'Novelle'*, p. 36) perceives the work as an imitation of Boccaccio, plus a moralizing element.

21 Glyn Tegai Hughes, *Romantic German Literature* (London: Edward Arnold, 1979), p. 32; Bennett (*A History of the German 'Novelle'*), p. 57.

22 The 1836 translation, along with others of the period, is listed by Norman W. Ingham, *E. T. A. Hoffmann's Reception in Russia* (Würzburg: jal Verlag, 1974), p. 276. For Odoevsky's remarks (in his notes for the subsequent unpublished Collected Works), see *Russian Nights* (1997), pp. 27–8. On the structural differences between the two works, see Ingham (p. 190). See also, on this topic: Passage, *The Russian Hoffmannists*; and A. B. Botnikova, *E. T. A. Gofman i russkaia literatura* (Voronezh, 1977).

23 See L. Iu. Romanenko, '"Florentinskie nochi" G. Geine i "Russkie nochi" V. F. Odoevskogo', in *Sbornik trudov molodykh uchenykh*, vyp. 3 (Tomsk, 1971), pp. 63–74.

24 For an account of the latter, see Cornwell, *Odoevsky and Romantic Poetics*, pp. 136–44.

25 Rado Pribić's study, *Bonaventura's 'Nachtwachen' and Dostoevsky's 'Notes from the Underground': A Comparison in Nihilism* (Munich, 1974), while seeing extensive parallels between the two works, is unable to produce any evidence that Dostoevsky even knew of 'Bonaventura' (although the possibility is not excluded). However, a suggestion that there is 'a clear affinity' between *Russian Nights* and *Die Nachtwachen* has been made: see Arsenii Gulyga, *Shelling* (Moscow, 1982), pp. 290–1; this stems in part at least from Gulyga's revival of the view (pp. 140–8) that Schelling was the real Bonaventura all along.

26 See Belza's afterword to the 1968 Russian translation, pp. 571–95; and S. Landa's (untitled) preface to D. Gorbov's Russian translation (*Rukopis' naidennaia v Saragose. Roman*, translated from the Polish by D. Gorbov with preface and notes by S. Landa (Moscow: Terra, 1997), 2 vols., vol. 1, pp. 5–34). Landa's preface, seemingly first published in 1971, has not been updated to take account of the new French edition of 1989 (while Gorbov's Russian translation remains that taken from the 1965 Polish edition).

27 Belza (*Rukopis'*, pp. 571–2) reprints the Pushkin fragment ('Al'fons saditsia na konia'): Alphonse, warned of dangers ahead, rides off intrepidly to pass the gibbet bearing the swinging bodies of the 'robber-chief brothers'. Although the action of Pushkin's fragment does not correspond exactly with the opening of *The*

Manuscript, its inspiration clearly derives from the early passages of 'The First Day'. On Pushkin, Viazemsky and Potocki, see Landa, pp. 31–2. For more on Pushkin and Potocki, see Belza, 'Pushkin i Ian Pototskii', including intriguing speculation (pp. 130–4) on a link in Pushkin's mind (relating to a planned but unwritten drama on Paul's assassination in 1801) between Potocki and the emperor Paul I, deriving from their alleged affiliations with the Supreme Order of St John of Jerusalem (or the Maltese Knights).

28 Landa, pp. 6 and 31, according to whom (p. 16) the sole surviving copy of the Petersburg printings is held in the St Petersburg Public Library.

29 Belza, *Rukopis'*, pp. 572–4; Landa, pp. 8 and 31–2. Viazemsky too commented on 'the clear and true colours with which the distinctive flights of fancy of Arabic poetry and the no less distinctive Spanish mores and life stand out' (Landa, p. 32).

30 Alethea Hayter's introduction to Charles Robert Maturin, *Melmoth the Wanderer: A Tale* (Harmondsworth: Penguin, 1977), p. 25. On Melmoth in Russia, see M. P. Alekseev, 'Ch. R. Met'iurin i ego "*Mel'mot Skitalets*"' in his edition of the Russian translation: Charlz Robert Met'iurin, *Mel'mot Skitalets* (Leningrad, 1976), pp. 563–674 (652–74); see also Passage, *The Russian Hoffmannists*, pp. 147–8.

31 On the European impact of these an other such texts, see Neil Cornwell, 'European Gothic', in *A Companion to the Gothic*, edited by David Punter (Oxford: Blackwell, 2000), pp. 27–38; see also some of the essays in *European Gothic: A Spirited Exchange, 1760–1960*, edited by Avril Horner (Manchester: Manchester University Press, publication forthcoming, 2002).

32 J. de Maistre, *Les soirées de Saint-Pétersbourg ou entretiens sur le gouvernement temporel de la providence*, fifth edition, vol. I (Paris, 1845), p. 11.

33 Maclean, 'Introduction' to Potocki, *The Manuscript Found in Saragossa*, p. xvi.

34 'V. F. Odoevsky [Predislovie k filosofskomu romanu]', published by L. A. Levina, *Vestnik Rossiiskogo universiteta druzhby narodov. Seriia Literaturovedenie. Zhurnalistika* 2 (1997), 95–8 (p. 96). See also Odoevsky's (later) 'Notes to *Russian Nights*', *Russian Nights* (1997), pp. 27–31.

35 Hughes, *Romantic German Literature*, p. 78.

36 Tzvetan Todorov, *Theories of the Symbol*, translated by Catherine Porter (Ithaca, NY: Cornell University Press, 1982), p. 170.

ADDITIONAL REFERENCES/READING

O'Brien, Fitz-James, *The Fantastic Tales of Fitz-James O'Brien*, edited by Michael Hayes, London: John Calder, 1977

Odoevskii, V. F., *Russkie nochi*, edited by B. F. Egorov, E. A. Maimin and M. I. Medovoi, series 'Literaturnye pamiatniki': Leningrad: Nauka, 1975
    Sochineniia v dvukh tomakh, Moscow, 1981

Odoevsky, Vladimir, *The Salamander and Other Gothic Tales*, translated by Neil Cornwell, London: Bristol Classical Press, 1992

Potocki, Jean, *Manuscrit trouvé à Saragosse*, new integral edition edited by René Radrizzani, Paris: Le Livre de Poche, 1992

Pototskii, Ian [Pototsky], 'Puteshestvie v Turtsiu i Egipet, sovershennoe v 1784 godu', introduction and annotations by M. S. Mater, in *Vostok – Zapad: Issledovaniia. Perevody. Publikatsii*, Moscow, 1985, pp. 35–82

Rukopis' naidennaia v Saragose, translated by A. S. Golemba, with afterword essay and notes by I. F. Belza, Moscow: Izdatel'stvo 'Nauka', 1968

Rukopis' naidennaia v Saragose, translated by D. A. Gorbov, Moscow: Khudozhestvennaia literatura, 1971

Rukopis' naidennaia v Saragose, translated by D. A. Gorbov, Moscow: Khudozhestvennaia literatura, 1989

Rukopis' naidennaia v Saragose, translated by D. A. Gorbov, Moscow: Khudozhestvennaia literatura, 1992

Rukopis' naidennaia v Saragose, translated by D. A. Gorbov, Moscow: Izdatel'stvo Prozerpina, 1994

Rukopis' naidennaia v Saragose, translated by D. A. Gorbov [?], Moscow: Ripol, 1994

Rukopis' naidennaia v Saragose. Roman, translated from the Polish by D. Gorbov with preface and notes by S. Landa, Moscow: Terra, 1997, 2 vols

Belza, I. F., '*Rukopis*', *naidennaia v Saragose*', in Ian Pototsky, *Rukopis' naidennaia v Saragose*, Moscow: Nauka, 1968, pp. 571–95

'Pushkin i Pototskii', in *Iskusstvo slova*, edited by K. V. Pigarev et al., Moscow: Nauka, 1973, pp. 125–34

Chernobaev, V. G., 'K istorii nabroska "Al'fons saditsia na konia ..."', in *Pushkin. Vremennik Pushkinskoi komissii*, kniga 4–5, Moscow and Leningrad, 1939

Frantsev, V., *Poslednee uchenoe puteshestvie grafa Iana Pototskogo, 1805–1806*, Prague, 1938

Istoriia romantizma v russkoi literature. Romantizm v russkoi literature 20–30-kh godov XIXv (1825–1840), edited by S. E. Shatalov et al., Moscow: Nauka, 1979

Istoriia russkoi literatury, edited by N. I. Prutskov et al., vol. 2: *Ot sentimentalizma k romantizmu i realizmu*, edited by E. N. Kupreanova, Leningrad: Nauka, 1981

Landa, S., 'Ian Pototskii i ego roman "Rukopis' naidennnaia v Saragose"', in Ian Pototskii, *Rukopis' naidennaia v Saragose*, Moscow, 1971, pp. 5–34; Moscow, 1989, pp. 5–38; Moscow, 1992, pp. 5–38

Preface and annotations to *Rukopis' naidennaia v Saragose*, Moscow, 1997, vol. 1, pp. 5–34; vol. 2, pp. 307–35

Orlovskaia, N. K., 'Ian Pototskii i Gruziia', *Trudy Tbilisskogo universiteta. Literaturovedenie*, no. 163, Tbilisi, 1975, pp. 119–29

Pol'skaia literatura v russkoi i sovetskoi pechati: Bibliograficheskii ukazatel', vol. 1: *Pol'skaia khudozhestvennaia literatura XVI – nachala XX veka v russkoi i sovetskoi pechati*, complied by I. L. Kurant, Warsaw [etc]: Izdanie Natsional'noi biblioteki, 1982

APPENDIX I   *A tentative genealogy of the 'frame-tale'*

Novella tradition		Philosophical tradition
Europe	*Russia*	
		Plato's dialogues
The East		
Pańcatantra etc.		
The 1001 Nights		
The Decameron		
The Canterbury Tales		Giordano Bruno
Cervantes		Diderot, *Le Neveu de Rameau* (1761)
Goethe, *Unterhaltungen deutscher Ausgewanderten* (1794)		*Jacques le fataliste* (1773)
Tieck/Wackenroder, *Phantasien über die Kunst* (1799)		
[anon.] *Die Nachtwachen des Bonaventura* (1804)		
Potocki, *Manuscrit trouvé à Saragosse* (1804–13)	(first part published anonymously in St Petersburg, 1804)	
Wieland, *Das Hexameron von Rosenhain* (1805)		
Tieck, *Phantasus* (1812)		
Hoffmann, *Der Serapionsbrüder* (1819–21)		de Maistre, *Les Soirées de Saint-Pétersbourg* (1821)
W. Irving, *Tales of a Traveller* (1824)		
The Alhambra (1832)	Pogorel'sky, *Dvoinik, ili moi vechera v Malorossii* (1828)	
Heine, *Florentinische Nächte* (1836)	(complete Russian translation of *Der Serapionsbrüder* and partial translation of *Florentinische Nächte*, 1836)	
	Odoevsky, tales (from 1831)	
	'Noch' pervaia' (1836)	
	Russkie nochi (1844)	

APPENDIX 2   *Alexander Pushkin: 'Al'phons saditsia na konia'*
(*1836*)

Alphonse mounts his horse;
The innkeeper holds his stirrup.
'Señor, listen to me:
Now's not the time to be on your way,
The mountains are dangerous and night is nigh,
The next *venta* is far away.
Stay here: your supper's ready;
A fire's laid in the grate;
There's a bed – you need some rest,
And your horse is hankering for his stall.'
– 'I'm used to travelling
Both day and night – I've a fancy for the road',
he replies – 'it wouldn't be the thing
For me to have fears.
I'm a nobleman – neither devil nor robbers
Can hold me back,
When I'm off on active service.'
And Don Alphonse spurred his steed
And off he moves at a trot. Before him
Runs only the track to the hills
Through a gorge, narrow and remote.
So, as he rides out into the valley,
What picture greets his eyes?
All around is wilderness, wild and barren,
While to one side looms a gibbet,
And on that gibbet are two bodies
Hanging. Cawing away, there flew off
A black flock of ravens,
Just as he rode up to them.
They were the corpses of two gypsies,
Two famous robber-brothers,
Long since hanged and there
Abandoned, an example to thieves.
With its rains the sky has soaked them,
And the torrid sun has dried them,
The wild wind has swung them,
The raven has swooped down to gnaw them.

And talk had it among the simple folk
That, breaking free at night,
And at liberty 'til morning, they
Cavorted, taking vengeance on their foes.

Alphonse's horse gave a snort and side-on
Went stepping past them, then
Dashed off sharply, at a light gallop,
Carrying his intrepid rider.

(literal translation: Neil Cornwell)

Comparative Criticism 24, pp. 141–165.   Cambridge University Press 2002
DOI: 10.1017/S0144756402005504   Printed in the United Kingdom

Potocki and the spectre of the postmodern

YVES CITTON

'A spectre is roaming through Europe: the Postmodern'.[1] Readers of
Jan Potocki's 700-page novel *The Manuscript Found in Saragossa* are
accustomed to seeing spectres, ghosts and other forms of *revenants*.
Such otherworldly creatures make up a remarkably high proportion of
the dozens of characters presented in the novel, which was written in
French by the Polish nobleman between 1797 and his suicide in 1815.
Of course, the protagonist, Alphonse van Worden, never encounters
Postmodernity as such – even though he seems to meet everybody else
(and her sister) during the sixty-six days of his journey through the
Sierra Morena, from enlightened Encyclopedists to American-Indian
princesses, from succubi to inkmakers, from a Wandering Jew who met
with Christ to the devil himself, from hermits and sheiks to bankers and
rats. And yet, as I would like to suggest in this article, what we have
come to identify today by the term 'postmodern' is in fact little more
than a *revenant*, returning to haunt us from the depth of Potocki's
historical and narrative imagination. Is it a pure coincidence that the
Manuscript's return from the dead in the 1990s, after two centuries of
quasi-oblivion,[2] corresponded with the multiplication of popular
anthologies anatomizing the Postmodern debate, in a phase Charles
Jencks characterized as the publication of 'critical summaries of the
Post-Modern paradigm'?[3]

By now, this 'bizarre novel', as it presents itself on its first page, has
received a considerable amount of critical attention, shedding precious
light on its textual history (Zoltowska[4]), its narrative stakes (Rosset[5])
and its thematic complexity (Fraisse[6]). However, many of the
philosophical implications of Potocki's work still remain to be unfolded.
Dominique Triaire's essay[7] gives a remarkably rich picture of the
author's worldview, particularly of his epistemology, his political
attitude and his conception of history; Günter von Kirn,[8] for his part,
investigates quite thoroughly the inscription of the *Manuscript* within
the ideological and philosophical context of the Enlightenment and of

141

early Romantic thought.[9] Yet, to my knowledge, the precise relation between the *Manuscript* and what our postmodern age has defined (accurately or erroneously) as 'modernity' has never received the full attention it deserves. My point of departure in this article will therefore be the following question (borrowing back from Richard Rorty[10] a terminology he himself borrowed from literary criticism): *what would a 'redescription' of the* Manuscript *through the 'vocabulary' of postmodernism look like?* Beyond the rather pointless exercise of a merely 'determining' judgment (*is Potocki postmodern?*), I hope that such an apparently meaningless question will in fact lead us to a more substantive exercise in 'reflective' judgment, i.e. to a questioning of the very categories originally put in play. Redescribing the *Manuscript* as postmodern may tell us less about the novel itself than about some of the conceptual weaknesses and oversimplifications on which the Modernity/Postmodernity divide commonly relies.[11]

To be sure, the question I just articulated does not really lead us into a *terra incognita*. Without explicitly referring to any of the major voices involved in the postmodern debate, a critic like François Rosset did in fact present the *Manuscript* as a very Baudrillardesque world of simulacra. As we will see in more detail below, Dominique Triaire offered striking echoes of Jean-François Lyotard's statements when he described Potocki's political attitude in terms of *souplesse*. On a deeper level, many scholars have discussed, albeit never in a very satisfactory manner, Potocki's problematic and complex relation to the *philosophes*. Insofar as postmodern theory has defined itself, for better or for worse, in contrast with an 'Enlightenment project' identified (somewhat loosely) with the Encyclopedists and their allies, this relation has a direct bearing on my question. A certain consensus emerges, which considers the novel as 'a document of a skeptical attitude which aims not only at the fantastic and its secrets, but also at the rational methods of "explaining" such secrets'.[12] 'The *Manuscript* sets itself at a critical distance as much towards the orthodoxy of the Church as towards the intellectual systems of the Enlightenment which, in their false radicality, build new dogmatic forms of constraint.' 'A unique attempt at a synthesis of the Enlightenment, classicism and romanticism',[13] the novel is commonly portrayed in the position of a *hinge*, deeply anchored in, and indebted to, the new spirit brought about by the *philosophes*, but already opening the door to further critical horizons which will use the Enlightenment's tools to undermine the Enlightenment's house.

In order to explore such intuitions a little further, let's suggest a few keywords which would describe the formal features of the novel, and the first impressions it produces on its readers. This should allow us to have a first, if superficial, glimpse at the postmodern dimension of the *Manuscript*, before moving on later to its broader and deeper ideological stakes.

1. *Indeterminacy*. Doesn't the *Manuscript*, at least in its first hundred pages which are paced by the maddening rhythm of multiple awakenings under the gallows, each making the reader doubt the reality of the previous one, offer one of the most radical experiences of ambiguity, rupture, and displacement known to world literature? After such a shock treatment, indeterminacies do in fact pervade all interpretations and constitute the reader's world.

2. *Fragmentation*. Even if the novel does eventually put all its threads together into one single consistent narrative structure, its mode of presentation – through the interruptions of the days, the jumps from one narrator to another, the parallel montage of multiple story lines – demonstrates a remarkable 'openness to brokenness' and seems decided to resist tooth and nail any attempt by the reader to totalize the stories into one closed and self-contained meaning.

3. *Decanonization*. Many scholars have stressed the 'derision of authority' at work whenever a paternal figure is staged in the novel – van Worden, Soarez, Avadoro seniors immediately come to mind.[14] Here again, what is the *Manuscript*, if not a constellation of *petites histoires* spread along the widest variety of heterogeneous language games (gothic novel, picaresque tales, history of religion, geometrical demonstration, pledge of secrecy, metaphysical speculation, erotic compulsion, moral prescription), which obstinately resist our best attempts at subsuming them under one single 'metanarrative' or 'mastercode'? The process of delegitimization at the heart of postmodernism is remarkably prefigured by the novel's perverse *jouissance* in staging unbelievable and untrustworthy figures of authority.

4. *Self-less-ness. Depth-less-ness*. Problematically enough for those critics eager to place the novel on the side of Romanticism, Potocki's characters are desperately devoid of any psychological depth. None of them demonstrates the type of pathos usually associated with the hypertrophied conception of interiority which was developing in the Europe of the time. Even when their sense of self is not openly 'challenged' (in the PC sense of that word, as it is the case for Pèdre Velásquez), even when the narrative fails to multiply them into hardly

distinguishable reduplications of the same (sister-sister, father-son, etc.), they all seem affected by a radical 'fake flatness' which prevents any serious possibility of identification on the part of the reader.

5. *The Unpresentable, Unrepresentable.* Something in the *Manuscript* fundamentally repels mimesis: no less than the flatness mentioned under the previous heading, what prevents any immediate adherence to the fictional world is the very multiplication of such flat surfaces (characters, story lines, language games), endlessly reflecting each other in the absence of any solid and stable core reality. As François Rosset has brilliantly shown in his book, the representative process is always-only liminary, staging and contesting only the modes of its own representation. At the hollow centre of this constellation of *petites histoires*, there is an intolerable, unthinkable, abject absence (the absence of ultimate truth). The horror of the gallows which haunts the first days of the narrative is in fact highly reassuring and comforting, compared with the radical negativity – an 'intolerably free exchange between signs and death' – on which the novel turns its last page with inhumane indifference. It is precisely this remarkably pure and deadly beautiful form of negativity which Jean Fabre alludes to in his comments upon the ending of the narrative, which he compares to a 'bulle de savon' or to the 'cigarette de Mallarmé dont la fumée monte comme une pure néantisation, une rêverie du néant'.[15]

6. *Irony.* That irony assumes a central function in the economy of the *Manuscript* has become a commonplace among critics. As early as 1847, Zygmunt Kasinski described the book as 'a remarkable work, but hyper-ironic and reckless (*archi-ironique et effréné*)',[16] while Günter von Kirn stressed more recently the 'ambivalence' and the 'distanciation through irony' displayed by the novel.[17]

7. *Hybridization* and 8. *Carnivalization.* Such a carnivalization is openly thematized by the Bohemians' lifestyle, where jesters cross-dress as Wandering Jews or demon-ridden lost souls. It reaches its high point in Avadoro's endless metamorphoses across genders and social status, from Elvire, a 'future vice-queen', to a nameless beggar, to the Marquis Castelli, a courtier plotting among the highest spheres of wealth and power. More generally, the ludic and subversive nature of the polyphony staged in the *Manuscript* leaves the reader constantly wondering about the seriousness and the real meaning of every scene: from the gory depictions of demons and *revenants* to the extended dissertations on Egyptian religion, from the most outrageous claims of scientific arrogance to the most desperate scenes of suicide, one is never sure

where the pathos starts and where the pastiche begins. In this wealth of textual thefts and intertextual *clins d'œil*, clichés and plagiarism seem to be the only stable game in the Sierra. This travesty of a novel constantly borrows and multiplies contradictory voices, in a polyphonic process of hybridization pushed to the point where no genre, no opinion, no ideology, no point of view can any longer be identified as authoritative, or even simply authorial.[18]

9. *Performance, Participation*. Within the *Manuscript*'s fictional world, most sub-narratives 'invite performance' in the sense that they are 'performed' by various actors (playing a Wandering Jew, Pacheco, a hermit) rather than being simply told. Not only do the Bohemians function as a performing band, but the 'gaps' and 'indeterminacies' left in their stories also invite a constant involvement on the part of their narratee (van Worden): the Venta Quemada is uncannily close to these virtual universes generated in our postmodern age by interactive computer games where the viewer/player is swallowed into the diegetic world and finds himself in the double position of the audience (for whom the whole fiction is staged) and of a character (whose fate is being determined as the story develops). On a higher level, it is the real history of the book's publication which illustrates, in the most striking manner, 'art's vulnerability to time, to death, to audience, to the Other': the manner in which this *found manuscript* was indeed quasi *lost* for two centuries, the polemics generated by its recent resurrection[19] are no less *romanesque* than the *roman* itself. 'Gaps must still be filled' in the text currently at the public's disposal. The indeterminacies and decanonizations staged in the fiction have infiltrated the published book itself, for which we still lack a definitive and canonical edition. Here again, the limits between the inside and the outside, reality and fiction, the stage and the audience are uncannily blurred, in a manner reminiscent (or rather anticipatory) of the interactive and open-ended practices favoured by postmodern artists in their games, installations and websites.

10. *Constructionism* and 11. *Immanence*. François Rosset has shed full light on the essential self-containment, self-referentiality (*immanence*) and self-announced artificiality (*constructivism*) ruling the game played by the *Manuscript*: functioning as a 'theatre of the romanesque', the 'construction' of the novel displays 'a gigantic narrative machine which refers only, in the last analysis, to its own movement': 'in this carnival of a novel, the play/game (*le jeu*) ends up proclaiming the vanity of discourses, the erosion of meaning, the tragic inanity of knowledge' (back cover).

The reader familiar with the 'Postmodern debate' will have recognized by now the list of 'The Eleven "Definiens" of the term Postmodern' provided by one of its first 'coiners', Ihab Hassan.[20] Even if it is a well-recognized feature of the Postmodern (and probably the only one universally agreed upon) to elicit any attempt made to capture it in a non-ambiguous definition – hence its spectral nature: 'this amorphous thing remains ghostly'[21] – the *Manuscript*'s rich response to the stimuli suggested by Hassan's (deceptively) handy checklist should suffice to catch our attention. The main question, however, remains to be tackled: under the surface of its narrative presentation, is there anything in the *intellectual attitude* expressed by the *Manuscript* which resonates with the 'postmodern condition'?

I will address this question from the point of view of four issues which play a central role in the postmodern debate as well as, I believe, in Potocki's work: lack of self-confidence, the aporia of judgment, political *souplesse*, and the debunking of human pretensions to mastery.

Lack of self-confidence. According to Zygmunt Bauman, 'the concept of postmodernity refers to a distinct quality of intellectual climate, to a distinct new meta-cultural stance, to a distinct self-awareness of the era [...] The most poignant of the postmodern experiences is the *lack* of self-confidence. [The postmodern period] tries to reconcile itself to a life under conditions of permanent and incurable uncertainty; a life in the presence of an unlimited quantity of competing forms of life, unable to prove their claims to be grounded in anything more solid and binding than their own historically shaped conventions.'[22]

As we have already noted above, the world of 'indeterminacies' into which the reader is thrown by the novel leads her, along with the protagonist, to being on the verge of 'losing her reason' (*Manuscript*, p. 108/128).[23] While the first hundred pages of the book certainly constitute a challenge to the rationalist attitude often associated with the (French) Enlightenment, it is important to notice how Potocki subtly but dramatically displaces the Cartesian framework with which he plays. As in the *Méditations métaphysiques*, van Worden and the reader are led to a position of radical doubt, where the distinction between being asleep and awake vanishes, where everything they perceive seems to be no different from the 'playful mystifications of dreams' (*ludificationes somniorum*):[24] 'all that I had seen over the last few days had so perplexed my mind that I no longer knew what I was doing, and if anyone had tried they could have made me doubt my own existence' (*Manuscript*, p. 93/113).

Behind the obvious and numerous similarities, however, one should note at least three significant displacements. First, the situation is not so much framed in terms of *identity* as in terms of *action* ('I no longer knew what I was *doing*'): the real question with which Alphonse finds himself faced is no longer 'who/what am I?' ('*quisnam sim ego ille*') (p. 52), but rather 'what should I do?' or, more precisely even, 'what should I (not) say?'. Second, the '*genium aliquem malignum*' (*ibid.*) whose profile is sketched behind the hypothetical 'if anyone had tried' is no longer, as in Descartes, an abstract and extreme theoretical possibility: in van Worden's case, the 'evil genius' is a reality, incarnated by the sheik and his accomplices. Moreover, the agency in which the hypothesis of the Cartesian *si me fallit* materializes no longer belongs to the supernatural realm of the divine (or demonic): in Potocki's world, humans are manipulated, fooled, deceived and lured *by other humans*. Third, the rock of certainty on which Descartes could rebuild the modern skyscraper of human knowledge (*ego existo, certum est*) is itself contaminated by doubt in Potocki's rewriting. Other humans can not only deceive me in what I perceive, they could also 'make me doubt my own existence' (should they choose to do so). The foundation of confidence on which Descartes laid the groundwork of modern science is radically undermined, condemning us from now on to live and act 'under conditions of permanent and incurable uncertainty'.

It is significant in this regard to find this lack of confidence stated by one of the characters most often described by the secondary literature as a representative of the *philosophes* (of the deist persuasion), Pèdre Velásquez. After having expressed his hope to reduce human emotions as well as human history to geometrical equations, this caricature of a scientist can't help but recognize the limits of scientific reason (and the correlative necessity of faith) in our making sense of our world: 'we are blind men who can feel some walls and know the ends of several roads. But we mustn't be expected to know the map of the whole city' (*Manuscript*, p. 417/447). In describing the physicist as 'always striving to understand' but 'always half-understanding' (*Manuscript*, p. 408/439), Velásquez and Potocki do more than express a typically postmodern feeling of 'opprobrium on totalization'. To go back to Bauman's already cited view, they put forth 'a new distinct meta-cultural stance', where scientific knowledge and the Christian revelation, or even cabbalism and the Muslim prophecy, appear merely as competing (and incommensurable) forms of understanding, which are ultimately 'unable to prove their claims to be grounded in anything more solid and binding than their own historically shaped conventions'.[25]

The aporia of judgement. For Potocki as for his postmodern grandsons, such a relativist attitude bears its most problematic consequences when the human subject has to use her faculty of judgement. Velásquez feels compelled to limit the scope of reason because he cannot resort to 'expose the faith of ethics to the mercy of sophistry' (*Manuscript*, p. 410/441). Faith, openly based on 'prejudices' (the traditional enemy of the Enlightenment project), is necessary to 'offer man a surer mainstay than reason' (*ibid.*) when the time comes to move from the question 'who am I?' to the question 'what should I do?'. And here again, this aporia of judgement is directly presented by the *Manuscript* through a character explicitly and precisely located in his relation to the Enlightenment: Blas Hervas is, literally, the son of an Encyclopedist, the son of this branch of the *lumières* which fell into the double (and specifically modern) hubris of totalization and atheism.[26] After having witnessed his father's demise and suicide, Blas sees his philosophical spectre return in the form of Don Bélial, who leaves little doubt about his own intellectual filiation: 'I am one of the principal members of a powerful society whose aim is to make men happy by curing them of the vain prejudices which they suck in with the milk of their wet-nurse, and which afterwards get in the way of all their desires. We have published very good books in which we demonstrate admirably well that self-love is the mainspring of all human actions' (*Manuscript*, p. 521/560). Whether one recognizes La Mettrie, Helvétius, Sade, Voltaire, d'Holbach, Diderot and/or 'toute la morale du XVIIIe siècle',[27] it is clearly the French Enlightenment gathered around the *Encyclopédie* which appears under the mask of the Devil. And the main point of this *mal masqué* is to stress the moral relativism taught by the *philosophes*:

'just and unjust [...] are relative qualities. I will make you see this with the help of a moral fable: Some tiny insects were crawling about on the tips of tall grasses. One said to the others: "Look at that tiger near us. It's the gentlest of animals. It never does us any harm. The sheep, on the other hand, is a ferocious beast. If one came along it would eat us with the grass which is our refuge. But the tiger is just. He would avenge us." You can deduce from this, Señor Hervas, that all ideas of the just and the unjust, or good and evil, are relative, and in no way absolute or general.' (*Manuscript*, p. 521/560)

Even if the moral dilemma facing Blas Hervas is rather crude (save an innocent victim or satisfy his own selfish desires), the fact that he makes the 'wrong' choice, and the fact that the novel ultimately fails to provide any convincing argument as to why this choice was wrong at all, contaminates the whole moral philosophy conveyed by the narrative with a feeling of uneasiness. To Don Bélial's unfettered logic of personal interest, the only alternative is provided by Enrique Velásquez, Pèdre's father, who describes himself as a 'strangely (*bizarrement*) constituted' creature, 'in whom selfishness is scarcely perceptible'; among the few members of this 'proscribed race', 'some are passionate about the sciences, others about the public good' (*Manuscript*, p. 269/293). Here again, however, the son reveals the weaknesses of the father: Enrique's selflessness and his feeling of being 'part of a great unity' take a purely ridiculous turn in the *géomètre*'s 'absent-mindedness', as if losing one's mind is the price to pay for endeavouring to cultivate a disinterested reason. Enrique's *désintéressement* is not a solution, nor even a true alternative to the 'morale du XVIIIe siècle', but merely a 'bizarrerie', an 'aberration of nature', or simply another 'idea of the just and the unjust', no more absolute or general, or valid, than any other.

At the end of all these ironic twists, the narrative leaves its reader with a feeling which anticipates the aporia described by many a postmodern thinker. Whether they emphasize the impossibility legitimately to deduct a prescriptive from a descriptive[28] or whether they evoke the 'ghost of the undecidable' raised 'in every event of decision',[29] they all describe a situation which fits perfectly with van Worden's (and the reader's) dilemma. One has to judge, one has to take sides (between the cousins and the hermit, between commitments made to different churches, between allegiance to conflicting parties, between various interpretative hypotheses) without being in a position to know for sure either the real nature of the choice or its real consequences. On which basis should van Worden determine whether his cousins are demoniac temptresses or victims in need of protection? How could he decide to oppose or follow the Gomelez family's conspiracy, when every bit of information concerning them seems to be a product of their very conspiracy? Even more cruelly, how can he direct his actions when the main concept which used to guide his previous moral choices (*l'honneur*) was shattered during his first days in the Sierra Morena? In the absence of a satisfactory system grounding the 'idea of the just' in a consensual description of reality (and giving it the strength of a concept), the moral agent is condemned to a scattered and case-by-case approach, exposed to the vicissitudes of trial and error, under the constant pressure of an 'urgency that obstructs the horizon of knowledge'.[30] 'Here lies the basis

for an ethical demand in the postmodern [...] We must judge: there is
no escape from the necessity of judging in any specific case. Yet we have
no grounds upon which to base our judging. [...] We must behave justly
towards the face of the Other; but we cannot do that accordingly to a
predetermined system of justice, a predetermined political theory'.[31]

Political suppleness. For, of course, such aporias in the definition of
the just bear considerable consequences on the conception of politics.
Dominique Triaire's description of Potocki's political attitude resonates
strongly with the positions taken by the Jean-François Lyotard of
Instructions païennes or *Just Gaming*. Both seem to prefer to 'stay as close
as possible to the event' rather than 'elaborating in the abstract grand
theories'; both value 'a great theoretical suppleness'; for both, 'politics
provides only a temporary fix (*un raccommodage*)', and for both,
'perfection is a dangerous *chimère*'. Both seem to share a common
resistance to producing 'a general representation of politics'[32] which
would systematize their thought and provide a totalizing map for further
action. Convinced that 'there is no science of the political'[33] both refuse
to play the role attributed in the modern period to the Intellectual. One
could trace such political suppleness all the way to the personal choices
made by both writers, from Potocki serving the Russian empire (which
had just invaded his country) to Lyotard denouncing the dead ends of
technoscience and of the *logique du capital* from the hometown of CNN
and Coca Cola. No less than Avadoro, who provides an almost
pathological example of 'suppleness', 'tolerance' and 'svelteness'[34]
throughout his endless personal and political metamorphoses, the duke
of Sidonia illustrates the posture of 'disillusionment' (see Coccaro) so
central to postmodern politics. Having learned the hard way 'that it was
not enough to want (*vouloir*) to do good, one [also] had to know (*savoir*)
how to do it' – even if, as we have just seen, one simultaneously and
contradictorily realizes that politics cannot be the object of a true
savoir – the duke hangs on to 'prudence' as a safer substitute for the
dangerous 'chimères' of his youth (*Manuscript*, p. 315/341), anticipating
Lyotard's call 'to distinguish intelligence from the paranoia that gave
rise to "modernity"'.[35]

The postmodern incredulity towards master-narratives implies a
similar incredulity towards *la raison politique* as such. The various forms
of Stalinism which littered the twentieth century with millions of
corpses have scarred a whole generation's political sensitivity, and –
legitimately or not – have led many to echo Velásquez's early warning:
'reasoning [...] is a dangerous instrument which can easily harm the

person using it. What virtue has not been attacked by reason? What crime have people not tried to justify by it?' (*Manuscript*, p. 410/441) While many participants in the postmodern debate have carefully resisted all attempts to enlist them under openly reactionary banners, it would be hard to ignore the convergence between postmodernity's second thoughts about the dangers of the political reason in which the Enlightenment grounded its emancipatory efforts, on the one hand, and, on the other hand, the direct filiation popularized by neo-conservative historians between Jacobinism and Stalinism, as if Robespierre's *terreur* and the Gulag were both necessary consequences of any attempt to force a human project of emancipation onto the spontaneous inertia of the existing state of things.[36] Here again, it would be (too) easy to suggest parallels between the socio-historical positions of unjustifiable privilege enjoyed by Potocki (as a member of the highest Polish nobility) and by late twentieth-century theorists of the postmodern (as members of wealthy Western societies) – who both would have much to lose in rocking their social boat too harshly.

What seems undeniable however is that, across two centuries, a similar political attitude of *suspension* appears to be shared by Potocki and his grandsons, an attitude he perfectly expressed in a comment on a Greek word which was to elicit abundant reflection in postmodern circles:

'The Ancient Greeks used to express with the verb *epochein* this attentive rest (*ce repos attentif*) after which one starts again to act in new erring endeavors (*nouveaux errements*). *Carneades*, in order to explain the value of this word, says that the *Epoché* is like the posture of an athlete who tries to estimate the strength of his enemy or the attitude of a charioteer who holds his horses ready to enter the field (*qui retient ses chevaux prêts à entrer dans la carrière*).'[37]

Lyotard's description of his own 'paganism' is stated in the similar vocabulary of 'a move in a context', on a field which is 'a place of ceaseless negotiations and ruses', where 'there is no reference by which to judge the opponent's strength; one does not know if s/he is a god or a human'.[38] This moment of suspension wherein one stops to wonder whether the enemy is 'a beggar' or 'a god' (or an enemy at all) is linked to a sharp awareness of one's own fragility: the postmodern political subject always remembers that 'there is no possible discourse of truth on the situation', that he 'has to judge therefore by opinion alone, that is, without criteria',[39] that all his moves are 'always tactical', and *only* tactical, mere 'instructions' reduced to a local context, never to be understood as 'slogans', for 'a slogan belongs to a general strategy' which is precisely what he can no longer pretend to devise.[40] What many critics of the postmodern movement have condemned as a mere 'withdrawal' from the political sphere is perhaps more accurately conceived, as Potocki helps us to do here, as a form of *epoché*, a *retenue* which in no way excludes the possibility of active interventions, as long as these are purely 'defensive and local',[41] but which remains always wary of getting carried away by its own horses into a career of thoughtless commitment.

The debunking of human mastery. This prudence leads to my last point of convergence, the status of human mastery. In the straw man standing for 'the Enlightenment' in postmodern discourse, three interconnected features are usually taken as main targets for denunciation: universal reason, emancipation and autonomy. All three come together in the figure of 'the modern subject' as master-of-his-destiny. The process of emancipation implied in the notion of *Enlightenment* or *Aufklärung* leads to a state where the subject can 'de-subjectify' himself, gain access to 'objective' knowledge and give himself the best possible laws which he will have devised thanks to his universally rational knowledge. At the horizon of this process lurks Laplace's dream of a Central Intelligence Agency which could trace the current position of every object in the universe, understand the laws of physics, and therefore be in a position to determine all future movements of every single body. At the higher level of complexity represented by human societies, a similar enterprise of measurement, understanding and calculation, developed by the 'social sciences', will allow mankind to devise for itself laws capable of maximizing its common happiness. Condorcet's *Esquisse* usually gives a historical (and historically highly pathetic) face to this emancipatory project (eloquently summarized by Lyotard in many letters of his *Postmodern Explained*).

How does the *Manuscript* stage such a project? The overarching structure of the narrative seems indeed articulated precisely along the lines of an (individual) process of emancipation. If, as Docherty puts it, 'the Enlightenment aimed at human emancipation from myth, superstition and enthralled enchantment to mysterious powers and forces of nature through the progressive operations of critical reason',[42] van Worden does indeed ultimately free himself from his fanatical subservience to honour, from his various religious prejudices, as well as from his episodic fear of the supernatural. Dominique Triaire goes as far as presenting the protagonist as an image of the Enlightenment's triumph: 'The *Manuscript* is [...] a metaphorical narrative of the Revolution: Alphonse appears in the first days as a child of the Ancien Régime, but he will manage to adopt the ideals of the young bourgeoisie, the daughter of the Enlightenment. Van Worden represents an anti-Potocki, the Revolution as successful; he will find his place in the new social order'.[43]

Moreover, the novel also presents another striking image of truly impressive mastery in the Gomelez family. Here is a Central Intelligence Agency capable of controlling every aspect of van Worden's reality, of manipulating it (and him) in exactly the direction they had planned for their own purpose. Nothing seems to escape their grip, to the point where the most inconceivable events of the first hundred pages eventually make perfect sense, once the organization's unlimited power to delude is ultimately revealed. In a paradox remarkably suggestive of a central contradiction of modernity, it is by going through a phase of *total alienation* (during which he is completely subjected to the Gomelez family's machinations) that van Worden ultimately becomes *free*.

This gleaming illustration of human mastery is in fact much more 'modern' than the caricatural master portrayed by postmodernity. Rather than focussing on an individual (Robespierre, Stalin, Pol Pot, etc), the novel locates the Agency in an *organization*. More than the sheik, who never appears particularly powerful as a character, it is the power of the Gomelez family as a collective agent which the novel conveys to us most forcefully. As we have already seen, Potocki brings down from heaven into a purely human world the figure of the all-powerful god (or evil genius) in the deceptive face of which Descartes constructed his self. It is now other humans, associated into a omnipotent organization, which can control my universe, manipulate me in the labyrinth of their inextricable deception, and even make me doubt of my very existence.

Is this to say that the *Manuscript* prefigures Orwell's *1984*? Obviously not: Potocki's tale is too interested in twin sisters to leave much room for any Big Brother. What the novel stages is rather a systematic debunking of any figure pretending to occupy a position of mastery. The 'archi-ironique' tone of the novel is the first device which prevents any character, any institution, any system, any ideal from gathering enough credibility to appear as threatening. Seen through the eyes of his fool, no master is likely to command much respect. On another obvious (thematic) level, the novel multiplies the depictions of ridiculous attempts at mastery: Diego Hervas (in his pretension to master the complete circle of human knowledge), van Worden senior (in his fanatical concern to master the infinite subtleties of the *point d'honneur*), as well as all the father figures in their hopeless efforts to guide the behaviour of their children.[44] All illustrate the fatal failure of any would-be master, invariably condemned by the logic of the narrative to bite the dust in the end.

And yet, what about the two central examples we just encountered? Doesn't Alphonse become an enlightened master of his destiny? Aren't the Gomelez clan sufficiently skilled at manipulating illusions to become masters of the world? Precisely not! And since this may be the most strikingly postmodern feature of the whole narrative, we may need to pause and reflect on the status of the novel's controversial ending. A good example of the controversy is provided by a discussion which took place during the Warsaw Conference dedicated to Potocki in 1972. Karel Krejci stressed the 'superficiality and banality of the ending, which contrasts with the refinement of the exposition' and which could be explained, according to him, either by Potocki's depressed mental state during the last years of his life, or even by the fact that the novel may have been left unfinished by its author, and completed hastily by its first translator, Chojecki.[45] Krejci was in fact expressing a feeling that most readers of the *Manuscript* have certainly experienced as they closed the book: after 700 pages of a masterly narrative build-up, the epilogue *does* indeed appear botched and leaves the reader somewhat disappointed. True, we are given a final display of fireworks, but the explosion takes place underground, sounding very much like a narrative dud. As the sheik provides a rational explanation which dissolves all the disturbing illusions displayed during the previous sixty-five days, one can hardly help wondering what was the real point of such a virtuosic display.

It is precisely the absence of reality in the ending of the novel which has appealed to other interpreters. During the discussion following Krejci's remarks, Maciej Zurowski objected that, on the contrary, the 'finale was a masterpiece', whose main achievement, according to Jean Fabre, consisted in its very nothingness ('une pure néantisation, une rêverie du néant').[46] In their rich and multidimensional analysis of the epilogue, both François Rosset and Luc Fraisse stressed the central void which the novel's ending designates at its very core: like a last curtain drawn on the *théâtre du romanesque*, the epilogue both covers up and denounces the emptiness of the stage as well as the irreality of the fiction which briefly filled it with illusions; in its very refusal to provide the comfort of a final message, the ending forces the reader to look at the narrative construction itself as the sole raison d'être of the literary enterprise;[47] the exhaustion of the (supposedly inexhaustible) goldmine on which the Gomelez family had built their power is at the same time a metaphor of the author's exhausted inspiration and a send-off signal for the literary work; as the fictional world (*mine tarie*) passes the baton to the real book (*manuscrit conservé*), reality appears as what shuts off the production of meaning: 'once the labyrinth has been destroyed, once the education has been completed, then starts true life, which is to say that there is nothing left to narrate'.[48]

All these interpretations are certainly correct in focussing on the way the epilogue stages the juncture between reality and fiction, since it is at this juncture that the question of *meaning* is raised most vividly.[49] The end is *disappointing* because of its refusal to make a *point*, that is, a point which would go beyond the inner play of the fiction. In other words: after the sheik's rational explanation of all the spectres and mysteries which haunted van Worden's experience, everything *makes sense* but, simultaneously, everything appears as *devoid of any satisfactory meaning*. The virtuosic display of illusions falls flat – of a flatness, a depthlessness considered by some as 'the supreme formal feature' of postmodern artifacts.[50] As we have already seen above, Potocki denies his reader any 'depth of meaning' by preventing his characters from gaining any real psychological consistency. The 'waning of the affect'[51] constantly illustrated in the *Manuscript* contributes to the anti-climactic nature of its epilogue: Alphonse mentions his father's death with the same brevity and unaffected tone he will use to list his military promotions. The novel ends without any of the weight of pathos a narrator is expected (by us modern readers) to bring to his final words. The affective dimension implied in the experience of putting an end to an enterprise (producing a sense of loss, sadness, nostalgia, hope, etc) is erased from the narrative – just as, according to Jameson, the depthlessness of Andy Warhol's *Diamond Dust Shoes* prevents the affective interplay of expression and projection that takes place in front of Van Gogh's *Pair of Boots*. Such 'waning of the affect' deprives us of the 'human meaning' we have come to expect from (post-Romantic) novels.

But, more importantly in my view, if the last pages of the *Manuscript* have been perceived by many as lacking in depth of meaning, it is mostly because they do not attempt to anchor the *petites histoires* told by the novel in a superior master-narrative, which would provide a 'message' transcending the fictional world to guide the reader in her real-life (ideological, existential, political, etc) dilemmas. On this level, the *Manuscript* perfectly satisfies Lyotard's requirement that a 'postmodern fable' be 'in no way finalized towards the horizon of an emancipation'.[52]

To be sure, Alphonse is enlightened by his sixty-six days in the Sierra Morena. But what does this enlightenment lead to? A few successful financial investments, the title of general, a few meetings with his cousins and the children born from their unions, the position of governor bringing him 'the charms of a quiet life' (*Manuscript*, p. 631/669) as well as the opportunity to copy and seal his manuscript for his family's future records. Good for him, the reader might say, but what does that leave *us* with? Alphonse did indeed 'find his place in the new social order', as Triaire noted, but, as Fraisse also suggested, of such a flat and bourgeois definition of success, there seems to be nothing meaningful to say.

Similarly, the Gomelez clan are *perfectly good* at manipulating their victims in their world of delusions, but they ultimately appear to be *good for nothing*. Granted, they manage to enrol Alphonse in their ranks and get offspring of his blood, which was the purpose of their three-month-long machination. But this brilliant success can scarcely hide the extent of their overall collapse. The almost all-powerful organization built over generations of patient efforts in order to conquer the world and convert it to Islam finds itself, in the last pages, out of troops, out of resources and, worst of all, out of project. As is the case for the novel itself, their success in enlisting van Worden has *no point*. It will make no difference for their doomed future. Nor, by the way, does the defeat of a Muslim conspiracy give anyone reason to salute a Christian victory. The religious, political, ideological framework which would give meaning to such words as 'defeat' and 'victory' has simply been pulled from under the feet of History's agents. The Central Intelligence Agency may be all-powerful in manipulating Alphonse's experience in the Sierra Morena, but what we witness in the book are the last sixty-six days of its existence, before its unglamorous self-destruction in the mine's final implosion.

It is significant that this implosion apparently causes no human casualty. To paraphrase a famous postmodern anthem, it's the end of the Gomelezes' world as they knew it, but everybody feels fine. As each conspirator walks away with his share of the common loot (from 50,000 to a million *sequins*), they all have reasons to cheer. The real victim is left unmourned: it is *the organization* itself. It looks as if, like

Margaret Thatcher, nobody among the Gomelez clan believed in (secret) 'societies' because all they ever encountered were only 'individuals'. And along with the organization goes its project. Lyotard is certainly right in presenting the *project* as that which 'gives modernity its characteristic mode': during the modern period, legitimacy has come from 'a future to be accomplished', a 'universal Idea', or the 'Idea of a universal subject' whose emancipation would justify (and provide meaning to) our actual practices. He also describes perfectly the *Manuscript*'s ending when he argues – against Habermas – that 'the project of modernity (the realization of universality)' is not merely 'incomplete', but has been 'destroyed, "liquidated"'.[53] This is precisely what is at stake in the epilogue. As the Gomelez clan's project of world mastery is eventually traded for a few *sequins*, it is very literally 'liquidated', transformed into liquid assets – which the banker Moro suggests Alphonse should invest in an already global market: 'you must buy property in Brabant, in Spain and even in America. Please allow me to see to this' (*Manuscript*, p. 627/665). The frustration felt by the readers of the epilogue (wondering what is the meaning of Alphonse's success) echoes very closely the one experienced by the postmodern subject faced with the 'victory' of capitalism: 'Success is the only criterion of judgment technoscience will accept. Yet it is incapable of saying what success is, or why it is good, just, or true, since success is self-proclaiming, like a ratification of something heedless of any law. It therefore does not complete the project of realizing universality, but in fact accelerates the process of delegitimation'.[54]

The novel's ending is indeed a masterpiece, crowning the masterly build-up of the narrative construction with a radical debunking of mastery. Such is probably the most truly postmodern dimension of the *Manuscript*, if one follows Jameson in equating postmodernism with 'the cultural logic of late capitalism'. It portrays the human subject as caught in a web of simulacra artificially generated by other humans to lure him under meaningless banners, emptied of any substantial allegiance, and ultimately resorbed into cash benefits. Unprecedented means of manipulating our human world coalesce into Decentred Unintelligent Agencies which have given up any socio-political project and strive mainly to maximize their short-term profit in a heedless race towards the self-destruction of their source of wealth and power. The corpses, spectres and ghosts faced by Alphonse at the beginning of his journey prefigure the spiritual death and the *revenants* his postmodern grandsons will have to face after the exhaustion of their *revenus*.

'Modernity was lived in a haunted house'.[55] Look for spectres and you will probably see them everywhere. The same is certainly true of the 'ghostly' postmodern. So – apart from the minor (but vital) profit a literary work makes by lending itself to such exercises – what is to be gained through a redescription of Potocki's novel in the vocabulary of the postmodern?

First, it could invite us to exert more prudence in our characterization of modernity. The Enlightenment, in its French incarnation at least, was everything *but* 'an era of certainty': as Bauman himself acknowledges later, only a gross oversimplification can allow us to pretend that modernity 'seems never to have entertained similar doubts [to those raised in the postmodern age] as to the universal grounding of its status'.[56] If an author like Diderot deserves to be counted among the tenors of the Enlightenment, the most superficial reading of his work should convince anyone of the profound uncertainty at work at the very core of modern thought. The fact that Potocki wrote at the very end of the Enlightenment (in particular after the trauma of the French Revolution) should not prevent us from seeing that he expressed doubts already voiced by many among the *philosophes* themselves. As a consequence, his skeptical staging of the excesses of rationalism and his pessimism about the possibility of human mastery are less a *condemnation* than a *furthering* of the thought developed by the Enlightenment. Günter von Kirn had already clearly indicated that 'Potocki pushes the critical thinking characteristic of Enlightenment philosophy against the Enlightenment itself, not in order to attack it, but in order to further its skeptical attitude by turning it against itself'.[57]

Potocki, as well as Diderot, provides a concrete illustration of 'the implication of the postmodern within the modern itself'.[58] The point has already been made countless times that, in spite of its deceptive labelling, the 'post'-modern is less to be conceived as what comes *after* modernity than as its ever-present darker side. Lyotard, among others, has been particularly clear on this issue:

'Rather we have to say that the postmodern is always implied in the modern because of the fact that modernity, modern temporality, comprises in itself an impulsion to exceed itself into a state other than itself. [...] Modernity is constitutionally and ceaselessly pregnant with its postmodernity. [...] Postmodernity is not a new age but the rewriting of some features claimed by modernity, and first of all modernity's claim to ground its legitimacy on the project of liberating humanity as a whole through science and technology. But as I have said, that rewriting has been at work, for a long time now, in modernity itself'.[59]

It is this active and unceasing 'rewriting' of modernity by itself which may legitimate the exercise in redescription carried out in this article. Beyond easy oversimplifications, (re)writers like Potocki or Lyotard are the ones who carry the furthest the unsettling questions planted by the *philosophes*.

A basic precaution in order to clarify our ideas could consist in questioning the equation established among most participants in the postmodern debate between Modernity and Enlightenment. The disturbing historical gap between the 'ideological' breakthrough of modernity (reaching full speed around 1750) and its 'aesthetic' counterpart (maturing in the second half of the nineteenth century) should warn us of a possible major flaw in our periodization. One can only wonder what would have happened if the debate about the 'project of modernity' had coalesced around the 1880s rather than around the 1780s, i.e. on the other side of the major trauma constituted by the Industrial Revolution.

In a reflection which attempts, precisely, to situate the postmodern in relation to transformations in the productive process (the 'formal' vs. the 'real' subsumption of labour within capital, the latter corresponding roughly to the development of the IT revolution, 'globalization' and Jameson's 'late capitalism'), Antonio Negri asks whether 'the post-modern is a new form of romanticism' in its 'negation of the revolution of the Enlightenment'.[60] In other words: does one find anticipations of the postmodern in Potocki simply because our culture, for two centuries, has been oscillating between a brighter (1780s, 1960s) and a darker (1810s, 1980s) side of Modernity? Even though such a circular and disenchanted view seems to please many of our contemporaries, Negri suggests that, while both romanticism and the postmodern symptomatize a transformation in the relation between subjectivity and capitalist domination, they each react to a very different phase in the development of the productive process. The characteristic feature of our age, according to Negri, is to be found in the fact that most of the Western populations are now being transformed into intellectual workers, who carry their productive tools (fixed capital) within their brain. This evolution will have far-reaching, and still inconceivable, consequences: by identifying the main means of production with the intellectual potential of the workers themselves, by making it necessary for the reproduction of capital to invest in the education of the labour force, by relying always more heavily on the production and communication of information, by encouraging the flexibility (suppleness) of the work force, by having to take into consideration the body's affects in order to guarantee proper functioning of the worker's brain, a drastically new logic of production of subjectivity[61] is taking shape under our very (short-sighted) eyes.

Now, isn't it precisely such a process of production of subjectivity which is investigated and displayed throughout the *Manuscript*? It is difficult to imagine a more striking illustration of the emancipatory promise, as well as of the inherent dangers, of 'productive biopolitics'[62] than the collective production of offspring for the Gomelez family through the necessary (re)education of van Worden's brain and the manipulation of his body's affects. Drugs and fascinations, 'sociétés du spectacle' and parodies of moral maxims, history lessons and geometrical demonstrations, all concur in a formative enterprise made successful by an artful mastery of an *in-formation technology*: while Alphonse is originally attractive as a mere source of semen (and of *proles*), it is clear from the beginning that the real stakes of the narrative concern his self-consciousness, with all its lures, delusions, lapses, aberrations, contradictions, incompleteness and plasticity. At the end of the process, a re-born and re-tooled subject has learned to be flexible, to play his role and find his place in the collective network of power and communication which produced him, and which will in turn be reproduced through his ephemeral participation.

Such is the story that modernity keeps rewriting from Diderot and Potocki to Lyotard and Negri: the constant metamorphosis of a spectral subject. Like all lost souls, the subject is given no natural place in the world. Like all ghosts, it refuses to die. Like any old *revenant*, it is now coming back under a scary and unrecognizable guise: collective rather than individual, means of production instead of end-in-itself, object of manipulation as much as source of agency.

The role played by the spectre (of the subject) in this work of 'rewriting' is perfectly illustrated by the story of Athenagoras, adapted from Pliny and inserted into the Eleventh day of van Worden's travels – in a tale which provides a striking model for the *hauntology* which Derrida evokes as the *revenant* of classical ontology.[63] After having acquired at a 'reasonable' (i.e. bargain) price a haunted house, the philosopher Athenagoras, afraid of imagining 'idle phantoms', 'concentrated his mind, his eyes and his hands on his writing'. As the spectre came around and loudly rattled his chains, the philosopher 'went on writing as though nothing untoward had happened'. Invited by the ghost to follow him into the courtyard where the apparition soon vanished, he put some grass and '*feuilles*' ['leaves' but also 'sheets of paper', 'pages'] on the ground to locate its place of disappearance. He had it dug out the following day, uncovering bones caught in chains – for which he provided a proper burial: 'and ever since the corpse was paid its last respects, it no longer disturbed the peace of the house' (*Manuscript*, p. 126/147).

In the haunted house of modernity, nobody believes any longer in ghosts, not even the theorists of the postmodern, who flatly acknowledge their incapacity to define the idle phantom they pursue. Yet, no matter how much one writes, one cannot make oneself totally deaf to the calls for emancipation coming from long forgotten victims: no (ir)rationalization can let us ignore the obvious fact that someone (or something) at our gates or within our inner cities is in chains, and in pain. Our senseless but not meaningless task consists therefore in heeding the call of this *spectre en souffrance* (in the existence of which nobody dares to believe), and in devoting a few of our pages to marking its point of vanishing, which may some day be its point of surprising resurgence. I know of no more suggestive depiction of the task of the literary critic in the postmodern age.

NOTES

1 Paolo Portoghesi, 'What Is the Postmodern?' in Thomas Docherty, *Postmodernism. A Reader* (New York: Columbia University Press, 1993), p. 208.

2 Potocki's novel appeared for the first time in its entirety in French in 1989, edited by René Radrizzani (and published by José Corti); the first nearly complete English translation by Ian Maclean appeared in 1995. Apart from important but relatively rare and obscure studies published mostly in Poland throughout the twentieth century, the three main books analysing the novel have also appeared over the last decade (see notes for references). The recent forcing of the *Manuscript* into mainstream media is due to the much publicized re-release of the 1964 film adaptation directed by Wojciech Has – restored thanks to the passion and financial support of such icons as Martin Scorsese and the late Jerry Garcia. For Postmodernity's fascination with spectres, see Jacques Derrida, *Specters of Marx* (New York: Routledge, 1994).

3 Charles Jencks, 'The Post-Modern Agenda' in Charles Jencks, *The Post-Modern Reader* (London: Academy Editions, 1992), p. 17.

4 Marie-Eveline Zoltowska, 'Un précurseur de la littérature fantastique: Jean Potocki et son "Manuscrit trouvé à Saragosse"', Yale University, dissertation, 1973.

5 François Rosset, *Le théâtre du romanesque: Le Manuscrit trouvé à Saragosse entre construction et maçonnerie* (Lausanne: L'âge d'homme, 1991).

6 Luc Fraisse, *Potocki ou l'itinéraire d'un initié* (Nimes: Lacour, 1992).

7 Dominique Triaire, *Potocki: Essai* (Arles: Actes Sud, 1991).

8 Günter von Kirn, 'Jan Potockis "Die Abenteuer in der Sierra Morena". Ein Roman zwischen Aufklärung und Romantik, zwischen Revolution und Restauration', dissertation, Universität Hannover, 1982.

9 For a survey of the earlier discussions among Polish scholars on the philosophical background of the *Manuscript*, in particular the contributions by Tadeusz Sinko and L. Kukulski, see Stanislaw Frybes, 'Les recherches polonaises sur le roman de Potocki' in *Jean Potocki et Le Manuscrit trouvé à Saragosse: Actes du colloque de Varsovie* (Warsaw: Les Cahiers de Varsovie, Centre de Civilisation française de l'Université de Varsovie, 1972), pp. 125–34.

10 Richard Rorty, *Contingency, Irony and Solidarity* (Cambridge: Cambridge University Press, 1989).

11 For a comparable endeavour on a different author, see Philip Watts, 'Postmodern Céline' in R. Scullion et al. (eds.), *Céline and the Politics of Difference* (Hanover: University Press of New England, 1995).

12 Kazimierz Bartoszynski, 'Structure et Signification du *Manuscrit trouvé à Saragosse*' in *Jan Potocki & the Writers of Enlightenment*, Literary Studies in Poland/Etudes Littéraires en Pologne no. XXIII (Wroclaw, 1990), p. 61.

13 Kirn, 'Potockis "Die Abenteur"', pp. 275 and 3.

14 See Janet Coccaro, 'Illusions and Disillusions: the Search for Truth in Jan Potocki's Manuscript Found in Saragossa', dissertation, University of Pittsburgh, 1999, chapter 3; also Marie-Eveline Zoltowska, 'La démocratisation de l'idée de l'honneur dans le *Manuscrit trouvé à Saragosse* de Jean Potocki', *Etudes sur le XVIIIe siècle* 11 (1984), 39–52.

15 Jean Fabre in one of the discussions recorded in *Jean Potocki et le Manuscrit trouvé à Saragosse*, p. 219.

16 Quoted in Z. Markiewicz, 'L'aspect préromantique du *Manuscrit trouvé à Saragosse*, sa réception par les romantiques français', *Revue de littérature comparée* 50 (1–2) (1976), 76.

17 Kirn, 'Potockis "Die Abenteuer"', p. 206.

18 Commenting on a paper by Jean Decottignes which focussed on the 'polyphonic' nature of the *Manuscript*, Jean Fabre stressed that 'polyphony should be understood not only as a plurality of voices in discourse (in the ordinary sense), but as some sort of perpetual dissonance within each theme' (*Jean Potocki et le Manuscrit*, p. 204).

19 See Daniel Beauvois, 'Jean Potocki méritait mieux', *Dix-huitième siècle*, 22 (1990), 441–7.

20 Ihab Hassan, 'Pluralism in Postmodern Perspective' in Jencks, *The Postmodern Reader*, pp. 196–9. Let's quote the terms provided by Hassan to define his categories:

1. '*Indeterminacy*, or rather indeterminacies. These include all manner of ambiguities, ruptures and displacements affecting knowledge and society. [...] Indeterminacies pervade our actions, ideas, interpretations; they constitute our world' (p. 196).

2. '*Fragmentation*. The postmodernist only disconnects; [...] his ultimate opprobrium is "totalisation"' (p. 196).

3. '*Decanonisation* [...] We are witnessing [...] a massive "delegitimation" of the

mastercodes in society, a desuetude of the metanarratives, favouring instead *les petites histoires* which preserve the heterogeneity of language games' (p. 196).

4. '*Self-less-ness. Depth-less-ness.* Postmodernism vacates the traditional self, stimulating self-effacement – a fake flatness, without inside/outside – or its opposite, self-multiplication, self-reflection' (p. 196).

5. '*The Unpresentable, Unrepresentable.* Postmodern art is irrealist, aniconic [...] its hard, flat surfaces repel mimesis. [...] It becomes liminary, contesting the modes of its own representation. [...] "What is unrepresentability?" Kristeva asks. [...] "That which, through meaning, is intolerable, unthinkable: the horrible, the abject" [...] "the exchange between signs and death"' (p. 197).

6. '*Irony.* In the absence of a cardinal principle or paradigm, we turn to play, interplay, dialogue, polylogue, allegory, self-reflection – in short, to irony. [...] These express the ineluctable recreations of mind in search of a truth that continually eludes it, leaving it with only an ironic access or excess of self-consciousness' (p. 197).

7. '*Hybridization,* or the mutant replication of genres, including parody, travesty, pastiche' (p. 197).

8. '*Carnivalization* [which] further means "polyphony" [...] in its ludic and subversive elements that promise renewal' (p. 198).

9. '*Performance, Participation.* Indeterminacy elicits participation; gaps must be filled. The postmodern text, verbal or nonverbal, invites performance [...] As performance, art (or theory for that matter) declares its vulnerability to time, to death, to audience, to the Other' (p. 198).

10. '*Constructionism.* Postmodernism [...] "constructs" reality in post-Kantian, indeed post-Nietzschean, "fictions"' (p. 198).

11. *Immanence.* This refers, without religious echo, to the growing capacity of the mind to generalize itself through symbols. Everywhere we witness problematic diffusions, dispersal, dissemination [...] Languages, apt or mendacious, reconstitute the universe [...] into signs of their own making, turning nature into culture, and culture into an immanent semiotic system' (p. 198).

21 Thomas Docherty, 'Introduction' to Docherty (ed.), *Postmodernism. A Reader* (New York: Columbia University Press, 1993), p. 1.

22 Zygmunt Bauman, 'The Fall of the Legislator' in Docherty (ed.), *Postmodernism,* p. 135.

23 In the quotes from the *Manuscript,* the first page number will refer to the English translation by Ian Maclean (Jan Potocki, *The Manuscript Found in Saragossa,* Harmondsworth: Penguin, 1995); the second page number will refer to the French original in its most common current edition (Jean Potocki, *Manuscrit trouvé à Saragosse,* Paris: Livre de Poche, 1992). All translations of articles originally published in French or German are mine.

24 René Descartes, *Méditations métaphysiques,* ed. Beyssade (Paris: Livre de Poche, 1990), p. 44.

25 Claiming a double (and incommensurable) standard of truth for 'natural philosophy' and for the Christian religion was, obviously, in no way a 'new stance' in 1815. The novelty resides in the fact that (1) religions are historicized (i.e. cut loose from any immediate anchorage in the divine) by the Wandering Jew's narrative, but that simultaneously (2) purely human accounts of our human reality

are nevertheless perceived as radically untenable. But, as we will see later, this is an essential dimension of the modern (as much as of the postmodern) experience.

26 See Kirn, 'Potocki's "Die Abenteuer"', pp. 262 ff.

27 See Marian Skrzypek, 'Les sources françaises de la théorie de la religion chez Jean Potocki (Potocki et Volney)' and the discussion that follows in *Jean Potocki et le Manuscrit trouvé à Saragosse*, pp. 69–74.

28 Jean-François Lyotard, *Just Gaming* (Minneapolis: University of Minnesota Press, 1985), pp. 19–32.

29 Jacques Derrida, 'Force of Law: the "Mystical Foundation of Authority"', *Cardozo Law Review* 11: 5–6, (July/August 1990), 965.

30 *Ibid.*, p. 967.

31 Docherty, *Postmodernism*, p. 26. For an extremely suggestive reinscription of this (supposedly postmodern) aporia of judgment within the opposition between 'Romantic Common Law' and 'Enlightened Civil Law', see Vivian Grosswald Curran, 'Romantic Common Law, Enlightened Civil Law: Legal Uniformity and the Homogenization of the European Union', *Columbia Journal of European Law* 7: 1 (Fall 2000).

32 Triaire, *Potocki*, pp. 77, 104, 105, 93.

33 Lyotard, *Just Gaming*, p. 28

34 Jean-François Lyotard, 'Tomb of the Intellectual' in *Political Writings* (Minneapolis: University of Minnesota Press, 1994), p. 7.

35 *Ibid.*, p. 7.

36 For a remarkable denunciation of this constant temptation in postmodern thought, see Alain Badiou, *Ethics: an Essay on the Understanding of Evil* (New York: Verso, 2000).

37 Quoted in Triaire, *Potocki*, p. 86.

38 Lyotard, *Just Gaming*, p. 43.

39 *Ibid.*, p. 43.

40 *Ibid.*, pp. 54–5.

41 Lyotard, 'Tomb', p. 7.

42 Docherty, *Postmodernism*, p. 5.

43 Triaire, *Potocki*, p. 219.

44 Coccaro, 'Illusions and Disillusions', ch. 3.

45 Karel Krejci, 'Le roman du comte Jean Potocki: sa génologie et sa généalogie' in *Jean Potocki et le Manuscrit trouvé à Saragosse*, pp. 215–16.

46 *Ibid.*, pp. 218–19.

47 Rosset, *Le théâtre du romanesque*, pp. 198–205.

48 Fraisse, *Potocki*, pp. 128–38.

49 For a symptomatic and stimulating rumination on the status of meaning in a postmodern world, see Jean-Luc Nancy, *Le sens du monde* (Paris: Galilée, 1993), especially pp. 11–30.

50 Fredric Jameson, *Postmodernism, or the Culture of Late Capitalism* (Durham: Duke University Press, 1991), p. 9.

51 *Ibid.*, p. 10.

52 Jean-François Lyotard, 'A Postmodern Fable' in *Postmodern Fables* (Minneapolis: University of Minnesota Press, 1997), p. 92.

53 Jean-François Lyotard, *The Postmodern Explained* (Minneapolis: University of Minnesota Press, 1988), p. 18.

54 *Ibid.*, pp. 18–19.

55 Bauman, 'The Fall of the Legislator', p. 140.

56 *Ibid.*, p. 135.

57 Kirn, 'Potockis "Die Abenteuer"', p. 222.

58 Nick Kaye, 'Thinking postmodernisms. On T. Docherty, *After Theory*, and F. Jameson, *Postmodernism*', *Comparative Criticism* 14 (1992), 217.

59 Jean-François Lyotard, 'Rewriting Modernity' in *The Inhuman* (Stanford: Stanford University Press, 1991), pp. 25, 34.

60 Antonio Negri, 'Postmodern' (1986) in *The Politics of Subversion. A Manifesto for the Twenty-First Century* (Cambridge: Polity Press, 1989), p. 201.

61 'The real paradox is that the more mobile and flexible the human quality is, and the more abstract the productive capacity is, the more collective the world and the subject are. The "primitive accumulation" of capital, as it is described by the classics, broke every natural and social tie and reduced the subject to a mere quantitative entity and a purely numerical existence in the market. On the contrary, the abstraction which is formed today is the one that permeates human intercommunicability and which, on this level, constructs the solidity of communitary relationships on the new reality of the subjects' (Negri, 'Postmodern', p. 207).

62 See Antonio Negri, *Exil* (Paris: Mille et une nuits, 1998), pp. 17–36, in particular p. 30.

63 Derrida, *Specters of Marx*, p. 10.

Comparative Criticism **24**, pp. 167–192. Cambridge University Press 2002
DOI: 10.1017/S0144756402005516 Printed in the United Kingdom

A film saved from the scissors of censorship

ANNE GUÉRIN-CASTELL

TRANSLATED BY CHARLOTTE PATTISON AND
GAIL GREENBERG

When he undertook the adaptation of *The Saragossa Manuscript*, Wojciech Has, for whom, like André Bazin,[1] literature and cinema are permeable arts, had already manifested his attachment to making films from literature. Five of his first six feature-length films spring from literary works of art. These films have surprised and often irritated those who thought they knew the authors being adapted. Has does not concern himself with the question of truthfulness in its usual sense. Visual richness of a work of art is not what interests him: 'Liczy się dla mnie przede wszystkim chęć przełożenia na obraz tej warstwy literatury, która nie jest filmowa'[2] (What matters to me in the first instance, is the desire to transmit in images the layer of literature that is not cinematic). For this, he tries above all to understand the perspective of the author, convinced that the modifications imposed on the work of art by the screenplay cannot alter either its impact or its meaning.[3]

The film-maker devoted two years to the writing of the script and the cutting of the film *Rękopis znaleziony w Saragosie* (The Saragossa Manuscript). His ambition was to 'tenter d'approcher le roman sur le plan des idées et des formes, saisir quelque chose de sa vérité et de sa poésie'[4] (attempt to approach the novel at the level of ideas and form, to seize something of its truth and its poetry), and conscious of having embarked on a risky route, he never stopped asking 'Can this be filmed?'. Thus he has contributed one of his major works to the art of cinema. This perspective, which at the time was one adopted by only a small circle of amateurs, appears to have imposed itself more widely these days.[5] Yet the film was very nearly lost forever through late and deliberate attempts by the censors to mutilate the original negative.

The opening of Has's film, leading to the manuscript's discovery

Has, with his usual finesse, understood that it was Potocki's choice of the fictional form which allowed him to avoid Russian censorship and to communicate a religious and philosophical subject, subversive at that time. One hundred and fifty years later, with censorship once again rife in Poland, Has followed the example of Potocki in using as an alibi a period drama, consequently one very much removed from the contemporary historical scene.

The historical framework of the film is constructed via a succession of masquerades. On the surface, a few standard principal characters –

Rebecca observes van Worden arrive at the Cabbalist's mysterious castle

hidalgo, anchorite, possessed, mysterious horseman, jealous husband, old fogey, insolent women, conniving duenna – and a whole series of secondary characters – hired killers, crippled beggars in church doorways, hawkers, clients, mocking, loose girls, fortune tellers, gawking onlookers, and a baroque accumulation of macabre objects – skeletons, bones and skulls – serve to create a stereotypical Spain: 'Rzecz się dzieje w Hiszpanii, we śnie o Hiszpanii. [...] Nie jest to Hiszpania, ale ma cos z niej: jej wygląd, w każdym razie przez nas wyobrażony, i obyczaj, i atmosferę, ktora nam całkowicie wystarcza'[6] (The whole thing happens in Spain, in a dream of Spain. [...] It isn't Spain, but there is something of Spain: its image, at least as we imagine it to be, and its customs, its atmosphere, which is enough for us).

The stressed hispanicisms mixed into the Polish language, notably the very numerous 'señors' and 'señoras', underline the conventional Spain depicted in eighteenth-century literature.[7] It is above all the spirit of that century, its particular wit,[8] which the film-maker has tried to convey through the lightness of the film, its elegance and its irony which is so cheerful as to lend an air of apparent amusement.

Has adds a third framework by introducing minute details referring to Poland, with some ironic anachronisms. Thus the character of Alphonse's father can be identified with an aristocratic Pole, thanks to the dual reference to the work of Sienkiewicz[9] – during his wedding, the innkeeper speaks with an exaggerated Polish rural accent – and the fox-fur hat, a head-dress typical of the ancient Polish provincial aristocracy, he wore in his castle. Polish spectators are thus warned, albeit with humour, that this film, apparently removed from the contemporary historical scene, does deal with their country.[10]

This framework acts as a sounding board for the bold staging, giving a deliberately corrosive character to the film. Has never was a conformist film-maker, and just like Potocki, takes the opportunity to ridicule some human weaknesses.[11] This is why he takes a rather sly pleasure in multiplying minor scenes, where religiosity and bigotry are derided with a Buñuelian impertinence: signs of the cross made too late (Toledo); everyday gestures accomplished with priestly rituality (Alphonse holding the skull-shaped goblet, like a chalice at the moment of the Eucharist; the Hermit sprinkling the floor of the chapel, as if blessing it with his broom cum aspergillum); the intonation of Busqueros when addressing Avadoro which imitates the psalmody resounding from the neighbouring church; the invocation of the two fabricated saints whose names form provocative anagrams, Aparisote and Parasite. The most daring provocation is the picture of the Virgin Mary used as a Punch-and-Judy figure by the monk of the Inquisition to knock out first Alphonse and then Velásquez: during Alphonse's arrest, the monk can be seen moving into the foreground shaking the picture perpendicular to the angle of shot, thus revealing the temptation of Eve in the painting of the Virgin Mary.

The Inquisition, ridiculed several times during the film, constitutes a privileged target.[12] We can note, for example, the comic effect provoked by the stupefaction of the Dominican during the irruption of the two female cousins who come to rescue Alphonse in the middle of being interrogated, or by his untimely intervention in the cave of the Cabbalist's castle. A further example is the scene of Velásquez's arrest, completely imagined for the film, in which the men of the Inquisition are shown in a less than flattering light: cases of mistaken identity, shameless contradictions, blasphemy, maltreatment of an 'innocent', and once innocence is recognized, a continued effort to treat him as guilty. And naturally, they refuse to offer even the slightest of apologies to Velásquez (who treats them openly as 'bandits' and later speaks of them as 'uneducated scoundrels'). Thus, behind the Inquisition as portrayed in the film, we can detect a certain contemporary police force.[13]

Add to the above, the eroticism which distinguishes this film from those produced in Poland at the time makes a clean break with the puritanism inherited from socialist realism: low-cut décolletés, effects of transparency or naked breasts; desire and sexual relationships evoked in scenes in which the women are far from passive; and above all the threesomes' love scenes which, picking up on one of the most important among the recurrent motifs of the novel, balance on a thin wire, somewhere between pornography and a faded vision, using a play on the off-camera shots highlighted by the expressive looks of one of the feminine partners.[14]

We can note too, that father figures are largely ridiculed. Has exploits a characteristic aspect of the novel, namely the derision of the paternal role via the use of original characters whose lives are regulated by a few rigid principles, whereas their sons' upbringing goes completely against those principles.[15] However, Has modifies some minor details, so that in the film it is the fathers who make themselves ridiculous under the watchful eyes of their sons: as for example when Alphonse returns to the family castle only to find his father listening to a story whilst crawling around on all fours; while a short time after, the father, quickly disarmed by Alphonse to whom he pretended to be teaching a secret thrust, like a child goes to be consoled by his wife. If this derision of fathers is part of the theme of the father–son relationships of which we can find traces throughout the work of the film-maker,[16] Has is perfectly aware that the dig is for the Communist regime, characterized by the paternalistic attitude of its leaders.[17]

However, the film-maker has found two passages in the text which will allow him to make more direct political allusions. The first concerns the beginning of the scene of Alphonse's interrogation by the Inquisition (Fourth Day). The second is the comparison by the Cabbalist of the methods of Hungarian and Polish vampires and those of Spanish vampires (Eleventh Day).[18]

In the first case, Has initiates the interrogation by the Dominican with this declaration: 'My, wedlug naszego systemu ... zostswiamy winowajcy wolność oskażania samego siebie ... Wyznanie tackie, jakkolwiek nieco wymuszone, ma jednak swoją dobrą stronę, zwalszcza ... gdy winny raczy wymierić współwinowajców'[19] (We, according to our system, leave to the guilty the liberty of accusing himself ... Such a confession, even if somewhat forced, does have its good side ... especially when the guilty one wants to reveal the names of his accomplices). This declaration cannot fail to evoke in Polish spectators the 'system' under which they live their daily lives, and the ghost, that appears with every tightening of the screw of freedom, of a police and a justice

system based on 'free' self-criticisms and denunciations extracted with
the help of blackmail or torture, which during the years 1948 to 1956
sent thousands of Polish men and women to labour camps.[20]

The second case is that of the Cabbalist, who, whilst leaving the
Venta Quemada in the company of Alphonse, evokes: 'upiory wegierskie
i polskie, które są po prostu trupami, wychodzącymi śród nocy z
grobów dla wysyania krwi ludzkiej, i upiory hiszpanskie, które wchodząc
w ...' (Hungarian and Polish vampires, who are nothing more than dead
bodies leaving their graves at night to suck the blood of human beings;
and Spanish vampires, who penetrate in ... (Film dialogue)). At the
time this film was made, the association of the word 'vampire' with
'Hungarian' and 'Polish' was filled with particular connotations.

In Adam Mickiewicz's celebrated play *Dziady* (Forefathers), which
since 1832, the year of its appearance, was regularly prohibited due to
its very marked anti-Russian content,[21] lending it legendary status for
the whole of Poland, the poet proceeded to effect a reversal of the
Voltairian metaphor of the vampire, the word 'vampire' no longer
designating tyrants or profiteers feeding off the people,[22] but victims
ready for revenge[23]. Moreover, the heroic and tragic events binding
Hungary and Poland were present in everyone's minds in 1965: from
the support offered by a regiment of patriotic Poles to the 1848
Hungarian Revolution – a revolution crushed by Austria, assisted by
Russia – to the protests at the origin of the Hungarian insurrection in
1956, a century later, a march by tens of thousands of students
acclaiming Poland which had succeeded in making the Soviet Union
give in.[24]

Has uses a comparable method for both of these allusions. He ensures
that the text of the dialogue at this precise moment follows that of the
literary original word for word. From the very beginning this cunning
move allows him to neutralize any attempts at intervention from the
censors, who could hardly demand that a passage be cut which follows
the dialogue of a text in standard published form, with uncontested
literary merits and written over a century before.[25] And Has adds a
number of cinematic procedures with the purpose of framing and
underlining the allusions made.[26]

As for Alphonse's interrogation, the Dominican's entrance is preceded
by a cut-in which constitutes a diversion from the classic point-of-view
shot.[27] Then, the film-maker gives the traditional angle/reverse angle
a twist – the two alternating series of shots (three with the Dominican
and two with Alphonse) depicting places which could be disjoined,

where the eyes of the two characters could never meet, with hetero-geneity from one series to another (light, depth of shot) – which ends as soon as the allusion has ended, just as the sound of the drums ends, a sinister tolling whose rhythm, long and insistent, lends the beginning of this interrogation a gravity which is in opposition to the general mood of the film. The peculiarity of the first cut-in draws the attention of the spectator, then the framing and cutting into false angle/ reverse angle compete to isolate the Dominican in space. The two sentences that he utters are thus detached from the diegesis. As soon as the allusive elements of the dialogues have ended, the technique is modified clearly, the diegesis assuming its course once again.

With regard to the Cabbalist's words, the allusion is preceded by Alphonse interrupting the Cabbalist, which produces a curious abrupt change of subject in the Cabbalist's remarks.[28] And immediately on hearing the syntagm 'Hungarian and Polish vampires', the Cabbalist's voice, the level of which is quite clearly reduced, is quickly covered by music through which his remaining words are lost. To this framing device is added the exaggerated play of the comedian and forced gesture accompanying the expression 'Hungarian and Polish vampires'. His extended arm points to a place located within the cinema audi-torium, making reference to Mickiewicz's play: the vampires are among the spectators.

This did not, however, escape the attention of the authorities, and Has's seventh full-length film, despite not being subjected to any official censorship at its opening, was the object of a hidden plot, the effects of which were felt during the next three decades.

The film finished in December 1964, was about to be released for Christmas, a particularly favourable time of the year; however, its *première*, initially fixed for 25 January 1965, did not take place until 9 February. This delay already counts as a clue. The film, 4,966 metres long, which corresponds to a length of 178 minutes, was projected in two parts, separated by an interval. The Polish public turned out *en masse*,[29] attracted by the novelty of a Polish period drama featuring the best actors of the day. However, even whilst singing its praises, the critics were of the opinion that the film was too long[30] and two authors felt impelled to show that one should not try to establish even the smallest connection with the Poland of the time.[31] On the other hand, the unusual silence of the review *Perspective polonaise*,[32] which did not dedicate a single article to *The Saragossa Manuscript* and failed to mention any of the prizes it had won, should be noted for the fact that of three articles on Polish cinema published in France and Italy at the beginning of 1965[33] and written by Polish authors, none mentioned the film, whilst all three dedicated a couple of sentences to *Popioły* (Ashes) by Wajda and *Faraon* (Pharaoh) by Kawalerowicz, both films being far from finished at the time.[34] We can thus assume the existence of a strategy with the objective of limiting the impact of the film, in Poland as well as abroad.

The Saragossa Manuscript was shown at the Cannes festival in 1965, but only outside the competition during a retrospective dedicated to Wojciech Has. It was at this moment that a French film distributor showed interest in the film, on condition that a shortened version be made available. On his return from the festival, Has composed a version of 3,587 metres, a length of 124 minutes, from which the two political allusions were removed.[35] It was this version that was sent to other festivals,[36] which was shown in Parisian auditoriums a year and a half later, and which was projected in several European countries and the United States. The short version may justify the long version not having left Poland.[37]

In its short version, the film had a mixed reception. During its showing in Paris, critics were divided. The film was not much appreciated by the French critics. For example, Marcel Martin thinks that it is 'superb and surprising spectacle' but regrets that 'malgré son ampleur, l'œuvre manque de la richesse qui rendrait exactement compte de l'original et du rythme qui en ferait autre chose qu'un monument magnifique mais pesant' (despite its abundance, the work lacks a richness which would be true to the original and a rhythm which would make the film something more than a magnificent but heavy monument).[38] And Claude Mauriac rates the film, 'plaisant mais froid et même glacé dans sa sensualité' (pleasant but cold, even frozen in its sensuality); it is more literary than cinematographic because it addresses the soul more than perception.[39] Yet the article which carries the most consequence is that of Serge Daney in *Les Cahiers du Cinéma*.[40] It is a brilliant and polemical text, clearly within the tone of the journal at that time. Daney, in a virulent three-part demonstration, demolishes a film which he sees as being nothing but a failed attempt to illustrate the vertigo caused by thoughts on infinity and the idea of the eternal return. Daney makes several allegations of gratuitousness: 'les gestes inutiles des personnages sont accompagnés par des mouvements de caméra complexes mais gratuits',[41] 'répétitions mornes, ennuyeuses et gratuites, passée la première surprise de l'esprit [...]

comment cet ennui, cette gratuité ne menaceraient-ils pas le film lui-même?'[42] (the unnecessary gestures of the characters are accompanied by complex but gratuitous camera movements ... gloomy repetitions which are boring and gratuitous, once the first surprise has passed [...] how could this boredom, this gratuitousness not affect the film itself?); and finally 'Wojciech Has, cinéaste artificiel et sans doute mineur, a réussi un film gratuit sur la gratuité; c'est-à-dire qu'il a échoué, tout film sur l'inutile devant être grave et rigoureux'[43] (Wojciech Has, artificial cinematographer and without a doubt a minor one, has produced a gratuitous film about gratuitousness, that is, he has failed, every film on uselessness needing to be grave and rigorous). This verdict carries an executionary force: never shall the celebrated journal mention Has again.[44]

However, a few independent minds do display their enthusiasm. Robert Benayoun, for whom the film was one of the best shown at Cannes in 1965, wrote a very complimentary article in *Positif*.[45] Jean-Louis Bory did as much in *Le Nouvel Observateur* on the occasion of the film's release in Paris.[46] And Jean d'Yvoire, in *Télérama*,[47] demonstrated that the film had its fair share of contemporary resonance:

L'énigme du sort de l'homme, l'illusion de l'action, l'illusion du bonheur? mais on ne parle que de cela aujourd'hui. Le mélange inextricable du rêve et de la réalité, de la vie et de la mort, du ciel qui cache l'enfer et des enfers qui peuvent, d'un rincanement, vous ramener à la saine compréhension de la terre? C'est tout le problème des valeurs convenues, bousculées et remises en cause dans la tornade de l'histoire. [...] Profondes, pétillantes, couverts de vagues noires au crêtes blanches – le film est en noir et blanc – les eaux espagnoles où navigue Has restent proches des rivages de Pologne. [...] Mais Saragosse en ruines, la Sierra désolée et peuplée des fantomes du passé, c'est peut-être l'Europe et le monde déchirés qui cherchent leur raison de vivre. Qui donnera son sens au manuscrit de Saragosse?[48]

(The mystery of human fate, the illusion of action, the illusion of happiness? but one talks of nothing else these days. The inextricable mixture of dream and reality, of life and death, of heaven that hides hell, and infernos which with a snigger can bring you back to a sane comprehension of earth? It is the problem of conventional values, shaken and put into question by the whirlwind of history. [...] Profound, scintillating, covered in black waves with white crests – the film is black and white – the Spanish waters that Has navigates are close to the banks of Poland [...] But Saragossa in ruins, the desolated Sierra, populated by phantoms of the past, that is perhaps a ravaged Europe and world, searching for their reason to live. Who will give its meaning to the Manuscript of Saragossa?)

Nevertheless, something very peculiar occurred between the film and its French spectators: thanks to word-of-mouth, the film continued to be shown for more than seven weeks, from 17 December 1966 to 8

February 1967.[49] Even more striking is the fact that for several decades, without the slightest publicity, the film returned periodically to Parisian screens. Its spectators cover a wide spectrum of the population and all ages. Through word-of-mouth, *The Saragossa Manuscript* became known in France even by those who had never seen the film, while paradoxically many a cinema lover is ignorant of its maker's name.[50]

The film has not been similarly successful in other countries where it has been screened. For example, Richard Roud, at the festival of Cannes in 1965 for *Sight and Sound*, who only saw the first 100 minutes due to an electrical fault, recognizes some elements of bravura in the film's pastiche, but for him it is 'All done rather heavily'.[51] This reproach of heaviness was shared by a number of British critics, disorientated by a film which for them counted as a failure.[52] The only exception was Derek Elley, a follower of the film-maker virtually since his beginnings in feature films.[53] On the whole, no matter which country, when the encounter with the film worked, it greatly affected its spectators, which led *The Saragossa Manuscript* to acquire the status of a cult film.[54]

Western spectators still only had access to the short version. Once the long version was reclaimed in 1984 for showing at the Avignon festival in homage to Wojciech Has, the copy received from Poland labelled the 'long version' revealed itself as lasting less than the three hours initially announced. Film Polski offered no explanation at the time and continued to send the same version until 1996, always with the false description of 'long version', which was shown on several occasions in auditoriums in Paris between 1990 and 1993.

The length of this version, 4,465 metres, corresponds to 150 minutes, so it is half-way between the long version and the short version produced by Has. A comparison with the genuine long version shows five cuts, each of differing lengths. Ninety-one shots have completely disappeared and eight have been shortened either at the beginning or the end, in ways more or less important to its continuity. The modifications affect ninety-nine shots out of 560, twenty-seven minutes having been eliminated, almost a sixth of the film.

An inquiry in autumn 1996 by the film-maker's followers discovered an order, dated 1984, by the Polish Ministry for Culture demanding that a new version of the film be produced.[55] The cuts were made to the film's original negative, so that it was irretrievably lost.[56] The investigation also discovered that this version appeared in the Film Polski archives under 'the second shot version'. So it was with full knowledge that the firm sent this censored version under the false pretences of the long version. One might be tempted to attribute this to a certain inertia or disorder due to recent political changes. The analysis of the segments that had been cut has led us to believe that the real cause lies elsewhere.

We can note that all the shots of the short version are in this version, at least as long. It is thus an 'intermediate version', the result of a meticulously fraudulent procedure. In fact, if the first two cuts reproduce exactly those made by Has himself for the short version of his film, it is an entirely different story for the remaining three cuts: they are peculiar to this version, and the continuity has visibly been manipulated in a manner imitative of the editing style of Has himself. An analysis of the continuity thus imitated allows us to discern some rather grave errors. Yet the fact is that the hoax worked for several years.[57]

The two political allusions disappeared with the first two cuts. The second one, which corresponds to a length of $2'33''$, is the scene in which one sees Alphonse and the Cabbalist leaving the Venta Quemada together. It has the visible goal of suppressing the moment when the Cabbalist invokes the Hungarian and the Polish vampires. The instance of the first cut is somewhat more complicated. It is the longest segment to be removed, with sixty shots corresponding to $10'46''$ and comprising the following scenes: Alphonse's awakening at the hermitage and his departure, his arrest by the Inquisition, his interrogation and his release, the fight between Zoto's and the Inquisition's troops, the encounter of Alphonse and his female 'cousins' in the room of the Venta Quemada, and the intervention of the Sheikh, who makes Alphonse drink a potion which renders him unconscious. Even a novice can see that it would have sufficed to remove the five shots of the false angle/reverse angle by which the interrogation commences for the political allusion to have been removed. The hypothesis of political censorship does not fully explain this cut, nor does it allow for an explanation of the three remaining ones.

However, all becomes clear once we envisage the possibility of a concomitant religious censorship. The first cut targets two micro-scenes already mentioned: the first, placed at the beginning of the censored segment, shows the Hermit sprinkling the floor of the chapel with a brush as if he were blessing it; the second, which forms part of Alphonse's arrest, shows the monk to be shaking the image of the Virgin Mary in such a manner as to reveal the 'impious' anamorphosis. Since the removal of these scenes is not possible without the total excision of

Alphonse's departure from the hermitage and his arrest, it was necessary to suppress all the following episodes until Alphonse awakes under the gibbet.

The third cut, 4'15" long, stretches from the arrival of the Cabbalist accompanied by Alphonse and Velásquez at his castle to the moment when Alphonse, responding to an invitation by the Cabbalist, examines the content of his library, altogether eleven shots. The cut has the purpose of removing one of the Cabbalist's replies.[58] Alphonse having communicated his intention of leaving the castle to go to Madrid, the Cabbalist objects, saying that the Inquisition is still monitoring the roads. Alphonse points to the castle courtyard. One can see Velásquez, accompanied by Enrico, walking towards the cellar, whilst hearing Alphonse say that perhaps Velásquez will find good counsel. The Cabbalist replies: 'To niedowiarek!' (He's a non-believer!). This reply plays on the double meaning of this word, which can equally well mean the belief in the occult sciences, dear to the Cabbalist, as well as religious belief.[59]

Obviously, Has appears to have made Velásquez his spokesperson.[60] The adaptation erases Velásquez's manias as well as his absent-mindedness, which in the novel make him a slightly ridiculous character. Several scenes of the film, on the contrary, depict a character who unites the power of observation with sensitivity of thought, who does not lack courage, and who practices a wisdom tinged with hedonism. And his interventions during the two scenes where the narrators of Avadoro exchange impressions contribute to detach the accounts from the anecdotal to include them in a philosophical and metaphysical reflection, which allows the film-maker to communicate his own vision of the world and of the art of film-making.

The fourth cut, the shortest, 47", suppresses the three shots of Avadoro's journey from the Lover's Inn to Toledo's house. Its purpose is to ensure the disappearance of a cape decorated with a Maltese Cross lying on the patio of Toledo's house.[61] The view of this cape, revealed through a panning shot, creates a surprise effect through its unexpected manner of appearing in the frame, the movement of the camera crossing the movement of Avadoro, whereas until then the camera was following the character. This effect of rupture, in which we can recognize one of the film-maker's stylistic features, polarizes attention onto the cape: it is in the foreground, between the spectator and Avadoro, literally exhibited – thus it is not a subjective shot. As can be understood from the next shot, it is its presence which indicates to

Avadoro that he has arrived at the house he was searching for. And at that instance the spectator understands that Toledo belongs to the Order of Malta, a detail which could easily be missed by those not having read the complete version of the novel, the title of 'Knight' added to his name on his first mention in the film possibly passing simply for an aristocratic title.

If the Toledo of the film is, like the one of the novel, a libertine whose religious sentiment is essentially grounded in the fear of chastisement in the beyond, the display linked to the passage into cinematographic form stresses these personality traits. Thus he is often shown to be drinking or smoking. And two scenes full of a malicious irony reinforce the image of Toledo as being just as inconsequential in religion as in love.

In the first of these scenes, Toledo, shaken by the 'revelations' made by the voice of his friend killed in a duel and ready to meditate on his life, dressed as a penitent, makes a solemn exit. Yet once at the bottom of the stairs, he changes his mind and backtracks. It is only when he is surprised by Avadoro, that, changing his mind once again, he really will do penance.[62]

In the second scene Toledo, who appears to be penitent, is in fact fast asleep on the steps of the church: it is the time of siesta. Woken by Avadoro he quickly tries to take on a posture of penitence. Yet as soon as he realises that the voice he heard was that of Lope Soarez, he gets up quickly and hurries to leave the square. A glance exchanged with a woman accompanied by her duenna brings him back to Avadoro, whom he asks if, in his opinion, his mistress is still faithful to him. Reassured by the reply, he leaves humming to himself.[63]

There are thus two of the film's characters censored in this manner: Velásquez, spokesperson of a Polish film-maker, cannot be a non-believer, and the inconstant and frivolous Toledo cannot belong to a prestigious religious order whose seat is in Rome.

The fifth cut, 8'13" in length, deals with the encounter of Avadoro and Busqueros, and the machinations which raise obstacles to the union of Lope Soarez and Ines, all in all sixteen shots. The cut has certainly been instigated to suppress two segments placed right at the beginning. One, already mentioned, shows Busqueros imitating in his speech the psalmody resounding from the church. The other concerns a dialogue which follows soon after. Busqueros informs Avadoro that Gaspar Soarez is in Madrid and asks him where a new arrival from the provinces can go. After some hesitation, Avadoro replies: 'Visit a church.' Busqueros triumphs: Avadoro is mistaken and the spectator learns, together with Avadoro, that the provincial coming to the capital does not visit churches but the handiest drinking houses.

The suppression of these two micro-scenes only indicates the disappearance of the first two shots of the segment. Nothing in the remaining censored segment seems to arise specifically from either of the two forms of censorship, unless it is the manner in which paternal authority is flouted in the torrent of scenes which show Gaspar Soarez falling into traps set by Busqueros and ridiculing himself in front of his son. These are liable to displease the defenders of religion as well as the authorities in place in 1984.

This double censorship, which twenty years later confirmed the corrosive character of the film, is surprising on more than one account. With regard to the late nature of this measure, we can imagine that, from its release in cinemas, the film has been subject to a note carefully preserved, which states that the long version of the film should not leave Poland, so that the request on the occasion of the Avignon festival caused a re-evaluation of the matter. The fact that in 1984 the two political allusions were still of contemporary interest, and the necessity to respond to a precise request for the long version, resulted in the ministerial decision to make a third version. Yet, how should the occurrence of religious censorship at this time be explained? If in 1984, Cardinal Glemp, new primate of Poland, led a policy of moderation and even reconciliation with the authorities, the predominantly Catholic opposition was strongly supported by the Polish Church. Could there have been during this period a kind of pact between the authorities and those close to Solidarnosc to carry through this work of censorship? The destruction of the original negative is testimony to a wish to close for good the problems caused by the film and translates the passionate character of this affair. The sending of the false film by Film Polski, long after the change in power, came to validate a disquieting *a priori* hypothesis.

The fabrication of this version, which required far from negligible means – cutting room, mixing room, laboratory work – could not have been produced without a number of accomplices within Polish filmmaking. The circle of Polish cinema, centred around a few places, formed a professional group where everyone – directors, technicians, employees, scriptwriters, critics – knew more or less everyone else. This is the reason why Has could not imagine that his film could have been modified without his, in one way or another, having been informed.

Later, when he had to face up to the facts, he replied to my attempt to approach this matter as follows: 'C'est une chose qui est souvent arrivée à des réalisateurs américains' (This is something that has often happened to American directors). Which was a way of saying that he would not pursue this topic any further. However, he had probably reinterpreted certain past events, in particular the role played by the short version, because immediately afterwards, he firmly asserted that he recognized but one version of the film, the long one, the only version of which he is the real and complete author.

NOTES

1 Has's view on adaptation, explained in an interview dated 1959, takes up several arguments of André Bazin's celebrated text, 'Pour un cinéma impur, defense de l'adaptation', in *Qu'est-ce que le cinéma? Le Cinéma et les autres arts* (Paris: Les Editions du Cerf, 1959), pp. 7–32. See Stanislaw Janicki, 'Film współczesny czy optymistyczny, O kompleksach i szerokim ekranie, Romans z literaturą, Rozmowa z rezyserem Wojciechem Hasem' (On the subject of complexes and the big screen: a romance with literature, Interview with the director Wojciech Has), *Film* 51/52 (1959), 19.

2 Wojciech Has, interview with Tadeusz Sobolewski, 'Wybieraji nieosiagalne' (Choose the inaccessible), *Kino* 7 (1989), 2. We can once again note a convergence of opinions, this time with Eisenstein: 'Le protocole visuel de l'écrivain est précisément ce qui nous importe le moins. Ce qui importe, c'est le type de production de la pensée de l'auteur [...] C'est la chose la plus utile car, finalement, si l'on est incapable de voir l'image à travers le prisme de son domaine propre et de ses possibilités propres, à quoi bon devenir réalisateur?' (The visual protocol of the writer is exactly what matters the least to us. What does matter is the type of production of the author's thoughts [...] It is the most useful thing because, in the end, if one is incapable of seeing the image through the prism of one's own domain and one's own possibilities, then what is the good of becoming a director?). S. M. Eisenstein, 'Le cinéma et la littérature (de l'imagicité)', in *Le Mouvement de l'art*, edited by François Albera and Naoum Kleiman (Paris: Les Editions du Cerf, 1986), p. 28.

3 Cf. Wojciech Has, interview with Jerzy Peltz, 'O realizacji *Jak być kochaną*, o pracy z aktorami, o przyczynach niepowodze nia *Złota* mówi Wojciech Has' (Wojciech J. Has s'exprime à propos de la réalisation de *L'Art d'être aimée*, du travail avec les acteurs, de l'échec de *L'Or*) (Wojciech Has on the making of *How to be Loved*, work with actors, and the failure of *Gold*), *Film* 1, no. 5 (1963), p. 6.

4 Jerzy Parvi, 'Le *Manuscrit trouvé à Saragosse* à l'écran, quelques problèmes de l'adaptation', *Les Cahiers de Varsovie* 3 (1975), 77.

5 See, for instance, the interest created by its being on the programme of a variety of cinemas in the United States these last years, under the patronage of Jerry Garcia and Martin Scorsese: after its showing at the Walter Reade Theatre in New York on 21 May 1999, the film was viewable at the Cinémathèque of Los Angeles on 17 June 1999, since then at a variety of different North American institutions and art

centres, such as Portland, San Francisco, Berkeley, San Raphael, Cleveland, New York, Hartford, Minneapolis, Honolulu, Santa Fe, Toronto, Pittsburgh, Seattle, Houston, Austin, Albuquerque and Brooklyn. Cf. the site of Cowboy Booking International dedicated to Has's film, http://www.cowboybi.com/saragossa.

6 Aleksander Jackiewicz, 'Has w hiszpańskim kostiumie' (Has in Spanish Dress), *Zycie Literackie* 8 (1965), 5.

7 Fiction was then largely influenced by Spanish literature. Cf. François Rosset, *Le Théâtre du romanesque*, Manuscrit trouvé à Saragosse *entre construction et maçonnerie* (Lausanne: L'Age d'homme, 1991), p.155.

8 Cf. Wojciech Has, interview with Cl. Brelet, 'Cybulski/Has à propos du Manuscrit/Entretien avec Has', *Midi-Minuit* 17 (1967), 38.

9 Sienkiewicz (1846–1916), with *Krzyzacy* (The Knights of the Cross) or his trilogy – *Ogniem i mieczem* (With Fire and Sword), *Potop* (The Deluge) and *Pan Wolodyjowski* (Messire Wolodyjowski) – by immersing his readers in the glorious pages of their national history, enabled them to endure foreign domination. The 'spiritual nourishment' has contributed powerfully towards the creation of the myths constituant of 'Polishness', still very vibrant under Soviet domination.

10 This has been clearly expressed by the critic Zygmunt Kałużynski on the release of the film in Poland:

Ale największą osobliwością owego dzieła [...] jest, że nie ma ono nic, ale to absolutnie nic wspólnego z Polską. Ale zaraz! Nie za szybko! Ta satyra na fanatyzm ... na fanfaronadę ... na fałszywy romantyzm: 'Trzy polskie F!' Czy Hiszpania nie była zawsze, w naszej literaturze – jako klasyczny kraj katolicko – szlachecki – zastepczym 'symbolem' Polski? Nie łudzmy się! Nawet z okazji dziwactwa takiego jak 'Rękopis', nie uda nam się uciec, bo wszystko co robią Polcay, i również najsmielsze ich brednie [...] muszą dziać się en POLOGNE ...? (But the largest singularity of this 'work' [...] is that it has nothing, absolutely nothing in common with Poland. But not so fast! This satire of fanaticism ... of fanfaronades ... of false romanticism: the three Polish 'F's'! Has not Spain in our literature always been, in terms of being perfectly catholic and noble, the replacement of the Polish 'symbol'? Let us not delude ourselves. Even in the case of chimeras as with those of the 'Manuscript', it is not an evasion that is brought to us, because all that concerns Poles, and even their most daring ravings have to take place in POLAND ...), Zygmunt Kałużynski, 'Dziwy w filmie polskim!' (Of the Strange in Polish Films!, *Polityka* 6 (1965), 12 (The quotations marks are Kaluzynski's, the last two words in French, and the last word in capitals).

11 Cf. Wojciech Has, interview with Maria Oleksiewicz, 'O rożnych szufladkach 'Saragossy' (The Different Draws of 'Saragossa'), *Film* 10 (1965), 7.

12 Which is not the case in the novel, ignoring the scene of Alphonse's interrogation during the Fourth Day.

13 'J'allais dire: il n'y a plus d'Inquisition. C'est faux, bien sûr. Ce qui a disparu, c'est le théâtre de la persécution, non la persécution elle-même: l'auto-da-fé s'est subtilisé en opération de police ...' (I was about to say: the Inquisition is no longer. It is false, certainly. What has vanished is the theatre of persecution, not persecution itself: the auto-da-fé has refined itself into a police operation), Roland Barthes, 'Le dernier des écrivains heureux' (Preface), in Voltaire, *Romans et contes* (Paris: Gallimard, 1988), p. 9.

14 The spectator is thus riveted on the 'perversity' of a production which whilst sparking his curiosity keeps him at a distance.

15 Cf. Dominique Triaire, *Potocki* (Arles: Actes du Sud, 1991), pp. 153–5.

16 Notably in *Pozegnania* (Farewells), *Zloto* (Gold), *Szyfry* (The Code) and *Sanatorium pod Klpsydra* (The Hourglass Sanatorium).

17 This paternalism he denounces openly in an interview in 1983: 'My zás często stykamy się z postawą protekcjonalnego poklepywania po ramieniu. Daje nam się do zrzumienia, ze wielu rzeczy nie wiemy i nie pojmujemy. Istnieją oczywiście włajemniczeni, ci, co widzą wszystko za siebie i za nas' (We found ourselves faced with a protective attitude. We are made to understand that there are many things of which we are ignorant, which escape our comprehension. Those who are part of the secret know and see all for us), Wojciech Has, interview with Maria Kornatowska, 'Kino trudne' (A Difficult Cinema), *Film* 48 (1983).

18 Do the two passages themselves constitute an allusion in the novel? It seems likely for the first one.

19 Film dialogue. The suspension points indicate a change of shot.

20 Shortly afterwards, the film shows Alphonse enduring the 'première épreuve', which differs radically from the torture as described by the Dominican in the novel: Alphonse, hands tied behind his back, is suspended from his wrists by a system of ropes and pulleys, a method of torture which could easily be a contemporary one.

21 During this period, the simple possession in Poland of a copy was punishable with deportation to Siberia or death. The first performance was staged in Cracow, in 1901, at a time when Austrian censorship displayed a certain leniency. The performances were once again banned in Poland after 1945 and during the Stalin period, that is until 1955. Finally, when the piece was performed in Warsaw in January 1968, in a production which highlighted its anti-Soviet character, the public demonstrated noisily at certain passages. The prohibition on pursuing the performances launched an important movement in university circles which was equally harshly reprimanded.

22 'On n'entendait point parler de vampires à Londres, ni même à Paris. J'avoue que dans ces deux villes il y eut des agioteurs, des traitans, des gens d'affaire qui sucèrent en plein jour le sang du peuple, mais ils n'étaient points morts quoique corrompus' (One did not hear talk of vampires in London, not even in Paris. I swear that in these two towns there were speculators, spies, and business men who in broad daylight sucked the blood of the people, yet they were hardly dead, even if corrupt) and 'Les vrais vampires sont les moins qui mangent aux dépens des rois et des peuples' (The true vampires are the monks who feed at the expense of kings and the people), Voltaire, *Questions sur l'encyclopédie par des Amateurs* (Lausanne: Carmer, 1775), vol. 6, p. 448 and p. 452.

23 Conrad's song, repeated by the chorus:

> My song was in the grave, already cold –
> But blood it smells, from the ground it spies.
> Hungry for blood, like a vampire, it grows bold –
> And 'Give me blood, blood, blood!' it cries.
>
> So vengeance, vengeance, vengeance on the foe,
> With God – or sans God if it need be so!

My Song says: 'Now an evening stroll I'll take.
First, I must bite my brother, fellow Poles' –
In someone's soul my claws I now must slake,
A ghost like me must drink the blood of souls.
So vengeance, vengeance, vengeance on the foe,
With God – or sans God if it need be so!

And then I'll drink foeman's blood in pails!
I'll cut his body open with an axe,
I'll fix his hands down and his legs with nails,
Lest he should rise and claim a vampire's tax.

Adam Mickiewicz, *Forefathers*, extract from Part III, translated by Count Potocki of Montalk (London: The Polish Cultural Foundation, 1968), pp. 161–2.

24 In the night of 19–20 October 1956, a Polish delegation faced Khrushchev, attending together with an impressive array of Russian marshals and generals, to restore 'order' in Poland's affairs.

25 Polish directors, in principle, have the 'final cut' and the censorship consists in inciting them to carry out the 'suggested' cuts and modifications. The most critical moments are the examination of the script by the Commission which decides whether or not the project is acceptable, and the viewing of the film by the 'Commission of Qualification' which issues visas of exploitation, for distribution both within Poland and abroad. On this matter, see Anne Guérin-Castell, 'La place de *Manuscrit trouvé à Saragosse* dans l'œuvre cinématographique de Wojciech J. Has', doctoral thesis under the supervision of Guy Fihman, Université de Paris VIII, 1988, vol. 1, pp. 71–3.

26 We can bring together the procedures of interruption as used by Potocki and as brought up to date by Tadeuz Sinko: 'Chaque fois qu'il attaque, au nom de la raison, le christianisme ou, plus généralement, la naïveté de ceux qui croient aux forces surnaturelles, le récit s'interrompt au moment décisif, le commentaire se fait attendre ou bien le lecteur est invité discrètement à conclure lui-même' (Each time he attacks, in the name of reason, christianity or, more generally, the naivety of those who believe in supernatural powers, the narrative is interrupted at the decisive moment, the commentary is postponed or the reader is discreetly invited to draw his own conclusions), Stanislaw Frybes, 'Les recherches polonaises sur le roman de Potocki', *Les Cahiers de Varsovie* 3 (1975), 128.

27 The viewer has just heard a muffled human cry, its origin not visible in the shot. The cry makes two monks, dressed in black, turn back on themselves to reveal their masked faces. It is at this moment that the shot is cut. The start of the following shot, instead of revealing, as in a classic point-of-view shot, the object of the monk's attention – and thus the origin from which the cry emanated – shows a scene completely devoid of human beings: one sees only a collection of immobile pulleys and ropes. It is only after a period of no movement at all that, from the left, the Dominican enters. His silent entrance and his calm attitude deny that he could have been the person to have produced that sound. The origin of the sound is only revealed in the next shot, which shows Alphonse in the hands of the executioner.

28 The Cabbalist started with obscure thoughts on the fundamental texts of the Cabbala. To Alphonse, who having asked whether he should repeat the

incomprehensible words, the Cabbalist replies 'Cela agrémente mon chemin' (That will embellish my way) before switching without transition to the different types of vampires.

29 Cf. Konrad Eberhardt, *Wojiech Has* (Warsaw: Wydawnictwa Artystyczne i Filmowe, Biblioteka 'X Mura', (1967), p. 65.

30 See, for example, the criticism of Alexander Jackiewicz, 'Has w hispańskim kostumie', *Życie Literackie* 8 (1965), 5, or the explicit title of that of Jan Alfred Szczepánski, 'Mniej bywa czasem więcej' (More is Sometimes Less), *Film* 8 (1965), 5.

31 One of them is none other than Zygmunt Kałużynski' 'Kwiat tuberozy w panoramie' (The Tuberous Flower in Panorama), *Polityka* 8 (1965), 6, who thus completes a remarkable U-turn as he stated the complete opposite in an article published two weeks beforehand in the same journal (cf. note 9). The other is the writer Wojciech Żukrowski, 'Zabawa dla mądrych' (An Amusement for the Wise), *Kultura* 8 (1965), 5.

32 With the duty of promoting a socialist Poland, this journal, edited in Warsaw in several languages, was sent to around thirty countries. A regular column was dedicated to cinema, whereas notes in the cultural pages indicated the participation of Polish films at different events and their releases in Western cinemas.

33 The following articles are concerned: Jerzy Toeplitz, 'Venti anni di cinema polacco: le tradizioni e le prospettive' (Twenty Years of Polish Cinema: Traditions and Prospects), *Filmcritica* 153 (1965); Tadeusz Pallasz, 'Sintomi di una ripresa' (Symptoms of a Renewal), *Cinema Sessanta* 50 (1965), and Jerzy Toeplitz, 'Les perspectives du cinéma polonais' (Perspectives of Polish Cinema), *Perspective polonaises* 3 (1965).

34 *Popioly* was released on 25 September 1965 and *Faraon* on 11 April 1966.

35 The cinematographer proceeded via light cuts, shortening certain shots at the beginning or the end; other, somewhat heavier cuts, affect segments which are quite long. The disappearance of the first allusion is easily explained: it belongs to a long block of dialogue. But the suppression of the second allusion only leads to a saving of 2′33″. Perhaps Has followed what purported to be disinterested advice. It is more likely that he himself decided to remove a passage, which in his opinion was of concern only to Polish spectators, from a version which was intended for the French.

36 For example, the festival of San Sebastian in Spain, which follows closely the Cannes festival. Those responsible for Polish cinema sent a copy of very poor quality, made from the positive which served to create the short version, and this without notifying the film-maker that his film had been selected for the festival.

37 On this note the following is of interest:
1. The Cannes retrospective dedicated to Has – more likely intended to make up for the fact that his last film was not selected, in contrast to *Pierwzy dzién wolności* (The First Day of Freedom), an academic and declamatory work of Aleksander Ford, highly influential on Polish cinema during this period – was organized by the association 'Pleins Feux sur le monde et les hommes';
2. The request for a distribution visa made in September the following year for the short version in Paris stems curiously from the same organization, as documented by the file on the film conserved at the Film Archive of Bois d'Arcy.

38 Marcel Martin, 'Présence d'un terrible passé', in *Lettres françaises*, 28 October
1965. One might be surprised by the use of this reference to the original literary
work to belittle the film, a procedure which can be found to have been used by other
French critics of that period, at a time when Potocki's novel was only published in
the abridged version by Roger Caillois. With this same tactic abundantly used by
Polish critics, one could believe that the opinions expressed resulted from
exchanges with the spokespersons of Polish criticism.

39 This allows him, after having evoked 'the most beautiful images that the novel
could have inspired', to dedicate the rest of his article to the novel. Claude Mauriac,
'*Le Manuscrit trouvé à Saragosse* de Wojciech Has', *Le Figaro Littéraire*, 22
December 1966.

40 Serge Daney, 'La fin de l'éternité', *Les Cahiers du Cinéma* 187 (1967) 69–70.

41 *Ibid.*

42 *Ibid.*

43 *Ibid.*

44 This will not be without consequence for the work of the film-maker. That is how
it came about that the Cinémathèque Française does not possess a single copy of
the film, which never forms part of its programme, just as it does not hold any of
Has's other feature-length films.

45 Robert Benayoun, 'Des zakouski de résistance', *Positif* 71 (1965), 39–40. In his
article, Benayoun protests with humour against the principle of the short version:
'Aux distributeurs qui annoncent déjà leur intention de mutiler ce chef-d'œuvre,
je crie: Méfiez-vous! L'auberge de la Venta Quemada n'a pas encore lancé son
dernier sortilège et vous dépêchera ses fantômes vengeurs' (To the distributors who
already announce their intention to mutilate this masterpiece, I cry: Beware! The
Venta Quemada has not yet cast its last spell and will send you its revengeful
phantoms), p. 40.

46 Jean-Louis Bory, 'Le Cinéma du Père Noël', *Le Nouvel Observateur* 28/12 (1966),
43.

47 Jean d'Yvoire, '*Le Manuscrit trouvé à Saragosse*, Le Grand livre de la vie ou sa
brillante illusion?', *Télérama* 885 (1967), 60.

48 *Ibid.*

49 *The Saragossa Manuscript* was first shown in two cinemas, Studios *Marigny* and
Saint-Séverin, and in January, solely at *Saint-Séverin*. The showings which were
supposed to finish mid-January were continued to the end of the month. In
February, after a day at *Calypso*, the film moved to the *Casino Saint-Martin*.

50 This obvious rapport between the film and its French spectators can be explained
by the intelligence, the consistency and the drive with which Cartesian logic is
disturbed.

51 Richard Roud, account of the festival of Cannes 1965, in *Sight and Sound* 43
(Summer 1965), 119.

52 Cf. The note, 'Has, Wojciech (Jerzy)', in John Wakeman, *World Film Director*
(New York: H. W. Wilson Company), vol. 2, p. 417.

53 In his study of Has, Derek Elley writes:

The Saragossa Manuscript amazed audiences when it first appeared, since few were prepared
for such a massive demonstration of the director's capabilities. [...] The print available outside
Poland is cut by fifty-one minutes, the missing sections being continuations of existing tales:

though nothing is missing of the basic structure, the lost hour only increases the film's puzzling effect and confuses instead of clarifying. Some memorable imagery is clearly lost in the present version, but *The Saragossa Manuscript* still retains the power to delight, mystify and entertain at repeated viewings.

Derek Elley, 'Wojciech Has', in *International Film Guide 1963–1975*, edited by Peter Cowie (London: Tantivy Press, 1975), pp. 41–2.

54 Has loved to tell the story that the film was shown so often at Berkeley that it had been reduced to just twenty minutes. Let us note among the admirers of the film, the guitarist Jerry Garcia, whose favourite film it was, and the film-maker Buñuel, who personally bought a copy of the film.

55 This late date is explained by the fact that neither Has nor Koukou Chanska, in charge of the society Jeck Film, and holder of the film rights (in particular the rights for France since 1984), have ever wanted to listen to the arguments that I have been putting forward since 1990: Has, whom I have interviewed several times on this matter, was convinced that I was confusing the long and the short versions. This certainty was crushed at the end of the summer of 1996, when the organisers of the festival of Telluride (US) who wanted to show the long version of the film protested to Jeck Film that the length of the film received was a lot shorter than expected.

56 By chance a 'lavender' (special soft print made from the original negative) was found, which has allowed some copies to be made of the long version. This, which required the creation of a new negative to maintain it and a subtitled copy, was co-financed by the Pacific Film Archive (with funds bequeathed by Jerry Garcia) and Martin Scorsese. However, it is in no way a restoration, as is made clear on the web site of Cowboy Booking International.

57 For a precise analysis of these cut-in scenes, see Guérin-Castell, 'La place de *Manuscrit trouvé à Saragossa*', pp. 452–5.

58 *Ibid.*, pp. 391–2.

59 In the video copy of the long version destined for the Italian public (*Manoscritto trovato a Saragozza*, Cecchi Gori Editoria Elettronica, Rome), the Cabbalist's reply is translated as 'Non credo' (I do not believe) instead of 'Non crede' (He does not believe). A skilful falsification which succeeds in creating an alibi from a simple typographical error.

60 As we know, this role is attributed to several characters in the novel.

61 Cf. Guérin-Castell, 'La place de *Manuscrit trouvé à Saragossa*' p. 389.

62 This scene is without equivalent in the novel.

63 This scene is inspired by a scene in the novel, but it adds the impertinent details of the siesta and the glance exchanged with the woman walking towards the church.

Bio-filmography of Wojciech Jerzy Has

The Polish film-maker Wojciech Jerzy Has, who was born on 1 April 1925 in Crakow and who died on 3 October 2000 in Łódz, directed fourteen feature-length films which he could call entirely his own, and this without ever possessing party political membership, or abandoning his vision of cinema as art. Despite encountering numerous obstacles he always refused to be considered as a 'doomed film-maker'.

Like the majority of young Poles, he was forced to interrupt his studies when Germany invaded Poland. He then worked as a miner. However, he succeeded in publishing three small books containing his own illustrations, thus enabling him to be admitted to a school of applied art, which secretly concealed an academy of fine art behind the façade of a technical education (the only one to be tolerated by the Germans).

At the end of the war, Has studied painting at the Academy of Fine Art at Crakow. Interested in animated films, he also took classes at the Warsztat Filmowy Młodych (Cinematographic Youth Workshop) which had just been created by Antoni Bohdziewicz: in the morning he studied painting, and in the afternoon, until late at night, the cinema. He received his diploma from the Academy of Fine Arts in 1948. His professors wanted to send him to Paris to continue his studies, but Has refused. Between painting and cinema, he had already made his choice.

The difficulties started immediately. His first feature film, a medium-length film called *Harmonia* (Harmony) (1948) was not distributed, and during the congress of Wisla, which in 1949 imposed social realism on Polish film-makers, Has was one of the film-makers that were under suspicion. The documentary on Warsaw, *Ulica Brzozowa* (Brzozowa Road) (1949) which he directed with Różewicz, was not distributed either. Has worked at the Documentary Film Studio in Warsaw (WFD) and made several films for Polska Kronika Filmowa (Polish Newsreels). Yet, following the making of a very personal impressionistic film about Crakow, *Moje Miasto* (My Town) (1950), he was sent to the Educational Film Studio in Lódź (WFO). In this quiet and isolated location, he made a few short films, notably *Karmnik Jankowy* (The Manger of Janek) (1952).

When the liberalization of the mid 1950s occurred, he felt sufficiently prepared to attempt feature films, and this not only technically speaking. The years of exclusion had allowed him to mature and build up his resistance to pressure, ruses and harassment. Resolute in his intention not to produce just films, but *his* films, he refused the proposition made by Jerzy Zarzycki to direct a first long feature film, *Ziemia* (Earth), for which he would have been nothing but a kind of super-assistant.

Shortly after, he wrote a screenplay based on a novel, *Pętla* (The Noose), by Marek Hłasko, young anti-conformist writer and provocateur. Made in 1957, the film which shows the wanderings of a talented and alcoholic painter in a hostile town, was sharply criticized on its release. The main reproach to Has was that he did not sufficiently portray the social aspects of alcoholism; however, the critics did welcome the appearance of a new film-maker.

For several years, Has was able to make film upon film, tackling various topics. The provocative blackness of *Pętla* was followed by the sweet-sour tonality of *Pożegnania* (Farewells) (1958), based on the novel by Stanisław Dygat (the meeting of a young aristocrat and a bar hostess, rebelling against their milieux, on a background of war and the collapse of values). Then, the absurd tragedy with *Wspólny Pokój* (One-Room Tenants) (1959), based on the novel of Zbigniew Uniłowski (four young people, none of whom finds a place in society, share a room in a poor neighbourhood of Warsaw); the sentimental comedy *Rozstanie* (Partings), based on a short story by Jadwiga Żylińska (an actress who returns to her home for her grandfather's funeral meets her family of aristocratic origin, her besotted cousin, old acquaintances, and has a short romance with a young student she met on the train); the impossible quest for an elsewhere in *Złoto* (Gold) (1961), based on an original screenplay by Bohdan Czeszko (a young man who believes he has run over a cyclist reaches the industrial complex of Turoszów where he hopes to cross the border); reminiscences of a painful past with *Jak być kochaną* (How to be Loved) (1962), based on the short story by Kazimierz Brandys (an actress, famous thanks to a radio serial, takes an aeroplane for the first time and relives her past, from her debut as Ophelia to the tragic suicide of Wiktor, the man she loved and sheltered during the war).

These six films, with their characters who are subjected to events and situations beyond their control, build a pessimistic vision of the world, albeit without bitterness, which the film-maker's perception of society's defects colours with subversive irony. These films were equally occasions for formal experiments – camera angle jumps, *regards caméra*, depth of field, *plans-séquences*, very personal work with jump cut and off-screen – which in their transgressions of the code of classic cinema constitute as many questions about cinema itself.

The success of *Jak być kochaną*[1] enabled Has to envisage more ambitious projects. Tadeusz Kwiatkowski suggested that Potocki's *Manuscript Found in Saragossa* be brought to the screen. Despite a few decision-makers who deemed it not to be 'educational' enough, the screenplay was eventually accepted. Presented at the fringe of the Cannes Film Festival in 1965, the film *Rękopis znaleziony w Saragossie* (The Saragossa Manuscript) was given an award at the festival of San Sebastian, and awarded the First Prize at the Edinburgh Festival the following year.

His next project, the adaptation of a short story by Chekhov, *Nieciekawa Historia* (An Uninteresting History), having been rejected, Has submitted a script based on a short story by Andrzej Kijowski, *Szyfry* (The Code), which was accepted. On its release (in December 1966), the film did not make it to the more prestigious cinemas, and the critics considered it a minor film, a late offspring of the 'Polish School'. It is, on the contrary, an essential film; the film-maker uses the intrigue of Kijowski – a father returns to Poland to research into the disappearance of his son twenty years previously in the war – to investigate the views of the Poles on the extermination of the Jews, and to affirm his ethical position on the representation of history in the cinema.

Having had a further script refused – a film on Wyspiański, based on his major work *Wesele* (The Wedding) – Has took on a project which Jan Rybkowski had intended to but could not direct: the adaptation of a novel by Prus, *Lalka* (The Doll). He chose to limit the screenplay to the main intrigue – the love of a rich Warsaw merchant for the daughter of a ruined aristocrat – which takes place during the last quarter of the nineteenth century, and to film in colour for the first time. The characters of Prus were an opportunity for him to draw a portrait of contemporary Polish society, and he took advantage of a line spoken by the main character to take a stand against the anti-semitism raging in Poland at the time. On its release in Poland in 1968, the film was attacked by all the critics, who unanimously claimed that Prus's novel had been distorted.

Has then presented a project which he had been considering for a long time: the adaptation of Bruno Schulz's short stories. His first screenplay having been refused, he insisted, in a less than favourable political climate, on presenting nothing but successive versions of the same project. The situation was opened up with the arrival at the end of 1971 of a more liberal Minister for Culture and the Arts, and Has managed to film *Sanatorium pod Klepsydrą* (The Hourglass

Sanatorium) in the autumn of 1972. Once the editing was completed, the film-maker, fearing that his film would not be distributed – he had refused to remove a scene which constituted a clear allusion to the recent wave of anti-semitism – arranged to leave Poland with a copy of his film, which he showed to the organizers of the Cannes Film Festival in Paris. The film was selected and was given the jury's special award. Released in Poland seven months after the festival, this film too was subject to a virulent campaign denouncing its alleged betrayal of the original literary lines.

Has knew perfectly well that the moment had arrived for him to pay for his independence. He accepted a teaching position at the school of cinema in Łódz. None of his next projects succeeded[2] since he continued to refuse to submit to the dictates demanding contemporary subjects, whether they emanated from the authorities or the critics of that period. His enforced 'silence' lasted ten years.

In 1981, during the brief 'Solidarnosc Spring', the artistic and literary directors of the 'Zespoły' (Production companies),[3] which since 1956 were traditionally designated by the authorities, were for the first time elected by the representatives of the profession in a direct and secret ballot. Has, made director of one of the 'Zespoły' for the first time, found himself in a more favourable position to accomplish his own projects.

While Poland was engulfed in the deep night of the Jaruzelski dictatorship, Has directed his three darkest films: in 1982, *Nieciekawa Historia* (An Uninteresting History), after Chekhov (twenty-four hours in the life of an insomniac medical professor, who knowing that he is the victim of an incurable disease, breaks his ties with the world, one by one); in 1984, *Pismak* (The Scribbler), based on a novel by Władysław Terlecki (a satirical journalist, shut away in a prison in Lublin at the beginning of World War I, who shares his cell with a safe-breaker and a murdering priest); in 1985, *Osobisty Pamiętnik grzesznika ... przez niego samego spisany* (The Intimate Memoirs of a Sinner ... Transcribed by Himself), an adaptation of a novel by James Hogg (*Confessions of a Justified Sinner*, a young man who, incited by the Devil, killed his half-brother and then his parents). This last film was banned for several months, the censors fearing that the relationship to the murder of Father Popiełuszko in October 1984 would be made.

In 1988, Has directed a co-production together with France, *Niezwykła podróż Baltazara Kobera* (The Extraordinary Voyage of Balthasar Kober), based on the novel by Frédéric Tristan, *Les Tribulations héroïques de Balthasar Kober*. He was still teaching at the school of cinema at Łódz, where he was elected rector from 1990 to 1993. He gave up this post in 1996, because he was still hoping to direct a film in co-production with France, 'L'Ane qui joue de la lyre', inspired by Apuleius. He died without having succeeded in raising the necessary funds to start his fifteenth feature film.

NOTES

1 Selected for the 1953 Cannes Film Festival, it won three awards that year (Grand Prize, Best Screenplay and Best Actress) at the San Francisco Film Festival.

2 The screenplay, from the novel by Jarosław Iwaszkiewicz, *Czerwone tracze* (The Red Shields), was initially refused, then subsequently accepted, but whilst the film was in production, and following a substantial amount of documentation and research, the production was finally cancelled. The screenplay of *Nieciekawa Historia*, presented twice during this period, was refused each time. The projects to adapt *The Sorrows of Young Werther* by Goethe, for which Has had contact with a producer in West Germany, and *Zmory* (Nightmares) by Emil Zegladowicz suffered the same fate.

3 Created in 1956, they were the cornerstone of the Polish film industry.

Comparative Criticism 24, pp. 193–216. Cambridge University Press 2002
DOI: 10.1017/S0144756402005528   Printed in the United Kingdom

Dialectics of enlightenment: notes on Wojciech Has's *Saragossa Manuscript*

PAUL COATES

Synopsis of Has's film *Rękopis znaleziony w Saragossie* (*The Saragossa Manuscript*)

In the middle of a battle, an officer enters a building where he finds a book. He is captured, and the book also interests his captor's commanding officer, who says it concerns his grandfather. As they read of the Spanish district of Sierra Morena, where gypsies and bandits prey on travellers, we cut to Alphonse van Worden lying on the grass in that area as one of his two servants – Mosquito – warns against a neighbouring haunted inn, the Venta Quemada. In an uncanny landscape of animal skeletons, snakes and vultures, Mosquito vanishes with the provisions. Alphonse rides on alone to the ill-reputed inn. Here a black serving-girl invites him to supper with two foreigners. As he ravenously falls on the food, the glamorous foreigners arrive. They identify themselves as Emina and Zibelda, term Alphonse a close relative, call themselves Moslems and regret his Christianity – for they want to marry him. They embrace him in turns, but he suddenly finds himself under a gallows. Running back to the inn, he finds the previous night's room full of rats and bones. Riding on he meets a hermit, who asks him about his upbringing. Alphonse describes his father's duel over the overturning of his carriage. Run through by his opponent, lying on a cart, van Worden senior offers to sell his soul for a sip of water. A girl suddenly appears with a jar. We then see his marriage, whose celebrations are interrupted by a summons to inherit an ancestral castle in the Ardennes. Brought up far from his father, Alphonse describes his father's decision to make him a captain of the guards. The hermit fears Alphonse's two women were in fact hanged bandits, and orders one-eyed Pacecho, whom he is exorcising, to tell his story, which may save Alphonse's soul. Pacecho met his father's wife and her sister, Inezilla, at the Venta Quemada, and also awoke under the gallows, whence the two hanged men pursued him, plucking out one of his eyes. On the hermit's recommendation Alphonse goes to the nearby chapel to sleep, mocking two male voices who claim to be his lovers. The next morning Alphonse leaves for Madrid but is captured by the Inquisition, which enquires whether he knows two African princesses. The sisters and their followers rescue Alphonse just as the torture is beginning. As they give him a talisman the Sheikh enters to punish him for being in the company of Gomelez women. He is forced to drain a goblet made of a skull and then awakes under the gallows beside the Cabbalist, who seems to have had a similar experience with two women. The two then head for Madrid, avoiding the road watched by the Inquisition. Meanwhile, the Inquisition ambushes Velásquez, mistaking him for Alphonse. Released, Velásquez encounters Alphonse and the Cabbalist and the three seek refuge in the Cabbalist's castle. Once there the Cabbalist takes his sister Rebecca aside and attributes their early arrival to unexpected circumstances. In the library Alphonse finds the book that so intrigued the officers at the outset and, recognizing the picture of the gallows, hastens to discuss it with the rationalist Velásquez. As he does so, the Cabbalist appropriates it and criticizes Rebecca for leaving it out: had Alphonse read it to the end 'the forthcoming events would have been pointless'. Rebecca is then introduced to the guests and the Gypsy chief Avadoro and his band arrive. Exhorted to tell of his adventures, he speaks of how a man hired him to watch his wife, whom he warned. He then meets the lady's lover, Toledo, who is extremely nervous following an apparent warning against libertinism by the spirit of a recently deceased friend. This story is interrupted when Avadoro is called away on business. He returns and continues his story, recounting Toledo's penitent despair and his own meeting with the injured Lopez Soarez, who tells his story. It concerns his merchant father's proscription of contact with nobles, particularly the House of Moro, and includes the father's story justifying the prohibition. Lopez then describes his own arrival in Madrid and how a nobleman called Busqueros attached himself to him. Busqueros repeatedly intervenes in his romance with Inez, who turns out to be of the House of Moro. As Lopez bewails this misfortune, Busqueros interrupts him with the story of his own affair with the flighty Frasquetta, which includes Frasquetta's own narrative of her marriage to the older man she cuckolded. Busqueros's story is interrupted by the arrival of a letter from Inez; he leads Lopez to her window, but as he climbs towards it, it opens and he falls. Toledo's head appears; it is the wrong window, and Toledo takes the wounded cries of Lopez for his friend's admonitions from beyond the grave. On hearing this Avadoro runs to inform Toledo, who immediately ends his penance. Although Rebecca asks him to continue his story, Avadoro is summoned away again. On returning he describes his own meeting with Busqueros, who drafts him into a plot to ensure that Lopez's father, recently arrived in Madrid, will permit his son's marriage to Inez. The plot succeeds. When Toledo, Avadoro and Busqueros are together, Toledo asks Busqueros for further particulars of Frasquetta's story. Busqueros tells how she rid herself of her husband and married her lover, then points her out on her way to visit Toledo. The three flee her. Avadoro and Busqueros then see Alphonse's father duelling. Avadoro's stories being over, Alphonse is summoned away on an important matter. A rider leads him to the Venta Quemada, where he finds the two sisters and the Sheikh. The latter explains that Alphonse was held long enough to determine whether his lovemaking had yielded the heirs needed by the Gomelez family, and how his honour and courage were tested. He will find all his experiences detailed in the book, and the Sheikh invites him to write in the rest himself. As the sisters leave, Alphonse fears never seeing them again. He asks who they really are. They step outside and he sees them meet his double, who returns to face him. They then reappear outside the inn where he is writing in the book, inviting him to supper. He mounts his horse and as he rides out the film ends. (For further details of the ending, see below, pp. 199–205, 213.)

1. HAS'S FILM: THIRTY YEARS LATER

To mark the 'Centenary of Cinema' in 1995 the leading Polish academic film journal, *Kwartalnik filmowy*, canvassed a series of prominent Polish

The seductive Emina entices van Worden to her bed in the first vision

critics to ascertain which Polish films they deemed most important. There was little surprise at the winner: Andrzej Wajda's *Popiół i diament* (*Ashes and Diamonds*, 1958). Two films by Wojciech Has featured in the top ten. The highest-placed was his *Sanatorium pod klepsydra* (*The Hourglass Sanatorium*, 1973), based on the stories of Bruno Schulz, which was equal fifth. *Rękopis znaleziony w Saragossie* (*The Saragossa Manuscript*) came equal seventh. Later, two issues of the journal featured essays on the majority of the top fifteen films. Krzysztof Lipka contributed one on *The Saragossa Manuscript*.[1]

Lipka is a paid-up Potockian, stating his love of the original novel, confessing to having read it four times, and even devoting more pages to it than to the film. While praising many aspects of the film – the fine camerawork and sets, the use of horror conventions, the surrealistic effect of such incongruous details as van Worden's 'Polish' fur hat worn in Spain – he has several objections. They are not so much to the loss of material: after all, the film's unusual length (176 minutes) clearly demonstrates a will to include as much as possible, and although as many as 23 of the 33 stories or stories-within-stories disappear, the only major omission is of the story of the Wandering Jew (whether this omission should be read as motivated aesthetically, ideologically or both is an issue to which I will return). Instead they concern the accentuation of the comic in the film's second half (the most frequent object of

Avadoro brings news of his beloved to the despairing Toledo

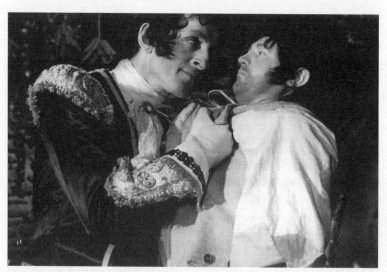

Pasheko insists that he will defy the ghosts of Venta Quemada

reviewers' criticism[2]), Zbigniew Cybulski's characterization of Alphonse van Worden (perhaps hardly surprising, as the choice of Cybulski for the role was a last-minute compromise following failed attempts to engage a supposedly French actor[3]), the elements of pastiche in

Krzysztof Penderecki's score, and the new ending (of which more later), which he sees as throwing the work into disarray.

2. THE ENDING: HAS AS AUTEUR?

Of these objections, the critique of the ending is the most serious, raising the issue of the terms upon which a filmic adaptation of a literary text – or, if one likes, its transposition or transference[4] – can revise the narrated events of its pre-text.[5] Of course, it may fruitfully be argued that the differential nature of the sign-systems of literature and film (the one more 'abstract' than the other, its characters at best line-drawings soliciting completion by the reader, the other generally linked 'indexically' to a 'pro-filmic event' the camera reproduces with automatic thoroughness) renders the recreation of a prototype a merely chimerical pursuit, freeing film-makers to comb originals for any usable material. Nevertheless, it is also true that different works adopt different attitudes to their originals. Some directors, be it out of genuine regard for the written text or because they and/or their producers covet the greater popularity achievable by a demonstrably 'faithful' work (a possible greater use-value to an audience now able to employ it cynically to displace 'the original'), do indeed profess a goal of 'fidelity'. Of course, the sheer length and variety of Potocki's work on the one hand, and the constraints of late sixties film distribution (unable as yet to take the option of producing 'amphibious' works to appear in shorter segments on TV and in larger units, or in toto, in the cinema),[6] translate 'faithful' into the pragmatic 'as faithful as possible'. And for all Has's stated wish to 'choose the impossible' and film works often deemed unfilmable,[7] the drastic editing of Potocki performed by Tadeusz Kwiatkowski's script follows the pragmatic version of fidelity. This version of 'fidelity' permits divergence: hence Lipka has no strong objections to the thinning of narrative strands. But does this liberal version of 'fidelity' encompass the framing of a new ending? Does Has's new ending (to be described and analysed later) seek to lend his film a status beyond that of illustrating the novelistic pre-text? Or might it even be a logical outgrowth of a declaredly faithful reading, representing a conclusion that is not only acceptable but perhaps even the only one possible in an artistically ambitious modern version of a much older text? Does this make the novel more pretext than pre-text?

The viability of a claim that the novel functions merely as pretext can of course help determine the degree to which Has's work is amenable to classification as a *film d'auteur*. As Ian Christie has pointed out, early foreign reviewers were unanimous that the work did not fall into this category[8] (Polish reviewers meanwhile generally praised it while voicing a certain disappointment[9]). Although it was not always stated explicitly, Has clearly lacked two of the key qualifications for achieving *auteur* status (for a certain circularity dictated that although *film d'auteur* was the supreme label of approbation, no film could achieve supreme status on its own merits but had to bear the legitimating signature of the *auteur*, to stand in a sequence of works).

The first qualification is the element of stylistic, thematic and ideological repetition. Indeed, Has motivates his decision to film Potocki's work with a desire to *avoid* repetition – and possible ossification – thereby denying the recognizability that was a key factor in the spectator's delectation of the unity of an *auteur*'s *œuvre*. Because *The Hourglass Sanatorium* – which Has mentions as his next project in discussions of the *Manuscript* – had not yet come into being, a typical 'Has strategy' of creatively reworking texts of the fantastic could not yet be identified (the perception of repetition depending after all on the existence of at least two similar works). Valorizations of 'the oneiric' as a key category of his work would come later, as would descriptions of it as preoccupied with time and isolated protagonists negotiating opaque worlds. In fact, Has's position may be seen as the extreme embodiment of a certain freedom offered directors under the Polish production system, whatever other constraints it may have imposed: the freedom to work with little thought of a film's subsequent box-office success. Attempted applications of an auteurist model to East European post-war directors may be misconceived, while a case such as that of Has may interrogate both auteurism and its possible complicity with capitalism, as the imperative to repeat becomes the self-commodification that establishes product recognizability, ensuring the capacity for further film-making (the limit-case being the one-man factory known as Fassbinder). In displaying the repetitiveness of the commodity form, the artist to some extent is scarred by the prevalent mode of production. In Poland, meanwhile, the artist's position as state functionary preserved him or her from this imperative, though – conversely – the non-requirement of profit could yield works of no real interest to anyone.

Another prerequisite for *auteur* classification Has clearly lacked was the status of writer-director. Whatever his contribution to the screenplays of his earlier films, it is not until *The Hourglass Sanatorium* that he figures as sole scriptwriter. Moreover, Has lacked the characteristic feature whereby both Poles and foreigners distinguished between their *auteurs* and their *metteurs-en-scène* – or, worse still, hacks: a foregrounded dissident political agenda. Wajda may seldom have figured as writer-director – through he co-wrote *Ashes and Diamonds* and was sole author of the screenplay of the astonishing *Wszystko na sprzedaż* (*Everything for Sale*, 1968) – but even though his *Popioły* (*Ashes*, 1965/65) inherited Has's sets, Wajda's ever-present political preoccupations (not to mention a stylistic propensity for 'Baroque' effects and such repeated motifs as the white horse) rendered his *auteur* status indubitable, if occasionally clouded. If Has's fabulation can be termed Cortázarian, as Ian Christie has argued,[10] that too could be held against it. In Wajda's *Człowiek z marmuru* (*Man of Marble*, 1976) an archival projectionist derides the apprentice film-maker Agnieszka by suggesting that her diploma film may be an *étude* based on – Cortázar! Gone were the days when 'formalism' posed a threat: by the time of *Man of Marble*, and perhaps by that of Has's film also, many viewed it as a comfortable demonstration of the artist's cultivation of his own garden, well away from the political front-line. If the authorities could not persuade artists to serve the cause directly, they could do so indirectly by demonstrating official tolerance of – even friendliness towards – the arts. That *Man of Marble* archivist might have seen *The Saragossa Manuscript* as safely spiralling away into nothingness. From this perspective, its prestige première at the Palace of Arts and Sciences would have been particularly damning.

3. 'FOR TO END YET AGAIN...': TOTALIZATION,
ENLIGHTENMENT AND MADNESS

If the ending of Has's *Manuscript* is important, it is also because endings often determine the degree to which the foregoing text is susceptible of totalization, with 'art cinema' offering defiantly open endings that encourage the viewer to do as Alphonse is enjoined to do here: 'resztę dopisz sam!': to make their own contribution to the text, select their own ending, or reflect on the grounds of the impossibility of choice. Totalization presupposes just such an overview as traditionally appears at the end of classical texts – the most signal instance being the retelling of the story in finally comprehensible miniature at the end of the detective story. Here, as in the philosophy of Hegel, totalization is anti-individualistic, like Potocki's text, which repeatedly immerses us in the seductive single voice only to then recall, rationalistically, that each voice not only inevitably leads to but *requires* another: that nothing is comprehensible in isolation, that the true, whole story is a constellation of voices. And, Alphonse's educative testing being complete, the Sheik appears at the end like the detective who shows things in their true colours. The single voice, the signifier of mere subjectivity, is deluded, even paranoid, in its limitation; and so, in Has's film, Alphonse does not perceive the winks, knowing glances and back- and off-stage business that may evoke our slight unease – a sense of another story potentially brewing behind and around the ostensible main one – and may seem to betray the final outcome prematurely, as Lipka argues they do[11] (an argument that presupposes a reader's projection of the known novel into the film, for the final outcome is far less clearly apparent to spectators – surely the majority even now – without prior knowledge of Potocki). Thus the spectator's perspective is as limited as that of the reader, who is more often and more patently and closely tied to the single voice in its isolation. Has's film may be far more precisely aligned *in the main* with the Enlightenment than the book that continually alienates the 'I' while reserving the revelation of a safe perspective outside it, beyond the undecidability of the cousins' identity, to the very end, but its final accent explodes all Enlightenment perspectives and, because of the weight usually accorded endings, may be taken as most characteristic of its position. Aleksander Jackiewicz may be over-sanguine in describing the film's dialectical reason as a form of 'good sense' that is 'magnificent precisely because it plays with nonsense, is in love with nonsense, the reason of the human imagination, wise and free'.[12] The unreason that inundates the ending is no silver lining tightly stitched into reason's cloud but profoundly disturbing. Has's totalization is not the Sheikh's reasonable explanation of Alphonse's confusion but a reimmersion in it. The film's final moment offers not explanation but an unstable paradox, combining the work's opposed strands by pairing the uncanny countryside with the classical music associated with the comedy of manners of its Madrid section. In so doing it braids into a single motto the *two films* it contains. For Has's own description of it as twice as long as a normal film[13] corresponds to its status as in effect two films (most Polish critics preferred 'the first',[14] the Romantic evocation of ghosts and the exotic set in the rocky Spanish hills, to the demystifying social comedy of the city). The final return to the uncanny does not so much prevent the film breaking in two as restart the first film, with the circularity of madness.

To speak of 'the ending' is of course to consider more than the last seconds' paradoxical combination of elements from the two halves. After the Sheikh has explained the purpose of Alphonse's adventures another four-and-a-half minutes elapse, during which the following events occur:

Alphonse asks the Sheikh and his cousins who they really are. They tell him to close his eyes, and when he hears his name they will follow. He opens his eyes to find the room empty, a goblet made from a skull in his hands. He picks up an oriental slipper and sees himself walking outside in the desert with the sisters, then returning to stand face to face with himself. As he confronts himself female laughter bursts out on the soundtrack and he finds himself under the gallows again, in the presence of his two pages. One asks if they'll make it before nightfall, and he says that this time they will. He saddles his horse and rides on ahead of them, clutching the book with the manuscript. We then see him in the inn where the manuscript was first found. Wearing an idiotic grin, he repeats what he is writing in it: about how he has long been considered to be lost, how his arrival evoked general joy, and only the Sheikh was displeased on seeing him so weak. On being told that two foreigners staying the night have invited him to sup with them he rises in some consternation, opens the shutters and sees them seated outside, a mirror between them. He places his finger on his lips, returns to the book, then casts it aside. We then see a horseman (doubtless Alphonse) in long-shot riding out with the gallows-topped hill in the background as classical music plays.

This sequence of moments has implications very different from those of Potocki's ending. Potocki shows Alphonse rewarded in various ways: with riches that include a blank letter of credit; by seeing his children at intervals in subsequent years; and, finally, by experiencing the conversion to Christianity of the daughter, who becomes his heiress. Has's return to the beginning, however, suggests a narrative without exit: its crowding enigmas mark the return of the uncanniness repressed by the film's second half, clouding everything, as Alphonse's sole reward is the book that fatalistically pre-records his experiences. If Potocki's novel finally explodes the Romanticism it seems initially to propose, the film sanctions its return, arguably executing a twentieth-century recognition of the collapse of Enlightenment trajectories of progress. Adorno and Horkheimer have described the Enlightenment project as two-edged, a simultaneous removal of fear and disenchantment of the world.[15] Has's apparent banishment of mystery in the film's second half may tactically permit Enlightenment's overextension to the point of dialectical reversal; adaptational fidelity may be the mimicry that becomes mockery. Insofar as Enlightenment agendas privilege number – as Adorno and Horkheimer also note[16] – Has himself may be secretly in league with mathematics, Anne Guérin-Castell having argued that his cutting obeys just such rhythms as Velásquez the mathematician's proposed alogorithms of various human experiences.[17] But insofar as such mathematical patterning insinuates a hidden order, invisible to viewers, it is cabbalistic, numerological, occult and possibly paranoid.

The decision to film Potocki's novel was itself of course often described as a form of madness, utterly Quixotic. Yet there may be particular justifications for its transposition onto film. Potocki's cascading narratives require an ideally continuous, uninterrupted perusal, lest the reader forget whose story is unfolding at any one moment. The narrator establishes his omniscience by establishing our impotence. The single, unbroken flow of images that is the usual form of film reception may be seen as aiding orientation, simulating in miniature an ideal reading situation. Nevertheless, at the same time film's sheer continuousness prevents the textual cross-referencing – the backflips across a few pages – occasionally needed to ascertain just whose story really occupies the now. Potocki's narrators may all *speak*, but his own work is utterly textual. Does film's denial of this facility – to say nothing of the lists of names with which Ian Maclean prefaces his translation, offering us an array of guiding threads – increase the probability of our losing our way? That is certainly what befalls Alphonse, and helps justify the labyrinthine ending. In fact, with its images of book and mirror, that ending is genuinely Borgesian, though in other respects (to which I will return) the film as a whole is not. Apparently vulnerable to criticism as typical of sixties art cinema norms – as merely conventionally ambivalent – the ending may in fact represent the moment at which Potocki's Romanticism remerges as modernism, as the dream in which the sisters said Alphonse could see them overwhelms the ostensibly wakeful mind.

In this context it is intriguing to note the film's resemblance to the work often deemed the first 'art film' worthy of the name (the first to conjugate a theory of narration into questions of isolation, doubling and paranoia): Robert Wiene's *Das Kabinett des Doktor Caligari* (*The Cabinet of Dr Caligari*, 1919). *Caligari* begins of course with a character called Francis narrating a story; a white-smocked woman drifts past as he does so, but the focus on him prevents us drawing any conclusions from her appearance. Only at the end of his tale of an insane asylum doctor who terrorized the nearby town in the guise of a mountebank does the actor who played the doctor reappear, benevolently seeking to help a Francis now revealed as an asylum inmate (the woman in white, his tale's love-interest, being another). Overlooking for a moment the controversial genesis of this ending – an apparent graft onto the original script[18] – the similarities to Has's are patent. Each work concludes as a vortex whose apparent outward spiralling towards others finally spirals inwards: the movement through the labyrinth ends not in liberation and self-knowledge but entrapment. Objections to Has's new ending, such as that of Krzysztof Lipka,[19] overlook the effects of Potocki's combination of a frame narration with chronic epistemological uncertainty. Spectators may accept madness as a plausible outcome, having themselves felt its undertow throughout the narrative. They may see themselves in the Alphonse who laboriously calculated who had been narrating to whom at the point of deepest encryption and concluded 'one could go mad'. Indeed, one may even suspect the secret purpose of the Cabbalist to be the subversion of his sanity: on the way to his castle he remarks that to think of Velásquez's experience might cause madness, then sows the seed of Alphonse's doubt in his own senses by pronouncing non-existent the book he had found in the library. Perhaps significantly, both these elements represent changes to the novel and so help prepare the new *dénouement*.

Adorno and Horkheimer describe the source of fear – that place where Romanticism seeks to rediscover the well-spring of the numinous – as the existence of 'outside'.[20] The first images of the ending show Alphonse going outside, then pulled back inwards to the place where his watching self stands. His gravitation back to the self may be taken as rejecting such key 'outsides' of the work as femininity and other cultures and religions ('the exotic'); their location in a desert carries the undertone of fear that justifies retreat. The self that had seemed capable of transformation – *Bildung*, integration with the Other – places its own change under the signs of loss and madness, reverting to an interior that has shed the innocence of the starting point and become perverse regression. The eternal return of and to primary narcissism conjugates into misogyny, xenophobia, and a self-splitting that may be the logical, alienated conclusion of the film-world's fall into two halves.

If Has's film finally documents a collapse of the Enlightenment project, this may be the merely inevitable concomitant of the transmutation of words – of readerly control of the story-flow's timing and degree of concretion – into images binding us to the time of their spell. The mirror, that final frame within the frame, may hold up the image of cinema itself, the social simulacrum of the dream of a helpless dreamer. For enlightenment has seldom been a cinematic project: mainstream cinema cannot countenance the Brechtian distanciation of late sixties Godardian historical-materialist film, with its theoretical welcome of spectatorial interruption. Potocki may allow his hearers to interrupt the stories with which they are presented – often to ask whether or not the hearer would have been afraid had *he* been in the situation under description ('if you had been Trivulzio, would you have been afraid?'), or simply because the Gypsy chief has been called away by unspecified business – and may even describe the story-book of van Worden senior as open at random, but interventionist readings or temporary shelvings of films are unfeasible (though video-cassettes, with different conditions of reception, may be treated thus). The sound bridges, matches on action and other suturing devices of mainstream narrative film mute the potential disruptiveness of cutting, that fundamental form of filmic interruption. If the audiences of the first silent films legendarily ducked when phantom trains steamed towards them, such fear would be institutionalized in the horror film, that most durable of genres, whose shock effects can fuse with those of modernist art, as they do here. The statement that 'a nobleman need never feel fear' may simply indicate the infrequency with which cinema has taken aristocracy as its target audience (piquantly echoing some early politically motivated reviews, Lipka wonders how Potocki would have viewed his story's movement from limited edition to mass art).[21] Has may make little use of the expressionist visual effects of horror (the most visually evocative moment being perhaps the one at which Pacecho peers through a hole in sack-cloth, the visibility of the single eye underlining its vulnerability rather as the non-painting of Hoichi's ears in Kobayashi's omnibus film of ghost-stories, *Kwaidan* (1964), allows demons to rip them off). Nevertheless, he skilfully deploys specifically filmic means to disturb and disorient, foregrounding skulls, vultures and snakes over human figures in the early scenes, allowing unlocalizable voices to skitter across the soundtrack (Pacecho's story), or using Penderecki's electronic sounds to sow unease. The movement from love to the gallows is abrupt, a shock-cut, while the repeated use of the same set-ups, camera angles and distances for different scenes (e.g. the figure approaching both Alphonse and Pacecho from behind at the inn) economically and instantaneously evokes uncanny circularity. Film's continuousness is more likely to engender claustrophobia and deep-seated fear than the intellectual detachment of a Brechtian theory eager to harness art to pedagogy. Has's ending may be *film's* dream of freedom, of revenge upon the theatrical conventions that had dominated both the rest of the work and a Polish cinema whose actors almost all worked on the stage – until the mid seventies and 'the cinema of moral unrest' saw a change.

4. QUESTIONS OF ADAPTATION

The ending may represent Has and Kwiatkowski's most radical and arresting reconfiguration – even drowning – of Potocki's magic book, but the re-reading in the main body of the film effects also deserves consideration. I intend to do so under several headings, beginning with the all-important question of narration.

'FIDELITY' AND NARRATION

'Fidelity' in adaptations has not always been deemed a prerequisite of their success, regardless of whether they be considered in New Critical isolation, as ideally complex aesthetic objects, or as fulfillments of a contract with the public. As noted earlier, the complexity of Potocki's work, and the concomitant extensive cutting required to adjust it to something like a traditionally 'filmic' length, surely render this a non-issue. As Maria Malatyńska remarks in an eloquent panegyric of the film, 'it would be ludicrous to check the film's fidelity to its novelistic prototype'.[22] But since Has himself describes his work as 'faithful',[23] it is legitimate to ask why, and in what sense. It may, for instance, be so in the sense of retaining the novel's most characteristic structural feature, its multiply framed narration. However many the excisions, Has and Kwiatkowski follow the narration's descent to its most dizzying level, after which the characters (as if coming up for air) comment on this peculiarity of their story-telling situation. The film thus preserves the work's characteristic vertigo and reflexivity and, because 'three things on the go' at one time is this novel's norm, even includes the moment of metaphorical self-reference at which Toledo describes his libertine method of overlapping affairs.

As shaped by Has and Kwiatkowski, the narrative falls into two halves. During the first, which circles and recircles the Venta Quemada, Alphonse tells the hermit about his father and Pacecho recounts his loss of an eye. As in traditional filmic flashback narration, these stories are dramatized, fading from the speaking voice into an apparent reality of events narrating themselves; as the Benveniste-influenced film theorist Christian Metz would put it, *discours* disguises the marks of its own enunciation and masquerades as *histoire*.[24] Finally, the Cabbalist recounts his night at the Venta Quemada, but this – tantalizingly – is not dramatized. The second half is set not in the Gypsy's camp but in the Cabbalist's castle, though the Gypsy chief Avadoro still functions as the main storyteller and guide through the deepening complication of stories. He recounts the stories told to him by Toledo and Lopez Soarez (the latter including the stories Lopez heard from his own father and from Busqueros, as well as the one Frasquetta told Busqueros), followed by the story of Frasquetta's husband, which Busqueros relayed to Toledo in his presence. Since Avadoro primarily mediates others' stories, the only elements of his own still preserved are those linking him to the other storytellers named above. Consequently, his own childhood and loves are deleted.

Potocki's novel may not tell multiple stories simultaneously, but it does evoke a sense of simultaneity by prompting us to try to retain a memory of all levels to preserve our bearings. Has's film does not place simultaneity in the mind's eye but stages it physically in the busy, cluttered *mise-en-scène*, as Mieczysław Jahoda's camera frequently tracks past a densely populated clutch of mini-scenes whose foregrounding prevents their overlooking. And just as the tracking camera emphasizes the range of material and potential stories in the foreground, the depth of field and frequent strong contrasts of foreground and background enact the film-world's extensibility in depth. If the most spectacular instance is the tiny horse on the horizon seen through another horse's legs near the film's end, the most frequent is the erotic dalliance viewed through Lopez Soarez's window (highlighted by its mid-screen positioning) as he and Busqueros sit at table. The totality of Potocki's narrative may lie beyond Has's reach, but he purposively stretches the co-ordinates of his *mise-en-scène* to intimate a potentiality underscored by the widescreen format of traditional epic cornucopia.

In this context, it is worth considering the point in the story at which Has and Kwiatkowski allow us to think it has developed a loose end, begun (understandably) to unravel. As Busqueros lies in bed with Frasquetta, a young man with a bloodied head appears at the window. We may suspect his use by Frasquetta in her plot to make her husband feel haunted. Since the new figure's appearance ought logically to generate another story explaining his arrival, its absence may be taken as indicating the true irrationality of the storytelling situation (the law of 'six degrees of separation' meaning that telling 'the story' would require telling the stories of almost all humankind: 'almost all', of course, for Potocki never reaches the final (*sixth?*) level that would reveal the interconnection of all human tales). For a moment it seems as if the vertiginous nesting of narratives means that the preservation of reason requires one story to flutter away into the abyss, for to attempt to 'grasp everything' would indeed be madness. Twenty minutes later, however, the loose end is recaptured and woven in by Busqueros. But if the text does indeed thereby validate the pursuit of the classical madness of the closed system, may it not thereby generate the actual madness of the new ending, rendering it a critique of the consequences of classical storytelling? Could the brief flapping of the loose end have indicated the existence of a safety valve, an openness to 'outside', and its tying in that valve's closure?

Like so many works of 'epic' length, Has's film falls into halves, though without any formal interval for reel-changing, drinks or cigarettes. Their separation is reinforced, however, by a changed treatment of the stories. Those of the first half, albeit different, all conjugate the same scenario, whose repetitiveness breathes a demonic suspension of temporality: Alphonse, Pacecho and the Cabbalist all experience a night with two women then find themselves under the gallows (the contrast of ecstasy and disillusionment possibly representing two aspects of the experience of hanging, the eros of the former fantastically lining the moment of death). As in Freud's evocation of the uncanniness of walking the labyrinthine streets of a provincial Italian town only to find himself in the same place,[25] the doubling of events destabilizes apparently linear, successive time. The fantastic turns the line round into a magic circle: van Worden's initial intention of following a straight line to Madrid suffers definitive defeat. In the Enlightenment world of progress, repetition and circularity are demonized as the uncanny.

In the work's second half, however, the narrative situation changes. The famous narrative framings become more insistent and complex; their Baroque perspectival extensions acquire an air of comic unbelievability. Has's increasingly frequent momentary cross-cuts between narrator and story as the narrative approaches its deepest level (e.g. between Caspar Soarez and the events of his story) becomes an incredulous, near-neurotic checking and rechecking of the story's moorings (though the returns to Caspar also permit usefully rapid verbal transmission of complex explanatory material). The atmosphere of almost unbearably vertiginous narrative descent is intensified by the relative brevity of the most intricate narrative situations, whose embedding within other narratives requires their definition as more extensive. When Velásquez mentions his ability to name the infinite he articulates this sublime comedy; speaks, in fact, for the Kantian 'mathematical sublime'.[26] Remembering the uncanny of Freud, it is surely significant that Velásquez, by contrast, says walking in an unknown city can return us to the same place *in order to get us where we're going*: circularity need not suspend time disturbingly but can further its progress. Has's version of the story cycle is itself a circle, beginning and ending with stories concerning Alphonse's father.[27] Velásquez's 'gay science' may make him the *porte parole* for Has himself, as Anne Guérin-Castell has argued,[28] and as Jackiewicz's mention of 'wise nonsense' would suggest.[29] So when Alphonse says the nested narratives could drive one mad, his bewilderment is also the merely comic stolidity of the simple soldier. In retrospect, though, viewed from the perspective of its ending, it may anticipate his madness, its comedy being not funny but an idiot's grin. The position of Velásquez may be Has's own, *mise-en-abîme*, but – in a theme to which I will return – it is van Worden who is the contemporary man. And in Has's revised version of Potocki's world, a tale of deep deception for scant reward, the hero goes mad.[30]

JEWISHNESS: A 'STRUCTURING ABSENCE'?

As noted above, the rationale for Has's omissions of Potocki's material is obvious: it sprawls far beyond the scope of even an extended film format. But although omission is so necessary a structuring principle as to cause doubts whether any single one could be deemed significant, one deserves fuller discussion, a potentially controversial candidate for description as a 'structuring absence' by the ideological, symptomatic analysis that has dominated the history of academic film studies. It is the element of Jewishness in general, and of the Wandering Jew in particular.

I will begin with the simpler case of the Wandering Jew. Only one possible cause of his omission is potentially controversial. After all, his inclusion would breach the unity of the work's time-frame, *mise-en-scène* and perhaps even style. Films as widely separated as D. W. Griffith's *Intolerance* (1916) and Martin Scorsese's *Last Temptation of Christ* (1988) founder on the difficulty of plausibly rendering life in the Palestine Jesus knew. Including the Jew would mean building complex and expensive extra sets. Moreover, it would cause an intersection of fabular and historical space, either threatening the integrity of the fantastic or compromising the work's historicity by splicing together the real Jesus and the anti-Semitic legend. The Borgesian allegiances of Has's film do not embrace Borges's fusion of real and imaginary history to tantalize with the *fata Morgana* of a 'secret history'. Moreover, any imagining of Jesus, whose story is integral to that of the Jew, would have been controversial and probably undesirable to – censorable by – the Polish authorities. (Though, paradoxically, in a changed political climate, those authorities, dependent on the clergy to help ensure non-violence in the opposition, may have censored it in the eighties *to remove anti-clericalism*, as Guérin-Castell has argued.)[31]

Consideration of possible official response brings one to the final, most troubling possible reason for the Wandering Jew's excision: a possible general marginalization of Jewishness. Viewers ignorant of Has's other works – particularly his *Hourglass Sanatorium* of 1973 – might suspect this one of having been crafted to downplay it. Their brief for the prosecution might cite the depiction of Rebecca, who never discusses her religion. The casting of Beata Tyszkiewicz may indeed preserve the 'engaging blondeness' Potocki gives her, but the non-reference to her Jewishness (left merely implicit in her name) means that in the film, unlike the novel, her looks do not so much subvert stereotype as dispel all thoughts of ethnicity (as does the widespread Polish public knowledge of Tyszkiewicz's aristocratic descent). Nevertheless, an ancillary accusation of sexism may carry more weight. For if the removal of Rebecca's intellectuality subverts unattractive stereotypes of 'Jewish intellectualism', its replacement with coquetteish charms accentuated by low-cut dresses (only occasionally masked by a Siamese cat) and her repeated facing of the camera is also problematic. The Cabbalist's first words to her, 'make yourself beautiful', are not only *this* film's addition to *this* novel but express the spirit of mainstream film in general, which stages femininity as spectacle. Is it significant that the film omits his first description of her, evocative of her intelligence as well as her beauty? Its retention of reference to the Cabbala meanwhile could be dismissed as serving the exoticism on which epic spectacle feeds, as references to mainstream Judaism vanish. This may be attributed to the film-makers' rationalism (to which I will return when considering the conception of Alphonse), to a secularism welcomed by the Communist authorities, and/or to a desire to insulate the film from a belief-system too closely allied to the Polish Catholic one (the Old Testament having nurtured the New): a desire congruent with Said's analysis of Orientalism. On the other hand it may reflect fear of censorship by a Communist party containing anti-Semitic factions or even – the darkest and most dubious of suspicions – a desire to appeal to a public still sympathetic to anti-Semitism (a mere four years before an anti-Semitic campaign would sweep Poland, as the Party leadership followed the bandwaggon of one of its own factions). May Has and Kwiatkowski perhaps have deemed it better, at whatever level of consciousness, to censor themselves and retain control of their work than have it censored by others and lose it? (The partial censorship of their work at the time, discussed by Guérin-Castell, could otherwise have been far more extensive.) Such suspicions, however unwarranted, are hard to dispel, recorded statements of intent from the period being either cryptic or non-existent, and statements issued after 1989 open to criticism as opportunistic or too late for certain accuracy. One thing is certain, however: Has and Kwiatkowski cannot reasonably be accused of anti-Semitism. The valorization of Jewish culture in Has's other films is patent and has been documented by Guérin-Castell.[32] Indeed, upon completing the *Manuscript* he would declare his next project to be *The Hourglass Sanatorium*, based on the stories of the Kafkaesque inter-war Jewish writer Bruno Schulz. This project encountered much official resistance, culminating in a ten-year inability to make any films. Might it not have sought to restore, in a separate work, the Jewish elements excised from the earlier one? Might they have been excised from the *Manuscript* simply in order to render the later work possible, the omission being merely the prelude to their highlighting? Might Jewishness have simply been *set aside* for fuller later treatment? Or could it be that it was only the ferocious anti-Semitic campaign of 1968 that caused Has fully to grasp the possible implications of innocent excisions and take a stand upon the defence of Jewishness? If there is no better evidence of a commitment to Jewish culture than the price Has paid after filming Schulz's work, philosemitism may mark the *Manuscript* itself: the Wandering Jew may have been excised precisely because he sustains anti-Semitic legend.

A CONTEMPORARY DREAMBOOK?

The idea of 'the contemporary' haunts Polish cinema between October 1956, which marked the definitive end of the period of the country's darkest Stalinization by installing Władysław Gomułka as Party First Secretary, and 1976, when Andrzej Wajda's *Man of Marble* defiantly utilized the leeway offered by an unusually liberal Minister of Culture and launched 'the Cinema of Moral Anxiety', a multi-pronged cinematic lancing of official corruption. The idea of 'the contemporary' becomes a focal point in wider Polish debate, a Bakhtinian 'word in dispute', its importance underlined by its furnishing the title of a periodical, *Współczesność*. The changes in cultural policy associated with 'October' (1956) prompted attempts bluntly to interrogate contemporary Polish reality, jettisoning socialist realist schemata. The imperative to do justice to the present was complicated however by the one to confront the past, and in particular to provide truthful images of the fate of the Home Army (AK), the main Polish wartime resistance organization, whose members had languished and died in Polish jails, and been pilloried in Stalinist propaganda, between 1947 and 1953. Which should receive justice first – the present or the recent past? The ideally cunning solution was perhaps that of Wajda's *Ashes and Diamonds*, set in 1945 but deploying the anachronistically bejeaned existential hero of the late fifties, played by Zbigniew Cybulski, forging what Polish film critic Zygmunt Kałużyński termed a 'synthetic' portrait of post-war youth. (Has's film may deliberately evoke Wajda's by beginning in similar manner, with Cybulski prone on the grass.)

At the same time, though, the fact that the early sixties demand for 'the contemporary' echoed fashionable Western, *Nouvelle Vague* desiderata increased the authorities' desire to appropriate it to their own ends. Seeking justice both for Has and for literary adaptation in general, Guérin-Castell argues that adaptation may have troubled the authorities more than contemporary screenplays, which were easier to control[33]. Nevertheless, although certain moments in the Polish classical literary canon could be staged as implicit criticism of the régime, that régime supported such works and barely resented allusive pinpricks; indeed, 'liberal' Party factions could argue that these provided safety valves for critique, legitimated the Party's own authority by demonstrating a certain tolerance of (limited) opposition, and even allowed it to flatter itself on its ability privately to thumb its nose at its Soviet paymasters. It is also worth noting the obstacles to the filming of literary works that were canonic but thematized communism and revolution, such as Stefan Żeromski's *Pre-Spring*, whose screenplay by Wajda was vetoed. Ignoring the disputed status of 'contemporaneity', Guérin-Castell cannot explain why the most vigorously repressed Polish films of the sixties were precisely the most explosively contemporary ones: those associated with Jerzy Skolimowski, who either scripted, co-scripted or filmed them (e.g. *Nóż w wodzie* (*Knife in the Water*, 1962), directed by Roman Polanski; *Niewinne czarodzieje* (*Innocent Sorcerers*, 1960), directed by Wajda; and

Ręce do góry! (*Hands Up!*, 1967), directed by himself). Such films may have been 'political' – one element in the formula for contemporaneity the régime sought to persuade Has to adopt – but they hardly furnished the other ingredient he mentions: that of 'serving the authorities'.[34] Ironically, Has's *Manuscript* both helped meet and profited from the late sixties official demand for spectacular works commissioned with the age-old aim of providing circuses during bread-shortages. It is worth noting that he himself described the *Manuscript* as a second-choice work, his preference having been for a contemporary one![35] But could that not render it akin to *Ashes and Diamonds*, also a second-choice after official rejection of contemporary scripts, and may it not also richly secrete *a contemporary film* behind apparent escapism at both high (surrealistic) and low (historical romance) cultural levels?

Has's *Manuscript* is of course no cloak-and-dagger film, as Zbigniew Cybulski would stress – and not just because he sat uneasily on a horse. But is it 'contemporary', perhaps even the 'realistic' film Has declared he wanted to make?[36] In what way is the Poland of 1964, the site of recent devastating official criticism of *Knife in the Water* and *Innocent Sorcerers*, both about contemporary youth, present in the *Manuscript*, if at all?

Writing before the fall of the Communist state in 1989, and hence in a coded idiom, Andrzej Werner describes Has's vision of 'culture as a cemetery of props – nothing more' as embracing also the present.[37] This play with cultural masks resembles and may descend from surrealism, where everything can be cut up simply because it is dead, but a coded critique of the present is discernible in Has's description of Potocki's novel as 'a painful comedy, showing what lies concealed behind lyrical and poetic matters: a highly differentiated, complicated world'.[38] His statement that 'the contemporary world is also full of contradictions' may not have endeared him to Marxists bent on defining contradiction as characterizing capitalism alone. 'External forms have changed', he adds, 'but the methods of struggle – baseness and stupidity – still exist'.[39] To apply this to the *Manuscript* is to see Alphonse as cheated and finally driven insane by higher authority. His comic manipulation leaves a blackly bitter residue. Has does not spell out this reading of Alphonse's story, which runs deeper than Cybulski's own description of him as a 'contemporary man' with a quasi-eighteenth-century rationalism and 'more appetite for a real chicken leg than the unreal charms of the girls'.[40] Cybulski's version of 'contemporary man' of course hardly threatens the self-vauntingly 'scientific' Marxist excoriation of superstition-riddled pasts. What Cybulski terms 'van Worden's ironic relationship with the world of magic'[41] is 'contemporary' in the double sense of 'disenchanted'. But Alphonse's changed final relationship with magic dissolves all ironic distance. The new ending submerges him in the spell of an undivine comedy that is, as Has puts it, *painful*. And the joke surely lacerates the Polish cultural authorities also: the historiography of the Enlightenment, that officially cherished ancestor of 'real socialism', founders. The *contemporaneity* of the *Manuscript* invokes the recurrent Polish fate of an entrapment whose sole exit is madness: in the title of Has's next film, a world of *Ciphers*. And yet the film's ending is dialectical, sustaining the dream of escape, as surrealism becomes the true modern realism, literary adaptation the mere cocoon of an independent work. The ending may leave Alphonse trapped but it covers the escape of the viewer – and of Wojciech Has.

NOTES

Many thanks to Lisa DiBartolomeo and Ela Dziekońska for helpful provision of Has material.

1 Krzysztof Lipka, 'Miedzy epiką, retoryką i poezją', *Kwartalnik filmowy* 17 (77) (Spring 1997), 106–18.

2 See for example Jan Alfred Szczepański, 'Mniej bywa czasem więcej', *Film* 846 (1965), 4–5 and Aleksander Jackiewicz, 'Has w hiszpanskim kostiumie', in Jackiewicz, *Moja filmoteka: kino polskie* (Warsaw: Wydawnictwa artystyczne i filmowe, 1983), pp. 154–6.

3 For a reading of the failed attempt to engage this actor, and Cybulski's recruitment after an abortive first day's shoot, see Anne Guérin-Castell, 'La place de *Manuscrit trouvé à Sargosse* dans l'œuvre cinématographique de Wojciech Jerzy Has' dissertation, Université de Paris VIII (1998), p. 372. Guérin-Castell describes the actor as not really French and his recommendation as in all probability a sabotage attempt emanating from the circle of Wanda Jakubowska.

4 For the most sophisticated and useful recent meditation on the typology of adaptation, see Brian McFarlane, *Novel to Film: an Introduction to the Theory of Adaptation* (Oxford: Clarendon Press, 1996), pp. 3–30. The seminal text for this field of course remains George Bluestone's *Novels into Film* (Berkeley and Los Angeles: University of California Press, 1957).

5 Guérin-Castell describes Has's adaptation as 'surfidèle' (Guérin-Castell, 'La place de *Manuscrit*', pp. 462–3), without considering the degree to which the new ending transforms the work.

6 One (extreme) example would be Rainer Werner Fassbinder's fifteen-hour version of Alfred Döblin's *Berlin Alexanderplatz*. For an account of its all-night showing, with spectators arming themselves with thermos flasks and drifting in and out of

slumber, see Karsten Witte, *Im Kino: Texte vom Sehen und Hören* (Frankfurt am Main: Fischer, 1985), pp. 159–61. It is worth noting in this context that before Has began filming, Jerzy Bossak had proposed a four-hour version. (Wojciech Has in conversation with Jan Słodowski and Tadeusz Wijata, 'Projekty nie do zrealizowania' in Słodowski, *Rupieciarnia marzeń* (Warsaw: Skorpion, 1994, p. 11).) Has himself later proposed a twenty-part version to Polish television, whose counter-proposal was a twelve-part one. Nothing came of this because Has finally deemed the work ill-suited to television, where it would 'disintegrate into many independent stories whose various climates and styles would hinder their dramaturgical linkage through the figure of the main hero' (Leszek Bajer, 'Dlaczego Pan milczy?: rozmowa z Wojciechem Hasem', *Kino* 16:4 (April 1981), 5.)

7 Tadeuz Sobolewski, 'Wybieraj nieosiągalne', *Kino* 23:7 (July 1989), 1–5. Jan Alfred Szczepański, however, advocated even stricter abbreviation and criticized Has for following Kwiatkowski's script too closely (Szczepański,'Mniej bywa czasem wiecej'), his title (and argument) being 'less is more'.

8 See his paper on 'The Western Reception of Has's *Saragossa Manuscript*', elsewhere in this volume.

9 The mixed feelings are succinctly documented in the extracts from reviews assembled in the *Historia kina polskiego*, vol. 5, ed., Rafał Marszałek et al. (Warsaw: Wydawnictwa artystyczne i filmowe, 1985), pp. 230–1. Perhaps the most interesting example of mixed feelings is found in the film's second review by Zygmunt Kałużyński. Guérin-Castell usefully notes the disparity between the enthusiastic one he published initially and one published after the film's release had allowed the authorities to gauge the public's reaction and note its discernment of political comment in certain scenes (for instance, the parallel between the Inquisition's methods and those of the Polish secret police). The second review criticizes the Quixotic nature of Has's undertaking and stresses that social comment is not central to his agenda. (Guérin-Castell, 'La place de *Manuscrit*', pp. 377–80). One may note the particular cunning of the second comment, whose truth (see note 10 below) lends plausibility to the official strategy of defusing some of the work's elements by highlighting others (rather than allowing the simultaneous response on *multiple* levels solicited by Has).

10 See Christie. It is interesting in this context to note Has distancing himself from the 'cinema of moral unrest' inaugurated by Wajda and criticizing its lack of artistry (Bajer, p. 6).

11 Lipka, pp. 115–6.

12 Jackiewicz, pp. 155–6.

13 Mieczysław Walasek, *Rękopis znaleziony w Saragossie*, *Ekran* 370 (10 May 1964), 9. This being the case, it may be that Guérin-Castell's reading of the motives for the cutting of the film's export copy (Guérin-Castell, 'La place de *Manuscrit* ... ,' pp. 373–4) is excessively conspiratorial. The film's unusual length did indeed complicate its international distribution and invite the fate suffered by many a film of non-standard length. The cutting is surely less an example of censorship or of particular animus against Has (his political allusions being opaque to non-Poles) than of the authorities' philistine thirst to export at all costs.

14 C.f. both Szczepański and Lipka.

15 Max Horkheimer/T. W. Adorno, *Dialektik der Aufklärung: Philosophische Fragmente* (Frankfurt am Main: Fischer, 1971 (1944)), p. 7. The description of Potocki's work as suspended between Enlightenment and Romanticism is of course a topos of Potocki exegesis established by Roger Callois.

16 *Ibid.*, pp. 10 and 26.

17 See Guérin-Castell, 'La place de *Manuscrit*', pp. 190–253.

18 The classic account of the revision is given in Siegfried Kracauer's *From Caligari to Hitler: a Psychological History of the German Film* (Princeton, NJ: Princeton University Press, 1974 (1947)), pp. 61–76. Nevertheless, a typescript of the original screenplay lodged with the Deutsche Kinemathek in Berlin does indeed have a frame, casting doubt on the scriptwriters' claim of its late imposition by the producer, Erich Pommer. See S. S. Prawer, *Caligari's Children: the Film as Tale of Terror* (Oxford: Oxford University Press, 1980), pp. 168–9.

19 Lipka, p. 117.

20 Horkheimer/Adorno, p. 18.

21 Lipka, p. 118.

22 Maria Malatyńska, 'Twórca uwiedziony literaturą', *Kino* XIII, 1 (January 1978), 10.

23 Maria Oleksiewicz, 'O różnych szufladkach "Saragossy" – z Wojciechem Hasem', *Film* 848 (1965), 7.

24 C.f. Christian Metz, 'Story/Discourse: Notes on Two Kinds of Voyeurism', in *Movies and Methods II*, edited by Bill Nichols (Berkeley and Los Angeles: University of California Press, 1984), pp. 543–9.

25 Sigmund Freud, 'The 'Uncanny'', in Freud, *Collected Papers*, vol. IV (London: The Hogarth Press, 1950), pp. 389–90.

26 Immanuel Kant, *Critique of Judgment*, translated by Werner S. Pluhar (Indianapolis/Cambridge: Hackett, 1987), pp. 103–17.

27 C.f. Maxine Hong Kingston, *Tripmaster Monkey: His Fake Book* (London: Picador, 1989), where a character called Charley remarks: 'I saw *The Saragossa Manuscript* for the third time. The flick surprised me with logic. I love logic. I wouldn't have gone four times if I weren't getting intelligence' (p. 103). (Hong Kingston's contribution to the reception of Has's film is an intriguing one, for this character's summary of its plot is spectacularly inaccurate, perhaps intending to evoke the sheer difficulty of grasping it.)

28 Anne Guérin-Castell, 'Sztuka wierności własnej wierności', *Kwartalnik filmowy* 18 (Summer 1997), p. 115 n36.

29 Jackiewicz, p. 156.

30 Walasek, p. 9.

31 See Guérin-Castell, 'La place de *Manuscrit*', pp. 394–9.

32 Guérin-Castell, 'Sztuka wierności', pp. 111–12.

33 *Ibid.*, p. 116 n52.

34 Tadeusz Sobolewski, 'Wybieraj nieosiągalne', p. 2.

35 Walasek, p. 9.

36 *Ibid.*

37 Andrzej Werner, 'Film Fabularny', in *Historia kina polskiego*, vol. 5, 111.

38 Walasek, p. 9. Concealment of referents was of course common in the politically censored art of People's Poland. For Zygmunt Kałużyński – whose reviews tortuously and frustratingly mingle political time-serving and real insight – one

'Catholic' country (Spain) could stand for another, Poland ('Dziwy w filmie polskim!', *Polityka* 6 (1965), 12. And for Guérin-Castell 'La place de *Manuscrit*', pp. 361–70), the work contains two particularly strong political allusions: the parallel between the Inquisition's methods and Stalinism's invitations to 'self-criticism', and the mention of 'Polish and Hungarian vampires' that recalls the two nations' shared history of revolt, particularly their simultaneous protests in 1956.

39 Walasek, p. 9.

40 Quoted in Jerzy Afanasjew, *Okno Zbyszka Cybulskiego* (Łódź: Wydawnictwo łódzkie, 1987 (1970)), p. 250.

41 *Ibid*. In other statements, though, Cybulski advances a more complex conception of van Worden as 'tragic, and yet laughable'. See for instance Elżbieta Smoleń-Wasilewska, 'Dwa dni pod Saragossą', *Film* 813 (1964), 10.

Comparative Criticism 24, pp. 217–237. Cambridge University Press 2002
DOI: 10.1017/S014475640200553X Printed in the United Kingdom

A garden of forking paths: the Western reception of Has's *Saragossa Manuscript*

IAN CHRISTIE

Being chronically unseen and rumoured about suits it beautifully.

Michael Atkinson[1]

That Wojciech Has's *Saragossa Manuscript* (*Rekopis znaleziony w Saragossie*, 1964) has had a chequered career in distribution is undeniable. Its recent restoration thanks to a legacy from a dead rock star is only the latest twist in a truly Potockian saga. But apart from the poetic aptness of the film's uncertain fate paralleling that of its source, is there more to be gained from exploring its initial reception? I shall argue here that the intense climate of excitement and competition surrounding 'new' international cinema in 1966–67 was highly significant, providing unusual opportunities for this eccentric work to circulate more widely than might have been expected, but also posing problems of classification and interpretation. Comparison of its very different reception in Britain, France and the United States will also reveal something of the complexity of cinema culture at that time – a time before the concept of 'art cinema' began to be used to designate an elite category – and indeed before cinema became subject to academic study.

What can be learned from sampling this record is a more general lesson still inadequately recognized in cinema history. Although films can and do circulate internationally with much greater freedom than books or any other cultural artefact, the factors which give them any lasting presence in a specific national culture are complex and fragile. The route that led from festival screening to independent local distributor to specialist cinema release had only been established for little more than a decade by 1966, and would soon be subject to new pressures and alternatives. Criticism was also changing, with a generation of reviewers formed in the 1930s giving way to younger and more partisan writers, who could air their views in a wider range of publications and help foster passionate cults. Above all, by the mid 1960s cinema had returned to a position it achieved briefly in the 1920s, becoming a cultural sphere in its own right, related to yet distinct from traditional literary of 'high' culture. To be abreast of international cinema in this era, as a critic or viewer, was to have one's finger uniquely on the pulse of contemporary culture. But in an era before home-video, it was a 'virtual' culture of attendance, memory and citation, supported only by occasional magazine articles.

I

An important part of that culture, inescapable if often invisible, was the Cold War. In the decade following the Second World War, cinema everywhere found itself increasingly embroiled in the propaganda struggle between East and West. The visible component was a stream of explicitly propagandist films which had started in the late 1940s and would continue into the 1960s. Those emanating from the Soviet Union and its allies were assumed to be state-sponsored, while Western films with propaganda intent were officially private commercial ventures. In fact, as historians are continuing to discover, a variety of covert incentives and controls operated across the democracies in order to maximize anti-communist initiatives and minimize incoming 'socialist' propaganda.[2] Similarly, it has become clear that production in the Warsaw Pact states was neither as purposeful nor as co-ordinated as has sometimes been assumed. The relaxation of the Stalinist command system in the late 1950s had led to a cultural 'Thaw' in the USSR and more or less equivalent latitude in the satellite states of Eastern Europe. Film-makers, understandably in view of their medium, took longer than writers to test this new freedom, but by the early 1960s cinema provided the clearest evidence of a new permissiveness and diversity throughout Eastern Europe, with Poland very much in the lead.

This became most visible at the international film festivals which had proliferated during the 1950s: a renascent Soviet cinema scored major successes in Cannes in 1958 with *The Cranes Are Flying* (*Letaiut zhuravli*, 1957, Kalatozov) and in Venice in 1962 with *The Childhood of Ivan* (*Ivanovo detstvo*, Tarkovsky). But Polish cinema made its mark even earlier, when Wajda's *Kanal* was awarded a Special Jury Prize at Cannes in 1957, followed by the FIPRESCI critics' award for his *Ashes and Diamonds* (*Popiol i diament*) at Venice in 1959. Other East European countries would claim their recognition in subsequent years – a

Czechoslovak film took the main prize at Locarno in 1963 and a Hungarian film at Mar del Plata in the same year – as festivals became major arenas of cultural diplomacy, combined with business development. Against the background of political tension caused by such events as the suppression of popular uprisings in Hungary and Poland in 1956 and the Cuban missile crisis of 1962, films from Warsaw Pact countries with 'humanist' rather than overtly political themes had obvious propaganda value – in the same way that Western 'cultural freedom' was covertly promoted in the Cold War propaganda battle.[3] Festivals within the Eastern bloc also provided an opportunity for 'home' audiences to see the newest trends from abroad under controlled conditions. A celebrated example of this was the Moscow festival giving its main award to Fellini's autobiographical fantasy *Eight and a Half* (*Otto e mezzo*) in 1963, a decision which seemed to confirm the *de facto* tolerance of departures from 'socialist realism' by Soviet artists in many fields. However, after Khrushchev's removal from power in the following year, this policy would soon be reversed, with a general campaign against 'indiscipline' and stylistic experimentation in the arts, which included the trial of dissident writers Siniavsky and Daniel and the banning of many films already in production.[4]

By the mid 1960s cinematic diplomacy had become as complex as the political landscape it reflected. Bizarrely, one of the most controversial East European films of this period had no obvious bearing on the present: Tarkovsky's treatment of the life and times of the medieval Russian icon painter Andrei Rublev was begun in the last months of the Khrushchev regime, but ran into a series of criticisms and obstructions when it was completed in late 1966. Requested for Cannes in 1967, and refused by the Soviet authorities, it became 'the most famous [Russian] film *not* released in the Soviet Union',[5] a reputation further enhanced by an apparently 'accidental' screening out of competition in Cannes in 1969, at which it received the critics' prize. The Tarkovsky–*Rublev* affair had become an equivalent to the Pasternak–*Zhivago* scandal of a decade earlier, discussed at the highest levels within the Soviet government and tarnishing not only the image of Soviet cinema but also wider perceptions of the USSR in the era of 'détente'.

However, East European films were not only being seen at festivals, even if these provided an important focus for sales and promotion. By the mid 1960s, they had secured a distinct niche within the Western commercial cinema market and were widely shown in specialist cinemas and the thriving film societies. That this could happen was partly due to a perceived decline of Hollywood's ability to monopolize the global market. Not only were its films too expensive and too erratic in their aim, but they were increasingly felt to be out of touch with the turbulent 'contemporary reality' of the 1960s.[6] Here Polish cinema blazed a trail for others to follow, particularly due to the success of Wajda's war trilogy, with *Ashes and Diamonds* sufficiently well known in Britain to achieve a nomination for Best Film at the British Academy of Film and Television Awards in 1960. Although the specialist distributors who imported such films had often started from a political affiliation, they had also become substantial businesses; and by creating markets for East European films they were able to return invaluable hard currency to the producer-states.[7]

The typical post-war release pattern in most Western countries involved specialist distributors seeing films at festivals, or at special advance trade screenings, then bidding competitively for these, before launching them at first-run metropolitan cinemas. Depending on their success, the films would then go on to play at provincial cinemas and eventually at film societies, often on 16 mm. In Britain, from the early 1960s onwards they might also be sold to television, a trend accelerated by the launch of the BBC's second channel in 1964. Throughout this process, critical reputation was vital: first reactions recorded in festival press reports would be amplified by launch reviews, then the verdicts of specialist publications would be examined by film societies before making their selection. Since distributors and press critics were usually present at the same festivals, verdicts would often be canvassed on the spot, making this a system delicately balanced between risk-taking and cultural validation.

By the time that *The Saragossa Manuscript* made its appearance, a cultural network or system had emerged in many Western countries, one that set considerable store by its contemporaneity and its eclectic internationalism ('have you seen the latest Polish/Russian/Mexican/ French etc. film?'),[8] and that also required a considerable investment of what Pierre Bourdieu has termed educational and cultural 'capital'.[9] A willingness to read subtitles while listening to an unfamiliar language, to attempt pronunciation of the names of figures associated with such films (Wajda, Cybulski, Buñuel, Mizoguchi and the like), to identify films by director rather than star – all these involve competences which, as Bourdieu showed, are more common in the middle, professional and upper classes.[10] Yet it would be misleading to suggest that participation in this system was simply proportionate to the consumption of other 'high' cultural forms. Since cinema was still not taught at any level of formal education, familiarity with 'world cinema' could only be gained from a limited number of books and through membership of a film society or attendance at a repertory cinema. Information about new films and festival 'discoveries' came largely from specialist magazines. And due to the origins of the specialized or 'foreign' cinema movement in struggles to show Soviet films at a time when they were widely banned, there remained a strong link with socialist politics.[11] Autodidacticism and working-class radicalism were still more associated with an interest in foreign cinema than with other traditional cultural practices. Yet the potential audience was also large: numerically much larger than for any other contemporary art form, or for work in other media from foreign-language cultures. An influential British critic, pondering whether the leading directors had created this new audience or whether the audience had encouraged the filmmakers, wrote in 1963:

The fact is that audience and films are there; and even a phrase like minority cinema takes on a new meaning when the BBC transmits films such as De Sica's *Bicycle Thieves* or Andrzej Wajda's trilogy of wartime Poland to audiences of seven or eight million.[12]

II

By the early 1960s, Western art cinema and film society audiences had become familiar with Polish irony, celebrated in Wajda's trilogy, in Andrzej Munk's *Eroica* and in the 'new wave' films by younger directors such as Roman Polanski and Jerzy Skolimowski. Serge Daney would refer to this as 'a Polish constant' in his 1967 review of *The Saragossa Manuscript*.[13] They also appreciated the aesthetic shift from a vaguely socialist neo-realism, even if this had rarely been rigid, towards an increasingly dramatic expressionism and even modernism, which kept pace with the other great 'foreign film' cult of the period: Ingmar Bergman's probing of the Protestant conscience in such films as *The Seventh Seal* (*Det sjunde inseglet*, 1956) and *Wild Strawberries* (*Smultronstället*, 1957). And just as Bergman's regular actors gained stature from their association with his work, so Wajda's trilogy launched the Ukrainian-born Zbigniew Cybulski as the first Eastern European 'star' to gain an international reputation. Like his near-contemporary James Dean, who became a cult after his tragically early death in 1965, Cybulski seemed to embody a distinctively modern form of hero – narcissistic as well as rebellious – and his spectacularly choreographed death scene at the end of *Ashes and Diamonds* became a familiar icon for the international specialist film audience.[14] Cybulski's presence in *The Saragossa Manuscript* would provide an important point of contact for international audiences, as well as a diversification in the actor's repertoire.

Although Polish cinema had made an early mark abroad, by the beginning of the 1960s there was intense competition, not only from the French *nouvelle vague* but from similar 'new cinema' movements around the world. Poland would also participate in this trend with Polanski's *Knife in the Water* (*Noz w wodzie*, 1962) and Skolimowski's *Rysopsis* (1964), and with Wajda's own 'new wave' film *Innocent Sorcerers* (*Nie winni czaro dzieje*, 1960) and his contribution to the international 'portmanteau' *Love at Twenty* (1962), both starring Cybulski. Polish cinema, at least to some foreign eyes, was moving away from any lingering Cold War basis and successfully adapting to new trends and expectations, as Penelope Houston noted in her 1963 survey:

What gives films like Wajda's *Innocent Sorcerors* or Polanski's *Knife in the Water* their exemplary value [is that] they make contact, spark across the East-West frontier. They have absolutely nothing to do with the positive or the progressive; their standards are their own, their approach to life cool, sardonic and apprehensive.[15]

Export success also made feasible more expensive and exotic departures from Polish cinema's staple themes. The first of these was the veteran Alexander Ford's conventional but impressive *Knights of the Teutonic Order* (*Krzyzacy*, 1960). This was followed by Jerzy Kawalerowicz's more challenging account of the seventeenth-century case of mass hysteria in a convent, *Mother Joan of the Angels* (*Matka Joanna od aniolow*, 1961), which Aldous Huxley had popularized in *The Devils of Loudun* and Ken Russell would film, more controversially, in 1970.[16] *The Saragossa Manuscript*, starring Cybulski in his first costume role, appeared to be in a similar vein, bringing modern concerns to bear on a period subject. *Mother Joan*, however, benefited from the prestige of Huxley's study, and its association with the Salem witch trials which Arthur Miller had used as the basis for his powerful allegory of political persecution *The Crucible* (1953). But *The Saragossa Manuscript* had no such known pedigree, and its evidently playful self-reference may well have reminded many reviewers and audiences of the recent John Osborne–Tony Richardson burlesque of *Tom Jones* (1963), which had been a popular, rather than a critical, success.

'Polishness' was understandably less the perceived defining feature of Has's film than its picaresque narrative with supernatural trappings. In this respect, *The Saragossa Manuscript* fitted more closely within an international art cinema trend which had suddenly returned to prominence in the mid 1960s: the multi-episode or 'portmanteau' film. There were precedents, such as the early German trio of horrific tales *Waxworks* (*Das Wachsfigurenkabinett*, 1924, Paul Leni) and the Ealing ghost story compendium *Dead of Night* (1945, Robert Hamer et al.); and later Powell and Pressburger's *Tales of Hoffman* (1951), and Max Ophuls's two anthologies of linked tales by a single author: *La Ronde* (1950) drawn from Schnitzler and *Le Plaisir* (1952) based on Maupassant. But it was in 1962 that the transnational 'portmanteau' film emerged as a full-blown fashion, with Italy as its epicentre. Wajda and Cybulski contributed the 'Warsaw' segment to *Love at Twenty* (1962), co-produced between France, Italy, Germany, Poland and Japan. In the same year, *Rogopag* consisted of short fictions by Roberto Rossellini, Jean-Luc Godard, Pier Paolo Pasolini and Ugo Gregoretti; while *Boccaccio '70* (1962) brought together Fellini, Visconti, Monicelli and De Sica for an updating of four of Boccaccio's tales concerning the battle of the sexes.[17] Following the release of *The Saragossa Manuscript*, *Histoires extraordinaires* (1968) had two French directors, Roger Vadim and Louis Malle, and Fellini, each of whom contributes an adaptation of an Edgar Allan Poe story. Whether or not precisely because of these reminders, the *Decameron* and the *Arabian Nights* became common reference points in early reviews of Has's film, as indeed they had been for the original readers of the novel.[18] Similarly, the Gothic novel was mentioned by a number of reviewers, recalling the importance this genre had had for Potocki.[19]

Equally significant, however, for the film's mid 1960s reputation was the recent discovery of Jorge Luis Borges, following the award of the Prix Formentor in 1961.[20] Even if only a few contemporary reviews explicitly invoked the Argentinian essayist and contriver of ingenious 'fictions', there is good reason to believe that the film's reception was influenced by awareness of his distinctive concerns. Borges's encyclopaedic interests in world literature promoted a significant broadening of interest in the curiosities and continuities of literature, from ancient Greece and China, to classical Arabic and neglected medieval writers, alongside Romantics and unfashionable Edwardians. In the context of the eccentrics, both real and imagined, that Borges celebrates, Potocki and his novel are hardly strange. And among the earliest motifs to be considered 'Borgesian' were the story within a story and the imbrication of fiction and reality, in such stories as 'The Garden of Forking Paths', 'Death and the Compass' and 'Theme of the Traitor

Sixties-style poster for the 1997 reissue of *The Saragossa Manuscript*, 'presented
by Martin Scorsese and Francis Ford Coppola, in dedication to Jerry Garcia'

and the Hero'. Moreover, there is an important link between the
discovery of Borges and the emergence of the French *nouveau roman*
group, and the entry of both as a modernizing movement in cinema.

Borges was substantially translated into French in the early 1950s and
greeted enthusiastically by the future spokesman of the *nouveau roman*
group, Alain Robbe-Grillet.[21] Throughout the following twenty years,
awareness of and access to Borges increased rapidly, with English
translations first appearing in 1962,[22] and his influence beginning to be
discernible in cinema, in such films as *Performance* (1967–9, by Nicolas
Roeg and Donald Cammell) and *The Spider's Stratagem* (1970, by
Bernardo Bertolucci).

Meanwhile, his essays, both speculative and fictive, seemed to
anticipate ideas of 'textuality' even before the theoretical work of the
nouveaux romanciers, the journal *Tel Quel*, and Roland Barthes became
widely known. One product of this primarily literary avant-grade,

All is finally revealed to van Worden in the Cabbalistic book that doubles the
Manuscript in Has's film

however, did circulate widely and acquire its own
notoriety – underlining the extent to which cinema was now, to some
extent, in partnership with literature.[23] *Last Year at Marienbad*
(*L'Année dernière à Marienbad*, 1961), directed by Alain Resnais from
a script by Robbe-Grillet, dramatized the idea of a narrative without
external reference: a closed world in which characters' claims about past
encounters and relationships are contradictory yet unresolvable, since
the text offers no 'truthful' level of resolution. Another important
feature of *Marienbad* was its extensive use of *mise en abyme*, or reflexive
citation.[24] Examples of this trope in other media would be the character
in André Gide's *Les Faux-monnayeurs* (*The Counterfeiters*, 1925) who is
writing a novel similar to the one in which he appears, or the inclusion
of a figure in Velázquez's painting *Las meninas* which can be identified
as the artist himself, looking both at his sitters and at us, his viewers.[25]
In *Marienbad*, the famous 'match game' and the play which the
characters watch serve as figures of self-reference, underlining the sense
of a larger puzzle and the systematic uncertainty about what is illusory
or real. As filmed, *The Saragossa Manuscript* appears to use occult
symbols in similar fashion, to point to 'mysteries' which may or may not
be soluble. The English critic, Chris Auty, in addition to invoking
Borges, adopted this as the key to his reading of the film:

But the film's real (and secret) subject is the Gothic imagery of the Tarot and Cabbalistic traditions: multiple storyline, trains of resemblance, mysterious icons of Fate and Death.[26]

As we shall see, the mingled shadows of the 'new picaresque', the *nouveau roman* and a renewed interest in narrativity and reflexivity, as well as in the occult and the psychedelic, would all fall across the reception of *The Saragossa Manuscript* – ensuring a lively, if sometimes incoherent and uncomplimentary, response.

III

The Saragossa Manuscript made its international debut at the Cannes Festival in May 1965, not in the main competition, but in the *Semaine de la critique*, which was then the festival's only alternative selection.[27] According to Robert Benayoun, writing in *Positif*, the festival director, Robert Favre Le Bret, had refused 'this extraordinary film, certainly the best to be seen in Cannes', in favour of an academic work by Alexander Ford (*The First Day of Freedom*).[28] Benayoun, one of the leading Surrealist critics, continues with a eulogy which stresses how the film has tackled the novel's unusual construction and tone:

Potocki's superb novel has a crazy construction of episodes which multiply to infinity. Has has drawn from this a film that is truly picaresque, fantastic and pagan, with a fine sense of humour and making use of practically all the Polish stars [...] especially a Cybulski who is both subtle and truculent.

Assuming some familiarity of the novel as published by Gallimard, he goes on to indicate that the second part of the film draws on the 'Madrid stories' later discovered in Poland and used to 'diabolical' effect by the scriptwriter Tadeusz Kwiatkowsky. On the basis of this textual familiarity, Benayoun suggests that the combination of Kwiatkowsky's 'cheerful' humour with Potocki's 'cold and distant' tone produces sparks of intelligence. But clearly there was already talk among distributors about the desirability of shortening the film; and Benayoun ends with a mock-Gothic curse:

To the distributors who have already announced their intention of mutilating this masterpiece by a third, I cry: Beware! The Inn of Venta Quemada has not yet cast its last spell, and will send its vengeful ghosts ...

A difference of outlook between *Positif*, largely run by left-leaning Surrealist sympathizers, and its rival *Les Cahiers du cinéma*, originally inspired by the realist aesthetic of André Bazin, although increasingly eclectic in its enthusiasms and veering to the left, was inevitable at this time. In fact, *Cahiers* had published a special issue in December 1966 on 'Problems of cinematic and novelistic narrative', guest-edited by Claude Ollier and with contributions by many of the *Tel Quel* group. The review of *Saragossa Manuscript* by a rising young critic, Serge Daney, appeared in February 1967, and began with an epigraph from Borges on one of his familiar themes: only death gives meaning and pathos to human actions, whereas immortality implies the 'vertigo' of infinite repetition.[29] Daney deals briskly and somewhat dismissively with the trappings of the narrative – 'stories imbricated within each other, "paramnesia", eternal returns, gardens with forking paths, eroticism, etc'. The effect, he suggests, is at first striking and then boring, 'even if this boredom is accompanied by a certain fascination and facile mental pleasure'. He proceeds to analyse the film's failure under three headings. First, it maintains an even distance from its material, 'an elegant and ironic detachment'. Secondly, it falls into the trap of literalism, of portraying repetition and gratuitousness by being repetitive and gratuitous. And finally, applying Borges's maxim, where there are no limits, no mortality, there is no significance, no life and no art. The universe of Has's film, Daney concludes, has become like the 'experimental' reality of an Isaac Asimov story, in which the Manipulators of Time can make anything happen to humans as often as they wish, so that 'man's choice means nothing and his art little more (cf. W. J. Has)'.

This is typical *Cahiers* polemical criticism of the time, based on issues of 'principle' which the film is deemed to mishandle, and ultimately on the auteurist judgement that Has is an 'artificial and no doubt minor' director. Had he succumbed to the 'vertigo' implicit in Potocki's seeming infinite regress of stories, or had his irony been sharpened beyond the Polish norm, the failure might have been qualified; but for Daney, it is clear than 'any film about pointlessness must be serious and rigorous', and he cites as an example of this Alain Resnais's recent *The War Is Over* (*La Guerre est finie*, 1966), about the frustration of a Spanish exile working in France for Franco's overthrow.

For *Positif* and *Cahiers* to disagree was hardly unusual in the partisan world of French cultural criticism: indeed the former's endorsement may have helped ensure the latter's dismissal. Nor can these be regarded as typical of the spectrum of French response to the film. An illustrated feature from the time of the film's release speaks of its uniqueness in the history of cinema and as one of the most striking of all Polish films,[30] while a *Positif* report on Has's subsequent film, *Codes* (*Szyfry*, 1967), qualifies the earlier verdict on *Saragossa Manuscript*, describing it as an 'uneven though often happy illustration of Potocki'.[31] Clearly French responses were uniquely affected by a degree of awareness of the original novel, so that the film was considered to some extent as an adaptation, rather than an autonomous fantasy. Equally, underlying the polarized *Positif* and *Cahiers* verdicts are vestiges of, on the one hand, a traditional Surrealist-socialist *politique* in favour of Polish and East European work, and on the other, a renewed effort to define *Cahiers*'s aims in terms of commitment to 'new cinema', as well as a desire to engage with the new literary and critical theory emerging from *Tel Quel*.[32] At this moment in France, on the edge of the politico-cultural revolution of 1968, Has's film was entering an ideologically overdetermined space; and to find what was probably the majority verdict among French *cinéphiles* of the 1960s we have to turn to a less partisan source. Roger Boussinot published the first edition of his popular encyclopedia in 1967, and in this now-standard reference work, *The Saragossa Manuscript* is characterized as 'rich in colour, and full of good humour and optimism'.[33]

IV

The Saragossa Manuscript made its debut in Britain in a context that was also undergoing change, although less dramatically than in France or the United States. It played first at the Edinburgh Film Festival, in August 1965, where it created a stir in this hitherto staid event, previously much concerned with short films and documentaries, but also having a tradition of presenting East European work. Chosen as the provocative opening film, Has's film found the conservative *Daily Telegraph* critic, Eric Shorter, receptive to a departure from 'the beaten Polish track, sweeping us back to a vivid, swashbuckling Spain with devilish black comedy and Arabian nights fantasy'.[34] After appearing later that year in the newly launched London Film Festival, and apparently attracting little attention, it was acquired by Contemporary Films, a company with strong socialist and East European connections, as part of its growing commitment to 'progressive' world cinema.

Contemporary Films had an interest in the Paris Pullman Cinema, where the film opened in December 1966 to reviews which ranged from amused to dismissive. Perhaps surprisingly, the critic of the Communist Party's *Morning Star* was most hostile to its 'strange and gruesome fantasy', and despite its 'weird fascination' found Has's 'nodding and winking style of humour unbearably arch'.[35] However, aside from temperamental differences, this recalls a familiar Cold War pattern in which traditional Western socialists (especially those who had remained Communist Party members after 1956) were suspicious of the new styles and themes appearing in Eastern Europe, while apolitical or anti-communist critics were often keen to welcome signs of 'deviation' from the norms of socialist realism. Elsewhere, British newspaper reviewers' phrases ranged from 'persuasive' and 'engaging' to 'nutty' and, despite the cuts, 'overlong'. The British Film Institute's two journals were scarcely more encouraging. *Sight and Sound* gave it two stars, but only as a 'shaggy dog story', while the *Monthly Film Bulletin*, widely read by film societies, found it 'difficult to take very seriously'. Amid rising interest in, especially, Skolimowski and Godard, it fell short of both the moral seriousness associated with Polish film-making and the overt modernism of Godard, Resnais and Antonioni.

One review, however, did take the film more seriously, measuring it against relevant benchmarks. Writing in *Films and Filming*, a journal that managed to be both more populist and more eclectic than *Sight and Sound*, Raymond Durgnat invoked *Last Year at Marienbad*:

From one angle, the film may seem to be posing the *Marienbad* question, 'What is dream? What is reality?' But I suspect that [its] implications go the other way. Our hero is last seen running crazily towards two far-distant figures who may be the succulent girls but may also be the gruesome corpses.[36]

He then quotes from the film's original narration: 'People who allow themselves to be haunted by daydreams, by superstition, by religion, by honour, lose sight of reality and waste their lives in a futile delirium.'[37] Working within a Cold War paradigm, he concludes that the film 'is clearly a Marxist denunciation of religions as "the opium of the people", while the harping on devils is of course a way of sniping at Christianity as superstition'. Durgnat also speculates, within this honest and responsive review, that it offers a critique of the Polish cult of honour, and that its 'stress on horror and the erotic suggests another streak of satire, at the expense of the horror films which have been so conspicuous in Western film-fare of late'. His main thrust, however, is to identify the film's Surrealist aspect:

Though I found the second half patchy, the last twist has a derisory-tragic quality that's not at all unworthy of Buñuel, who is, in a sense, the film's spiritual godfather ... The key moments of horror and eroticism are fully effective, and I can't help thinking that if the film had caught more of the genuine fascination of the dreamworld, it could have made its criticisms even more disturbingly.

Durgnat was at that time one of the leading critics in Britain who professed a strong interest in Surrealism, with books on both of the leading surrealist film-makers, Luis Buñuel and Georges Franju, appearing in the same year as this review.[38] The terms of his praise for *The Saragossa Manuscript* chime with a typical Surrealist recuperation of works which share a common outlook without necessarily professing allegiance – rather as his account of Buñuel's then most recent film, *Belle de jour* (1966), implied some regret at the film's 'bland, pellucid line', while asserting that 'on reflection, the ellipses, mysteries, oddities, depths are there'.[39]

Durgnat's perception was borne out some years later when Buñuel revealed in his memoirs that, among a small canon of favourites, he 'adored' *The Saragossa Manuscript*, having seen it 'a record-breaking three times and convinced [his producer] to buy it for Mexico in exchange for *Simon of the Desert* (*Simon del desierto*, 1965)'.[40] Although both Buñuel's *The Exterminating Angel* (*El angel exterminador*, 1962) and *Simon* have some features in common with Has's film, in terms of dream-like repetition and 'magical' ellipsis for supernatural effects, it is probably his later film, *The Milky Way* (*La Voie lactée*, 1969), which bears a closer relationship and may even owe some inspiration to the *Manuscript*. This arcane 'road movie', seemingly out of joint with the era of *Easy Rider* (1969, Dennis Hopper), involves two modern tramps on a pilgrimage to Santiago de Compostela who encounter voluble exponents of most of the Christian heresies. The effect of gnostic and other heresies portrayed dramatically is as disconcerting as Has's direct realization of Potocki's tales, and had a similarly mixed response, before Buñuel developed this form of disjunctive picaresque into the structure of his magnificent late films.[41]

Durgnat's review was one of the few extended discussions of the film in Britain. My own recollection is that its minor cult reputation owed much to being spurned by the arbiters of official taste. Awareness of Poland's surrealist legacy was also beginning to spread, encouraged by the discovery of the animators Jan Lenica and Walerian Borowczyk, whose first live-action feature after emigrating to France, *Goto, île d'amour* (1968), would inspire a loyal avant-garde following. The late 1960s careers of Polanski and Skolimowski in emigration would also support this revaluation of Poland, less as a permissive Communist regime (a verdict soon to be savagely disproved) than as an alternative tributary in the broad stream of international Surrealism. Polanski's *Dance of the Vampires* (1967), although deplored by many of his former admirers, together with Skolimowski's *Adventures of Brigadier Gerard* (1970) revealed a taste for burlesque and a reminder of Surrealism's appetite for the exotic and the absurd, especially as these frequently co-existed in popular romance.

Although *The Saragossa Manuscript* quickly disappeared from the written record in Britain, there is fragmentary evidence that it continued to intrigue both old and young. Basil Wright, a veteran of the Grierson documentary movement, wrote in his memoirs published in 1974, that apart from Skolimowski's *Barrier* being 'the most stimulating film to come from Poland since Munk's *Eroica*', 'one should perhaps add Has's enticing phantasmagoria *The Saragossa Manuscript*'.[42] And in a 1994 interview, Sally Potter, originally a dancer and performance artist, now best known for her avant-garde features *Orlando* (1992) and *The Man Who Cried* (2001), recalled among her crucial late 1960s influences:

Around about that time, I was seeing films like *The Saragossa Manuscript* and *Last Year at Marienbad*, which I would have thought of as storytelling films but which were doing extraordinary things with storytelling and with time.[43]

V

The American premiere of *The Saragossa Manuscript* took place at the San Francisco Film Festival of 1966, placing it coincidentally at the heart of the emerging 'counter culture'. Fuelled in equal measure by the liberationist and utopian ideologies of the New Left and by the 'psychedelic revolution' proclaimed by Timothy Leary, this mixture of extravagant style and heavy drug use rapidly reached a global audience through its associated rock music. Before making their *Sergeant Pepper* album in 1967, the Beatles visited San Francisco, where the leading local band was the Grateful Dead, co-founded in 1965 by Jerry Garcia. Through an association with Ken Kesey, the Grateful Dead became integral to his 'Acid Test' events, described as 'LSD served up in a heady brew of amplified rock bands, strobe lights and free-form dance', and remained closely linked with the Haight-Ashbury hippie movement and its subsequent mutations.[44]

It is tempting to assume that Garcia's first encounter with *The Saragossa Manuscript* either took place under the influence of LSD, or strongly recalled the experience – 'turn on, tune in and drop out', in Leary's notorious mantra.[45] However, according to Garcia's friend and

future publisher, Alan Trist, it actually happened when Garcia, his
song-writing partner Robert Hunter and Trist were roaming 'the San
Francisco Bay area ... in search of art and entertainment', and found the
film playing at a cinema in North Beach, on a double-bill with another
exotic East European discovery of the period, Serge Paradjanov's
Shadows of our Forgotten Ancestors (*Teni zabytykh predkov*, 1964).[46]
According to Trist, Garcia and Hunter had already read Potocki's novel,
and Hunter remembers 'how tickled Jerry was with the scene where the
guy keeps moving his bed around so that death can't stand at the foot
of it'. Discovering recently that this scene does not actually appear,
Trist concludes:

it might as well have been there. It's archetypal to the movie, and it perfectly illustrates
the attraction this movie had for Jerry. [...] From the first dialogue – 'Captain, the
enemy is surrounding us. What shall I do?' 'Close the door, you fool, it's drafty ... can't
you see I'm admiring these drawings?' – a perfectly surreal world is created [...] As
story within story unfold and entwine in a potent mythic landscape, other qualities in
our hero – such as honor, courage, wit – are needed to resolve bizarrely cycling
dilemmas [...] Jerry couldn't get enough of this take on life.

Trist's memoir of his late partner's enthusiasm also suggests that
Krzysztof Penderecki's remarkable part-electronic score for the film was
important for Garcia, similar 'in feeling and arrangement with [the]
musical "space" to which Jerry always returned with the Grateful
Dead'.

Five years after its San Francisco debut, according to J. Hoberman,
the film 'attracted a New York hippie following' for late-night showings
at the Elgin, a shabby theatre near Greenwich Village, following that
theatre's remarkable success with Alexandro Jodorowsky's *El topo* (The
Mole, 1971), which played every night at midnight for over six months
in 1971.[47] The context is again significant. Just as *Shadows of Our
Forgotten Ancestors* had introduced a new visual language into Soviet
cinema, steeped in folklore and mysticism, *El topo* was a violent
mystical–absurdist Western, starring its Russian-born director as 'a
character none too subtly identified with Moses, Buddha and Jesus
Christ'.[48] Hoberman and Rosenbaum, chroniclers of the 'midnight
movie' fashion which spread through many cities during the 1970s,
propose a quasi-religious 'cultic' account of this phenomenon, and
quote a contemporary evocation of the Elgin's atmosphere:

It's midnight mass at the Elgin. Cocteau's *Blood of a Poet* (*Le Sang d'un poète*, 1930) has
just ended and the wait for *El topo* is a brief grope for comfort before sinking back into
fantastic stillness. The audience is young. It applauded Cocteau's sanguine dream as

though he were in the theatre, but as credits appear on the screen, it settles again into rapt attention. They've come to see the light – and the screen before them is illuminated by an abstract landscape of desert and sky – and the ritual begins again ... Jodorowsky is here to confess; the young audience is here for communion.[49]

Hoberman and Rosenbaum link *El topo* with 'the prestige of such hippie texts as *The Lord of the Rings*, Robert Heinlein's *Stranger in a Strange Land*, Hermann Hesse's *Steppenwolf* ... and Carlos Castaneda's *The Teachings of Don Juan*'. They also note how the Elgin cinema's success led to other midnight screenings in Manhattan, which included George Romero's neo-realist horror film *Night of the Living Dead* (1969) and the long-suppressed *Freaks* (1932, Tod Browning), and also from abroad Fernando Arrabal's *Viva la muerte* (1969) and the 'tropicalist' Brazilian black comedy *Macunaima* (1969, Joaquim Pedro de Andrade). This, then, was the eclectic context in which *The Saragossa Manuscript* began to acquire its 'underground' reputation.

It was also when the indigenous American avant-garde began to produce a range of dream-like, orgiastic performance pieces, epitomized by Jack Smith's notorious *Flaming Creatures* (1962–3) and Andy Warhol's increasingly ambitious works, culminating in his two-screen *Chelsea Girls* (1966). And, emerging from an earlier phase of avant-garde activity, in 1966 Kenneth Anger re-edited his ritualistic *Inauguration of the Pleasure Dome* (1954), a 'lavishly costumed magic masquerade party inspired by the neopagan rituals of Aleister Crowley', adding 'underworld' footage culled from *Dante's Inferno* (1935) and Janáček's *Glagolitic Mass* as soundtrack.[50] In such a context, Has's film would have looked far from strange, indeed somewhat quaint. Apparently never in full commercial distribution, its reputation faded as Paradjanov's and Tarkovsky's persecution by Soviet authorities attracted attention to their films during the 'second Cold War' of the 1970s and 1980s.

When the film was finally restored, with financial assistance – now posthumous – from Garcia and from Martin Scorsese, and largely thanks to the tenacity of Edith Kramer at the Pacific Film Archive, it played belatedly at the New York Festival 1997 and two years later at specialist venues around the United States.[51] Among the new reviews this occasioned, Hoberman recalled the film's original contribution to the new culture of 'cult cinema'; and Michael Atkinson attempted to place it for a new audience:

Larky, seductive and looking forward to both Lars von Trier and Terry Gilliam, Saragossa musters an utterly unique and antiquated cosmos.[52]

However, not all recent reviews have been as enthusiastic. The Shock Cinema website predicted that it 'will undoubtedly send most viewers screaming for the exits'; while *The Cutting Edge*, reviewing the video release, cautions that 'this distinctly literary exercise is not a film for the uncommitted or casual viewer ... Only the adventurous need apply.' So far, the restored version appears to have attracted no interest outside the United States.

VI

Whatever the circumstances of its production (see article by Anne Guérin-Castell in this volume), Has's *Saragossa Manuscript* reached its Western 'export' audience at the climax of what Arthur Marwick has termed the High Sixties like an unexpected guest at a party, or a series of rather different parties.[53] It arrived in a France gripped by passionate debate about the politics of culture and, like many earlier works (such as Poe's tales), found itself conscripted into a distinctively French scenario, in this case a 'revolution of the text'. In Britain, it provoked mainly bemusement, while helping mark a shift from the early socialist and liberal appreciation of East European films towards a new outlook coloured by the (re)discovery of Surrealism and of Polish modernism, in the work of Jan Kott and Witold Gombrowicz – the latter, appropriately, a longtime resident of Borges's homeland, Argentina. It also contributed to the formation of an emerging generation of British independent filmmakers, including Sally Potter, Peter Greenaway and Derek Jarman, who would all develop forms of labyrinthine and anachronistic narrative.[54] In the United States, it appears to have lived three separate lives: first as part of the West Coast 'summer of love' and its hippie aftermath, and as an ingredient in the eclectic New York 'cult movie' scene; and recently as a 'rediscovered classic' within the thriving archival cinema culture that has been stimulated by video and DVD in the United States.

Tracing its reception, even in outline, may also shed some light on the still-undervalued way in which cinema, since the 1960s, has become a crucial dynamic in contemporary culture: making connections, creating contexts, thrusting novel and exotic works across borders. Like Has's compelling dramatization of Potocki's opening chapter, it invites our absorption and leads us in promiscuous, unforseeable directions.

NOTES

1 Review of *The Saragossa Manuscript*, *Village Voice* (US), 18 February 1997.

2 See Tony Shaw, *British Cinema and the Cold War* (London: I. B. Tauris, 2001) for a recent study of the pervasive impact of the Cold War both on British productions and films entering Britain from Eastern Europe.

3 The revelation that the journal *Encounter* was secretly funded by the Central Intelligence Agency signalled a level of covert cultural activity largely unsuspected until the 1990s. See Frances Stonor Saunders, *Who Paid the Piper? The CIA and the Cultural Cold War* (London, 1999).

4 Siniavsky had led a double literary life, publishing in the USSR under his own name and abroad as 'Abram Tertz', in which role he mocked socialist realism. Many of the daring films that were 'shelved' until their release under *glasnost* in 1986–7 dated from 1965–7, when film-makers were still operating under relative freedom up to the point of final approval before release. See Ian Christie, 'The Cinema', in Julian Graffy and Geoffrey Hosking (eds.), *Culture and the Media in the USSR Today* (London: Macmillan, 1989), pp. 43–77.

5 Vida Johnson and Graham Petrie, *The Films of Andrei Tarkovsky: a Visual Fugue* (Bloomington: Indiana University Press, 1994), p. 81.

6 Ian Cameron, 'Introduction', in Cameron (ed.), *Second Wave* (London: Studio Vista, 1970), p. 5.

7 Both Stanley Forman, founder of Plato Films (later ETV) and Charles Cooper, founder of Contemporary Films, the distributor of *The Saragossa Manuscript*, were Communist Party members and active in 'peace movement' and 'broad left' campaigns of the 1950s–80s. See Margaret Dickinson, *Rogue Reels: Oppositional Film in Britain*, 1945–90 (London: British Film Institute, 1990), pp. 210–23.

8 An advertisement by Contemporary Films, the British distributor of *The Saragossa Manuscript*, in 1966 is headed 'Go globe trotting with Contemporary's international films', and lists films from twenty-one different countries (*Sight and Sound* 35, no. 2 (Spring, 1966), i).

9 Pierre Bourdieu, *Distinction: a Social Critique of the Judgement of Taste*, trans. R. Nice (London: Routledge, 1984). By an interesting coincidence, Bourdieu's surveys for this work were carried out in France in 1963 and 1967–8.

10 Bourdieu, *Distinction*, p. 530.

11 On the early distribution of Russian cinema in Britain and the film society movement, see Ian Christie, 'Censorship, Culture, and Codpieces: Eisenstein's influence in Britain in the 1930s and 1940s', in Al Lavalley and Barry P. Scherr (eds.), *Eisenstein at 100: a reconsideration* (New Brunswick, NJ: Rutgers University Press, 2001), pp. 109–20.

12 Penelope Houston, *The Contemporary Cinema* (Harmondsworth: Penguin, 1963), pp. 7–8.

13 Serge Daney, review in *Cahiers du cinéma* 187 (February 1967), 69–70.

14 Cybulski (b. 1927) would also die young, in a railway accident in 1967, and be commemorated in Wajda's fictionalized biography *Everything for Sale* (*Wszytko na sprezedaz*, 1968).

15 *The Contemporary Cinema*, pp. 137–8.

16 Huxley's book, published in 1952, served as the basis for a play by John Whiting

in 1961, which coincided with Kawalerowicz's film winning the 1961 Jury prize at Cannes. Russell's film, based on the play, was widely attacked for sensationalism, with Polish film praised for its restraint.

17 Pasolini would later turn to *The Decameron* as the first of his 'trilogy of life' in 1971, followed by *The Canterbury Tales* (1972) and *The Arabian Nights* (1974), all in approximate period settings.

18 Ian Maclean, Introduction to his translations of Potocki, *The Manuscript Found in Saragossa* (Harmondsworth: Penguin, 1996), p. xiv. Patrick Gibbs, in a wholly enthusiastic review in the *Daily Telegraph*, described it as 'an excellent example of that rare and difficult style, the picaresque' commending its 'romantic-sardonic, not to say erotic style that recalls now Boccaccio, now Baron von Munchausen' (9.12.66). Hibbin mentions *The Arabian Nights* disparagingly.

19 David Robinson, *The Times*; Raymond Durgnat, *Films and Filming*. Maclean, quoting a letter from Potocki, Introduction, p. xiv.

20 Borges shared this first Formentor prize with Samuel Beckett, and later wrote that, as a consequence, 'my books mushroomed overnight throughout the Western world'. 'Autobiographical Essay', quoted in Emir Rodriguez Monegal, *Jorges Luis Borges, a Literary Biography* (New York: Paragon House, 1988), p. 444.

21 See Robbe-Grillet's review of Bioy Casares's *L'Invention de Morel*, and its preface by Borges, *Critique* 54 (November 1951), 1002. I am grateful for this reference, and for a wider prespective on the impact of Borges on the *nouveau roman*, to Dorota Ostrowska.

22 *Fictions* published by Grove Press and Weidenfeld, 1962. Paperback in 1965.

23 Many of the *nouveau roman* and *Tel Quel* groups' members would make at least some direct involvement with avant-garde cinema, as Dorota Ostrowska's doctoral dissertation will show.

24 Defined, more technically, as the 'hypodiegetic reduplication of the diegetic', in Shlomith Rimmon-Kenan, *Narrative Fiction: Contemporary Poetics* (London: Methuen, 1983), p. 93.

25 Svetlana Alpers, *The Art of Describing* (Chicago: University of Chicago Press, 1983), pp. 69–70.

26 Chris Auty, review in *Time Out Film Guide* (London: Penguin Books, 1996, fifth edn), p. 709.

27 The 'Critics' Week' would be joined by a 'Directors' Fortnight' (*Quinzaine des réalisateurs*) after the festival's disruption in 1968. Subsequently other selections have been added, making Cannes today something of a shopping mall of competing displays.

28 Robert Benayoun, 'Des zakouskis de résistance' *Positif* 71 (September 1965), 38. All subsequent quotations from this page, in my translation.

29 *Cahiers du cinéma*, 187 (February 1967), 69–70.

30 Unidentified French magazine cutting on microfiche in BFI National Library.

31 Louis Seguin, Locarno Festival report, *Positif* 88 (October 1967), 39.

32 In issue no. 156, March 1966, Jean-Louis Comolli had defined *Cahiers*'s work as 'the support everywhere and by all means of New Cinema'.

33 Roger Boussinot, *Encyclopédie du cinéma* (Paris: Bordas, 1995), p. 1634.

34 'Polish Film Fantasy of Spain', *Daily Telegraph*, 23 August 1965.

35 *Morning Star*, 17 December 1966.

36 *Films and Filming*, March 1967, p. 32.
37 The film was cut by some 50 minutes for its UK and US release and, from memory, included the cautionary words quoted by Durgnat, which do not appear to be part of its restored version.
38 Raymond Durgnat, *Luis Buñuel* (London: Studio Vista, 1967); *Georges Franju* (London: Studio Vista, 1967).
39 Durgnat, *Luis Buñuel*, p. 146.
40 Luis Buñuel, *Mon dernier soupir* (Paris: Editions Robert Laffont, 1982); quotation from the English edition, translated by Abigail Israel, *My Last Breath* (London: Fontana/Flamingo, 1985), p. 224.
41 *Le charme discret de la bourgeoisie* (1972), *Le Fantôme de la liberté* (1974) and *Cet obscur objet du desir* (1977).
42 Basil Wright, *The Long View* (London: Secker and Warburg, 1974), p. 590.
43 Sally Potter interviewed in, Scott MacDonald, *A Critical Cinema 3* (Berkeley: University of California Press, 1998), pp. 404–5.
44 Theodore Roszak, *The Making of a Counter Culture* (London: Faber, 1971), p. 166.
45 Timothy Leary, *The Politics of Ecstasy* (New York: Putnam, 1968).
46 Alan Trist, manager of the Grateful Dead's licensing company, 'Seeing the Film with Jerry', Cowboy Pictures website Saragossa@cowboybi.com. All subsequent quotations from this source. The Georgian-Armenian Paradjanov had made his 'magic surrealist' film in the Carpathians in a dream-like style, intensifying its ethnographic detail and launching a new 'pictorial' style in the trans-Caucasus Soviet republics, which soon attracted official disfavour. Meanwhile the film won many awards abroad and made Paradjanov as famous as Tarkovsky among 'dissident' Russian film-makers.
47 *Village Voice*, 25 May 1999, p. 123.
48 J. Hoberman and Jonathan Rosenbaum, *Midnight Movies* (New York: Harper and Row, 1983), p. 80.
49 Glenn O'Brien, *Village Voice*, March, 1971, quoted by Hoberman and Rosenbaum, p. 94.
50 On Anger, see Tony Rayns, 'Lucifer: a Kenneth Anger Kompendium', *Cinema* (London) 4 (October 1969), 23–31.
51 Kramer's account of the protracted negotiations required to obtain a full-length print is included as an essay on the Cowboy Pictures website.
52 *Village Voice*, 18 February 1997.
53 Arthur Marwick, *The Sixties* (Oxford: Oxford University Press, 1998). Marwick identifies this period as 1964–9.
54 David Curtis informs me that *The Saragossa Manuscript* was shown regularly at the London Arts Lab, after this opened in Drury Lane in 1967, and became a box-office mainstay.

Sadly, Raymond Durgnat died in May 2002 while this volume was in press. He will be mourned by film scholars in Britain and throughout the world.

Comparative Criticism 24, pp. 239–254. © 2002 Cambridge University Press
DOI: 10.1017/S0144756402005541   Printed in the United Kingdom

Archetype and aesthetics of the fantastic: the narrative form in Chinese and French fiction

FANFAN CHEN

Theories on the fantastic (fantasy or *le fantastique* in French) have been considerably developed over recent decades, especially after the emergence of Tzvetan Todorov's *Introduction à la littérature fantastique*. Though remaining problematic, the genre (with its poetic and thematic uniqueness in fiction) is generally defined and received aesthetically on the basis of Todorov's seemingly strict or 'pure' definition. According to his definition, the fantastic (*le fantastique*) resides in the hesitation or ambiguity between the marvellous (*le merveilleux*) and the uncanny (*l'étrange*).[1] In an application of this restrictive definition of the fantastic to Chinese fiction, what is generally regarded as Chinese 'fantastic' fiction is not, then, fantastic at all. But does this type of fiction meet the definition of 'the marvellous' (*le merveilleux*)? According to general French theories on *le merveilleux*, such a story mostly starts with 'Once upon a time' (*Il était une fois*) and the setting is not realistic. But in Chinese tales, the setting and the characters are as real as realistic fiction, and the commencement of the fiction is not marked by any expression similar to 'Once upon a time'. Thus, critics often surmise that the genre of the 'fantastic' does not exist in Chinese literature.[2]

But, in fact, Chinese literature offers a special narrative genre – *zhiguai* – that is very close to Western fantastic tales and is generally translated into English as fantasy, or as supernatural, weird, or fantastic tales. The literary definition of *zhiguai* is based on the themes, such as ghosts and divinities, and most literary critics define this narrative form thematically. Generally, *zhiguai* is short fiction, written in classic Chinese (*guwen*), which depicts all events about supernatural, strange, improbable, or abnormal phenomena. Yu Ru-Jie defines the genre from a contemporary point of view which reflects his thematic, historic and aesthetic approaches: '*Zhiguai* is a bizarre, strange, *superextraordinary* (*guai* and *yi*)[3] and absurd kind of story; the images are divine and bizarre (*shen* and *guai*), the plots are extraordinary and *superextraordinary* (*qi* and *yi*) because logic is transgressed and reason and nature are violated.'[4] Most critics generally accept this definition of *zhiguai* fiction: the typical characters are *shen*, *xian*, *gui*, *guai*, *yao* (all sorts of supernatural beings, such as gods, ghosts, spirits, monsters) and also the events of this fiction are highly unlikely (*yi*).[5]

Mostly limited by linguistic knowledge, Western critics, theorists or anthologists rarely include Chinese fiction in their works. The generally perceived 'fantastic literature' may more appropriately be labelled as 'Western fantastic literature'. Even in Western fantastic literature, the Todorovian formalist theory of the fantastic cannot be applied without reservation to fantastic works in all languages. In fact, the fantastic fiction considered and studied in the theoretical work of Todorov is primarily French nineteenth-century fiction. His formalist analysis of the fantastic also focuses solely on the French language. Consequently, the texts included and studied bias critics' theories on fantastic literature, as Colin N. Manlove argues:

> Those theorists whose definitions differed from mine usually did so because they were applying them to quite different works or contexts: E. S. Rabkin, for instance, described what he saw as the fantastic in all literature (as, more recently, has Kathryn Hume); Rosemary Jackson discussed 'subversive fantasies' by Poe, Stevenson, Dostoevsky, Kafka, or Pynchon directed at criticism of our world; W. R. Irwin considered fantasies subscribing to his notion of 'play' or 'the game of the impossible'; Tzvetan Todorov was concerned with certain French works of the nineteenth century which produced a hesitation in the reader between 'supernatural' and 'natural' readings.[6]

Moreover, in contrast with Todorov's view that the fantastic disappears by the time Kafka's writing appears (like *Metamorphosis*), recent anthologies or studies of the fantastic still include certain works of Kafka. Furthermore, the fantastic survives and evolves in contemporary times under different forms as, for example, in the fantastic stories of Tolkien or many fictions of the fantastic or magical realism in Latin America.

Instead of getting into a debate over controversial definitions of the fantastic, a study and comparison of the fantastic in Chinese and French fiction will prove more enlightening. The Chinese texts included are generally considered or translated in French as *fantastique* (fantastic or fantasy), *merveilleux* (fairytale, marvellous) or *étrange* (weird). Although a formalist approach tends to exclude Chinese fiction, a comparative thematic approach will highlight the homogeneous themes recurrent in both Chinese and French fantastic fiction. Fantastic love, dreams, metamorphosis, mysterious or supernatural powers, the return of the dead, and the sublime nature of supernatural art are among the most recurrent themes in fantastic stories of both cultures. The range of this study will encompass French 'classic' fantastic fiction (mainly nineteenth-century fantastic tales) and Chinese 'classic' fiction (before the modernization movement at the beginning of the twentieth century) that is thematically fantastic. The general concern of this study is whether fantastic literature should be viewed as a thematic genre (as defined in Chinese theory) or as a narrative genre (as defined in most French theory). From the point of view of comparative literature and cultural studies, the issue of fantastic literature is more complicated than a pure issue of literary narrative. The genre is in reality a universal literary creation, and both writers' vision of the world and their language may influence the production of fantastic literature. As Todorov emphasizes, the narration is crucial to the development of the structural procedure of fantastic fiction, which can be called here 'fantastic syntax'. A comparison of the narrative form in Chinese and French fiction will display the homogeneity and heterogeneity of fantastic syntax in each culture. The different aspects of narration to be studied and compared in this article include the emphasis of narrative voices (homodiegetic, autodiegetic or heterodiegetic), narrative focalization (zero, internal or external focalization) and narrative level (extradiegetic or intradiegetic) in each culture.[7] This comparative study offers a more thorough viewpoint and illustrates the syntactical structure of fantastic fiction.

Given the thematic homogeneity in Chinese and French fantastic fiction, the fantastic genre is a kind of universal imaginary archetype, though the art of the narrative is quite different in the two cultures. Strada Vittorio, in his studies of Russian fantastic tales, assumes that the creation of the fantastic is a kind of *aestheticization* of human superstition, especially after the disappearance of myths. The difference and the sameness of this '*aestheticization* of superstition'[8] in the two cultures will be the focus of this study.

One of the most obvious features of French fantastic stories is the use of narration in the first person or homodiegetic narration. Some French critics (like Todorov and Malrieu) assume this is a main characteristic of the fantastic. Pointing to certain short stories considered as paradigms of the fantastic, Todorov notices the following: 'In the fantastic stories, the narrator usually says "I". This is an empirical fact that we can verify easily ... The exceptions are almost always texts that move away from meeting the standard definition of the genre known as the fantastic.'[9] Despite this trend of homodiegetic narration, numerous fantastic stories in French are told in a heterodiegetic manner. Take some French authoritative anthologies, such as that by Castex or Baronian, as an example. A considerable number of fantastic stories are in heterodiegetic narration, such as *L'élixir de longue vie* by Balzac, *Les Willis* by Alphonse Karr, or *Arria Marcella* by Gautier. Since some fantastic writers make use of heterodiegetic narration, this kind of narrative technique must possess certain important values for the function of fantastic writing. As to the narrative voice in Chinese fantastic fiction, the majority of the stories are heterodiegetic. However, the narrative focalization cannot be confused with that of French fairy tales. In Chinese narration, the narrative perspective is often limited to a single character or the presence of the narrator is so ignored that external focalization is frequently employed. Undeniably, homodiegetic narration exists in some stories by certain Chinese writers of the Tang Dynasty (618–907) or in stories by Pu Song-Ling in the Qing Dynasty (1644–1911). But a deeper analysis into the real voice and focalization of the apparently homodiegetic narrator reveals that the narrator 'I' is a forgery. The following study of fantastic fiction in both cultures illustrates the main difference in the narration of the fantastic.

1. HOMODIEGETIC NARRATION: PREDILECTION OF FRENCH FANTASTIC STORYTELLERS

French fantastic storytellers show a special predilection for narration in the first person, which is moreover a phenomenon in the Romantic age – also the golden age of the French fantastic. The individualism of first-person narration exploits the interior profoundly in poetry as well as in prose fiction. Thus from a thematic or rhetorical point of view, the homodiegetic narrator meets the creative needs of the writer of fantastic fiction. Homodiegetic narration can be characterized by the subjectivity of the fiction. Although the narrator tells his own experience and the presence of this character-narrator renders the story credible, the trick is the play on the subjectivity of the discourse. Not surprisingly, Todorov values homodiegetic narration in the fantastic genre. Also not surprisingly, Todorov's definition focuses on the hesitation felt by the hero (and the reader). And such hesitation results in a kind of ambiguity that operates in the fiction. Generally speaking, in the homodiegetic narration of fantastic stories, the narrator can be either the hero who suffers a nearly supernatural intrusion or a witness who sees from a certain distance what happens to the hero. Occasionally, the narrator may even be a supernatural character in the stories, like the ghostly narrator in *La seconde vie* (The Second Life) by Charles Asselineau. Nevertheless, the narrator here may not actually be a supernatural character himself, for an interpretation of the story as a mad man's discourse is also possible.

AUTODIEGETIC NARRATION AND THE DUBIOUS HERO

The autodiegetic narrator tells his own story retrospectively, i.e. everything is accomplished when he utters the story which is beyond his reasonable comprehension. He is the only one who knows what happened during the supernatural intrusion and, at the same time, he is the only one prey to the torturing experience. He tries to communicate with others in order to find a psychological exit. In addition, being the narrator, he is allowed to unveil the story that disturbs his reason. However, in many cases, the hero returns empty-handed from this trial of communication, for he hazards his reason and is often considered a lunatic. Examples can be found in numerous stories by Gautier, such as *La cafetière* (The Coffeepot), *Le pied de momie* (The Mummy's Foot) and *La morte amoureuse* (The Vampire in Love). The autodiegetic narrators in these stories tell their personal stories as if they were taking the readers or listeners into their confidence about the experiences of their youth. Since the event seems unlikely or unreasonable, this kind of communication is, in reality, an interior monologue of the hero through which his psychological status is transmitted to the reader.

The autodiegetic narration allows the reader to share the feeling of the hero. The story, presented as a diary or as a personal confidence, reaches the climax of the narrator's crisis as he encounters the supernatural intrusion. This kind of narrative mechanism plunges the reader into a *récit d'instant* (story of the moment). The reader ignores the sequence of the story just as the autodiegetic narrator is unable to control the development of events. In the course of the narration in *La bague antique* (The Antique Ring), by Berthoud, the narrator is led progressively towards destruction and the discourse is finished as the narrator is annihilated: 'Ah! There's the ghost coming back; it makes a sign for me to die. Adieu!'[10] The communication between the narrator and the person he addresses is in fact a subjective illusion. The real existence of the person named 'Edouard' – recipient of the letter (the story is in epistolary form) – is doubtful. That the narrator ('I') tells the fantastic story is all the more subjective because he is aware of his limited knowledge and is suspicious of his own objectivity. The narrator desperately needs the support of his friend as he experiences his grief. A similar narrative strategy by means of a dubious hero can be found in some of Maupassant's stories, such as *Le Horla* (Horla) or *La nuit* (Night). In both stories, the autodiegetic heroes end their narration as they face their destruction.

ORCHESTRATION OF ENIGMA THROUGH THE HOMODIEGETIC NARRATOR

As a witness, the homodiegetic narrator preserves a distance from the fantastic story. In many cases, the narrator is susceptible to the inexplicable events that he witnessed and his vision is thus disturbed. The narrator tries to show his readers the incredible events rather than looking for some kind of communication. The intention of the narrator to convince the reader to believe the story is quite obvious, if only implicitly. But the narrator's observation as witness may not be convincing to the reader. Take the homodiegetic narrator at intradiegetic level of *Le bracelet de cheveux* (The Hair Bracelet) by Dumas, for example. The narrator intends to make the audience in the story believe that the dead are not really dead and that a corpse is not a real corpse. However, the audience reveals a sceptical attitude towards the story. In addition, readers have the right to doubt the verity of the story since it is told from the narrator's point of view. The objectivity of the story can always be doubted. In contrast, the narrator–witness of Maupassant's stories seems more credible as the tale is told by someone trustworthy like a doctor or a scholar. For example, the narrator (intradiegetic and homodiegetic) in *Conte de Noël* (Christmas Tale) tells his audience that he witnessed supernatural events. The story is concerned with the supernatural cure of a woman possessed by an evil spirit. The doctor's sound reason and scientific training and his detailed observations on the whole confuse the reader and face him with an enigma. The fact of an evil spirit is unreasonable and unbelievable, but could the doctor tell a lie? Such erudite or learned characters also narrate the well-known short stories of Prosper Mérimée, such as *La Vénus d'Ille* and *Lokis*. The stories are all the more convincing and ambiguous as these narrators provide both a sceptical and a supernatural explanation.

The most confusing type occurs when a trustworthy narrator speaks for the mad character in the story. On several occasions, the narrator changes his reasonable and positivist demeanour at the time of the story's resolution, after his communication with the mad or nearly mad character. In this case, the narration turns out to possess a fantastic kind of contagiousness. Thus the narrator functions as a transmitter of the speech of the mad or someone considered nearly mad. Examples can be found in numerous stories of Nodier (who borrowed from Potocki) such as *Une heure ou la vision* (One O'clock or the Vision), *Lydie ou la résurrection* (Lydie or the Resurrection) or *Jean-François-les-Bas-Bleus* (The Bluestocking Jean François). The effect of the credible narrator contaminated by an insane person's viewpoint reinforces the story's ambiguity and contributes to the intricacy of the fantastic enigma.

2. HETERODIEGETIC NARRATION: CHRONICLE TRADITION AND NEUTRALIZED NARRATIVE VOICE IN THE CHINESE FANTASTIC

The ellipsis of the speaking subject in a language as ambiguous as Chinese provides the story with an open narration.[11] The author tries to erase the narrator's presence in order to create the effect that the narrator does not exist and the story is shown theatrically. If the aesthetic of the French fantastic texts on the basis of an ambiguous narration where the homodiegetic (naturally including autodiegetic) narrator serves as the best strategy, the Chinese fantastic makes the most of the heterodiegetic narrator to tell an unlikely or supernatural story from a 'historical' point of view. The narrative mechanism of ambiguity is not the main concern in Chinese fiction. Many stories start with the apparition of supernatural beings and then proceed to the impending reaction of the characters and the events that follow.

Actually, Chinese authors care about historiographic style because history is considered as a noble genre in Chinese narrative writing. Considering the minor position of fiction (*xiaoshuo*) in Chinese literature, it understandably adopts a historiographic style. Desiring to be recognized for their writing talents but at the same time being pushed by an impulsion of fictive and supernatural imagination, Chinese writers apply a historical viewpoint in writing fantastic fiction. For example, the fantastic stories (*zhiguai*) of the Six Dynasties are always narrated in the third person, the technique of which remains the norm until Pu Song-Ling's time. Though some stories are homodiegetic, especially in the Tang Dynasty, the stories with this type of narration are few. The majority of Chinese fantastic stories are still told through the medium of a heterodiegetic narrator.

FANTASTIC THROUGH LIMITED FOCALIZATION AND THE OBJECTIFICATION OF SILENCE

Although Chinese fantastic stories are heterodiegetic, readers do not know more than the characters. In fact, most of these stories are not narrated with zero focalization. Nevertheless, many critics assume that Chinese fantastic stories are no different from the occidental fairy tales. In contrast, Chinese objectification based on an aesthetic of silence reduces characters' psychological depth and limits the intervention of analepses or prolepses. A number of Chinese stories are told by a heterodiegetic narrator who takes a character's view and gradually unfolds the fantastic plot. Readers can only be sure of this character's thoughts and his vision as he is faced with the supernatural intrusion. Like this character, readers are not informed of the coming events. If readers have the impression that an omniscient narrator narrates Chinese stories, this is because the neutral tone of the narrator is a *trompe-l'œil* of omniscience. However, the heterodiegetic narrator is actually an individual like the character, his narration is underpinned by the character's vision. For example, the narrator tells the story of *Lujiang Feng'ao zhuan* (The Old Woman of Lujiang) through the vision of the old woman Feng. Like her, readers are ignorant of the real status (ghost) of the person she encounters. The narrative ellipsis of other possible hints limits the readers' knowledge. In any event, readers are always dependent on the character's vision until the last revelation: the character that the old woman met had been dead for a long time. Also, readers have to wait until the very end of the story in order to learn that a narrative pact exists between the narrator (who transcribes the story) and his friend Yue (who tells the narrator the story he has witnessed).

In the story *Hao Huahu* (Hao Paints the Tiger) by Jiang Xiu-Fu, the entire ellipsis of the interior and the external focalization on characters' behaviour leads the story to the point of the fantastic through cold observation of the gradual metamorphosis of the hero. Though the story starts with an indication of its origin communicated by the grandson of the hero as if this story were narrated at intradiegetic level, the narrative is in any event heterodiegetic. This is essentially concerned with the relationship between the indirect discourse and the free indirect discourse effected by the narrative activity. Obviously, a kind of anacoluthon makes the narrative discourse confusing. Even the beginning ellipsis of the personal subject produces an ambiguity between the homodiegetic and the heterodiegetic narrator. For instance, the translated version of modern Chinese usually adds a homodiegetic narrator (the witness) who expresses his inability to give the hero's name. In the original version in classical Chinese (*guwen*), the pronoun 'I' is omitted. With or without the 'I', the virtual situation of the heterodiegetic narrator is less important than the fantastic effect he intends to produce. In the course of the plot development, the heterodiegetic narrator describes the external changes of the hero's behaviour and temperament. In contrast, his psychological state is not depicted at all. Readers just follow the narrator and observe the hero's behaviour until the culminating point of the fantastic. Employing the modal expression 'ze huaweihu shiye' (the hero must have metamorphosed into the tiger) to end the story, the narrator is not aware of the real situation concerning the hero's disappearance. He is not able to affirm the metamorphosis of the hero into the tiger. The disappearance of the hero remains an enigma for the narrator as well as for the reader. Such examples can also be found in a number of Pu Song-Ling's stories.

THE OMNISCIENT NARRATOR AND READERS' EXPECTATION OF SURPRISES

In a number of stories, the reader knows more than the character about the supernatural events that the character is subjected to. If the fantastic narration plays on the character's innocence compared with the narrator's control over the fantastic events, this is because the readers' horizon of expectation usually relies on the character's reaction after the supernatural intrusion. The story *Huazhou canjun* (A Governor of Huazhou) by Wen Ting-Yun doubles the fantastic effect as the heroine (who is, in fact, dead) appears in front of the hero's house. Readers are actually aware of the real situation where the fictive discourse enters in the unreal part of the story without the hero's knowing about the death of his beloved (the heroine). Although the omniscient narrator (heterodiegetic with zero focalization) knows and controls everything, he never risks the aesthetic of silence. Even after the hero learns that his beloved is in reality a ghost, the story continues to develop on the basis of this revelation and the end of the story is all the more surprising. The ex-husband of the heroine accuses the hero of committing adultery with his wife (as a ghost), and this accusation is judged at the governor's court. In fact, many Chinese fantastic stories are characterized by a narrative procedure of multiple surprises – a more unlikely event succeeding a previous unlikely one. Or frequently these stories contain a second climax. After the revelation of the unreal event that functions as a first climax, a second unreal event emerges, i.e. the unreal out of unreal.

Pu Song-Ling is one of the storytellers that frequently make use of the omniscient narrator. In fact, his first concern in his narrative creation is to depict the behaviour and mind of his supernatural characters. The vision of the narrator is not limited to a unique character. In addition, he tends to stage the fantastic by a sort of sophisticated discourse that interweaves the events, the shifting of visions often being employed. Like the narration in Pu's *Huapi* (Paint on the Skin), the narrator shifts his vision from that of the hero to the Taoist master, and eventually to the vision of the hero's wife. The story does not end with the ghost's transformation and the hero's destruction. Readers may be astonished to proceed to the next part of the story, which is seen through the wife's vision. The wife will act as heroine of the story and undergo a series of incredible events to resurrect her husband. The narrative skill here can be found in other stories by Pu. Being a narrative master of describing dynamism in the fox-spirit (*huxian*) stories, Pu Song-Ling resorts to the omniscient narrator to capture the different temperaments of the fox-spirits as well as the behaviour of the hero facing intrusion by these supernatural figures. The supernatural characters are hence personified and the fantastic plot depends upon the interaction between the hero and the supernatural characters.

3. MINOR NARRATIVE VOICE IN CHINESE AND FRENCH FANTASTIC STORIES
THE PARTICULARITY OF THE HOMODIEGETIC NARRATOR IN THE CHINESE FANTASTIC

In Chinese fantastic stories, the narrative voice of the first person is considered quite exceptional. This is closely related to the world vision of Chinese people. Actually, Chinese are not used to uttering 'I' either in fiction or in poetry, for the vision centred on the subjective 'I' is not a usual way of thinking in Chinese culture. Even if a homodiegetic narrator tells the story, the teller does not say 'I' but says his name or the author's. Some Chinese critics view the story *Yimenglu* (Weird Dreams) by Shen Ya-Zhi or *Gujingji* (Antique Mirror) by Wang Du as being narrated in the first person. Yet the utterance 'I' does not appear in the course of the narration in either of these two stories. Readers can only see the name 'Shen Ya-Zhi' or 'Ya-Zhi' (name of the author) in the first story or 'Du' (the name of the author) in the second. Due to the lack of inflectional verbs, readers cannot tell, simply by virtue of the verbs, whether the narration is homodiegetic or heterodiegetic. Consequently, without recourse to the author, the story can be viewed as either heterodiegetic or homodiegetic. Another confusing narrative situation is the alternation between the proper noun and the pronoun 'I'. The story *Qinmengji* (Dreaming of the Qin Dynasty) of Shen Ya-Zhi is an example. Throughout the whole story, readers have an impression that the narration is heterodiegetic as the hero is addressed as 'Ya-Zhi'. However, at the end of the story, the 'I' arrives unexpectedly and abruptly, which disturbs the pact of narration, which until this point had remained heterodiegetic. To readers who are ignorant of the author's name, this 'cleavage' of the narration is abnormal and illogical, especially for readers coming from a linguistic background other than Chinese. Nevertheless, the ordinary homo-diegetic narration exists in Chinese fiction, though the examples are quite limited. The story *Zhouqinxingji* (Memory of a Voyage to the Zhou and Qin Dynasties) by Wei Guan is a real example of homodiegetism. In this story, the narrator telling his own supernatural adventure is an autodiegetic one.

Unlike most French autodiegetic narrators, the Chinese narrator focuses more on the story than on comments or meditation on the unintelligible phenomena. In most cases, Chinese fantastic stories in homodiegetic narration are *de facto* embedded stories, though the narrative levels are not explicitly shown. The narrator at the extradiegetic level communicates or transcribes the story told by another character or witness. Besides, the always absent 'I' who appears abruptly at the end of the story explains how the narrator receives the story. The following stories are examples of such embedded narration: *Lihunji* (The Separation of Soul) by Chen Xuan-You, *Lujiang Feng'ao zhuan* (The Old Woman of Lujiang) by Li Gong-Zuo, *Humeng* (Dreams of Foxes) by Pu Song-Ling, etc. These stories are substantially homodiegetic at extradiegetic level and heterodiegetic at intradiegetic level. Generally, it is not easy to tell the difference between the fictive narrator and the author. In short, the Chinese writers tend to 'objectify' the 'subjective' homodiegetic narration. The individual subject in Chinese fiction is erased by the neutralization of narrative voice.

NARRATION EXCLUDING 'I' IN FRENCH FANTASTIC STORIES

As emphasized earlier, heterodiegetic narrative does exist in French fantastic fiction. Some French storytellers employ this narrative voice to stage the fantastic events. They often adopt a more neutral and objective point of view through an internal focalization. In addition, if the narrator 'I', being the prey of the supernatural intrusion, is still capable of speaking to an implied listener, the heterodiegetic narrator tends to erase the character's existence as well as his speech following the fantastic intrusion.[12] For example, in the story *Arria Marcella* by Thoéphile Gautier, the heterodiegetic narration prevents the hero from communicating with others about his supernatural nocturnal experience. Nevertheless, the narrator keeps a distance from the story and from the character's position to let the readers judge. In *Gottfried Wolfgang* by Petrus Borel, narration at intradiegetic level can also illustrate this kind of communication blockade between the hero and others. The heterodiegetic narrator tells the night adventure of the hero by fixing on the hero's vision. Though the narrator tells the story as if he held an outer and objective point of view, the reality of the hero's encounter with the female ghost is still uncertain through the narrator's utterance.

Likewise, the character can be annihilated by the omniscient narration. His behaviour, reaction or feelings turn out to be secondary to the rhetoric of irony or allegory. For instance, the character M. Desalleux in the story *Le ministre public* by Charles Rabou is finally driven insane and sent to the asylum; and it is impossible for him to tell others of his encounter with the ghost, his victim Pierre Leroux. The narrator sees everything and knows everything about the supernatural reality in the story. He acts like God and laughs at the human condition. In *L'élixir de longue vie* (The Elixir of Long Life), Balzac also employs a heterodiegetic narrator. The narrator does not care to surprise readers by the supernatural intrusion, nor to go deeply into the interior universe of the character facing the supernatural presence. He simply describes the fantastic events and at the same time unveils the hidden recesses of the human soul.

CONCLUSION: FROM NARRATIVE SITUATION TO SYNTAX

With the respective emphasis of the homodiegetic narrative in French fiction and the heterodiegetic in Chinese fiction, the aspect of narrative mode can be illustrated distinctively. Although narration in fiction is generally a combination of two modes, 'telling' and 'showing', an obvious tendency to 'show' characterizes Chinese fantastic fiction (as the narrator objectively presents the unlikely events); and the mode of 'telling' distinguishes the fantastic in French stories (as the narrator meditates in the process of narration and goes more deeply into the subjectivity of the characters).

Whether the narrator is an 'I' who suffers or witnesses, or an agent's voice from outside the story, the stake of French storytellers is in the mechanism of ambiguous plotting. Normally, the story is developed from *the real* to *the unreal*.[13] In contrast, most Chinese stories are developed out of *the unreal* to a more unlikely *unreal* rhetoric that diffuses into a more *real* narration. This narrative mode, though apparently similar to Brook-Rose's 'the unreal as real' narration, is substantially a penetration into the real and the unreal beyond a dualist vision.

Different mechanisms of narrative in Chinese and French fantastic short stories result in three main different typological proceedings or fantastic syntax based on the discourse of the real and the unreal. Fantastic fiction functions by playing on these two propositions to form fantastic structure proceeding from the real to the unreal or from the unreal to the more unreal (normally unique to Chinese fiction), interweaving ambiguously the real with the unreal. In the Chinese fantastic, the writers tend to endeavour to stage the supernatural events and the character's behaviour in the stories or to stage a more stunning and unreal plot after the first unveiling of the unreal. In French stories, however, the homodiegetic or heterodiegetic narrator's meditation and hesitation on the unintelligible and nearly supernatural happenings occupy the plot. The fantastic in the former case often produces effect by a more incredible reaction of the character after a supernatural beginning. In contrast, the effect of the French fantastic grows in the course of the narration as a kind of tension; and the real epiphany of the fantastic appears near the end of the story. Obviously, the Todorovian hesitation felt by the character and the reader is hardly perceived in Chinese fantastic stories since the authors create the imaginary fantastic with the style of historiography that depicts the unreal without ambiguity. This difference in the narrative aesthetic of the fantastic is essentially related to the *Weltanschauung* in each culture. In the same way, the heterogeneity of fantastic narration illustrates the different characteristics of various languages and cultures. The influence of Taoism on Chinese literature results in an aesthetic of *Yi King* or nondualistic harmony in the fantastic narrative. With a Taoist vision, nothing is absolute; the distinction between the natural and supernatural is only temporary. There is always space for the character or reader to accept supernatural phenomena or revaluate the previous vision of the world. As to the French fantastic, both Christian and Cartesian vision creates a dubious ambiguity in the face of the supernatural or other dimensions beyond human knowledge. Interestingly, the ambiguous Chinese Taoist thought generates an unambiguous narrative; the clear-cut dualist French Cartesian and Christian metaphysics produces an ambiguous narrative. Henceforth, the symbolic image of *Yi King* ☯ may illustrate the Chinese aesthetics of the fantastic, in contrast, the image of a well-divided circle ◐ may illustrate the French aesthetics.

After this short study of Chinese and French fantastic narrative, the assertion that the fantastic can be defined by a certain fixed style of narrative or that a structuralist theory can comprehend the fantastic fictions of various cultures may be questioned. It would be more universal to interpret the fantastic as an archetype of human narrative creation about the unlikely or supernatural phenomena in the natural world or the perception of extra-dimensions, even though the aesthetic forms are different. In Chinese culture, superstition spreads widely and the view of the natural and the supernatural or of the real and the unreal is not based on the same way of thinking as that of the French. For example, a Chinese character who does not believe in supernatural beings would probably accept their existence after encountering them and thus reshape his vision of the world. It is not so 'unbearable (*insupportable*)' and 'heartrending (*déchirant*)'[14] for a Chinese character to encounter a supernatural being as for a French character faced with the same situation. Human imagination is influenced in so many ways by society, language and inborn sacred quality (which can be illustrated by the images of god(s)) in different cultures. Ghost stories exist in every culture, but the ways of telling ghost stories are various. A deeper and further comprehension of this fantastic phenomenon in narrative creation offers a better realization that the essence of the fantastic exhibits an archetype of human innate imagination of the supernatural or the unknown or the impossible. However, this homogeneous human imagination is aestheticized differently and conditioned by culture, society and language.

NOTES

1 Todorov defines the genre 'fantastic' by three elements: (1) The text obliges the reader to consider the world of the character as real. The reader has to hesitate between the supernatural (or the marvellous) and the natural (or the uncanny) explanations. (2) The character may also feel this kind of hesitation. Thus the reader identifies with character. (3) It is significant that the reader adopts a certain attitude towards the text: allegorical or 'poetic' interpretation must be refused. (Tzvetan Todorov, *Introduction à la littérature fantastique* (Paris: Seuil, 1992), pp. 37–8, my translation from French.)

2 French critic Roger Bozzetto and Sinologist Muriel Détrie are prudent in applying the term *fantastique* to Chinese tales of similar kind and doubt that the genre *fantastique* exists in Chinese literature. See Bozzetto, 'Peut-on parler de "fantastique" dans la littérature chinoise?', *Cahiers du CERLI* (1997). Détrie, 'Les contes "fantastique" chinois: questions de genre et de terminologie', *Cahiers du CERLI* (1997).

3 Here I employ the translation *superextraordinaire* (superextraordinary) of the French Sinologist André Lévy for the Chinese terms *guai, yi, qi*. Lévy, 'Introduction', *Histoires extraordinaires et récits fantastiques de la Chine ancienne*, vol. 2: *chefs-d'œuvre de la nouvelle (Dynastie des Tang. 618–907)* (Paris: Aubier, 1993).

4 Ru Jie Yu, *Xian, Gui, Yao, Ren – Zhiguai Chuanqi Xinlun* (New Critic on *Zhiguai* and *Chuanqi* Fiction) (Beijing: Zhongguogongren, 1992), p. 19.

5 Jian Guo Li, *Tangqian Zhiguai Xiaoshuoshi*. History of *Zhiguai* Short Stories before the Tang Dynasty) (Tianjin: Nankai University Press, 1984).

6 Colin N. Manlove, 'The Elusiveness of Fantasy', *The Shape of the Fantastic: Selected Essays from the Seventh International Conference on the Fantastic in the Arts* (New York: Greenwood Press, 1990), pp. 53–4.

7 In this article, I apply the terms of narratology theorized by Gérard Genette in his *Figure III*. The narration in the first person is *homodiegetic*. If the narrator is the hero himself, then the narration is *autodiegetic*. The third-person narration is *heterodiegetic*. As to the levels of narration, the embedded narrator inside the frame of story is *intradiegetic*; while the narrator of first level is designated as *extradiegetic*. Genette, *Figure III* (Paris: Editions du Seuil, 1972).

8 Strada Vittorio, based on the philosophy of Plato's myth of the cave, defines the creation of the fantastic as a general act of human imagination. This is a poetic procedure that *aestheticizes* superstition – the lost primitive myth is from the translation of Neil Cornwell in *The Literary Fantastic from Gothic to Postmodernism* (New York, London, Toronto, Sydney, Tokyo, Singapore: Harvester Wheatsheaf, 1990).

9 The quotation is translated from French: 'Dans les histoires fantastiques, le narrateur dit habituellement "je". C'est un fait empirique que l'on peut vérifier facilement. [...] Les exceptions sont presque toujours des textes qui, de plusieurs autres points de vue, s'éloignent du fantastique' (Todorov, p. 87).

10 The quotation is translated from French: 'Tiens! Voilà le fantôme qui revient; il me fait signe que je puis mourir. Adieu!' (Pierre-Georges Castex, *Anthologie du conte fantastique français* (Paris: José Corti, 1987), p. 82).

11 In Chinese, it is not necessary to utter the subject with a verb. However, it is not like Spanish (where subjects can also be omitted) where we can tell the subject according to the verb conjugation. Chinese is a language without inflectional verbs.

12 Joel Malrieu, *Le fantastique* (Paris: Hachette, 1992).

13 Christine Brooke-Rose, *A Rhetoric of the Unreal: Studies in Narrative and Structure, Especially of the Fantastic* (Cambridge University Press, 1983), p. 51.

14 Roger Caillois assumes that the intrusion of the fantastic shows a scandal (*scandale*), a tear (*déchirure*) and an unusual irruption (*irruption insolite*) that is unbearable for both the character and the reader in the real world ('De la féerique à la science-fiction', *Anthologie de la littérature fantastique* (Paris: Gallimard, 1966)).

ADDITIONAL REFERENCES

Baronian, Jean-Baptiste, *La France fantastique de Balzac à Louÿs* (Verviers: André Gérard Marabout, 1973)

Castex, Pierre-Georges, *Le conte fantastique en France: de Nodier à Maupassant* (Paris: José Corti, 1987)

Liu, Yong Lian, trans. and ed. *Zhongguo Zhiguai Xiaoshuo Xuanyi* (Anthology of Zhiguai Short Stories, translated into Modern Chinese) (Beijing: Baowentang, 1990)

Pu, Song Ling, *Liaozhai zhiyi* (Taipei: Dazhongguo, 1996)

Rochefort-Guillouet, Sophie, *La Littérature fantastique en 50 ouvrages* (Paris: Ellipses, 1997)

Steinmetz, Jean-Luc, *La Littérature fantastique* (Paris: PUF, 1990)

Tritter, Valérie, *Le Fantastique* (Paris: Ellipses, 2001)

Wang, Pi Jiang, *Tangren xiaoshuo* (Short Stories of the Tang People) (Shanghai Guji, 1988) (New Critic on *Zhiguai*)

Comparative Criticism 24, pp. 255–282.   Cambridge University Press 2002
DOI: 10.1017/S0144756402005553   Printed in the United Kingdom

The style of the Holy Spirit: Johann Jacob Junckherrott's translation of the New Testament (1732)

CHARLIE LOUTH

I

Johann Jacob Junckherrott's translation of the New Testament into German was published in 1732 and is virtually unknown.[1] Upon publication it was confiscated on account of its 'abenteuerlichen Deutschen Sprache' [adventurous German] and it has never been republished. The quotation comes from one of the few sources of information about Junckherrott, an encyclopaedia entry of 1787 which already remarks that his translation is very rare.[2] A copy was acquired by the British Museum Library in 1852 and a few other libraries have copies. Junckherrott is virtually untraceable; he has slipped through the fine net of the *Allgemeine Deutsche Biographie* and is included in no modern reference work.

The obscurity of Junckherrott and his book is clearly due to the nature of the translation itself. On its appearance it was dismissed as an aberration, an offence against good taste, and a work of ignorance. Junckherrott attempted to translate element for element, breaking the Greek down into its parts and then reconstituting these parts in German equivalents, usually privileging the etymological meaning of each element in isolation over the sense of the word as a whole. This practice results in a German text which is at many points unreadable and can never be read without difficulty. But the New Testament is more commonly reread than read. Junckherrott's translation is more readable than its technique would suggest because we can recognize the familiar stories through it. Like our reading, Junckherrott's translation is determined by the text it is a version of. It does not arbitrarily happen upon a method, it derives its method wholly from its source and justifies it in the material supplementary to the translation itself. The translation attempts to render not just the matter, indeed not primarily the matter at all, but the exact form and structure of its representation. The focus on the original wording is religious, and the sense of the translation resides there. The original is for Junckherrott the given, sole possible form, and this must be conveyed across, as unaltered as can be, into the new language. It is as if different languages did not exist – the form the Holy Spirit found, which happened to be in Greek, must be transferred intact and like a magnet constellate the German round it. This undertaking is highly contradictory, but it is also highly serious. The failure of the early reviewers to acknowledge the seriousness of Junckherrott's intent, their dismissal of his translation as *merely* eccentric, led directly to its neglect.

II

The translation *is* eccentric; but that aspect of it needs to be separated from the sound, entirely centred core which can usually be made out. The contemporary reviewers seized upon the obvious peculiarity and from it arrived at the conclusion that the translation was in its very nature, in its intent and in its substance, eccentric. This seems partly to have been due to what they knew about the character of the translator himself. Junckherrott has only one date attached to him, the date of the publication of his translation, *Das | Neue | Testament | des HERREN Unserer | JESU | Christi, | Eigentlich aus dem Griechischen Grund-Text gedollmetschet und in | das Teutsche übersetzt, | durch weyland | Johann Jacob Junckherrott. | Gedruckt im Jahr 1732. | Zu haben bey Henrich Christian Schäffer | in Offenbach [The New Testament of the Lord of Ours Jesus Christ, properly interpreted from the Greek original and translated into German by the late Johann Jacob Junckherrott. Printed in the year 1732. Available from Henrich Christian Schäffer in Offenbach]*. As this title page makes plain, he was by then dead. His first known reviewer, writing in Gottsched's *Critische Beyträge* in 1736, knew nothing about him at all: 'Wir wissen nicht, wer der weyland Hr J. gewesen ist, noch wo er gelebet hat' [we do not know who the late Mr J. was, nor where he lived].[3] The next source, from 1743, is better informed, and tells the story, repeated in the encyclopaedia entry I quoted from at the beginning, that Junckherrott had misspent much of his youth and perhaps not only his youth gambling, but with such success that he was able to donate 10,000 thalers to the poor. The translation is presented as a kind of penance:

Sein neuer Eifer vor die Frömmigkeit, riethe ihm auch, seinen Nächsten durch sein Exempel wieder zu erbauen, durch welches er ihn geärgert hatte. Der beste Weg schien ihm dieser zu seyn, wenn er eine, seiner Meynung nach, bessere Uebersetzung des neuen Testaments ans Licht stellete, welche er denn auch zum Stande brachte; aber darüber den Weg alles Fleisches gieng, daß sie erst nach seinem Tode, als eine unglückliche Geburth ans Licht getreten; wozu der Offenbachische Strumpf-Weber, Schäffer, und andre, als Hebammen, geholfen haben.[4]

[His newly acquired appetite for piety also recommended him to edify his neighbour by his own example to make up for having set him a bad one before. The best way seemed to him to be this, to present a, as he saw it, better translation of the New Testament, which he duly achieved; but in doing so went the way of all flesh so that it only saw the light of day after his death, an unfortunate birth which the Offenbach hosier Schäffer, and others, were midwives to.]

From the translation itself ('So aber jemals eine wunderliche und abgeschmackte Uebersetzung im Deutschen herausgekommen, so ist es gewiß diese' [If ever a curious and tasteless translation appeared in German, this is certainly it], p. 966) the writer concludes that Junckherrott was 'ein Mensch von [...] Unwissenheit und Unverschäm-theit' [an ignorant and shameless man] and discounts all thought that 'dessen abgeschmackteste Dinge' [his utterly tasteless products] might be considered 'Würckungen eines göttlichen Triebes' [results of divine inspiration] (p. 967). The same tones can be heard in the next writer, who repeats the judgements and scraps of biography we already know but adds some details about the fate of the book itself:

Der unausbleibliche Anstos, welchen dieses Buch versursachen müssen, hat die Obrigkeit bewogen, es aufs möglichste zu unterdrucken, und alle vorrätige Exemplare der ganzen auf des Verfassers Kosten veranstalteten Auflage in die gräfliche Kanzeley liefern zu lassen. Daher es sehr selten zu haben ist, indem es nie in Buchhandlungen gekommen, und nur wenige Exemplare vor gedachter Unterdrückung verschenkt oder verkaufet gewesen.[5]

[The offence inevitably caused by this book moved the authorities to do everything they could to suppress it and to have all available copies of the edition, which had been printed at the author's own expense, handed over to the count's chancellery. For this reason it is very hard to come by, never having reached the bookshops and only a few copies having been given away or sold before the aforementioned suppression.]

By the time of the encyclopaedia entry, which relies heavily on the earlier sources, Junckherrott has simply become 'ein seltsamer verrückter Kopf' [a strange, mad chap].

III

Biblical translation, as is obvious and well known, works at a special pressure because the words of the original are held to be divinely inspired and thus the endeavour of transferral becomes a theological undertaking, even a kind of rite, inseparable from the technical business of converting meanings from one language to another. That Junckherrott thought like this (and was far less influenced by the other pressure on biblical translators, the need to evangelize) is plain not only from the translation itself but from the various pieces appended to it. All these relate to the translation and its manner and *raison d'être*; there are no introductory remarks to the New Testament as a whole, though eighteenth-century bibles often included such. They show that Junckherrott was fully conscious of the oddity, even scandalousness, of his translation, and in the different prefaces, introductions, afterwords it is hedged round with he is at pains to pre-empt criticism by establishing the authority by which he proceeds: his work does not derive from expertise as a translator but from direct knowledge of the truth which the New Testament contains.

The pattern of Junckherrott's extra matter is partly conventional. The translation of the New Testament by J. H. Reitz, which had reached a fourth impression by 1730 and which Junckherrott refers to, has a similar apparatus.[6] Both translations have as their first page a list of 'Bemärcke' [remarks] explaining the meaning of symbols inserted into the text which are substantially, sometimes exactly, the same (relating to other possible translations or to words traditionally added). And both include a glossed list of non-German words that occur in the New Testament. Junckherrott seems then to be fitting himself into an established mould, giving his unconventional translation a conventional surround, though whether to emphasize the seriousness or to mask the extremity of what he is doing is uncertain. But he does situate his version among other German versions, referring to Luther as well as to Reitz, and thus to the best and most influential as well as to one of the most current and recent.

Though he can write plainly, in giving a general account of himself, as he does in the first of his pieces, 'Beygefügter Vorbericht, dem geneigten Leser' [preface appended for the interested reader], he uses language of great difficulty and peculiarity, so that the 'interested reader' has to make strenuous efforts to draw anything coherent from it. German prose in the early eighteenth century was still quite a primitive medium, particularly its syntax was often awkward and unsupple, but Junckherrott is deliberately cultivating a 'dark' style, which resembles the language he arrives at in his translation, a resemblance noted by the writers in the *Beyträge* (p. 317) and the *Nachrichten von merkwürdigen Büchern* (p. 315). It is reminiscent of the mystical style of Boehme and Hamann, but his declared model is the style of the Holy Spirit itself, as starts to emerge from the opening of his 'Vorbericht':

Gleichwie des Heil. Geistes Stilus in wenigem viel, der Menschen ihrer aber in vielem wenig da aushin drucket, also ist ein solches durch das gantze Neue Testament zu erkennen, zugleich aber auch in dessen Benahmetwerdung, *Ein Buch Werdungs JEsu Christi.*[7]

[Just as the Holy Spirit's style expresses much in few words, but humans', theirs, little in many, so this is to be seen throughout the New Testament, and equally also in its naming, *A Book of the Becoming of Jesus Christ.*][8]

This then is the beginning of his justification for attending to every scrap of possible meaning in the Greek – because in it the Holy Spirit has expressed 'in wenigem viel'. The most obvious instance of this economy, to which he later alludes, is the parable, and Junckherrott seems to let the parabolic mode colour his understanding of the expressiveness of the New Testament as a whole in that he sees its very language as essentially parabolic, meaning something other, and more, than it says. He adopts this idiom, as he perceives it and partly constructs it in his translation, for his own use. What follows now is an attempt to trace a route through the four pages of the 'Vorbericht', in which Junckherrott's basic principles are outlined.

At one point, in brackets, Junckherrott makes a clear statement: 'nicht daß man wolte suchen den Sinn der in andern Ubersetzungen etwa buchstäblich heraus kommt, sondern welcher nur irgend einem hierinnen möchte einleuchten' [not that one wanted to seek the sense that comes out literally in other translations, but only that which might appear to one here]. So he is emphatically doing something different from 'other' translations, and it is interesting that he characterizes those other translations as 'literal', since it might be thought, reading his own, that what best characterized its difference from previous versions was precisely an extreme literality. In seeking out only 'the sense [...] which might appear to one here', Junckherrott is trying to get at something directly, the truth, the essence, of the New Testament; he is trying to work it into some kind of illuminating manifestation which is beyond or apart from the literal. The work of the translation is 'den in dem Grund enthaltenen Sinn des Geistes [...] in mehrerm Lichtes scheinbahrwer-

dung da aushin zu drucken' [to express the sense of the Spirit contained
in the source in a greater manifestation of light there], to bring to light,
to illumine, the (Holy) Spirit hidden within. One aspect of this is 'das
noch meinst unerkandte gar subtill-würckende Geheimnüß der Setzung
fest sonder vestgesetztwerdung' [the still mostly unrecognized and very
subtly-working secret of fixing without becoming fixed].[9] This is the
mystery of fluid form; the Holy Spirit has found a form in the Greek
New Testament but as it is an apt form it cannot be a form which fixes
or constricts it, its 'Ewigkeiten' [eternities]. Junckherrott's realizing of
this, and even more his determined and serious attempt to avoid fixity
of form in his translation, is at once the main reason for the strange form
of language it has and the main reason for its importance and interest.

Junckherrott's attention to 'the Spirit's sense' arises from the
distinction he makes at the beginning of the 'Vorbericht' between the
Holy Spirit's style and man's. The exact relationship between the two,
and whether there is a point where they meet, is left open, but at first
there is no difficulty in seeing his drift. When Christ's disciples began
to speak the 'mysteries of God', to write down the books of the New
Testament, it was not, says Junckherrott, 'in beredeter menschlicher
Weißheit, aber in der Weißheit Gottes' [in the speech of human wisdom
but in the wisdom of God]. In God's language rather than man's.
For this reason, the 'ohngründlichen Grund' [ungroundable ground]
is 'noch verborgen' [still concealed], and translation is required to
reveal it.

Dieweilen nun Sprachen oder Zungen (*Geheimnüsse*) dieselbe auch sonder Dollmetschung nicht mögen erkannt werden, beydes aber sind Gaben, auch Schenkungen des
Heil. Geistes der (in eben denselben) hin giebet, das Licht, darinnen wir mögen sehen
das Licht; Dann auch in diesen, die Gabe dieser Dollmetschung [...] ist zu prüffen nach
der Schrift Heiliger, auch Zeugnüß des Geistes.

[In the way that languages or tongues (mysteries) these also without translation cannot
be recognized, but both are gifts, also donations of the Holy Spirit who (in precisely
these) gives, the light in which we might see the light; so also here, the gift of this
translation is to probe the Holy Writ, also a testimony of the Spirit.]

So translation is necessary if the mysteries of the New Testament are to
be recognized, the only possible implication being that the 'wisdom of
God' will thus be brought into 'the speech of human wisdom',
converted into a new, apprehensible form. Here we are forced to take
pause. If the texts are not fully realized without the aid of translation,
where does that leave the original Greek? Are the books which were the
main vehicle of the teachings of Christ to be considered defective?

Junckherrott cannot be read as meaning all this from a German perspective – he is not simply saying that as Germans do not understand Greek the 'sense of the Spirit' will remain concealed until it is translated into the vernacular. He is saying that the role of translation is to draw the Spirit's meanings into the human sphere.

This ends the first phase of the Preface. Junckherrott then says, in curious sentences without verbs, that it would be impossible, without 'leermachung des Creutzes Christi, auch des Geistes Sinn in demselben' [emptying the cross of Christ, also the Spirit's sense in the same], to translate into 'die übliche Teutsche Sprach und Red-Art' [normal German]. This allows a kind of retrospective take on what has gone before: if he is deliberately avoiding conventional speech, and also and thus avoiding the type of translation others have done before him (as he has said he is), then he could be construed as saying that what is needed is a *new* translation, a translation which would restore the original by translating 'against' the versions which have obscured the movements of the Spirit through using a language too fixed, too human. This idea, of translation as restoration, finds some support in the account Junckherrott then gives of the progress of his translating. It means his sense that the original has to be brought to light, to be clarified, is simultaneously a wish to return it to its enigmatic, compact mysteriousness.

At first, Junckherrott says, he translated into the language of men, for which he uses the analogy of God taking on human shape in Christ, integrating a quotation from Philippians (2:7) which expresses this event as a degradation, as taking on the form of a servant. The degradation, the becoming 'abgeschmackt' [tasteless] as Junckherrott puts it, which means taking on a familiar, non-spiritual, form (making himself 'of no reputation'), had to happen for God to impinge on the world, but this was only a temporary appearance whose full meaning was to emerge once it was over. Junckherrott intends a similar inference to be made about his own translation, I think, that another mode is entered on after a first crude transitional phase, but he expresses it through a different analogy, this time to the story of the woman of Samaria. This analogy complicates the first: Junckherrott compares himself to the people of Samaria, who initially are drawn by the woman's testimony (in English: 'Come, see a man, which told me all things that ever I did: is not this the Christ?', John 4:29) but then come to believe independently of her (the Samaritans 'said unto the woman, Now we believe, not because of thy saying: for we have heard him

ourselves, and know that this is indeed the Christ', John 4:42).
Junckherrott paraphrases both these passages and provides the corollary:
'auff diese Weise ein jeder, auch ich nicht mehr durch dieses des
Ubersetzers seiniger sprechung glaube da, dann selbst ich habe gehöret
auch weiß nun sichtbarlich, daß diese Zeugung ist Wahrheit in so fern'
[in this way everyone, I too, no longer by this the translator's own
speaking believe there, for even I have heard and know now visibly, that
this testimony is truth in so far]. He claims a kind of unmediated access
to the truth in the scriptures which allows him 'dahin auffpassend auff
den Winck der Zeigung des Lichtes' [looking out for the sign of the
showing of the light], to express the Holy Spirit directly, to write in the
language of God, not man. At the end of the Preface he refers to himself
not as a translator, but as 'ein Küsser der Wahrheit' [a kisser of the
truth]. This parallels Philo Judaeus's account of the translation of the
Septuagint, where the translators 'cease to be translators and become
"prophets of the mysteries"'.[10]

I V

The 'Vorbericht' is followed by 'Einige Gedancken des Ubersetzers,
betreffend die Dollmetschung Neues Testaments' [Some thoughts
relating to the translation of the New Testament], in which Junckherrott
moves to a further explanation of his translation, this time from a more
purely technical point of view.[11] This fits oddly with the identification
with the Spirit made just before, but from it some clear principles
emerge. And the shift to the details of technique is not in fact an
abandonment of the claims of spirituality since the rules, which is what
they amount to, are justified above all because they will guarantee that
the translator will not 'twist' the 'sense of the Spirit'. To translate with
direct access to the Spirit is to use the Spirit's language, and the way to
do this is to ensure that its lineaments are preserved in translation,
whence the rules. That those representatives of other versions, Luther
and Reitz, failed to preserve these lineaments seems to be the main
quarrel Junckherrott has with them, and they are arraigned for their lack
of discipline in his first rule. In giving an account of Junckherrott's
'Gedancken' I will quote freely, thus providing further examples of
Junckherrott's style, though here it is less opaque than elsewhere.

The first 'Thought' states: 'Soll eine wahre Dollmetschung heraus
kommen, so muß das Wort, einmahl wie das andere mahl, und nicht

einmahl so, und das andere und mehrere mahl, anderst, gedollmetschet werden' [if a true translation is to come out the word must be translated once and for all, and not the first time one way and the next and other times differently]. The example given is δαίμων and all words derived or made up from it. Giving a list of their various solutions, Junckherrott takes issue with Luther and Reitz for not making the links between all these words apparent and thus obscuring the unity and tight-knit quality of the original. 'Ab solcher Dollmetschung möchte einem wohl Entsetzen ankommen; wann einem Dollmetscher frey stehet, die Worte also auch mit einander äusserst contrairen zu dollmetschen, so kan einer sagen und setzen einen Sinn, welcher ihme nur kommlich ist' [such translation might well make one recoil with horror; if a translator is free to translate the words thus, with ones quite contrary to each other, he can say and put whatever sense suits him]. Against this is set, in the recurring phrase, 'eine wahre Dollmetschung', which seeks to eliminate the arbitrary, though doing so it obviously sacrifices what for Luther was vital, the idiomatic. Junckherrott's own (narrow) course is to keep the word and its compounds unaltered, and so *Daimon* duly appears in his glossary (see below).

The second of the 'Gedancken' brings the correlate to the first: every different word in Greek must have its own translation in German. This applies even (especially) to apparent synonyms.

The third states that compound words must not be expressed as simplex words. The composite form of the original word must be evident, each particle must be conveyed.

As a natural consequence of rules 1 and 3 comes the fourth:

Soll eine warhaffte Dollmetschung da heraus kommen, so muß die Signification des Simplicis oder Radicis beybehalten, die da hinzu gesetzte Particula mithin auch exprimiret werden, und nicht, wann αλλάσσω, (allásso) ich ändere, gedollmetschet wird, καταλλάσσω (katallássoo) ich versöhne, sondern vielmehr, ich verändere mich da gegenhin, (*der Geändertwerdung nach da gegenhin*) gedollmetschet werden, als welches den Grund der Versöhnung ausdrucket, dann wann ich mich verändere da gegenhin, werde ich als ein anderer da gegenhin angenommen.

[If a veritable translation is to come out there the signification of the simplex or radix must be preserved, the particles added to it be expressed with it too, and not, if αλλάσσω, (allásso) is translated by 'I change', καταλλάσσω (katallássoo) by 'I reconcile', but rather by 'I change towards there', (*according to the becoming changed towards there*), which expresses the ground of reconciliation, for if I change towards something there, I am accepted as another there towards.]

This is much more radical, also more doctrinaire, and begins to give an idea of what to expect of the translation itself. Words are not to be translated as units of meaning, but as structures, structures anatomized and transferred to German in pieces. Junckherrott sees this method of translating καταλλάσσω as expressing 'den Grund der Versöhnung' [the ground of reconciliation]. The notion of 'Grund' is an important one for him, we have come across it before in the 'Vorbericht', and in the 'Bemärcke' at the front of the book Junckherrott notes the use of a particular symbol in the text to signal a more conventional alternative translation, 'wiewohl den Grund nicht eigentlich ausdrückend' [although not properly expressive of the ground]. For Junckherrott the 'Grund' of something is the meaning held in the etymology of its *Greek* word, and the importance thus conferred on Greek is because it is the chosen language of the Holy Spirit. The 'Grund' of Greek, its etymological ground, is the reposing-place of the Spirit, and etymology is the path back to it. With the example of καταλλάσσω, Junckherrott argues for element-for-element translation because it allows access to the movement underlying the idea of reconciliation, but the real importance seems to be not this supposed insight but the etymological descent to that point beyond which etymology cannot lead and which therefore represents a final repair of the Spirit, 'the sense of the Spirit contained in the ground (or source)' ('Vorbericht'). The equation of etymological elements with the Spirit, coupled with the process of translation, in which the broken-down Greek meanings often become unrecoverable, is reminiscent of Walter Benjamin's later thought that through translation intimations of a 'reine Sprache', a pure language, might be felt, a kind of pre-language of total communication, which for Junckherrott is the Holy Spirit.[12] Language is no longer a vehicle of meaning, but of the Spirit, which is to say that it is actually a manifestation of the Spirit. Traces of human language adhere, the material is there, but its articulation is largely frustrated by the dominance of the mode of the Spirit itself, which is revealed as shifting, incoherent, in the process of constituting meaning that is never quite constituted in human terms. That is a way of understanding Junckherrott's intentions which we can test against the translation itself later. But we should note now how radical his conception is.

The fifth rule also concerns the transportation of Greek forms into German, this time grammar. Pronouns, Junckherrott says, should not be translated as (possessive) adjectives. So πατὴρ ἡμῶν ('our father', but literally 'father of ours') is to be rendered 'Vatter unserer' [Father of ours], not 'unser Vatter' [our Father] or even 'Vatter unser' as translations usually have it. Curiously this is not justifed simply because it accords with the form of the Spirit, but is followed by a long reasoning on theological grounds and in impenetrable language whose detail eludes me apart from the initial question as to 'what species of man' is permitted to call God a father, with the implication that only Christ can. This is then followed by the point that 'unserer' fosters a degree of significant ambiguity which exists in the Greek. Junckherrott suggests that in the sentence 'Our Father, which art in heaven, hallowed be thy name' to use 'unserer' means that 'our' can be applied to both heaven and name as well as to father, supplying citations which read tendentiously give possible grounds for entertaining this idea. The pattern is now familiar: the specific justifications are far-fetched, off-putting in their wilfulness, but the underlying intent of conveying the multiplicity of the Greek, of translating a network of possibilities rather than a single strand, is serious, and seriously pursued.

The sixth rule reinforces the point:

In der Dollmetschung muß auch kein Comma, oder andere den Gelehrten in den Buchstaben übliche Distinction gesetzt werden, dann wann ich wolte setzen Vatter unserer, der in denen Himmelen, so könte obiger sinn schon nicht heraus kommen, wie wann ich ohne Comma es setze, und das Wort *unserer* zu denen Worten – *der in denen Himmelen*, – auch nachgehends – auf *Nahmen* – ziehe.

[In the translation no comma or other distinction common among the scholars in letters must be placed, for if I were to put 'father of ours, who in those heavens' the above sense could not come out as it could if I write it without a comma and connect the words *of ours* to those words – *who in those heavens* – and also to the following – to *name*.]

Although he mentions it neither here nor anywhere else, Junckherrott uses the word 'da' instead of the comma, giving the translation (and sometimes his own writing) its most distinctive and eccentric trait. (See p. 270 for its use in the translation, and p. 262 for its use in his own writing.)

The seventh rule argues similarly with regard to the position of adjectives, which must be kept as in the Greek. If the adjective comes after the noun (as it quite regularly does in Greek) it should not be put in its normal German position before the noun, again because this might restrict its range. The example Junckherrott gives is revealing and provocative because it is a passage so routinely understood otherwise than the way he suggests: αὐτὸς ἡμᾶς βαπτίσει ἐν μνεύματι ἁγίῳ καὶ πυρί. Luther translates this as 'der wird euch mit dem Heiligen geist vnd mit fewer teuffen' (Matthew 3:11; Authorized Version: 'he shall baptize you with the Holy Ghost, and with fire'), and by repeating the 'mit' makes it doubly clear that 'heilig' belongs to 'geist' and not to 'fewer'.[13] Junckherrott proposes 'derselbe euch wird tauchen in Geiste heiligem auch Feuer' [the same will dip you in Spirit holy also fire] and adds: 'dann also kan und muß das Wort heiligem auff Geiste – nicht weniger auch auff Feuer – gezogen werden' [for thus can and must the word 'holy' be related to Spirit – no less than to fire]. There follows a string of references associating Christ with fire.

The next two rules are also to do with position: if pronouns occur in the Greek they must be translated *as well as* the person indicated by the ending of the verb (Greek uses no separate pronoun except for emphasis). So, to take the example Junckherrott refers to, ἐγὼ ἀπέστειλα ὑμᾶς ('I sent you', John 4:38) comes out as 'Ich hab geschickt ich euch' [I have sent I you].[14] As Junckherrott says, the pronoun has not been put in 'von ohngefähr' [at random] but because it has 'einen wichtigen Nachdruck' [an important emphasis]; but to give this as a reason for translating as he does is misleading because all his version does is register the presence of the additional pronoun, it doesn't express its effect. The proper German means of doing that is eschewed. There is thus a discrepancy between how Junckherrott proceeds and the reasons he gives for it, and the true motive seems to be the uncomplicated one of wanting to stick as closely as possible to the contours of the Greek. This is supported by the ninth rule, which insists that the words for 'not' should not be translated out of position so that the exact emphasis of the Spirit be retained.

The tenth of the 'Gedancken' says that ἀλλά and καί ('but' and 'and') must usually be translated by 'aber' [though] and 'auch' [also], not 'sondern' [but] and 'und' [and] which 'nicht so wohl zusammen binden' [do not join together so well] (Junckherrott tries to avoid them in his own prose too). As with the observation about punctuation, an interlinked, unimpeded text is the ideal.

The 'Gedancken' end with a return to the sentiments of the 'Vorbericht', invoking 1 Corinthians 12:10: 'Zungen, auch deren Dollmetschung ist eine Gabe des Geistes' [tongues, also their translation is a gift of the Spirit]. Despite the apparent setting out of principles the 'Gedancken' comprise, this is their core, the belief that for a 'pure and true translation' the translator must be inspired. And for Junckherrott an inspired translator will be just that and speak the language of the Spirit. To speak this language means reproducing the form of the original, for the Spirit lies in, is, the form. This explains the apparent paradox between a set of well-defined rules and the claim of divine inspiration.

What is the simplest way of describing Junckherrott's technique, the retention of Greek word-order, is not enunciated as such. Perhaps it emerges naturally from the ten rules (it is almost, but not quite, a necessary consequence of them); or perhaps it is such an obvious requirement for Junckherrott as to not need spelling out.

V

Next comes the glossary already mentioned. This extends over fifty pages and provides commentary on contentious words, most of which are transliterated Greek and familiar as such. The purpose of such lists was mainly to help the reader enter into the biblical world, and thus belonged to the clarifying, popularizing impulse behind Lutheranism. But though traces of this conventional purpose remain, Junckherrott has really turned the form to a quite different use and made it the principal means of presenting his differences with previous translators, specifically Luther and Reitz. The entries also allow us to shadow Junckherrott's extreme and often fantastic etymologizing, a process that goes on throughout the translation itself. 'Daimon' gets a representative treatment. The extravagant etymology is quite false and curious, but the style is by Junckherrott's standards clear, and the whole of the glossary is noticeably less marked by the stylistic mannerisms that affect the rest of the editorial matter.

Daimon [...] von δαίω ich weiß, und dann von μάω, ich suche mit Verlangen, dannenhero man sagen mögte, daß ein Daimon seye *ein Geist der das Wissen bloß da hinauf bey Verlangen suchet da auffhin*; Teuffel aber kan dieses Wort nicht in Warheit gedollmetscht werden, wie Luther gleichwohl fast in allen Orthen N. Test. thut, sintemahlen Διάβολος ist, auch wird gedollmetscht Teuffel insgemein, gleichwie aber dieses ein gantz ander Wort ist als Δαίμων, so wird auch damit ein anderer Geist durch den Buchstaben der Schrifft bezeichnet, dann gesetzt, daß Daimonen in das Königreich des Satans gehören, so ist doch umb dieses willen der auch der Daimon da nicht der Teuffel selbst; dieses Wort mag auch nicht geschicklich werden gedollmetschet, (unreiner) Geist, wie Reitz es dollmetschet. (pp. 7–8)

[*Daimon*, from δαίω I know, and then from μάω, I seek with desire, whence one might say that a daimon is *a spirit who seeks out knowledge only there up by desire there*; but this word cannot in truth be translated by devil, as Luther nevertheless does in almost all parts of the NT, since Διάβολος is also translated as devil in general, even though this is quite another word than Δαίμων and so with it another spirit is designated by the letters of the scriptures, for though admittedly daimons belong in the kingdom of Satan the daimon is not for that reason there the devil himself; this may also not well be translated by (unclean) spirit, as Reitz translates it.]

What we have is a justification for leaving the word untranslated, supported by criticism of other versions. The etymological paraphrase given is inconsistent, since the notion of 'Geist' is introduced even though Junckherrott's proposed derivation excludes it. And the point against Luther's use of 'Teufel' may seem a good one until we realize that Luther distinguishes between '*ein* Teufel' and '*der* Teufel', thus making the difference clear and also according with common usage. That kind of difference is too subtle for Junckherrott's focus on the 'letters of the scriptures' and doesn't interest him: the words appear differently in Greek and must appear differently in German. But this just underlines what Junckherrott has already insisted on, the relative unimportance of transposing into our terms, into a form of understanding which can be grasped, with attention fixed instead on the constituent parts and process of language, on the texture and substance of the original. One effect of this is to reveal the inconsistencies and heterogeneity of the Greek source, something Luther had tended to elide. The ideal is to bring the original across whole, as if its otherness, and thus its translatability, were not a fact. Junckherrott lies very close to Borges's fable of Pierre Menard, the translator who was actually a copier.

VI

There are straightforward ways in which we can compare Junckherrott's translation with the two others he explicitly invites comparison with, by Luther and Reitz. And we can see that on his own terms at least, there are significant advances. A simple example comes from the beginning of Matthew. It is a single word: γενέσις, which Junckherrott translates by 'werdung' [becoming]: 'Ein buch werdungs Jesu Christi' [a book of the becoming of Jesus Christ]. Luther and Reitz both use 'geburt' [birth], though Reitz indicates in a note that 'Werdung' would be a possibility. Junckherrott's choice is forced on him by the first of his 'thoughts', that variations on a particular root should be recognizable as such. The difference between 'geburt' and 'werdung' contains *in nuce* the difference between Junckherrott's translation and the others'. 'Geburt' clearly reduces γενέσις to one of its possibilities, narrows its spectrum of meaning to the one idea. 'Werdung' keeps that spectrum wide, allows a flickering and shift of meaning which ranges from beginning through a development to a completion all held together in one word. 'Werdung' is an odd word, but it is dense with the incipient, fluctuating meaning which Junckherrott identifies as being crucial to the New Testament as a whole when he says at the beginning of his Preface that 'des Heil. Geistes Stilus in wenigem viel [...] aushin drucket' and gives as his example precisely the word 'Werdung'. Junckherrott is quite aware of what he is doing and it is not in itself at all eccentric; the opening out of the Greek as against the accepted translations, the cultivation of a certain ambiguity, is also, in this case, more accurate. The theological intent is also a philological one.

This responsiveness to the Greek, as if translation could be something like tracing, appears altogether more oddly when it is a question of a continuous text. This is how Junckherrott renders the prologue to John's gospel, the title of which he reproduces word for word and without regard for German as 'Das nach Johanne Evangelium' [the according to John gospel]:

Im anfang ware die rede da auch die rede ware zu den Gott da auch Gott ware die rede da.

2. Diese ware im anfange da zu den Gotte da.

3. Alle durch derselben wurden da auch sonder derselben ward da auch nicht ein einiges welches ist worden da.

4. In derselben leben ware da auch das leben ware das licht derer menschen da.

5. Auch das licht in der düsterigkeit scheinet da auch die düsterigkeit dasselbe nicht hat genommen da gegenhin.

6. (*Nun*) ward ein mensch ein seyender geschickt worden von Gottes in so fern da abhin ein nahmen demselben Johannes da.

7. Dieser kame in eine zeugung dahin in dem bezeuget werden da daß solte geben er zeugung von des lichtes da in dem bezeuget werden damit alle möchten glauben durch desselben da.

8. Nicht war jener da das licht da aber daß solte geben er zeugung von des lichtes da in dem bezeuget werden.

9. Es wäre das licht das wahre da welches in lichte begabet allen menschen da kommendt in die welt dahin.

10. In der welt ware sie (*die rede*) da auch die welt durch derselben ist worden da auch die welt dieselbe nicht hat hat erkand da in so fern.

11. In die eigene kame die dahin auch die eigene dieselbe nicht haben genommen dabeyhin in so fern.

12. So viel etwa aber haben hin genommen dieselbe da gegeben hat sie denenselben dahin weesenheit da kindere Gottes zu werden da außhin denen seyenden glaubhaffte in den nahmen derselben da.

13. Die nicht auß bluhten auch nicht auß willens fleisches auch nicht auß willens Mannes aber auß Gottes wären gezeuget worden da.

14. Auch die rede fleisch wardt da auch hutchete sie in uns da auch beschaueten wir die geachtet seyung derselben eine geachtet seyung als eines gewordenen alleinigen in dem werden in so fern von Vatters erfüllt genade auch wahrheits da.

15. Johannes gibt zeugung von derselben da in der bezeugetwerdung auch hat gekryschen er redendt da dieser ware welchen ich sagte da der hinden nach meiner hinkommende da vor meiner ist worden da einhin da dieweilen ein vorderster meiner ware er da.

16. Auch auß der erfüllenden fülle desselben da wir alle wir haben genommen genade an statt danckes dahin.

17. Dann die festsetzung gesetzliche durch Mosis ist gegeben worden dahin die genade auch die wahrheit durch Jesu Christi ist worden da.

18. Gott da keiner hat gesehen jemahlen da der gewordene alleinige sohn in dem werden der seyende in den schooß des vatters da jener da hat (es) da einhin geführet da außhin.

[In the beginning was speech there also the speech was to the God there also God was speech there.

2. This was in the beginning there to the God there.

3. All through the same became there also without the same became there also not any thing which is become there.

4. In the same [speech] life was there also the life was the light of those people there.

5. Also the light in the darkness shines there also the darkness not took it there towards.

6. (Now) became a man one being sent down from God in so far there a name to him John there.

7. This man came in a witness there in the being witnessed there that he should give witness of the light there in the being witnessed that all might believe through the same there.

8. Not was he there the light there but that he should give witness of the light there in being witnessed.

9. It were the light the true there which gifts in light all people there coming into the world there.

10. In the world it (*speech*) was there also the world through the same is become there also the world the same not recognized there in so far.

11. Into its own came it [speech] there also its own the same not took in in so far.

12. As many though took in the same there it gave them there substance there to become children of God there to them being believers in the name of the same there.

13. Who not from bloods also not from will of flesh also not from will of Man but from God had been born there.

14. Also speech flesh became there also it hutted in us there also we looked upon the being-respected of the same a being-respected as of one become alone in the becoming in so far of the Father filled of grace also of truth there.

15. John gives witness of the same there in the becoming-witnessed also he shrieked speaking there this was whom I said there the one behind after me coming there before me has become there in there because one most in front of me he was there.

16. Also from the fulfilling fullness of him there we all we have taken grace on instead of thanks there.

17. For the fixing legally through Moses was given there the grace also the truth through Jesus Christ is become there.

18. God there none has seen ever there the become alone son in the becoming the being in the bosom of the father there he there has there set (it) in there out.]

Most of the local oddities speak for themselves and need no comment. It is obvious that Junckherrott is not in any normal sense *writing* German, he is using it to take an impression of the Greek. Divergences from German usage can usually be explained by reference to the Greek. For instance, the use of cases after prepositions is governed by the original, not by German requirements, so that in verse 1 we find 'zu den Gott' as a translation of πρὸς τὸν Θεόν, with similar transgressions (accusative for dative) in virtually every verse. This is clearly very extreme, and is not covered by any of the rules set down in the 'Gedancken'. Being made to behave like Greek, the German becomes freakish, outlandish, and its status as German is undermined (it is odder, though perhaps not harder to understand, than the attempted English translation). Translation appears as a form of violent incursion where one language invades another and twists it into its image. German bends to the Greek and in so doing comes close to ceasing to be a language at all. It is more an instrument of measurement. This seems to be Junckherrott's intention, but obviously there are limits that make the translation something different from a transliteration. Grammatical case, and to a slightly lesser extent word-order, are as far as Junckherrott is prepared to go in the realm of direct transposition. We might have expected gender to be treated similarly, but it is not.

Certainly one of the most curious and quirky aspects of the translation is its handling of participles, some verbs and fewer nouns. The practice seems to arise from the stipulation in the fourth of the 'Gedancken' that every element of a word should be attended to in its discrete etymological sense, but it far exceeds what can be explained by this. An expansion takes place, as in verse 7, where 'daß solte geben er zeugung von des lichtes da in dem bezeuget werden' translates ἵνα μαρτυρήσῃ περὶ τοῦ φωτός (that he should bear witness of the light), that is, the verb is reiterated by the addition of 'in dem bezeuget werden', as if Junckherrott were translating both the verbal sense and the infinitive which somehow still inheres in the word. Similarly, the noun μαρτυρία (witness) is given as 'eine zeugung [...] in dem bezeuget werden', a rendering which can perhaps be justified because the noun derives from the verb. Some words receive this treatment, and some do not, and it is impossible to identify any consistent reason why this should be so. In John 1:20 ὡμολόγησεν (he confessed) becomes the quite extravagant 'redete er sich hin|auß zusamt dem geredet werden in der geredetwerdung', whereas ἠρνήσατο (he denied) becomes simply 'laugnete er'. In verse 17 ὁ νόμος (the law) is rendered as 'die festsetzung gesetzliche' (perhaps because it derives from the verb νεμω?), whereas φῶς (light) is always rendered as 'licht' (but it too derives from a verb). A more interesting instance of such 'double' (or triple) translations is Junckherrott's practice of rendering various verbs of seeing and knowing as 'sehen mit wissen', thus acknowledging the etymological interconnexions between the words in Greek. John 1:29 is thus 'siehe mit wissen da das lamm des Gottes' [see with knowledge there the lamb of God].

If little can be deduced about the cause, something can be said about the effect of these translations. It is an effect of diffuseness, in which the Greek is undone into German. We can try to equate this with 'the sense of the Spirit contained in the ground' along lines suggested above, as if Junckherrott were transmitting not the literal sense, but the movements of the Spirit; and this must in fact be his intention. But even a reader sympathetic to such an enterprise must soon feel misgivings, at least about this particular instance, misgivings fed by the inconsistency and sheer esoteric nature of what is going on. It is especially odd that Junckherrott offers no comment on these expansions when he is at such pains to clarify other aspects of his practice.

Still, there are angles from which we can read his opening to John against Luther's and point to some advantages it has. Not to suggest that Junckherrott is better than Luther in this or that respect, they are too different in kind, but to try to identify what it may be about Luther (and implicitly other German versions) that Junckherrott wishes his translation to correct. In the first verse Junckherrott translates ὁ Λόγος as 'die rede' (Luther had 'Wort' and has nearly always been followed). Interestingly, this corresponds to Calvin's preference for *sermo* rather than *verbum*.[15] Another trace suggesting the influence of Calvin comes in a variant Junckherrott offers for 'ware': 'ist'.[16] This is uncharacteristic, since the Greek itself is clearly a past tense and Junckherrott usually renders tenses faithfully. But it points to an uneasiness about the word shared by Calvin. How can the verb expressing the *logos* be in the past tense, apparently limiting it, giving it an extent within time? Junckherrott's plumping for the past tense while signalling some discomfort with it through the variant is evidence of an awareness, in which accuracy prevails, of the special status of the word. The use of unexpected tenses of the verb 'to be' is part of the dynamic of the prologue, which reaches forward into the rest of John. A tension within the meaning of *being* is complemented by a counterpart, the idea of *becoming*. The placing and interacting of these verbs are important to the texture of John's text, and Junckherrott meticulously reproduces each thread, even if the final result does look more like the reverse of the tapestry than the clear pattern of the surface.[17] John is concerned with the threshold between being and becoming, the theological difference between the two, with the way words change their meaning, or have another resonance, depending on whether they attach to the human or to the sacred.[18] This comes through in Junckherrott, but is sometimes obscured, or at least reduced, in Luther.

The insistence on ἦν (was), used four times and in three separate ways in the first two verses, together with the unusual tense, confer on it a particular significance which its absence from verse 3 extends to the word of becoming ἐγένετο, which 'replaces' it. On each side of the line beween verses 2 and 3 there is a concentration of, before, words denoting *being* and, after, words denoting *becoming*. This balancing is maintained in Junckherrott, who in verse 3 uses three different forms of 'werden'. Luther runs otherwise: 'Alle ding sind durch dasselbige gemacht / und on dasselbige ist nichts gemacht / was gemacht ist' [all things are made by it, and without it is nothing made that is made]. The balance between being and becoming is thus upset, since even though it is only functioning as a passive auxiliary, the verb of being associates itself with the sphere of becoming, with the human sphere of the created. The reassertion in verse 4 of 'war' as pertaining to the divine *logos* has thus lost something of its weight.

The counterpointing of ἦν and ἐγένετο becomes particularly clear in verse 6 where the first word signifies becoming and is attached to a human, John the Baptist. Luther uses 'werden', but in such a way that it attracts a passive sense: 'Es ward ein mensch von Gott gesandt'.[19] Junckherrott uses 'werden' in an absolute sense, as in the Greek (and unusual too there), though he seeks to soften the effect a little by introducing a particle: '(*Nun*) ward ein mensch ein seyender geschickt worden von Gottes'. The latter half of this phrase is obviously open to the same strictures as Luther's 'ist gemacht' (though it is a participle, not a verb), but 'ward' carries its full weight. John the Baptist is expressly the one who was *not* the light (verse 8).

In verse 10 ἦν occurs with an implied masculine subject which in the Greek can encompass both God and the Word – the indivisibility of the two here has point. Luther, providing the subject 'das', maintains ambiguity but shifts it onto light and Word, where it is still meaningful.[20] Junckherrott clarifies by making it refer only to the Word, which in his version requires the feminine pronoun (for 'die rede'). This seems to diminish the compactness of the text, and doesn't correspond to his normal practice (or its result) of openness. Conversely, the next verse (11) shows up the shortcomings of Junckherrott's general method, as it fails to differentiate between τὰ ἴδια and οἱ ἴδιοι. The verse means literally something like: 'He/it came to his/its own (things [τὰ ἴδια], neuter plural]), and his/its own (people [οἱ ἴδιοι], masculine plural) received him/it not'. The subtlety of the Greek lies in the small shift from neuter to masculine: God-the Word-Christ came to the things his own because created by him, and those very things, in their human form but just as dependent on him as the rest of creation, rejected him. Junckherrott's literality cannot convey that, but he could be seen to be correcting Luther's 'Er kam inn sein eigenthum / vnd die seinen namen in nicht auff' [He came unto his property, and his own received him not], which distinguishes so sharply that the connection is in danger of escaping us.

In the dynamic of being and becoming verse 14 is crucial, the moment of transition when the divine becomes human and so the verb of becoming can be used of it – both Junckherrott and Luther have 'ward'. But the next verb, ἐσκήνωσεν, which Luther gives as 'wonet' [dwells] ('Und das Wort ward fleisch / vnd wonet vnter vns'), is actually a more provisional word, its root meaning tabernacle or tent; the temporary nature of the habitation is brought out by Junckherrott's 'hutchete', itself a makeshift word which seems to have been devised for the occasion. Being will only be part of becoming for a while. The continuing difference between the two is re-emphasized in verse 15 in John's riddling words on precedence: Christ the Word, though coming after him, has *become* (γέγονεν) before him (i.e. is far more important – the Authorized Version has 'is preferred before me') because he/it *was* before him. Junckherrott is faithful to these theological niceties, but Luther weakens the antithesis: 'Nach mir wird komen / der vor mir gewesen ist / denn er war ehe denn ich' [After me will come he who has been before me, for he was before me] relies on the force 'war' has acquired since the first verse, and on the change in tense, for a degree of contention with 'gewesen ist' to obtain.

These points do not demonstrate Junckherrott's superiority to Luther, but they do indicate something of the intention of the translation, which in many ways, and for good reasons, opposes Luther's. I have been attending to its qualities because its faults have already led to its virtual extinction. Its first readers saw only the inconsistencies, the wilfulness, and overlooked the deliberateness, the sustained rigorousness of the translation, its radical accuracy. And this despite the fact that Junckherrott provided a defence in the form of a dialogue appended at the end of the book. The explicit subject of this dialogue is the controversial nature of the translation.

VII

'Einiger Anhang eines Nachberichts, unter einem da zuvorhin gegangenen Gespräch: in mitte Cleophas, auch Timotheo, zur Prüffung, auch zum Uberzeugungs-Grund, in Schrifft dahin gesetzet' [A sort of appended epilogue in the form of a previously conducted dialogue between Cleophas, also Timotheo, set down in writing for examination, and as a reason for conviction] consists of Cleophas (the name given to one of Christ's disciples, who unwittingly spoke to him on the road to Emmaus[21]) asking difficult questions about the translation and Timotheo (the godfearer, Junckherrott's spokesman) giving resolutely difficult answers. There are no page numbers, but it is set out in numbered paragraphs. Cleophas speaks clearly, making exactly the objections the translation first brings to mind; Timotheo replies in riddles, in a dark style which is nevertheless cogent and considered, and so forestalls them for Junckherrott's readership. Cleophas's first complaint, that the translation is 'sehr wunderlich, ja [...] abgeschmackt' [very curious, even tasteless], provokes the longest response, which stands under the sign of the general claim that 'das buch des N. T. bezeuget lauter Geist [...] folglich muß dasselbe auch geistlich geurtheilet werden' [the book of the NT is a pure testimony of Spirit, accordingly it must be judged spiritually] (§2). Judgement can only be through the Spirit, and Timotheo warns against false judgement before comparing the translation to Paul preaching to the Athenians (they thought him a 'babbler', a 'setter forth of strange gods' (Acts 17:18), which of course he was): 'Daß auch diese übersetzung denen meinsten eine Gelegenheit etwas neueres zu sehen, zu reden, auch zu hören da irgend' [that this translation too is for most people some opportunity to see, to speak, also to hear something new there]. It *should* startle – Junckherrott sees himself as spreading the word in a 'hard', undigested form. He is trying to make it possible to see the New Testament with fresh eyes. That the idiom this intent results in will put people off, 'dieses hat der übersetzer selbst [...] voraushin wohl erkannt' [the translator himself has clearly recognized in advance], but, Timotheo explicitly insists, he has proceeded in full consciousness of what he is doing: 'nicht hat er getretten in Düstrigkeit da: aber gehabbt hat er das Licht des Lebens' [he has not proceeded in darkness there, but has had the light of life]. Timotheo suggests that a reader proceeding likewise will in the end come to understand the translation, even though it is 'anfänglich […] da aushin zu sinnen beschwerlich' [difficult to work out there at first]. From these points, which are all reinforced by biblical references, Timotheo goes on to anticipate another charge, that of the lack of logical connection or clear syntax. The terms are familiar but the passage is worth quoting. It reasserts the Pauline influence:

> Daß in diese übersetzung keine Connexion-Zusammenhang? Es ist bekannt daß in heiliger Schrifft zweyerley Sinn-Verstand, der eine ist buchstäblich, eignet sich dem Todt, der ander ist der Sinn des Geistes, welcher ist lebende 2 Cor. 3, 6 folglich ein jeder Sinn ins besonder seine Connexion-Zusammenhang, beyde aber im höchsten Grad einander entgegen; Wenn nun der Geist den todten Buchstaben macht lebende folglich muß er seine Connexion-Zusammenhang dem Eigenen nach verlieren, also bleibt nur dem Sinn des Geistes eine Connexion, jene ist getruncken oder ertruncken.

> [No coherent syntax in this translation? It is well known that in holy scripture there are two kinds of sense-understanding, the one is literal, suited to death, the other is the sense of the Spirit, which is living (2 Corinthians 3:6) accordingly each sense has its particular way of connecting, both though to the highest degree oppose each other; if then the Spirit makes the dead letter living it follows that it must lose its own coherent syntax, so there remains a connection only for the sense of the Spirit, that is drunk or drowned.]

This again makes the point that the aim is to express 'den Sinn des Geistes oder eigentlich daß Geistliche Wesen' [the sense of the Spirit or properly the spiritual essence] (§2). It is nothing less than to revitalize the dead letter. But it is typical of Junckherrott that he undermines the credibility of what he is arguing by an uncontrolled word-play ('getruncken oder ertruncken'), perhaps an example of the kind of 'Connexion' he thinks the Spirit makes but not likely to win Cleophas's confidence.

Cleophas's next question nevertheless accepts that the logic of the letter does not belong to the New Testament but asks where that leaves the problem of comprehensibility. Surely Christ and his disciples, if here now, would speak so as to be understood? (§3) Timotheo is consequential in his reply. Citing Luke 2:49–50 he points out that Jesus was ill-understood at first: 'wie nun gestern auch heute, lehret der Heil. Geist alle; Diesem nach nicht zu bewundern daß auch Lern-Jüngere des HErrn diese Dollmetschung anfänglich nicht verstehen' [then as now the Holy Spirit teaches all; accordingly it is not surprising that even disciples of the Lord do not understand this translation at first] (§4).

What, then, about the sheer oddity of the translation? Cleophas persists, quoting Matthew 1:18: 'Maria ward befunden im Wanste habende aus Geistes heiligen' [Mary was found with a belly of the Holy Ghost], which he finds not just peculiar, but 'eine Geringachtung' [disparaging] (§5). Timotheo's reply is interesting. He points out that 'seyende schwanger' [with child] is given as a variant but prefers the literal version because 'etwas thierisches' [something bestial] is meant, to emphasize Jesus's humble, bodily origin (§6). Cleophas cedes this but questions other instances, particularly the titles of individual books, whose eccentricity he finds trivial. They are certainly very odd. The Acts of the Apostles Junckherrott gives as 'Treibungen derer H. Apostolen da abhin' [doings of the Holy Apostles down there], and Timotheo himself quotes perhaps the oddest, 'Jacobi des geschickten da abhin schickung da überhin gäntzliche da gegenhin' (The General Epistle of James), and defends it: every detail counts and must be preserved. 'Der heilige Geist [habe] nicht ein einiges Strichlein oder Spitzlein sonder Grund auffzeichnen lassen. [...] nicht ein einiges Jota, welches unter des Geistes heiligen ist geschrieben worden, daß nicht solte erfüllet werden' [the holy Ghost did not dictate a single little stroke or dot without reason, not a single jot was written under the holy Spirit that should not be fulfilled] (§8). It is the translator's duty to fulfil the demands of the spiritual text.

Cleophas presses further with more specific instances, asking why 'die Schrifftgelehrten' (Luther's word for what is rendered in English by 'scribes') is rejected for 'die in dem Buchstaben Gelehrte' [those learned in the letter] (incidentally revealing that Junckherrott's old-fashioned grammar is something of an affectation, or at least a conscious design). Timotheo restates the importance of making the familiar appear in an unfamiliar light. Other expressions are used, 'den Sinn des Geistes, der in dem Grund enthalten in mehrem Lichtes scheinbarwerdung dadurch auszudrucken' [to express the sense of the Spirit that is contained in the ground in more light-manifestation] (§10), repeating a formulation from the 'Preface'. He continues in aphoristic fashion: 'wo ist nicht Unterschied, da ist keine Weißheit, dann Weißheit ist Unterschied' [where there is no difference there is no wisdom, for wisdom is difference]. The shift brings a new truth with it: the Pharisees do not, in Timotheo's view, have anything to do with *scripture*, for they merely meddle around with *letters*. There is a definite rationale, but Junckherrott doesn't mention *how* he has arrived at this translation, the method behind it, which is simply etymological, γραμματεύς deriving from γράμμα, one meaning of which is a letter, a character. The same is true of the other word Cleophas confronts Timotheo with, διάβολος, where an elaborate theological argument is given in place of the etymology that leads to 'Werffender dafürhin in dem geworffen werden da durchhin' [throwing there in the being thrown there through] (§12). The method expounded in the prefatory matter and practised in the body of the translation itself gains a wider vindication. In the dialogue Junckherrott shows he is not just pursuing an eccentric method but can justify it. He is a kind of spiritual fundamentalist, going back to the text which, 'von GOTT eingegeistert' [inspired by God] (§14), needs to have its true lineaments made clear. Only the translator who operates according to the Spirit can hope to make the operation of the Spirit discernible. Though the technique is mechanical, for Junckherrott it can coincide with a state of inspiration.

VIII

Though Junckherrott meets most of the objections that can be raised against his translation in the dialogue, his undertaking remains contradictory. The contradiction can best be expressed by saying that he is attempting to translate without translating, to carry the original across rather than to translate *from* the original into something else. This intent rests on the premise that the Greek original is the word of God, that its actual form is sacred and to be treated like a relic, preserved rather than altered. The essentially transformative nature of translation is thus denied or ignored. We know now that the koine Greek of the New Testament is itself a kind of translation, a compilation from various Hebrew and Aramaic sources.[22] Junckherrott's attribution of absolute status to the Greek is therefore unfounded, but there are precedents for the kind of biblical translation that submits as totally as possible to the source text, like the second-century Greek version of the Septuagint by Aquila de Pontos, which imposes Hebrew word-order on Greek, or the 1553 Ferrara bible, prepared for the Inquisition, which does the same ('traduzida palabra por palabra') with Spanish.[23] As far as I have been able to judge, Junckherrott outstrips even these versions in his literality, giving the original letter such authority that even a simple thing like a shoe is rendered etymologically and inscrutably as 'zubündenseyung da unterhin' [being-bound-up there below] (John 1:27). This is taking Jerome's affirmation 'verborum ordo mysterium est' to an absurd extreme.[24]

A probable source for that extremity lies in the success of Luther, whose version had established itself so firmly in the hearts, minds and language of the majority of Germans that it had secured the status of an original. The process in which translations come to be regarded as originals is a recurring pattern in the history of biblical translation; the Greek New Testament itself is already an instance of it, but the two main examples are the Septuagint and Jerome's Vulgate. With both of these, it was soon forgotten or ignored that they were derivative texts: they became originals, and as such sacred. In each case this was partly justified by the claim that the translators were divinely inspired – the seventy-two different translators of the Septuagint were supposed to have arrived independently at the same version, and Jerome stated that his task had been made possible by divine assistance. The claim of divine inspiration institutes a new original, and the process of translation is denied, or rather it becomes magical in that the dream of 'translating' from original to original comes true. Obviously this depends on the status of the new original's being accepted. Luther made no claims to have been divinely inspired, though others later did so for him, but his translation instated itself all the same. Junckherrott's undertaking can be understood as a reaction against this, against the way Luther's version had replaced the original (or the Vulgate as original) so that in much of Germany it had become not just the German version but to all intents and purposes the Bible itself. The original text, the divinely inspired word, had been left behind for something that was secondary. Junckherrott's intention was to return to the text, to translate so as to recover the original, a process he did not entrust to his method alone but supplemented with his claim of being guided by faith and understanding of the Spirit, asserting the status of an (alternative) original for his own version. In this, differing from Luther is an essential part of bringing the reader back, of renewing the text so that it may be seen again. In Junckherrott's eyes, Luther, far from being a window onto the original, had become a hindrance, not just because to him it might not be accurate, but because it had become so familiar. That is the sense of Junckherrott's dictum 'wisdom is difference'; the New Testament is to be brought home by emphasizing its foreignness.

The influence of Pietism can doubtless be felt here.[25] It was strong in Frankfurt, where Spener began it; Junckherrott's translation was published in nearby Offenbach. The strict return to the original text, and the emphasis on personal interpretation, which the translation both evidences and enables, are clearly Pietistic traits, and Pietism itself will have nourished the sense that Luther's version had too much authority, that it had come to annex and restrict the meanings of the original. As Timotheo is made to say in the dialogue, Junckherrott did not want to build on 'einen ausheimischen Grund', i.e. on something prescribed externally, but on 'den zuvoraushin in ihm liegenden Grund der Wahrheit welcher ist Christus' [not on foreign ground but on the ground of truth already lying within him which is Christ]. The effect of this deeply pietistic attitude is to put weight on the mystery of the scriptures, which again increases the individual's responsibility for interpretation. The clarity which is one of the main achievements of Luther's translation was for Junckherrott a fault, even a falsification, and, true to his identification with St Paul ('we speak the wisdom of God in a mystery, even the hidden wisdom', 1 Corinthians 2:7, a passage Junckherrott cites), he brings out, or as he sees it reverts to, the unclarity, the difficulty, the fluidity of the original.

My main intention here has simply been to present Junckherrott's translation, in the belief that it should be better known. Since the book itself is scarce, I have tried to give enough detail for a good impression to be formed. It is an extreme work, and its extremity has meant that it has had little influence, but it is also instructive in that it reminds us of the loosening, the undermining of language intrinsic to the act of translation, which whatever else it may also be is always an undoing of the text it works upon. Junckherrott anticipates a good deal, not only what Hölderlin did with Pindar, but also, in his revealing of the shifting nature of language through precise literality, the processes and insights of deconstruction. Junckherrott's text can seem like an actual realization of deconstruction's view of language, almost a parody. The undoing of translation can be productive in that new possibilities of language present themselves, but it needs to be accompanied by a constitutive element, which is something almost entirely lacking from Junckherrott. He does not have the binding rhythm or the flashes of beauty of Hölderlin's Pindar versions, but shares with them the process of altering our sense of the source through radically literal rendition and the implicit critique of received versions.[26] If he is readable at all, it is only because, as I said at the beginning, parts at least of what he is translating are likely to be familiar to us, and so the constitutive element can be supplied. What results is a curiously involved form of reading, in which meanings are at once articulated and dissolved.

NOTES

1 The only modern reference to it I have found is Anneliese Senger, *Deutsche Übersetzungstheorie im 18. Jahrhundert (1734–1746)* (Bonn: Bouvier, 1971), pp. 81–6. This is where I first came across it. I have written about the translation briefly before, in a specific context, in my book *Hölderlin and the Dynamics of Translation* (Oxford: Legenda, 1998), pp. 17–21. Here I wish to present it for its own sake.

2 Johann Christoph Adelung, *Fortsetzung und Ergänzungen zu Christian Gottlieb Jöchers allgemeinen Gelehrten-Lexico, worin die Schriftsteller aller Stände nach ihren vornehmsten Lebensumständen und Schriften beschrieben werden*, vol. 2 (Leipzig, 1787), entry under Junckherrott.

3 *Beyträge zur Critischen Historie der Deutschen Sprache, Poesie und Beredsamkeit, herausgegeben von einigen Mitgliedern der Deutschen Gesellschaft in Leipzig*, pt. 14 (1736), 316.

4 *Fortgesetzte Theologische Bibliothec, Das ist, Richtiges Verzeichniß, zulängliche Beschreibung, und bescheidene Beurtheilung der dahin gehörigen vornehmsten Schrifften, welche in M. Michael Lilienthals Bücher-Vorrath befindlich sind*, 2 vols. (Königsberg, 1740–4), II, pt. 18 (1743), 966.

5 Siegm. Jac. Baumgarten, *Nachrichten von merkwürdigen Büchern*, 12 vols. (Halle, 1752–8), VIII (1755), 318.

6 *Das Neue Testament, aufs neue aus dem Grund verteutschet, und mit Anziehung der verschiedenen Lesungen, und vieler übereinstimmenden Schrift-Oerter, versehen*, translated by J. H. Reitz, 2 vols., 4th impression (Büdingen, 1730).

7 There are no page numbers. All quotations from Junckherrott are given exactly as they appear, even when, as in later quotations, there are oddities and inconsistencies which may derive from the printer.

8 The English translations (particularly of Junckherrott's own translation later) are somewhere between an (as if interlinear) aid and an attempt to render something of Junckherrott's manner and style.

9 Junckherrott is also alluding to punctuation (*Zeichensetzung*) and type-setting (*Setzung*) here.

10 Willis Barnstone, *The Poetics of Translation: History, Theory, Practice* (New Haven and London: Yale University Press, 1993), p. 172.

11 Again, the pages are unnumbered.

12 See 'Die Aufgabe des Übersetzers', in Walter Benjamin, *Gesammelte Schriften*, edited by Rolf Tiedemann and Hermann Schweppenhäuser, 7 vols. (Frankfurt am Main: Suhrkamp, 1972–89), IV, 9–21. In English: 'The Task of the Translator', translated by Harry Zohn, in Walter Benjamin, *Selected Writings*, vol. 1: *1913–1926*, edited by Michael W. Jennings (Cambridge, MA, and London: Belknap, 1996), pp. 253–63.

13 Martin Luther, *Biblia/das ist/die gantze Heilige Schrifft Deudsch* (Wittemberg, 1534; repr. Leipzig: Reclam, 1983).

14 Quotations from the Greek New Testament are from Η ΚΑΙΝΗ ΔΙΑΘΗΚΗ, edited by Erwin Nestle and G. D. Kilpatrick, 2nd edn (London, 1958). Not identical to the recension Junckherrott used, but this does not affect the passages dealt with here.

15 See Frank Kermode, 'John', in *The Literary Guide to the Bible*, edited by Robert Alter and Frank Kermode (London: Fontana, 1997), pp. 440–66 (p. 442).

16 'Ware': Junckherrott's habit of adding e's, as also in 'kame', I have not been able to explain, but it suggests an attention to rhythm.

17 This is Cervantes's image for all translation, quoted by Hamann: Johann Georg Hamann, *Aesthetica in nuce*, in *Entkleidung und Verklärung: Eine Auswahl aus Schriften und Briefen des 'Magus im Norden'*, edited by Martin Seils (Berlin: Eckart, 1963), pp. 315–54 (p. 320).

18 See Kermode, 'John', p. 445.

19 Later, revised versions of Luther have: 'Es war ein Mensch, von Gott gesandt', which is both closer to and further from the Greek.

20 Revisions of Luther supply 'er', doing away with any significant ambiguity and confining the range of the Greek.

21 Luther also wrote Cleophas, but modern versions have Cleopas.

22 Cf. Barnstone, *The Poetics of Translation*, p. 174.

23 See *ibid.*, pp. 173, 196, 279.

24 Saint Jérôme, *Lettres*, with a translation by Jérôme Labourt, 8 vols. (Paris, 1949–63), III (1953), 60 (Letter 57).

25 Cf. Senger, *Deutsche Übersetzungstheorie im 18. Jahrhundert*, p. 85.

26 Hölderlin's Pindar translation is discussed by M. B. Benn, *Hölderlin and Pindar* (The Hague: Mouton, 1962), David Constantine, 'Hölderlin's Pindar: The Language of Translation', *Modern Language Review* 73 (1978), 825–34, and in chapter 4 of my *Hölderlin* (see note 1). Hölderlin both continued and varied his method in his versions of Sophocles's *Antigone* and *Oedipus the King*, which in a letter to his publisher (28 September 1803) he said were intended to bring out the 'oriental' ground of the original. Choruses from Hölderlin's *Oedipus* were translated by David Constantine, with brief comments, in *Comparative Criticism* 20 (1998). Complete versions are now available: *Hölderlin's Sophocles: Oedipus & Antigone*, translated by David Constantine (Newcastle upon Tyne, 2001).

Comparative Criticism 24, p. 283. © 2002 Cambridge University Press
DOI: 10.1017/S0144756402009332 Printed in the United Kingdom

Winners of the BCLA/BCLT 2001 Translation Competition

OPEN COMPETITION

First Prize

Silvester Mazzarella, for his translation from the Swedish of Agneta Pleijel, *Lord Nevermore*.

Second Prize

Brian Cole, for his translation from the Spanish of selected poems by Circe Maia.

Third Prize

Bernard Meares, for his translation from the French of Olivier Rolin, *Inventing the World*.

Commendations

Neil Bishop, for his translation from the French of Robert Lalonde, *The Devil Knows/The Trickster Teacher*.

Cecilia Rossi, for her translation from the Spanish of selected poems by Alejandra Pizarnik.

Anthony Vivis, for his translation from the German of Botho Strauss, *Her Letter about the Wedding*.

Comparative Criticism 24, pp. 285–301. Cambridge University Press 2002
DOI: 10.1017/S0144756402005577   Printed in the United Kingdom

Lord Nevermore: a chapter from a novel by Agneta Pleijel

TRANSLATED FROM THE SWEDISH

BY SILVESTER MAZZARELLA

Agneta Pleijel was born in Stockholm in 1940 and after university studies at Lund and Gothenburg worked mainly as a journalist till 1980, since when she has been a full-time writer, achieving success in prose, poetry, drama, reportage and criticism. Her first novel was published in 1987. *Lord Nevermore*, her fifth, came out in 2000 and has so far won four awards in Sweden. It is a fictional recreation of the lives of the famous Polish anthropologist Bronisław Malinowski and those close to him, particularly the avant-garde painter, writer and philosopher Stanisław Witkiewicz.

The first chapter of *Lord Nevermore* is reproduced here. The action begins in Zakopane, a town in the Tatra Mountains of South Poland. The time is around 1914.

1. ZAKOPANE IN SOFT RAIN

Now I'll tell you about two friends called Bron and Stas. No special reason, I just feel like it. Where shall we start? Might as well start on a street in the Tatra mountains in the south of Poland. Bronisław is just thirty; his glasses have round lenses and his dark hair is combed back from his brow. He's a thoughtful young man, not entirely without vanity. When a motor-car clatters past throwing up a shower of thick mud he takes refuge on the pavement. Those sounds! That relentless mechanical motion! It's morning in the health resort of Zakopane and the sky looks like the inside of a casserole lid, with water trickling from the gables of houses and dripping from trees. Shining brown puddles have formed in the most inappropriate places on the street. With his handkerchief he wipes moisture from his glasses in the hope of achieving a clearer view of the world. No use; the crest of mountain peaks ringing the town has vanished behind soft curtains of surging rain.

He sighs and continues on his way up the hill.

In the yellow house at the top of the street Zakopane's music teacher is playing her spinet which sits like a refined spider among coarse wooden furniture, *l'art nouveau à la Zakopane*. A veneer of educated people has moved into the town, and they've discovered the peasant style and enthusiastically made it their own. The door is opened by a housemaid with well-rounded cheeks and a childish dimple on each knuckle. She drops a curtsey and asks Bron to come in. The spider lifts its slender legs to the music and dances absent-mindedly amongst the rustic furniture. Through the doorway Bron catches a glimpse of the little woman who is making the music. The housemaid precedes him into the damp drawing-room, waves him to a heavy armchair full of cushions with brightly-coloured handwoven covers, and lays her forefinger across her lips. As she leaves the room Bron follows her with his eyes. Her apron-strings are tied in a white bow just above her bottom.

The bow bobs up and down. Bron rapidly undresses her. Now all she's wearing is the white bow bobbing and swaying and wiggling above plump buttocks. He shuts his eyes and the dripping notes and soft broken chords turn into the swell of waves on a distant shore. Mrs Wicz the music teacher is married to Mr Wicz, Zakopane's world-famous painter, whose pictures are such exact reproductions of nature that it gives you a shock. Mrs Wicz wraps herself in a raincoat of notes that grows longer and longer till it reaches her ankles. She gets tangled up in it. She fights and struggles and has problems with the pedals, and in the end gives up. When she lifts her hands from the keyboard the spider releases a soggy sigh. Then silence, apart from the sound of water rustling and whispering over rooftiles and murmuring in drainpipes. Mrs Wicz sits still.

She turns her eyes to the wet windowpanes.

The damp that permeates the room is as soft and fine as a young girl's hair. Bronisław slowly opens his eyes. All is soft, liquescent, watery and misty. The rain has softened everything, even the air. All the thoughts that cross and recross the world have grown soft and blunted and can no longer hold their shape. Bronisław looks up at the ceiling. He has no idea what Mrs Wicz wants from him. She has asked him to come: what can she be after? He gives a light cough to make his friend's mother aware that he is there.

Mrs Wicz shoots from the piano stool like a cork from a champagne bottle and stumbles eagerly towards him in her long cloak. She draws his head down to her breast, kisses his cheeks, fusses over him and hugs him tightly. Her hands run everywhere and her breath mists up his glasses all over again. Bronisław struggles at the bottom of a lake.

He tries to take his glasses off to wipe them but his movements are slow and laboured as if under heavy pressure. It's difficult to grasp anything because Mrs Wicz's hands are constantly in the way. In the end he manages to hold his glasses out of her reach and simultaneously search in his breast pocket for his handkerchief.

Finally she lets him go with a friendly smile.

What a wet spring we're having, Mr Bronisław.

Yes indeed, says Bronisław, blinking.

Polishing his glasses, he has a strong sense of being under threat, but he doesn't know where from. Everything is just as it should be. Trade is flourishing throughout the Empire and the boundaries of knowledge are being extended. Freud has discovered the Oedipus Complex and with it the step humanity has taken from nature to culture. And Bronisław has been awarded a grant by the British Association for Scientific Development to further his ethnographic studies in Australia and New Guinea.

He holds up his glasses and looks through them at Mrs Wicz. She is small and blurred. When he puts them on again she is sharply defined and all of a piece, with a gaze that pierces the damp like a searchlight. He bows, pressing his glasses firmly into place on the bridge of his nose. Mrs Wicz moves about the carpet energetically swinging her short arms, collecting herself together. Then she stands still, turns towards him and says:

I've had an idea.

Yes? says Bronisław, bowing again.

I want you to take Stanisław with you to the South Seas.

The change of air will do him good. He'll find new subjects for his brush. It'll distract him. He'll get over his unhappy love affair. And he'll be a help to you on your journeys into the unknown. You'll have someone to share your thoughts with out there among those wild people. He'll be able to draw the natives for you. Mr Wicz and I will take care of his travel expenses. You'll be his road to spiritual health.

She doesn't wait for Bronisław to respond.

But stands on tiptoe, takes his face between her hands and kisses his cheeks. He feels his head rise from his neck and sail away like a balloon bouncing off walls and pictures and windows and bumping into the leather spines on the bookshelf. He feels dizzy without his head. He wants to run and catch it and press it back down firmly between his shoulders but he can't.

Mrs Wicz holds his hands fast between her own small, damp, musical hands.

It's not only that more and more things have now been researched but also that, corresponding to this, the more we research the more we find still remains to be researched. The greater the order we establish, the greater the chaos that remains. Scientists can no longer rely on God to guarantee order. Some maintain that evolution follows the laws of mathematics: if something is mathematically possible, it'll happen, and if it's not mathematically possible it won't happen. And if impossible things do happen they're called wonders or miracles.

And of course there's always chance.

But chance is no miracle. Chance just shakes up the accepted pattern then goes back to logic again. Bronisław feels rebellious towards logic. No, rather towards the antagonism between logic and chaos. He intends to be an empiricist. He will collect facts and put them together so as to slowly build up hypotheses he can test. He's in search of humanity in its most primitive form but he suspects human logic isn't the same everywhere. Do men in all societies long to stick knives into their fathers and copulate with their mothers? That's what Dr Freud thinks. What exactly *is* a man, anyway?

According to Dr Freud in Vienna a man is a neurasthenic paying a visit to Dr Freud in Vienna. The very core of Bronisław's being rebels against this. The ways of evolution are many and complex. Perhaps European man does suffer from an Oedipus complex and want to kill his father while secretly lusting after his mother's womb; could this be what has formed Europe as we know it with its wars, its melancholy soul, its death instinct and its destructive dreams? And why did his fiancée take her own life?

Not his own fiancée, Stanisław's. Bronisław scarcely even met her. He remembers her as a red-haired demi-mondaine with sparkling eyes, a volcano on the verge of eruption. That's what Stanisław's women are like. But does Bronisław really remember her, or is what he remembers the portrait of her Stanisław painted? How much do we actually see with our own eyes, and how much is the influence of others responsible for deceiving us into thinking we are seeing with our own eyes?

This thought stops Bronisław half-way down the hill on his way from Mrs Wicz. He looks round at the scenery. The Tatras are hidden by draperies of fine rain, with only a few dark green and blue outcrops visible here and there. Colours form and dissolve again; everything is constantly shifting, billowing, changing shape. How would Daddy Wicz depict this phenomenon? Stanisław's father – who is also his son's teacher – does not paint what is shifting and changeable, he paints reality.

Nature as it is. History as it was.

In Mr Wicz's paintings you experience reality more sharply than ever before, a reality which asserts itself in every leaf and blade of grass. The knight on horseback in shining armour wears a coat of mail in which every link is visible. Every crease and fold stands out in the shawl the peasant woman wraps round her shoulders as she lifts her face to the hero. This is how to present the strong and the weak, man and woman, the honour of the fatherland. But might what is so uncompromisingly clear in fact be horribly untrue to reality?

My dishonest father paints not what he sees but what he wants to see, Stas tells his friends. So where can we look for the real foundation of knowledge?

His fiancée died. We can't deny that.

She shot herself beside a rocky outcrop in the Tatras.

They say God's ways are inscrutable.

Yet there must an explanation for everything. Philosophy searches for the primal source and in the process dissects everything, even in the end itself. Where can we find a solid basis for our thinking? Why did this woman take her own life? What *is* woman? According to Dr Freud woman has no place in culture. She's a sort of empty space that man passes on the road to himself. Woman is inconceivable. Fundamentally incomprehensible.

Perhaps she's nature, what's left of nature in culture.

But how can nature take its own life?

The portrait Stanisław painted of his fiancée was exaggerated and hysterical: thick hair snaking about her brow, uneasy shadows flickering over white skin and burning lava streaming down her dress. What I paint, says Stas, is pure form. Bronisław stands motionless on the hill; the damp brings him whiffs of acrid resin, pine trees, heavy clay and sodden graves where dead kings have been sleeping a dreamless sleep for centuries.

Heroes, fighting men and clan chieftains.

That's Europe. He's going to leave Europe.

Or be called away from it, to be more accurate. Yet bewitched by his friend's solicitous mother he very nearly let her hectic appeals get the better of him. He just managed to break free in the nick of time.

Drawing a deep breath, he turns his face up to the sky. For a moment he feels carefree and happy. Soon he will be on his way and he plans to stay away for a very long time. He opens his mouth wide; rain trickles under his tongue, filling his throat with the taste of salt. He knows he has no idea what his friend's fiancée looked like, he just has a vague memory of someone sensitive and fragile. But he does remember what Stas painted. A fantasy, a feverish nightmare. How to interpret it? Perhaps as man's fear of woman. Or as Europe's fear of its own strange empty space?

This is not something he wants to take with him to the other side of the world.

A velocipede with a big front wheel swishes past him and dissolves into a cascade of shining streaks. Bronisław shuts his mouth and draws his index finger across his lips as if to seal them. No, he has no intention of pulling Stas along with him on this first field trip to the tropics, for which he has been awarded a grant by the English and which is to be the start of his scientific career. He presses his hat down on his head and goes on.

It's getting dark. Down in the town you can just make out weak light coming from Morskie Oko, eye of the sea. Not the lake itself but the restaurant which has been named after that round and bottomless lake whose dusky gaze encourages the people of Zakopane to think they have a secret underground link with the sea. And why shouldn't they?

A flickering lantern fringed with water-drops shows Bronisław the way in.

In the hallway he brushes water off his hat and coat and smooths rain out of his sparse moustache before entering what appears to be an empty room. No sign of Stanisław. He must be with some woman. In his studio. Somewhere. Not here. Makes no difference. Next morning Bronisław will be leaving Zakopane by train; meanwhile he's hungry and thirsty. Ready-laid tables are drawn up in formation as if expecting to be attacked by some army. The waiter Methuselah, nearly a hundred years old, emerges from the background trailing behind him his insect-like shadow, which looks about to take off from the wallpaper and flutter away. Bronisław has earned himself a bit of rest and refreshment.

No, he had told Mother Wicz.

I'm most awfully sorry, but it's not possible.

At this Mrs Wicz had let go of his hands.

She hadn't wanted to insist. It was just an idea she'd had. To give her dear son a chance to think about something else after his fiancée's death, after his own illness, in his great unrelenting grief. In the South Seas one would be bound to find other things to think about. Don't you, Mr

Bronisław, find new things to think about when you are among friends who love you? Her eyes had blazed with white fire but when Bronisław stared at the wall and stubbornly continued to shake his head the white fire died down. Something turned over in his heart.

It's not easy for a man to refuse a woman.

But now he must pull himself together and eat and drink something.

With a ceremonious gesture the waiter indicates a table. Bronisław chooses a different one. Methuselah shrugs his shoulders. His tired watery eyes are red at the corners. He shuffles off to fetch the menu. The curtains flutter. Bronisław looks through the window. It's dark outside, with small flickering lights moving like a string of pearls up in the mountains. A procession of shepherds? A train of dead souls? Once again he feels his head become unstable and begin floating away. He recaptures it and presses it down between his shoulders, keeping it in a firm grip. Not only Stanisław's mother, but Stanisław himself has this effect on him. Even when he's not present.

A sense of floating and flying, a gliding vertigo.

It must be possible to map out the functions of relationships.

One needs to travel a long way to be able to make sense of one's own. To learn to identify what is individual in the familiar net of relationships in which one is imprisoned. One needs to see what seems normal and universal and unchangeable in the light of what is different and alien. Only then – perhaps – will one be able to see through and understand both Europe and oneself.

To achieve this one must be alone. Not take Europe along in one's tent, babbling and chattering, sleepless and filling the air with drunken ideas like Stas. People are formed in families. The evolution of Europe has been an evolution of families. He must get away from the whole lot and from Stas. Without Stanisław Bronisław would never have become what he is. But who is Bronisław on his own? As the waiter puts the menu down in front of him he becomes aware that there is another customer in the restaurant. A woman. He recognizes her.

One of Stanisław's friends.

Bronisław has met her once or twice at parties. One summer evening he even danced a tango on a veranda with her. A good many years ago. In another life. Now she's sitting half hidden by the pillar at the other end of the restaurant smoking a cigarette in a long holder, red hat tilted at a slightly coquettish angle on her dark hair. Watching him.

He half-rises and bows, hand on heart.

Yes, he does recognize her. She gives him a smile.

What *is* woman? What is this woman doing here? On her own, smoking, half-hidden but equally half-visible, a glass of wine in front of her, distressingly lonely but at the same time seductively solitary.

When Stas paints portraits he reveals his own character.

But – and one must be honest about this – his own character is often the actual subject of the portrait. Stanisław has often used Bron as a sitter. These portraits show Bron's obstinacy and sharpness of intellect and his hatred of conformity. Flattering traits. But they also show something else: what? There's a charcoal sketch in which Bronisław is sitting with a scarf thrown round his neck pressed against a wall of rough logs. He seems paralysed.

His hands are thrust into over-large gloves with knitted fingers that droop like sorrowful rabbit-ears. It was cold and they'd just had a violent quarrel. About the fundamentals of art, no less. Stas had laughed at him and Bronisław hadn't yet recovered. He glares from the sketch with pursed lips. He has no wish to be laughed at or used for a portrait either.

But Stanisław does what he likes.

Stanisław has made portraits of everyone in Zakopane from green-eyed girls to white-skinned old gentlemen; and of half Kraków, from drunken painters and brilliant scientists and their wives some of whom have been Stas's lovers, to the small pale intelligent girls who are the daughters of these wives. He has portrayed vampires and moorhens, firemen and cobblers, Jews and psychoanalysts, famous prima donnas and obscure dentists. He has described a whole world in portraits. An inner world, he calls it.

Philosophy is in his portraits too. And the coming war.

Naturally he has painted his father, Daddy Wicz the famous nature painter, whose only son he is. And Mrs Wicz, much-loved mother of this only son. And, many times over, he has painted himself, with demonic eyebrows and curling lips. A devil dressed like an urchin. All rapid lines and quick movements.

Rather depict a cabbage-head well than Socrates' head badly, Daddy Wicz used to maintain, and he would have a cabbage-head brought in and placed in front of his son, and tell him to get on with it.

Art is craft. Art is producing an exact image of your subject.

Art is pure form, counters Stas, it has nothing to do with outer appearance. Form is the fire under the ashes, the wind that blows through everything, the power that transforms substance, the balance between life and death. Pure form triumphs over the irrelevant, defeats the accidental, overcomes meaninglessness and loves chaos.

Bronisław agreed with him, intoxicated by his friend's words.

He often backed his friend against Daddy Wicz, when he and Stas were alone together. When Stas felt isolated and depressed, an incompetent failure, Bronisław comforted him and urged him to have the courage of his convictions and let them take him wherever they would. But there can be no place for Stanisław's chaos in anthropology, which studies humanity from a rather different angle. But which angle?

This is what this research trip will show.

It's not meaninglessness he'll need to overcome but real mountains.

The woman has moved to Bronisław's table. He asked her to, for a bit of company on a lonely evening. She nodded, left her table and sat down at his, apparently unsurprised. Her name's Irena. Her voice is a bit husky. She's not young, about his own age, perhaps a bit past thirty. Her soft mouth has a faint dark shadow above the upper lip and she has black eyes. Why did Stanisław's fiancée kill herself?

What do women really want, Miss Irena?

She shrugs her shoulders lightly and lets her gaze wander to the window. It's pitch black now outside. No more flickering lights. His eyes rest on her white blouse: its collar forms a funny little bell from which her neck rises like the stalk of a flower from a vase. Irena is a teacher of mathematics, she teaches algebra and equations to the sons of Zakopane's industrialists and doctors. She's a modern woman, self-supporting and unmarried.

She knew the dead fiancée quite well. But she can't think of an answer to Bronisław's question. In the end she looks at him and asks what he himself thinks about love between man and woman. Is it possible at all?

I hope so, says Bron simply.

Stanisław's very highly strung, says Irena.

Bronisław knows that.

He has the soul of a woman, says Irena. Bronisław doesn't comment. It's because he's so sensitive and so incredibly talented that he's so unhappy, she adds. Bronisław knows all about Stanisław's misfortunes. He'd rather find out something he doesn't know. He wants to know what woman is – and what she herself thinks she is – in relation to culture. Perhaps an absurd question, but he's not afraid to ask Irena. He's not thinking of the dead fiancée, he explains.

He's not talking about Irena either. But woman *per se*. Irena laughs but he persists. They drink more wine. He asks her to tell him what love is. This makes Irena draw a deep breath and think for a long time.

Man and woman look for each other, she says.

Inevitably, she adds and laughs.

How does love begin? asks Bronisław.

In the eyes, says Irena. Then comes awareness. Through the skin of the palm of the hand. Then the skin of all the limbs. Then the person in love wants to go further. Beneath the skin. The two lovers press into one another. Not just the man into the woman, that's not what I mean, but the woman into the man as well. It's an obsession, a mania. Like diving down into Morskie Oko in search of your own reflection.

Bronisław listens with his chin cupped in his hands.

He's getting excited. This is the kind of insane love he lived through himself with Toskia. Irena reminds him of Toskia, the woman Bronisław recently finished with when he left the London School of Economics. Irena's expressing thoughts he's had himself. Thoughts he's ready to go a long way to escape from.

Love tries to get us to melt into one another, says Irena in her husky voice. This is true of men but it's true of women too. Then the surface of the water breaks and the mirror-image shatters and you fall to the bottom and nearly drown. Love leads to death. You just have to decide whose.

Either love's death. Or your own.

She says nothing more.

A group of drunk men is now sitting on the other side of the restaurant and making a lot of noise. Irena looks down at the table. Bronisław senses the wind blowing under her skin, a great storm. He wants to argue with her but can't find the words. He fills his glass. She has pulled the cork of the wine-bottle to pieces and is laying little bits out on the table in a meandering pattern. Her nails gleam.

The gentlemen near the pillar are calling in loud voices for Methuselah.

Bronisław once again sees Toskia under a streetlamp on Blackfriars Bridge with her dark eyes and her anger. He longs to cover Irena's hand with his own and help her solve the puzzle with the bits of cork, but holds back. When she doesn't speak again he's unable to keep quiet any longer.

Miss Irena, he starts softly.

Women really do want to be free. In London suffragettes march through the streets. They want a more rational order of things. Some believe that love will only be possible when women have won their freedom. Another sort of love, a love that doesn't lead to death. D'you think it could be possible to find such a love, Miss Irena?

At this Irena turns on him a gaze as bottomless as Morskie Oko.

The knife twists till Bronisław can hardly breathe.

You have to press forward down narrow passages, past deep ravines, through small spaces and grottoes inhabited by gnomes, you never know how far you'll have to go, the air might not last out, you may suffocate. Invisible bats squeak and shriek in those tunnels under the mountain. This is the route to love, and it's hideous. It would be a wonder, a miracle, to arrive safely. The guardians of the established order block the way, wearing uniforms and carrying sabres, deploying cavalry and cannons. But there is no other way forward to freedom and love.

Man through woman. Woman through man. The oppressed through their oppressors. Everything through everything else. The established pattern must be shaken up. For the sake of love. For the sake of freedom. This is why he broke with Toskia, but the pain of his loss shakes him like an earthquake. A task has been laid on his shoulders: the burden of changing himself. He knew this when he left London. But how can he achieve it?

That impossible relationship with Toskia.

That all-consuming agony of love.

When he says goodnight to Irena outside the magnificent patrician villa in which she, teacher of mathematics, rents an upstairs room, he still feels a shuddering in the entrails of the earth. But Irena's eyes are no longer like Toskia's. The moment of confusion has passed. Irena's eyes have become vague.

She wishes him all the best for his journey.

Just now, when she gazed at him across the table with Toskia's eyes, Bronisław wanted to fall between her thighs and weep. He resisted the temptation, and now he's exhausted. He has to get some sleep. As they part Irena lays her hand lightly on his lapel. He takes it and turns it over and kisses her palm. Then he lets it go and raises his hat.

He's finished with Zakopane.

God or someone else has led him back to his own path, the path of sobriety. He'll get back his common sense. He'll be transformed. Eventually he'll find love. There's still one goodbye to be said, the hardest of all: his mother. He can't wait to come to her in her dark flat in Kraków to complete that too. He's grateful to Irena for her disinterested friendliness. He stays at the gate while she walks towards the house, but on the point of going in she changes her mind and runs back to him with rapid steps. The white bell round her neck gleams in the darkness.

He's so scared his heartbeat quickens.

If she asks him in he won't have the power to say no. She lays both her hands over his on the gatepost. To avoid responding to the flicker of excitement in her eyes he kisses her hand again. But she doesn't invite him in. She asks him to say hello to Stanisław and to tell him to get in touch with her.

If I see him, answers Bronisław, which isn't likely.

Then she begs him to send her a letter or a picture-postcard from the other side of the world. She collects exotic stamps. He promises he will. Then he goes on his way. It has stopped raining and the sky is full of stars. Everything smells clean and freshly washed and he can hear the croaking of frogs. He needs to sleep. He has to get up early and catch the train. He has to pack, he has to travel, he has to forget.

He's going to be alone, alone for many years.

But as he nears his room in the dark corridor of the boarding house he sees a streak of light on the carpet from under his door. Full of misgivings, he opens the door, which creaks. His armchair has acquired long legs and light-coloured trousers ending in boots. It has also acquired arms, white shirt-sleeves and slim white hands. One of these holds a half-empty glass, while a spent but half-smoked cigar rests in the other.

At last! says Stas. Where the hell have you been?

Stanisław, says Bronisław.

Stas has something on his knee, a tropical pith helmet. Bronisław sits down heavily on the narrow bed. Stas lights his cigar and puffs; the match flares and a cloud of smoke envelops him. His eyes are pale and very clear. He grins encouragingly as he slowly fills a tooth-glass to the brim with vodka and holds it out to Bronisław.

No thanks, says Bronisław, taking it.

Stanisław strokes the pith helmet gently like the gravedigger in *Hamlet* with Yorick's skull. He smiles. I'm sure you're not going to believe me, he tells Bronisław, but I bought this topee here in Zakopane. It took me a bit of time to find it. It must be the only topee in town. It belonged to a man who travelled in Africa and died wearing it. His widow was a bit sentimental and took some persuading. But in the end she gave in.

What d'you think, Bronio?

Brilliant, says Bronisław, are you off to Africa?

He takes a swig of vodka and throws himself backwards on the bed with his arms over the pillow. He can feel the worn-out wallpaper with the ends of his fingers. On the ceiling is a stucco surround of pale plaster roses hooked into one another endlessly in eternal movement. In the furthest corner the rose-chain disappears into the shadows only to emerge again on the other side. Rose after rose, in tireless embrace, an unending cavalcade. What on earth can the plasterer have been thinking of?

The lamplight casts a halo round Stas's oval face.

His face is white as paper. From deep inside the cloud of tobacco his pale, friendly eyes gleam. He's drunk but still resembles an angel. Stas is never so lucid, sober or decisive as when he's drunk. He fishes his jacket up from the floor with the toe of his boot and carefully arranges the topee in it like a little girl putting her doll to bed. Then he caresses it in silence.

Have you any idea what the time is, says Bronisław.

My dear Bronio, says Stas with a laugh in his voice.

What is it you want, Stas, says Bronisław.

I've got a present for you, says Stas. Our youth is past, Bronio. We must be men now. Time for us both to haul in our anchors. Let's together leave this muddled place called Europe. Let's go and study wild people and unfathomable customs. Let's leave the women, both living and dead; they've all caused us too much pain. I'll follow you to Australia and New Guinea and the end of the world, Bronio. I want to paint the unacceptable.

Impossible, says Bronisław brusquely.

I shall follow you as Sancho Panza followed Don Quixote, continues Stas unruffled. I shall be your clown and armour-bearer. I shall save you from every windmill. You can't do without me, Bronio. You're easily led and on your own you always get into difficulties. Four eyes see better than two. Four legs will conquer every mountain peak. We'll stick together as we always have done.

No, Stasio, says Bronisław, not this time.

Think about it, Bron, says Stanisław.

You will never again get me involved in such nonsense, says Bronisław.

Dear Lord Nevermore, says Stas mildly.

Bronisław heaves himself up on one elbow and gropes about on the carpet for his glass. He empties it; the vodka burns his throat and makes him cough. He can see the young boy he first came to know one summer holiday in Zakopane long ago: slim, with a quicksilver tongue and squirrel ears, in tattered silk shirts and velvet trousers with holes at the knees, simultaneously spoilt and neglected.

Insufferable and lovable.

Stanisław on the front lawn early in the morning. Fishing rod on shoulder and pockets full of tobacco and apples when Bronisław is still on the stairs in his pyjamas. Good morning, dormouse, have you woken up at last? That was the summer Bron's father died.

Come on, pull yourself together, we're going fishing today.

Hey, listen to my latest play.

Can I show you the book my aunt brought from Warsaw?

Stanisław, who trades insults with the Zakopane boys when they mock Bronisław for his ill-health. Stanisław, who invents butterfly-tunes on his flute to comfort his friend Bronisław. Stanisław, who plays chess with Bronisław all night long, hundreds of games on end, to help him cope with his grief for his dead father.

And later, Stanisław at the Art School in Kraków, convinced of his inferiority as a painter, misunderstood by the teachers and bullied by his father who despises all art schools; only Bron believes in him. Stas could open his heart to no one else as he could to Bron. And Bron could talk to no one else as he could to Stas: about philosophy, sex, female anatomy, science.

There was no one else he could get so angry with.

And no one else it was so easy to make up with again.

And here was Stanisław whose young fiancée had killed herself; why did she do it? Of course Stas ought to get away from Zakopane for a while. But it would be madness for Bron to go away with Stas. This research trip is too important to fritter away as a prank. He rises slowly from the creaking bed and plants his feet on the floor. Reaching for the vodka bottle, he fills his glass and lifts it to Stas.

It won't work, Stasio, he says frankly. I've got to be alone. I mean it seriously this time.

Stas gives him a beautiful bright smile.

Bronisław is aware how tired he is. He drinks, spins his glass, drinks again. It's not only women it's difficult to say no to. It's just as difficult to say no to Stas, if not more so. It exhausts and depresses him, makes him incapable of action. He looks down into his vodka-glass.

Stas changes the subject. Are you any good at photography?

Bronisław shakes his head and studies the way the vodka rotates when he spins the glass, a little vortex which seems to move faster than his hand. It was horrible rejecting Toskia. She never wanted him to go. But she didn't want to leave her husband either. Perhaps she couldn't. Should he have stayed in London? But that would have been impossible. He was falling apart with jealousy. He managed to break away. Now her anger's pursuing him. Or perhaps it's not her anger, just his own sense of loss.

As for me, I'm the best photographer in Zakopane, Stas goes on.

I'm preparing a one-man show. Pity you won't be able to see it. It's going to be a sensation. I've done lots of research into Australian history, also geography, topography, climate and monsoon winds. Captain Cook had a whole retinue of botanists, zoologists and geographers with him when he discovered the southern continent, perhaps you didn't know that? I've planned to do a good deal of painting in oils if the climate allows it. D'you think one can use oils in the tropics? Gauguin did, of course.

But the main thing is I'm a good photographer. Modern science can't do without the art of photography.

Bronisław stops spinning his glass. Silence.

Somewhere down the corridor a door squeaks. An invisible resident tramps down the carpet past the room where they are sitting. It doesn't take much to make the floorboards creak. A twig scratches the window-pane. Out in the garden a cat mews, headstrong and obstinate, followed by a hissing that sounds like the sea, then a violent commotion and hideous cry of distress. The cat must have come across another cat. Then all is silent again.

I'm afraid I'm about to go mad, says Stas.

It's very bad this time. But if you really don't want me with you, Bronio, we'll say no more of the matter. But at least let me give you this. Have you got a topee?

Bronisław shakes his head again.

You have now, says Stas.

He carefully unwraps the jacket and places the topee on Bronisław's head. I bought it for you. That's the truth, it was for you.

Bronisław can't help smiling. He's moved by Stas's thoughtfulness. They continue drinking. They chat, about other things, about women. About Toskia, about Krystyna who shot herself beside the rocky outcrop. She'd made herself a wreath of flowers which was found close to her body.

Krystyna, says Stas, transformed her death into a fantastic still life. He sighs.

It's strange with life and art, he says.

They're so alike they almost mix together. They're certainly connected in some way. But they aren't the same. You mustn't confuse them. An abyss separates life from art. It's not easy to live in that abyss. So you have to choose one or the other. What to do? Turn your life into a work of art, perhaps? Well, that's always a possibility.

You can try to see yourself as an object.

At a distance. At a sufficient distance and with sufficient detachment for the chaos of life not to make you sick and incoherent. I often discussed this with Krystyna, says Stas. But the funny thing is, when you look at yourself from afar, as if through binoculars, you get cut off from something. From what? You could say that you get cut off from yourself. But what is this strange *yourself*? I'm damned if I know.

I consider myself responsible for Krystyna's death, says Stanisław.

Bronisław doesn't know what to say to this. It could be true. Hot and cold alternate incessantly with Stas. He's a good son, even an exemplary one. He goes along with Daddy Wicz in everything despite the fact that fundamentally he believes the opposite. He's a slave to women yet constantly lets them down. He loves without moderation or restraint, then he cuts himself free in such a way that everything round him falls apart.

This is because he tries to be himself all the time.

But no sooner has he found himself than this *himself* has already changed into a terrifying prison from which he will have to release himself yet again. It seems that in Stas opposites are so closely connected that he needs to switch constantly from one point of view to its exact opposite to hold himself together. Or to hold the world together. Or maybe to reach a reality beyond all the opposites.

It's your artistic genius, Bronisław maintains.

While Daddy Wicz paints what's real, you're making painting itself real. Which enables a previously unseen reality to emerge, more inward and more true.

But there's another reality beyond that one too, Stas objects, and beyond that *yet another*.

So you have to paint, write poetry and prose and think untiringly in order to reach the form that lies beyond all forms: pure form.

I remain eternally a dilettante, says Stas towards morning.

Someone of whom people will say: he never made it. Neither in art or life. But I've broken with that psychoanalyst who thought he could psychoanalyse me back to health. I told him I thought I had an embryo-complex. The idiot thought I was having him on, says Stas with a hearty laugh. Then in the end he came to believe I really was suffering from an embryo-complex.

I couldn't put up with him any longer after that.

Bronisław too shakes with laughter. Embryo-complex, for heaven's sake!

The air in the room is thick with tobacco smoke and the vodka bottle's empty. Bronisław switches off the light and throws the window wide open. In the boarding-house garden little patches of mist are dancing between the fruit-trees. They go out. The air outside is cold and fresh. Stas makes a close examination of the buds on one of the plum trees and says he is guilty, utterly guilty, of Krystyna's death.

Because of his embryo problem.

One moment he's totally cut off from everything. The next he's flowing out into other people and things, there are no limits, he's completely divided up and atomized. No one could feel loved by such a chameleon. Except perhaps you, Bronio. And Stanisław throws his arms round the trunk of the plum-tree and turns his white angel-face towards the dawn and doesn't laugh.

The grass is wet with dew.

A fox lopes by near the outhouse.

And the sun rising round and brilliant and immense over the Tatras is dispersing the mist. It's a ravishing morning. They see the first butterfly of spring, little and white, fluttering away among the bushes. They see the mountains lift their peaks to the sun. It's not quite clear how, but in that moment it's decided that Stas is going to come with Bron on the journey.

NOTE

This translation was awarded First Prize in the 2001 BCLA/BLTC Translation Competition.

Comparative Criticism 24, pp. 303–316. Cambridge University Press 2002
DOI: 10.1017/S0144756402005589 Printed in the United Kingdom

Selected poems by Circe Maia

TRANSLATED FROM THE SPANISH BY BRIAN COLE

Circe Maia is a Uruguayan poet, born in 1932, widely recognized in South America but little known in Europe. She spent her working life as a teacher of philosophy and languages, and has written poetry since her early days – with regular publication. In 1997 she was the subject of a thirteen-page tribute in the influential Argentinian *Diario de Poesía* – not the first time that organ had reported on her work. Susan Wicks wrote (for the Poetry Book Society): 'If a poet were to write a poem about the last straw that broke the camel's back, Circe Maia would be the one to write it. What she cares about is the subtle gradations of things, the precise distinctions between things that may or may not strike us alike.'

The poems translated here were originally published as follows: Circe Maia, *Cambios*, *Permanencias* (Ediciones de la Banda Oriental, Montevideo 1978), p. 79; *Dos Voces* (Ediciones Siete Poetas Hispano-americanos, Montevideo 1981), p. 44; *Superficies* (Ediciones de la Feria, Montevideo 1990), p. 47; *de lo visible* (Asoc. de Impresores del Uruguay, Montevideo 1998), p. 52.

THERE WILL NOT BE ...

Constructing the days one by one
it may well happen that we lose an hour
– perhaps only an hour –
or more or much more, but rarely to excess.

They are always missing, missing for us.
We would love to steal them from the night
but we are tired
already our eyelids are heavy.

So we go to sleep and the final image
– before we plunge into dreams –
is of a new day, with long hours
like the plains stretched out, like wind.

A pitiful deception.

There will not be unexpected bubble-days,
surprising, open.

The juice of this elapsed day
is filtered through the edge of early morning
and is already eating into it.

CHANGES

Sometimes change prepares itself
in subterranean form but explodes
suddenly, openly:
a nova in the sky
a fissure in the earth
a flood of light in the middle of the night
a tongue of fire
appears surprisingly in the eye
of the other, become Other, become alien.

Other changes take place
imperceptibly.
By obscure methods
and silent
means
what was not is and what was
is destroyed

But so gradually
that there are always remains:
of the sight, some
spark
sometimes.
Of the voice, some echo
(a word not yet
cooled down).

DESCENT

Abandoned to themselves they go down
they go back, gradually, in a form
not visible,
covertly.

Green moss is growing in the stone
rotting timber
eyes clogged with dirt
dusty expressions.

Abandoned.

Inertia. Dead weight.
A persistent current.
Gentle. Destructive.

A heavy foot. An opaque
word. Who is approaching?
What is coming?

Like death: to return. To be empty of life.
A blunted blade.
A thread without fibres.

Abandoned.

THE WINDOW

Do you see there was no total
of distinct days and nights and minutes?
Only one point, unchanging, in the field of vision.

It does not move even though the waves fall
blue bubbles come down, clear skies
all around, fickle days in radiance
fade and fade.

Although the nights blow up winds of darkness
dull sounds and points of silence,
it does not change,
it does not move.

You are always revealed
in the same window.

ONEIRICA

That in one class full of muffled noise
darkness falls and the students walk out,
except perhaps for some
who are distracted, distant.

That this occurs in seconds, quite unexpectedly,
in the middle of a phrase and while turning the head
to write a name
turning again, the phrase hangs from
a ravelled thread dispersed in the wind of the half-light.

The room itself has evaporated, opened.
The windows bore the weight of the walls
and the light flickers, sinister.

A cold wind has begun to blow.
Powdered chalk eddies, drowns.

DESTRUCTION OF THE LANDSCAPE

Three tones: green water, earth, sky-grey.
The tiny human figures
see each other with difficulty:
they are smaller spots
in the explosion of light: they do not stand out.

The great diamond enfolds them,
swallows them. There exists only
sharp clarity: bright air-water.

A spot of snow stands out
positive, precise, fixed.
And no single thought resists it
– invisible phantoms – within? without?
of little many-coloured spots.

However ...

The landscape devoured by the eyes,
reduced to ashes of memory,
floating briefly and then repelled,
backwards, backwards, now faded,
now blurred, vague – (as were,
as were the mountains, water, stones
– was there any cloud?)

Like a leaf sailing and then sinking
the landscape is engulfed.

ONE VOICE

Through a labyrinth of sounds comes
one voice, a thread in a tangled skein,
an invisible thread, disentangling itself.

Anxious
           faces.
Chains, stairs by which the voice rises
by ancient custom, familiar tread.

And then everything is in order again,
the hidden structure,
the necessary rhythm.

There open fans of sonorous brilliance,
and the music falls
– a secret rain –
arrows of delicate sound rend the air,
or slow drops fall,
round,
           dark.

ROBBERY

For children
the day holds broad spaces
and the hours are clear streets,
open avenues.

For us, time
narrows in such a way
that everything is squeezed and pressed.

Time runs away with itself.

One day hardly gives place to the other.
Before it is properly dawn
the light founders
in rapid noon
and you have scarcely looked on it
when it flees to evening
into wells of darkness.

A voice says:
From one turn to another
the day runs away from me.

Some mysterious
robber
is stealing away my life.

LOSSES

A child weeps for the broken bicycle,
his knee grazed,
and someone there, standing
as if looking for something ...
What have you lost?

– He has lost the desire to ride a bicycle.
He has lost the desire to weep
and a certain connection, a density of life,
also lost.

Softly night draws on and the colour of the evening
changes from pale pink to a candid blue.

(As if the passage of time declares
its total innocence.)

IF P, THEN Q

A very strong net, of steel thread.
Affirmation and denial interlock,
succeed each other, separate like drops
of molten lead, which escape
firom the premises, as from smelting furnaces.

No one cuts these threads.
No one pinches the skin of logic.

The finest fingers throw
their net over things.

        However
the net is pulled in empty.

CONTRADICTORY VOICES

Each hour comes with an axe
to cut the trunk of the dead hour.

Water-darkness falls and drowns the day
and another day appears
– nimble, forgetful –
whose splendour in its turn is also an axe,
        a destroying blaze, an arrow.

– It is not certain, it is not certain.
Each hour in its turn draws on the others
concentric lines.

Encircled, protected,
the old hour does not fall to the axe:
beneath and behind, it is alive.

THE LEAST FORESIGHT

The sound is heard of music from rare instruments
which have not yet been invented.

Voices are heard, but we do not hear them
and even if we could, we should not understand them.
(Language of years to come; what signs, what sounds?)

There will be a million things ... a million? – countless,
we have not the remotest idea, we know nothing ...

Nevertheless
if there are leaves
if there is air
the leaves will wave like this
the light will skip
over the bright green
and the earth will be covered with pools of brilliance.

Gestures of the water cannot vary much either,
can they?

Good, there is this, at least.

SUNSHADES

Here we are
installed in the middle
of the heart of the day
– multicoloured mushrooms on the coast –
each one with its circle of shade.

Dim circular thoughts
surround us as well; nothing comes
out of them, they overrun us
like the obstinacy of gentle waves.

And as the wind pushes the water to a lower level
memory brings up its recollections
of little density, with little edge,
ready to melt away like foam.

But at some moment
as if one would lift up some stone
of a more intense colouring,
it happens that an image breaks away
from the rest
water stone that strikes
unexpectedly
and tears the summer day to shreds.

CONCEALMENT

All the fires make haste, always,
to conceal the death of the old flame
                              (*Lucretius*)

The green
makes haste
and a triumphant entry:
Let a new wind now blow! – it says –
Let the memory disappear
of the dry stalk, of the blackened leaf!

New eyes open
hungry to see everything new

and the sun makes an effort, the light explodes
over yesterday in retreat
and although the old light filters through
the smallest chinks
everything on the scene conceals it
          and imagines it does not exist.

THEY PROTEST

When you discover
that reality is seen through language
when you see that it clothes itself in colourful costumes
all that before was vague and ill-defined,
you see yourself as a lord, a king, or at least
a page in the cortège that is still processing
giving names to things, saying to them:

'You are
this and you have
this other name and now you must
answer to the name of such-and-such ... Now
there are no more games of being-not being, nor unexpected
changes, no entrances no exits
from the stage that are not prepared
by some previous text ... Be very careful
with your tone and your manners'.

And the brilliant costumes
are extinguished, discolour and shrink:
in the word 'rain' there is not the sound
of the rain in the leaves
and the ess of 'sun' hardly shines.
Folded into language, the real is contained
inside the words;
every idiom adds to it a belt and a noose.

And so they stay wrapped up with ten turns
and knotted with knots
of various kinds,
all things, from the smallest
like a tiny seed or an insect's eye
to the most extensive like the mist
on the ground over the plain.
And sometimes – with hands tied – they thrash about
because they are not resigned to it
and sadness says, for example:
This little name,
singular, feminine, does not suit me
I remain a little austere and already worn out.
Let's see – it asks us – if we can change it
a little, at least,
so that it can be seen in the street
and not clash with the asphalt.

UNITY

You want to be dazzled?
Hurry then,
Because only at this hour
– ten twenty five in the morning –
the sun shines full on the face
of the clock tower. Blue,
the tiles change
into a vibrant violent sword
which marks the height.

And what does this luminous sword carry
that scars the retina?
Perhaps the distant voice of Plotinus, saying:
Unity cannot be looked on.

But the sudden attack
of the sublime is short.
Ecstasy escapes.
The jaws of light
have already released the clock tower.

At half past ten
once again the blue tiles
are visible. (Some
rather worn.)

ROOTS

This morning
we had to pull out some weeds
that were growing in all the crevices.
The weeds were pulled out
and lay there in the sun with roots trembling
as if very surprised ... why so?
From the dark to the light in an instant?

Inverted death, strange:
from the closed-in, blind earth
to the blue eye, that violates all that.

To open out to the four winds: to be lost.
To break through to full light: also to be lost,
say the roots,
trembling.

PRISONER

the city has to follow you. (*Kavafis*)

So, there is no way to get free:
you only have to turn round to see that.
There it comes following you,
moving – apparently slowly –
and in reality very fast.
And if you run away, for a moment you hear
very far away the noise of the streets:
arguments, motors and noise and horns
are a dull murmur.
                          And from so far away
now the light hardly shines from the highest windows,
say from a bell-tower.

But when you finally come to another
place, to another unknown city,
your city has suddenly caught up with you.
Now there is no question of turning round. Inside,
deep inside it you go for a walk
and in the other you ask it to wait for you,
not to go too far away ...

The other does not move, but it fades,
loses warmth, its sounds grow faint,
its odours are hardly perceptible

and the old aroma of what envelops you
will not let you go.

FIRDUSI

You have to jump back a thousand years, to Persia
and to Firdusi, who is growing old.
He laments, of course, among other problems,
not being able to make the swift movement
of turning the head
when the lance-thrust is already skimming the eyebrows.

So
that is old age: a reflex
which does not work in time and fails
for a tiny moment.

Does the hand fail?
The eye?
Thought?

Everything is being lost little by little
and by minuscule bits, tiny scraps
of pulverized time.

THE BIRD

The ancients saw it as a sign of good fortune
when birds flew on the right.
(Imagine the fear of seeing a large black bird
appearing on the left-hand side.)

This bird, however, does not give a clear message:
it appeared in front of me, it took an ambiguous flight
– a little to the right, then back again to the left –
and it vanished unexpectedly, swallowed up by the fog.

Its message – if it had one – remained unclear.
Its flight was an unfinished curve, a stretch
of a completely unforeseeable flight
apart from the little that could be seen ...
                                           However
the eye looks intently for it.

I wish it would show itself again! I wish it would fly again –
a hook, its little outline on the grey, I wish it would appear!

(The Delphic voice refuses to repeat its words
and is silent, however much we press it.)

Comparative Criticism 24, pp. 317–323. © 2002 Cambridge University Press
DOI: 10.1017/S0144756402005607   Printed in the United Kingdom

Books and periodicals received

COMPILED BY ANDREA BRADY

Allen, Carolyn and Judith A. Howard. *Provoking Feminisms*. Chicago and London: University of Chicago Press, 2000

Allnutt, Gillian. *Lintel*. Tarset: Bloodaxe, 2001 (poems)

Anderson, Linda. *Autobiography*. The New Critical Idiom. London and New York: Routledge, 2001

Armitage, David, Armand Himy and Quentin Skinner, eds. *Milton and Republicanism*. Cambridge University Press, 1995

Ashcroft, Bill. *Post-Colonial Transformation*. London and New York: Routledge, 2001

Ashcroft, Bill and Pal Ahluwaalia. *Edward Said*. Routledge Critical Thinkers. London and New York: Routledge, [1999] 2001

Barth, Ulrich and Claus-Dieter Osthövener, eds. *200 Jahre 'Reden über die Religion': Akten des 1. Internationalen Kongresses der Schleiermacher-Gesellschaft Halle, 14.–17. März 1999*. Berlin and New York: Walter de Gruyter, 2000

Bertens, Hans and Theo D'haen. *Contemporary American Crime Fiction*. Crime Files. New York and Basingstoke: Palgrave, 2001

Boccaccio, Giovanni. *Famous Women*. Edited and translated by Virginia Brown. I Tatti Renaissance Library. Cambridge, MA: Harvard University Press, 2001

Bozorth, Richard R. *Auden's Games of Knowledge: Poetry and the Meanings of Homosexuality*. New York: Columbia University Press, 2001

Bromley, Roger. *Narratives for a New Belonging: Diasporic Cultural Fictions*. Tendencies: Identities, Texts, Cultures. Edinburgh University Press, 2000

Brown, Marshall, ed. *The Cambridge History of Literary Criticism*. Volume v: *Romanticism*. Cambridge University Press, 2000

Bruni, Leonardo. *History of the Florentine People*. Volume 1: Books 1–iv. Edited and translated from the Italian by James Hankins. I Tatti Renaissance Library. Cambridge, MA: Harvard University Press, 2001

Buchanan, Ian and John Marks, eds. *Deleuze and Literature*. Edinburgh University Press, 2000

de Burine, Claude. *Words Have Frozen Over*. Translated from the French by Martin Sorrell. With an Introduction by Susan Wicks. Arc Visible Poets. Todmorden: Arc, 2001

Burrow, J. A. *The Gawain-Poet*. Writers and Their Work: Tavistock: Northcote House, 2001

Burwick, Frederick. *Thomas De Quincey: Knowledge and Power*. Romanticism in Perspective: Texts, Cultures, Histories. New York and Basingstoke: Palgrave, 2001

Çapan, Cevat. *Where Are You, Susie Petschek?* Translated from the Turkish by Michael Hulse and Cevat Çapan. With an Introduction by A. S. Byatt. Arc Visible Poets. Todmorden: Arc, 2001

Carter, Ronald and John McRae, eds. *The Routledge History of Literature in English: Britain and Ireland*. With a Foreword by Malcolm Bradbury. Second edition. London and New York: Routledge, 2001

Castle, Gregory, ed. *Postcolonial Discourses: an Anthology*. Oxford: Blackwell, 2001

Cattafi, Bartolo. *Anthracite*. Translated from the Italian by Brian Cole. With an Introduction by Peter Dale. Arc Visible Poets. Todmorden: Arc, 2000

Cavallaro, Dani. *Critical and Cultural Theory*. London and New Brunswick, NJ: The Athlone Press, 2001

Chard, Chloe. *Pleasure and Guilt on the Grand Tour: Travel Writing and Imaginative Geography 1600–1830*. Manchester University Press, 1999

Cheyette, Bryan. *Muriel Spark*. Writers and Their Work. Tavistock: Northcote House, 2000

Cixous, Hélène and Jacques Derrida. *Veils*. Translated from the French by Geoffrey Bennington. With drawings by Ernest Pignon-Ernest. Cultural Memory in the Present. Stanford University Press, 2001

Cobley, Paul. *Narrative*. The New Critical Idiom. London and New York: Routledge, 2001

Colebrook, Claire. *Gilles Deleuze*. Routledge Critical Thinkers. London and New York: Routledge, 2002

Connah, Roger. *How Architecture Got Its Hump*. Cambridge, MA, and London: MIT Press, 2001

Coupe, Laurence, ed. *The Green Studies Reader: From Romanticism to Ecocentrism*. With a Foreword by Jonathan Bate. London and New York: Routledge, 2000

Culler, Jonathan. *The Pursuit of Signs: Semiotics, Literature, Deconstruction*. London and New York: Routledge, [1981] 2001

Day, Gary. *Class*. The New Critical Idiom. London and New York: Routledge, 2001

Dayre, Eric. *Les Proses du temps: Thomas De Quincey et la philosophie kantienne*. Paris: Honoré Champion, 2000

Delbanco, Nicholas. *The Lost Suitcase: Reflections on Literary Life*. New York: Columbia University Press, 2000

Dharwadker, Vinay, ed. *Cosmopolitan Geographies: New Locations in Literature and Culture*. Essays from the English Institute. New York and London: Routledge, 2001

Dictionnaire des termes littéraires. Edited by Hendrik van Gorp, Dirk Delabastita, et al. Paris: Honoré Champion, 2001

Diderot, Denis. *Lettre sur les aveugles; Lettre sur les sourds et muets*. Edited by Marian Hobson and Simon Harvey. Paris: Flammarion, 2000

Ditsky, John. *John Steinbeck and The Critics*. Rochester, New York: Camden House, 2000

Edwards, Mike. *E. M. Forster: the Novels*. New York and Basingstoke: Palgrave, 2002

Engelberg, Edward. *Solitude and Its Ambiguities in Modernist Fiction*. New York and Basingstoke: Palgrave, 2001

Ficino, Marsilio. *Platonic Theology*. Volume I, Books I–IV. Translated from the Latin by Michael J. B. Allen with John Warden. Latin text edited by James Hankins with William Bowen. I Tatti Renaissance Library. Cambridge, MA: Harvard University Press, 2001

Finch, Alison. *Women's Writing in Nineteenth-Century France.* Cambridge Studies in French. Cambridge University Press, 2000

Forter, Greg. *Murdering Masculinities: Fantasies of Gender and Violence in the American Crime Novel.* New York and London: New York University Press, 2000

Fritzsche, Peter. *Reading Berlin 1900.* Cambridge, MA, and London: Harvard University Press, 1996

Godeau, Florence. *Récits en Souffrance: Essai sur 'Bartleby' (Herman Melville), 'La Métamorphose' et 'Le Terrier' (Franz Kafka), et 'L'Innommable' (Samuel Beckett).* Paris: Editions Kimé, 2001

Grabes, Herbert, ed. *Innovation and Continuity in English Studies: a Critical Jubilee.* Bamberger Beiträge zur Englischen Sprachwissenschaft. Frankfurt am Main: Peter Lang, 2001

Grady, Hugh, ed. *Shakespeare and Modernity: Early Modern to Millennium.* Accents on Shakespeare. London and New York: Routledge, 2000

Guy, Josephine M. ed. *The Victorian Age: an Anthology of Sources and Documents.* London and New York: Routledge, [1998] pb 2002

Haase, Ullrich and William Large. *Maurice Blanchot.* Routledge Critical Thinkers. London and New York: Routledge, 2000

Hansen, Erik W. *The Synchronic Fallacy: Historical Investigations with a Theory of History.* Odense University Press, 2001

Hawlin, Stefan. *The Complete Critical Guide to Robert Browning.* London and New York: Routledge, 2002

Hill, Geoffrey. *Speech! Speech!* London: Penguin, 2000 (poems)

Hill, Selima. *Bunny.* Tarset: Bloodaxe Books, 2001 (poems)

Hoving, Isabel. *In Praise of New Travelers: Reading Caribbean Migrant Women's Writing.* Cultural Memory in the Present. Stanford University Press, 2001

Howard, Jean E. and Scott Cutler Shershow, eds. *Marxist Shakespeares.* Accents on Shakespeare. New York and London: Routledge, 2001

Hudgins, Christopher C. and Leslie Kane, eds. *Gender and Genre: Essays on David Mamet.* New York and Basingstoke: Palgrave, 2001

Huggan, Graham. *The Postcolonial Exotic: Marketing the Margins.* London and New York: Routledge, 2001

Huhndorf, Shari M. *Going Native: Indians in the American Cultural Imagination.* Cornell University Press, 2001

Johnston, Dillon. *The Poetic Economies of England and Ireland, 1912–2000.* New York and Basingstoke: Palgrave, 2001

Knellwolf, Christa and Christopher Norris, eds. *The Cambridge History of Literary Criticism.* Volume IX: *Twentieth-Century Historical, Philosophical and Psychological Perspectives.* Cambridge University Press, 2001

Knight, Wilson. *The Wheel of Fire: Interpretations of Shakespearian Tragedy.* With an Introduction by T. S. Eliot. London and New York: Routledge, [1930] 2001

Korte, Barbara, Ralf Schneider and Stefanie Lethbridge, eds. *Anthologies of British Poetry Critical Perspectives from Literary and Cultural Studies.* Internationale Forschungen zur Allgemeinen und Vergleichenden Literaturwissenschaft. Amsterdam and Atlanta: Rodopi, 2000

Krutikov, Mikhail. *Yiddish Fiction and the Crisis of Modernity, 1905–1914.* Stanford Studies in Jewish History and Culture. Stanford University Press, 2001

Lansdown, Richard. *The Autonomy of Literature*. Basingstoke and New York: Macmillan, 2001

Lane, Richard J. *Jean Baudrillard*. Routledge Critical Thinkers. London and New York: Routledge, 2000

Large, Duncan. *Nietzsche and Proust: a Comparative Study*. Oxford Modern Languages and Literature Monographs. Oxford: Clarendon Press, 2001

Larson, Jil. *Ethics and Narrative in the English Novel, 1880–1914*. Cambridge University Press, 2001

Lawrence, D. H. *The Letters*. The Cambridge Edition. Volume VIII: Previously Uncollected Letters and General Index. Edited and compiled by James T. Boulton. Cambridge University Press, 2000

The Low Countries: Arts and Society in Flanders and the Netherlands. Yearbook 9. Rekkem: Flemish-Netherlands Foundation, 2001

Lu, Tina. *Persons, Roles, and Minds: Identity in* Peony Pavilion *and* Peach Blossom Fen. Stanford University Press, 2001

Lucas, John. *Ivor Gurney*. Writers and Their Work. Tavistock: Northcote House, 2001

Lyotard, Jean-François. *Soundproof Room: Malraux's Anti-Aesthetics*. Translated from the French by Robert Harvey. Stanford University Press, 2001

Maia, Circe. *Yesterday a Eucalyptus*. Translated from the Spanish by Brian Cole. Amersham: Brindin Press, 2001

Makinen, Merja. *Feminist Popular Fiction*. New York and Basingstoke: Palgrave, 2001

McLaughlin, Martin, ed. *Britain and Italy from Romanticism to Modernism: a Festschrift for Peter Brand*. Legenda. Oxford: European Humanities Research Centre, 2000

McQuillan, Martin, ed. *Deconstruction: a Reader*. Edinburgh University Press, 2000

McQuillan, Martin. *Paul de Man*. Routledge Critical Thinkers. London and New York: Routledge, 2001

Mengham, Rod. *Charles Dickens*. Writers and Their Work. Tavistock: Northcote House, 2001

Miller, Lindy. *Mastering Practical Criticism*. Palgrave Master Series. New York and Basingstoke: Palgrave, 2001

Murphet, Julian. *Literature and Race in Los Angeles*. Cultural Margins. Cambridge University Press, 2001

Neill, Michael. *Putting History to the Question: Power, Politics, and Society in English Renaissance Drama*. New York: Columbia University Press, 2000

Palmer, Bryan D. *Cultures of Darkness: Night Travels in the Histories of Transgression [from Medieval to Modern]*. New York: Monthly Review Press, 2000

Partridge, Eric. *Shakespeare's Bawdy*. With a Foreword by Stanley Wells. London and New York: Routledge, [1947] 2001

Paulson, William. *Literary Culture in a World Transformed: a Future for the Humanities*. Ithaca and London: Cornell University Press, 2001

Pfister, Manfred. *Laurence Sterne*. Writers and Their Work. Tavistock: Northcote House, 2001

Popkin, Margaret. *Peace without Justice: Obstacles to Building the Rule of Law in El Salvador*. University Park: Pennsylvania State University Press, 2000

Rabaté, Jean-Michel. *Jacques Lacan, Psychoanalysis and the Subject of Literature*. Transitions. New York and Basingstoke: Palgrave, 2001

Radnóti, Miklós. *Camp Notebook*. Translated from the Hungarian by Francis Jones. With an Introduction by George Szirtes. Arc Visible Poets. Todmorden: Arc, 2000

Rand, Richard, ed. *Futures of Jacques Derrida*. Cultural Memory in the Present. Stanford University Press, 2001

Rescher, Nicholas. *Process Philosophy: a Survey of Basic Issues*. University of Pittsburgh Press, 2000

Richards, I. A. *Principles of Literary Criticism*. London and New York: Routledge, [1924] 2001

Roberts, Adam. *Fredric Jameson*. Routledge Critical Thinkers. London and New York: Routledge, 2000

Roosevelt, Eleanor. *It Seems to Me: Selected Letters*. Edited by Leonard C. Schlup and Donald W. Whisenhunt. Lexington: University Press of Kentucky, 2001

Roston, Murray. *The Search for Selfhood in Modern Literature*. New York and Basingstoke: Palgrave, 2001

Ruthven, K. K. *Faking Literature*. Cambridge University Press, 2001

Rutter, Carol Chillington. *Enter the Body: Women and Representation on Shakespeare's Stage*. London and New York: Routledge, 2001

Saglia, Diego. *Poetic Castles in Spain: British Romanticism and Figurations of Iberia*. Internationale Forschungen zur Allgemeinen und Vergleichenden Literaturwissenschaft. Amsterdam and Atlanta: Rodopi, 2000

Sartre, Jean-Paul. *What is Literature?* Translated from the French by Bernard Frechtman. With an Introduction by David Caute. London and New York: Routledge, [1948] 2001

Sas, Miryam. *Fault Lines: Cultural Memory and Japanese Surrealism*. Cultural Memory in the Present. Stanford University Press, 2001

Sauerberg, Lars Ole. *Intercultural Voices in Contemporary British Literature: the Implosion of Empire*. New York and Basingstoke: Palgrave, 2001

Scarry, Elaine. *Dreaming by the Book*. Princeton University Press, 1999

Shirane, Haruo and Tomi Suzuki, eds. *Inventing the Classics: Modernity, National Identity, and Japanese Literature*. Stanford University Press, 2000

Silk, M. S. *Aristophanes and the Definition of Comedy*. Oxford University Press, 2000

Skilleås, Ole Martin. *Philosophy and Literature: an Introduction*. Edinburgh University Press, 2001

Smith, Peter D. *Metaphor and Materiality: German Literature and the World-View of Science 1780–1955*. Legenda Studies in Comparative Literature 4. Oxford: European Humanities Research Centre, 2000

Strachan, John and Richard Terry. *Poetry: an Introduction*. New York University Press, 2001

Strunge, Michael. *A Virgin from a Chilly Decade*. Translated from the Danish by Bente Elsworth. With an Introduction by John Fletcher. Arc Visible Poets. Todmorden: Arc, 2000

Tambling, Jeremy. *Becoming Posthumous: Life and Death in Literary and Cultural Studies*. Edinburgh University Press, 2001

Tamen, Miguel. *The Matter of the Facts: On Invention and Interpretation*. Stanford University Press, 2000

Ten Years of Atlas Press: a brief history, bibliography, prospectus of the Arkhive *series &*

an appendix demonstrating the occasional felicities of unsolicited mail. London: Atlas Press, 2000

Thurschwell, Pamela. *Sigmund Freud.* Routledge Critical Thinkers. London and New York: Routledge, 2000

Walder, Dennis, ed. *The Nineteenth-Century Novel: Identities.* London and New York: Routledge, 2001

Warner, Marina. *The Leto Bundle.* London: Chatto and Windus, 2001 (novel)

Wettlaufer, Alexandra K. *Pen vs. Paintbrush: Girodet, Balzac and the Myth of Pygmalion in Postrevolutionary France.* New York and Basingstoke: Palgrave, 2001

Williams, Alison. *Tricksters and Pranksters: Roguery in French and German Literature of the Middle Ages and the Renaissance.* Internationale Forschungen zur Allgemeinen und Vergleichenden Literaturwissenschaft. Amsterdam and Atlanta: Rodopi, 2000

Wilson, Richard, ed. *Julius Caesar.* New Casebooks. New York and Basingstoke: Palgrave, 2002

Wolfreys, Julian, ed. *Introducing Literary Theories: a Guide and Glossary.* Edinburgh University Press, 2001

Wolfreys, Julian, Ruth Robbins and Kenneth Womack. *Key Concepts in Literary Theory.* Edinburgh University Press, 2002

Wolfreys, Julian. *Victorian Hauntings: Spectrality, Gothic, the Uncanny and Literature.* New York and Basingstoke: Palgrave, 2002

Xenophon. *The Education of Cyrus.* Translated from the Greek by Wayne Ambler. Ithaca and London: Cornell University Press, 2001

Young, Robert J. C. *Postcolonialism: an Historical Introduction.* Oxford: Blackwell Publishers, 2001.

Zong-Qi Cai, ed. *A Chinese Literary Mind: Culture, Creativity, and Rhetoric in* Wenxin Diaolong. Stanford University Press, 2001

PERIODICALS AND JOURNALS

Books from Finland 35:2 (2001)

British Journal for Eighteenth-Century Studies 23:1 (Spring 2000)

The Coleridge Bulletin 16 (New Series) (Winter 2000), 27 (Summer 2001)

Configurations: A Journal of Literature, Science, and Technology 2:1 (Winter 1994), 8:3 (Fall 2000)

The George Eliot Review: Journal of the George Eliot Fellowship 32 (2001)

Journal of Contemporary China 10:26 (February 2001)

MHRA: Annual Bulletin of the Modern Humanities Research Association 73 (February 2001)

The Modern Language Review 93:1 (January 1998), 96:1 (January 2001), 96:2 (April 2001)

New Comparison: A Journal of Comparative and General Literary Studies 26 (Autumn 1998), 27/28 (Spring/Autumn 1999), 29 (Spring 2000)

PBS Bulletin 188 (Spring 2001)

The Persephone Quarterly 9 (Spring 2001)

PMLA 111:5 (October 1996), 115:3 (May 2000), 115:5 (October 2000), 115:7 (December 2000), 116:1 (January 2001), 116:2 (March 2001)

Proceedings of the British Academy 105 (2000)

Profession 2000

Science as Culture 10:2 (June 2001), 10:3 (September 2001), 10:4 (December 2001)

SLS Decodings: The Newsletter of the Society for Literature and Science 10:2 (Summer 2001)

The Thomas Hardy Journal 17:1 (February 2001)

Weissbort, Daniel, ed. *European Voices. Modern Poetry in Translation* 18 (New Series) (2001)

Yearbook of Comparative and General Literature 48 (2000)

Comparative Criticism 24, pp. 325–346. Cambridge University Press 2002
DOI: 10.1017/S0144756402005619 Printed in the United Kingdom

Bibliography of Jan Potocki

COMPILED BY FRANÇOIS ROSSET

EDITIONS OF WORKS BY POTOCKI

Only works currently in print are listed here. For a complete list of Potocki's works, see Dominique Triaire, *Œuvre de Jean Potocki – Inventaire*. Paris: Champion, 1985, 342 pp.

The Manuscript Found in Saragossa
Bulgarian

Rakopis nameren v Saragosa, Radrizzani text translated by Ana Perikliiska, Sofia: Beva Pres, 1992, 272 pp.

Danish

Manuskriptet fra Zaragoza, Radrizzani text translated by Lars Bonnevie, Viborg: Samleren, 1996, 554 pp.

Dutch

Manuscript gevonden te Zaragoza, Radrizzani text translated by Jan Versteeg, Amsterdam: Wereldbibliotheek, 1992, 554 pp.

English

The Manuscript Found in Saragossa, Radrizzani text translated with an introduction by Ian Maclean, New York: Viking, 1995; Harmondsworth: Penguin Books, 1996, 631 pp.
Articles and reviews (selected):
Weightman, John, 'Extravaganza in Progress', *The New York Review of Books*, 30 (Nov. 1995), 40–2
Wolff, Larry, 'Love Beneath the Gallows', *The New York Times Book Review*, 14 Jan. 1996, pp. 15–16
Elukin, Jonathan, 'A Thousand and Two Nights', *The American Scholar* (Washington), 66 (1997), 152–4
Furbank, P. N., 'Nesting Time', *London Review of Books*, 26 Jan. 1995, pp. 14–15

French

Manuscrit trouvé à Saragosse, Paris: Gallimard 'L'étrangère', 1996, 320 pp.
[Incomplete text edited by Roger Caillois, published by Gallimard 1958, reissued 1972 in 'Folio' collection under the title *La Duchesse d'Avila*.]

Manuscrit trouvé à Saragosse, first integral edition edited by René Radrizzani, Paris: José Corti, 1989, 680 pp. New edition, Paris: José Corti, 1992, 714 pp.; reissued in Le Livre de Poche, 1995, 701 pp.

Articles and reviews:

Decottignies, Jean, review, *Revue des Sciences Humaines* (Lille), 81 (1989), 225–6

Coward, David, 'The Mistery Remains', *The Times Literary Supplement* (London), 4515 (13 Oct. 1989), 1111–12

Péju, Pierre, 'Un étrange et gigantesque roman', *La Quinzaine littéraire* (Paris), 536 (16 July 1989), 5–6

Żółtowska, Maria Evelina, 'Rękopis znaleziony w tezie', *Kultura* (Paris), 506 (Nov. 1989), 116–23

Radrizzani, René, reply to M. E. Żółtowska, *Kultura* (Paris), 514 (July–Aug. 1990), 207–9

Taillade, Nicole, review, *Littératures* (Toulouse), 21 (autumn 1989), 181–4

Beauvois, Daniel, 'Jean Potocki méritait mieux', *Dix-huitième Siècle* (Paris) 22 (1990), 441–9

Review, *Revue d'Histoire Littéraire de la France* (Paris), 90: 4–5 (July–Oct. 1990), 833–5

Roger-Taillade, Nicole, review of the new edition (1992), *Littératures* (Toulouse), 26 (1992), 278–9

Piva, Franco, review, *Studi Francesi* (Turin), 36 (1992), 374–5

Kibédi Varga, Aaron, 'Un chef-d'œuvre du xviiie siècle', *Rapports – Het Franse Boek* (Amsterdam), 63 (1993), 28–31

Saras, Kalliopie, review, *Nineteenth-Century French Studies* (Fredonia, NY), 22 (1993/94), 582–3

German

Die Abenteuer in der Sierra Morena oder die Handschriften von Saragossa, Kukulski text translated with commentary by Werner Creuzinger, afterword by Leszek Kukulski, Zurich: Haffmans-Verlag, 1991, 940 pp.

Die Handschrift von Saragossa, Radrizzani text translated by Manfred Zander, Zürich: Haffmans-Verlag, 2000, 951 pp.

Review: Ingold, Felix Philipp, 'Der totale Roman', *Neue Zürcher Zeitung*, 4 Jan. 2001, p. 49

Italian

Manoscritto trovato a Saragozza, Radrizzani text translated with an introduction by Giovanni Bogliolo, Parma: Guanda, 1990, 751 pp.; 2nd edition, Milan: TEA, 1995

Polish

Rękopis znaleziony w Saragossie, Kukulski text translated by Edmund Chojecki. Wrocław: Siedmiogród, 1998

Romanian

Manuscrisul gasit la Saragosa, Radrizzani text translated with an introduction, chronology and notes by Adriana and Mihai Mitu. 2 vols. Bucarest: Nemira, 1997, 380 and 366 pp.

Russian

Rukopis' naidennaia v Saragose, Kukulski text translated by D. Gorbov with preface and notes by S. Landa. 2 vols. Moscow: Terra, 1997

Spanish

Manuscrito encontrado en Zaragoza, Radrizzani text translated by Amalia Alvarez and Francisco Javier Muñoz, preface by Federico Arbos, Madrid: Palas Atenea, 1990, 603 pp.

Manuscrito encontrado en Zaragoza, Caillois text translated by José Blanco, Barcelona: Minotauro, 1996, 318 pp.

Manuscrito encontrado en Zaragoza, Radrizzani text translated by Mauro Armiño, Madrid: Valdemar Colección Gótica, 1996, 592 pp.

Travel writing

An almost complete edition of the travels has been produced by Daniel Beauvois, Paris: Fayard, La Bibliothèque des voyageurs, 1980 (2 vols.). This essential edition is unfortunately out of print

Viaggio in Turchia, in Egitto e in Marocco, translated by Barbara Ferri and Pietro Veronese, Rome: Edizioni e/o, 1990, 196 pp.

Au Caucase et en Chine, une traversée de l'Asie par l'auteur du Manuscrit trouvé à Saragosse *(1797–1806), avec six dessins de l'auteur*, edited by Jean-Pierre Sicre; Paris: Phébus, 1991, 265 pp.

Article:

Delon, Michel, 'Voyageur (presque) de naissance', *La Quinzaine littéraire* (Paris), 588 (1 Nov. 1991), 28

Le Voyage de Hafez: récit oriental, n.p., Editions Novetlé, 1995, 67 pp.

Nelle steppe di Astrakan e del Caucaso: 1797–1798, edited, translated and introduced by Giovanni Battista Tomassini, Milan: Mondadori, 1996, 223 pp.

Voyage dans l'empire du Maroc: fait en l'année 1791, introduction and notes by Jean-Louis Miège, Paris: Maisonneuve et Larose, 1997, 191 pp.

Article:

Laroui, Fouad, 'Le premier touriste', *Jeune Afrique* (Paris), 2000–2001 (1999), 150–2

Mémoire sur l'ambassade en Chine, edited with an introduction and notes by Daniel Beauvois, Alexandre Stroev and Dominique Triaire, 'Jean Potocki rentre de Chine trop tôt ...', *Dix-huitième siècle* (Paris), 31 (1999), 345–76

Voyage en Turquie et en Egypte, edited by Serge Plantureux, Paris: José Corti, Collection Romantique no. 71, 1999, 166 pp.

Dramatic works

Parades, Les Bohémiens d'Andalousie, dramatic works edited by Dominique Triaire, Arles: Actes Sud, 1989, 127 pp.

Reviews:

Ryba, Janusz, review, *Pamiętnik Literacki* (Wrocław), 81: 4 (1990), 356–62

Vercruysse, Jeroom, review, *Nouvelles Annales Prince de Ligne* (Brussels), 5 (1990), 224–5

Dębowski, Marek, review, *Dix-huitième Siècle* (Paris), 24 (1992), 586–7

Decottignies, Jean, review, *Revue des Sciences Humaines* (Lille), 226 (April–June 1992), 217–19

L'Aveugle, an unpublished proverb edited with an introduction and notes by Dominique Triaire, *Dix-huitième Siècle* (Paris), 25 (1993), 295–303

Political and miscellaneous writings

Ecrits politiques, collection with introduction and notes by Dominique Triaire, Paris: Champion 1987, 338 pp.

Essay d'aphorismes sur la liberté, extracts published without name of editor on website. *Points de Fuite en Ligne*, http://www.citeweb.net/pdef/Restitution/Potocki.htm

Correspondence

Listy Jana Potockiego do A. K. Czartoryskiego 1807–1814 [Letters from J. Potocki to A. K. Czartoryski 1807–1814], edited with an introduction by Daniel Beauvois, in *Studia Historyczne* (Cracow), 18: 2 (1975), 251–3

Trois lettres de Jean Potocki à son frère Séverin, edited with an introduction and notes by Dominique Triaire, in Marthe Molinari and Dominique Triaire (eds.), *Paroles et révolutions*, Paris: Champion, 1992, pp. 211–18

Listy Jana Potockiego do Henryka Lubomirskiego z 1794 r [Letters from Jan Potocki to Henri Lubomirski], edited with an introduction and notes by Maria Evelina Żółtowska, *Wiek Oświecenia* (Warsaw), 10 (1994), 21–41

Correspondance inédite de Jean Potocki sur l'ambassade russe en Chine (1806–1810), edited with an introduction and notes by Alexandre Stroev and Dominique Triaire, in *Dix-huitième Siècle* (Paris), 26 (1994), 251–67

Treize lettres inédites de Jean Potocki, edited with an introduction and notes by Dominique Triaire, *Studies on Voltaire and the Eighteenth Century* (Oxford), 317 (1994), 117–35

Quatre lettres inédites de Jean Potocki, edited with an introduction and notes by Łukasz Kądziela, Alexandre Stroev and Dominique Triaire, in *La Culture française dans l'Europe du XVIIIe siècle*, Actes du colloque franco-russo-allemand tenu à l'Université de la Sarre en 1992 (to appear)

Quatre lettres inédites de Jean Potocki, edited with an introduction and notes by Dominique Triaire, in Izabella Zatorska and Andrzej Siemek (eds.), *Le Siècle de Rousseau et sa postérité. Mélanges offerts à Ewa Rzadkowska*, Warsaw: Uniwersytet Warszawski, 1998, pp. 217–28

Correspondance de Jean Potocki avec son frère Seweryn (1802–1808), edited with notes by Dominique Triaire, in François Rosset and Dominique Triaire, *De Varsovie à Saragosse: Jean Potocki et son œuvre*, Louvain and Paris: Peeters, 2000, pp. 39–62

Correspondance de Jean Potocki avec sa nièce Maria Potocka (1809–1812), edited with notes by Dominique Triaire, in François Rosset and Dominique Triaire, *De Varsovie à Saragosse: Jean Potocki et son œuvre*, Louvain and Paris: Peeters, 2000, pp. 63–85

Drawings

'Szkicownik Jana Potockiego z jego podróży do Cesarstwa Marokańskiego' [Potocki's sketchbook from his journey to Morocco], edited by Jerzy Wojciechowski, in *Konteksty. Polska Sztuka Ludowa* (Warsaw), 242–3: 3–4 (1998), 57–60

SECONDARY WORKS

Andrzejewski, Jerzy, '*O Rękopisie znalezionym w Saragossie*. Kartki z dziennika lektury' [On *Manuscript Found in Saragossa*. Pages from a lecture journal], in *Odrodzenie*, 4: 46 (16 Nov. 1947), 7

Antonowicz, Kaja, 'La tresse et la corde: les vampires du *Manuscrit trouvé à Saragosse* de Jean Potocki', in Michel Porret and François Rosset (eds.), *Le Jardin de l'esprit. Textes offerts à Bronisław Baczko*, Geneva: Droz, 1995, pp. 11–25

Audo, Yves, *Lecture du* Manuscrit trouvé à Saragosse: *apprentissage littéraire de la raison*, thesis, Université de Toulouse-Le Mirail, 1993, 967 pp.

Aufrère, Sydney H., 'Le comte Jean Potocki et l'Égypte du *Manuscrit trouvé à Saragosse*', *Egypte* (Paris), 6 (Sept. 1997), 31–8

Aufrère, Sydney H., 'L'influence du savoir égyptien issu de la tradition de l'Antiquité tardive', in Jan Herman, Paul Pelckmans, François Rosset (eds.), *Le* Manuscrit trouvé à Saragosse *et ses intertextes*, Actes du colloque international, Leuven – Anvers, 30 March–1 April 2000, Louvain and Paris: Peeters, 2001, pp. 73–89

Avalle-Arce, Juan Bautista de, 'El conde Jan Potocki: Polonia y España en el siglo XVIII', *Cuadernos de ALDEEU* (Erie, PA), 11: 1 (April 1995), 9–15

Baliński, Michał, 'Jan Potocki wędrowiec, literat i dziejopis' [Jan Potocki Traveller, Man of Letters and Historian], *Pisma historyczne*, Warsaw, 1843, vol. III, pp. 137–209

Barbier, Antoine-Alexandre, *Dictionnaire des ouvrages anonymes*, 3rd edition, vol. III, Paris: Paul Daffis, 1872, pp. 327, 1102–3, and vol. IV, Paris: Féchoz et Letouzey, 1882, pp. 57–8

Barrena, Inmaculada, 'El vizcáino grotesco o el endemoniado en el *Manuscrito encontrado en Zaragoza*', in Rosa de Diego and Lydia Vázquez (eds.), *De lo Grotesco*, I, Vitoria-Gasteiz, 1996, pp. 81–7

Bartoszyński, Kazimierz, 'O budowie i znaczeniu *Rękopisu znalezionego w Saragossie*', in *Pamiętnik Literacki* (Wrocław), 80: 2 (1989), 27–45 (reprinted under the title *Rękopis znaleziony w Saragossie* – "szkatułka" i powieść', *Powieść w świecie literackości*, Warsaw: IBL – PAN, 1991, pp. 11–28; French version: 'Structure et signification dans le *Manuscrit trouvé à Saragosse*', *Literary Studies in Poland – Etudes littéraires en Pologne* (Warsaw), 23 (1990), 41–62)

Beauvois, Daniel, 'Entre l'analyse et l'action politiques, Jean Potocki voyageur "éclairé"', *Modèles et moyens de la réflexion politique au XVIIIe siècle*, vol. I, Villeneuve d'Ascq: Presses de l'Université de Lille, 1978, pp. 39–63

'Un Polonais au service de la Russie: Jean Potocki et l'expansion en Transcaucasie 1804–1805', *Cahiers du monde russe et soviétique* (Paris), 19: 1–2 (1978), 175–89

'Jan Potocki a cenzura wileńska w roku 1814' [Jan Potocki and censorship in Vilna in 1814], *Przegląd Humanistyczny* (Warsaw), 22: 12 (1978), 137–43

'Le "Système asiatique" de Jean Potocki ou le rêve oriental dans les Empires d'Alexandre Ier et de Napoléon 1806–1808', *Cahiers du monde russe et soviétique* (Paris), 20: 3–4 (1979), 467–85

'Jean Potocki voyageur' in Jan Potocki, *Voyages en Turquie et en Egypte, au Maroc, en Hollande*, Paris: Fayard, 1980, pp. 7–41

'Du cosmopolitisme à l'impérialisme', in Jean Potocki, *Voyages au Caucase et en Chine*, Paris: Fayard, 1980, pp. 7–26

'Les relations de Jean et Stanislas-Félix Potocki d'après quelques documents des archives de Kiev', in Dominique Triaire (ed.), *Continuités et ruptures dans l'histoire et la littérature*, Paris: Champion, 1988, pp. 1–7

'Czego Jan Potocki szukał w Czeczeni?' [What was Jan Potocki Looking for in Chechenya?], *Biuletyn Towarzystwa Literackiego im. Adama Mickiewicza* (Warsaw) (1996), pp. 49–56

'Un proche bien encombrant de Stanislas Auguste: Jean Potocki et ses papillonnements politico-diplomatiques entre la Grande Diète et le voyage au Maroc (avec une lettre inédite)', *Wiek Oświecenia* (Warsaw), 15 (1999), 229–46

'Les sinuosités politiques du comte Jean Potocki', *Europe* (Paris), 863 (March 2001), 26–45

Bellemin-Noël, Jean, 'L'érotisme dans le fantastique chez Jean Potocki', *Revue des Sciences Humaines* (Lille), 131 (1968), 415–25

Belza, Igor, Postscript to the Russian edition of *Manuscript Found in Saragossa*, Moscow: Nauka, 1968, pp. 571–95

'Jan hrabia Potocki – kawaler maltański' [Count Jan Potocki, Knight of Malta], *Portrety romantyków*, Warsaw: IW Pax, 1974, pp. 107–29

'Potocki i Puszkin' [Potocki and Pushkin], *Portrety romantyków*, Warsaw: IW Pax, 1974, pp. 131–41

Berchtold, Jacques, 'Le *Manuscrit trouvé à Saragosse* et les parfums tentateurs de *Cleveland*', in Jan Herman, Paul Pelckmans and François Rosset (eds.), *Le Manuscrit trouvé à Saragosse et ses intertextes*, Actes du colloque international, Leuven – Anvers, 30 March–1 April 2000, Louvain and Paris: Peeters, 2001, pp. 151–66

Bernoussi, Mohamed, *Le Roman noir français dans la seconde moitié du XVIIIe siècle. Exemples Cazotte, Potocki, Sade, Prévost, Ducray-Duminil*, thesis, Université de Tours, 1995

Bessière, Irène, *Eléments de littérature fantastique au XVIIIe siècle. 'Le Diable amoureux', 'Vathek', 'Le Manuscrit trouvé à Saragosse'*, thesis, Université de Paris X Nanterre, 1972, 299 pp.

Le Récit fantastique. La poétique de l'incertain, Paris: Larousse, 1974, *passim*.

Bialas, Sbigniew, '*Fabula Interrupta*: on Taking (Textual) Liberties', *Comparative Criticism* 24, Cambridge: Cambridge University Press, 2002, pp. 111–20

Bittoun-Debruyne, Nathalie, 'La visión de España en el *Manuscrit trouvé à Saragosse* de Jean Potocki', in Jaume Pont (ed.), *Narrativa fantástica en el siglo XIX (España e Hispanoamérica)*, Lleida: Milenio, 1997, pp. 41–60

Błoński, Jan, 'Jan Potocki i jego powieść' [Jan Potocki and his Novel], in *Życie Literackie* (Cracow), 1: 5 (April 1951), p. 11

Bogliolo, Giovanni, 'Jan Potocki', *Cinquantadue trame di capolavori della letteratura francese dell'Ottocento*, Milan: Rizzoli, 1991, pp. 242–53

Bokobza Kahan, Michèle, 'Dispositif romanesque et statut des personnages féminins dans les récits de Don Juan d'Avadoro', in Jan Herman, Paul Pelckmans and François Rosset (eds.), *Le Manuscrit trouvé à Saragosse et ses intertextes*, Actes du colloque international, Leuven – Anvers, 30 March–1 April 2000, Louvain and Paris: Peeters, 2001, pp. 59–71

Bradecki, Tadeusz, 'Le *Manuscrit* théâtral', *Europe* (Paris), 863 (March 2001), 177–85

Brückner, Aleksander, *Jana hr. Potockiego prace i zasługi naukowe* [The Works and Scientific Merit of Count Jan Potocki], Warsaw: Gebethner and Wolff, 1911, 123 pp.

Brunet, Mathieu, 'Hybridation, encyclopédisme et fausse monnaie: l'association comme principe créateur chez Diderot, Du Laurens et Potocki', in Jan Herman, Paul Pelckmans and François Rosset (eds.), *Le* Manuscrit trouvé à Saragosse *et ses intertextes*, Actes du colloque international, Leuven – Anvers, 30 March–1 April 2000, Louvain and Paris: Peeters, 2001, pp. 167–77

Brzękowski, Jan, 'Spóźniony prekursor' [A Late Precursor], *Kultura* (Paris), Jan.–Feb. 1959, pp. 218–19

Caillois, Roger, 'Préface', in Jean Potocki, *Manuscrit trouvé à Saragosse*, Paris: Gallimard, 1958, pp. 7–24 (Caillois's incomplete text), reissued 1961 with modifications

Introduction to *Six parades* by Jan Potocki, in *Théâtre populaire* 34 (1959), 51

'Destin d'un homme et d'un livre: le comte Jean Potocki et le *Manuscrit trouvé à Saragosse*' with 'Extrait de la préface de la première édition (1958)', *Manuscrit trouvé à Saragosse*, 2nd edition, Paris: Gallimard, 1967, pp. 7–43 (Caillois's incomplete text published by Gallimard in the 'Folio' collection under the title *La Duchesse d'Avila*, 1972, later in the collection 'L'Etrangère', under the title *Manuscrit trouvé à Saragosse*, 1996)

Cano, José Luis, 'Nota biográfica del autor', in Jan Potocki, *Manuscrito encontrado en Zaragoza*, Madrid: Alianza, 1970, pp. 15–23

Caro Baroja, Julio, 'Prólogo para uso del lector de la traducción española', in Jan Potocki, *Manuscrito encontrado en Zaragoza*, Madrid: Alianza, 1970, pp. 7–14

Chojecki, Edmund, 'Krótka wiadomość o życiu i pismach Jana hrabiego Potockiego' [Brief Information on the Life and Writings of Count Jan Potocki], in Jan Potocki *Rękopis znaleziony w Saragossie*, 2nd edition, Leipzig: Księgarnia zagraniczna, 1857, pp. i–xv (reprinted in the Brussels edition, 1862)

Chołoniewski, Stanisław, 'Proroctwo Józefa de Maistre w Petersburgu przesłane Janowi Potockiemu, r. 1810, sprawdzone w Uładówce R.P. 1841' [Prophecy of Joseph de Maistre at St Petersburg addressed to Jan Potocki in 1810, verified at Uładówka in the year of our Lord 1841], in *Obrazy z galeryi życia mego*, Lvov: Gubrynowicz and Schmidt, 1890, pp. 179–200

Cieśla, Maria, '*Rękopis znaleziony w Saragossie* rozpisany na głosy' [*The Manuscript Found in Saragossa*, a novel in several voices], *Pamiętnik Literacki* (Wrocław), 64:4 (1973), 43–68

Citton, Yves, 'Potocki and the Spectre of the Postmodern', *Comparative Criticism* 24, Cambridge: Cambridge University Press, 2002, pp. 141–65

Coates, Paul, 'Dialectics of Enlightenment: Notes on Wojciech Has's *Manuscript Found in Saragossa*', *Comparative Criticism* 24, Cambridge University Press, 2002, pp. 193–216

Coccaro, Janet, *Illusions and Disillusions: the Search for Truth in Jan Potocki's Manuscript Found in Saragossa*, thesis, University of Pittsburgh, 1999, 218 pp.

Colucci, Michele, 'Jan Potocki e i "motivi italiani" nel *Manoscritto trovato a*

Saragozza', in Vittorio Branca (ed.) *Italia, Venezia e Polonia, tra Illuminismo e Romanticismo*, Florence: Olschki, 1973, pp. 273–92

Cormier, Jacques, 'Réminiscences de *Don Quichotte* chez Challe et chez Potocki', in Jan Herman, Paul Pelckmans and François Rosset (eds.), *Le* Manuscrit trouvé à Saragosse *et ses intertextes*, Actes du colloque international, Leuven – Anvers, 30 March–1 April 2000, Louvain and Paris: Peeters, 2001, pp. 119–30

Cornwell, Neil, 'The European "Nights" Tradition: Potocki and Odoevski's *Russian Nights'*, *Comparative Criticism* 24, Cambridge: Cambridge University Press, 2002, pp. 121–39

Dahan, Jacques-Remi, 'Charles Nodier et le *Manuscrit trouvé à Saragosse'*, *Bulletin du Bibliophile* 2 (Paris), (1988), 161–74

'Une copie inconnue du *Manuscrit trouvé à Saragosse'*, *Revue d'Histoire Littéraire de la France* (Paris), 89: 2 (1989), 260–66

Dębicki, Ludwik, *Puławy (1762–1830), Monografia z życia towarzyskiego, politycznego i literackiego na podstawie archiwum ks. Czartoryskich w Krakowie* [Puławy (1762–1830), Social, Political and Literary Life, monograph from the archives of the Czartoryski princes in Cracow], Lvov: Gubrynowicz and Schmidt, 1888, vol. III, pp. 1–25

Dębowski, Marek, 'Oryginalność *Parad* Jana Potockiego', *Przegląd Humanistyczny* (Warsaw), 25, 1981, 3, pp. 159–78 (abridged French version: 'Originalité des *Parades* de Potocki', *Studies on Voltaire and the Eighteenth Century*, (Oxford), 265 (1989), 1368–71)

'L'aristocrate et son *Comédien bourgeois* qui fait allusion à Jean-Jacques Rousseau', *Essais sur le dialogue. Les didascalies dans le théâtre européen XVIe–XXe siècle*, Grenoble: Institut des langues et cultures de l'Europe, Université Stendhal-Grenoble III, 1995, pp. 31–9

'L'éducation conjugale et sa dérision dans le théâtre polonais des Lumières', *Texte et Théâtralité. Mélanges offerts à Jean Claude*, Nancy: Presses universitaires de Nancy, 2000, pp. 277–84

Decottignies, Jean, 'Variations sur un succube. Histoire de Thibaud de la Jacquière', *Revue des Sciences Humaines* (Lille), 111 (1963), 329–40

'A propos du *Manuscrit trouvé à Saragosse*, décaméron et texte "polyphonique"', *Les Cahiers de Varsovie* (Warsaw), 3 (1974), 191–207

Delon, Michel, 'La bizarrerie de la nature', *Europe* (Paris), 863 (March 2001), 93–102

Didier, Béatrice, 'L'exotisme et la mise en question du système moral et familial dans le roman, à la fin du XVIIIe siècle, Beckford, Sade, Potocki', *Studies on Voltaire and the Eighteenth Century*, 152 (1976), 571–86

Doering, Ulrich, 'Die Abgründe der Lust. Jan Potockis *Manuscrit trouvé à Saragosse* (1805)', *Reisen ans Ende der Kultur. Wahrnehmung und Sinnlichkeit in der phantastischen Literatur Frankreichs*, Berne (etc.): Peter Lang, 1987, pp. 116–25

'Die Reise in die Welt der Schönheit. Jan Potockis "Histoire de Giulio Romati"', *Reisen ans Ende der Kultur. Wahrnehmung und Sinnlichkeit in der phantastischen Literatur Frankreichs*, Berne (etc.): Peter Lang, 1987, pp. 356–71

Domínguez Leiva, Antonio, *El laberinto imaginario de Jan Potocki. Manuscrito encontrado en Zaragoza. (Estudio crítico)*, Madrid: UNED, Coleccion Aula Abierta 150, 2000, 468 pp.

'Intertextualité et Talmudisme dans le *Manuscrit trouvé à Saragosse'*, in Jan Herman,

Paul Pelckmans and François Rosset (eds.), *Le* Manuscrit trouvé à Saragosse *et ses intertextes*, Actes du colloque international, Leuven – Anvers, 30 March–1 April 2000, Louvain and Paris: Peeters, 2001, pp. 91–105

Dorati, Marco, 'Jan Potocki interprete di Erodoto', *Annalli della Facoltà di Lettere e Filosofia dell'Università degli Studi di Milano* 54: 3 (2001), 3–34

El Bejaoui, Moufida, 'De quelques usages de l'altérité dans le *Voyage dans l'Empire du Maroc* (1791) de Jean Potocki', in Jean-Marie Goulemot (ed.), *Dialogisme culturel au XVIIIe siècle*, Tours: Université de Tours (*Cahiers d'histoire culturelle*, 4), 1997, pp. 47–54

Fabiański, Jan, 'Le Caucase septentrional à la fin du XVIIIe et au début du XIXe siècle à la lumière de la relation de Jean Potocki', *Etnografia polska* (Warsaw), 15: 1 (1970), 249–82

Fabre, Jean, 'Jan Potocki, Cazotte et le roman noir', *Idées sur le roman, de Madame de La Fayette au Marquis de Sade*, Paris: Klincksieck, 1979, pp. 228–315 (expanded version of article with same title in *Les Cahiers de Varsovie*, 3 (1974), 139–56)

Finné, Jacques, 'Jan Potocki et le *Gothic Novel*', *Revue des Langues vivantes* (Brussels), 36: 2 (1970), 141–65

Le Fantastique chez Jan Potocki, emprunts et originalité, mimeo, Université Libre de Bruxelles, 1967–8, 124+56 pp.

'Le Fantastique chez Jean Potocki, emprunts et originalité', *Revue des Langues Vivantes* (Brussels), 38: 1 and 2 (1972), 22–36 and 116–30

'Du fantastique chez Jean Potocki', in Albert Mingelgrün and Adolphe Nysenholc (eds.), *Ecritures à Maurice-Jean Lefèbvre*, Brussels: Editions de l'Université de Bruxelles, 1983, pp. 93–104

Forycki, Rémi, 'Joseph de Maistre i Jan Potocki' [Joseph de Maistre and Jan Potocki], *Res Publica* (Warsaw), 12 (38) (1990), 89–96

'Z pogranicza epok i mentalności: Joseph de Maistre i Jan Potocki' [At the Frontier of Epochs and Attitudes: Joseph de Maistre and Jan Potocki], in Ryszard Łużny and Stefan Nieznanowski (eds.) *Dzieje Lubelszczyzny*, vol. VI, 2, Lublin: LWN, 1991, pp. 235–46

'Le mal du siècle – duquel? Jean Potocki et Joseph de Maistre en Russie', *Le Bulletin de 'Lettre internationale'* (Paris), 3 (1995), 45–51

'Lumière dans les ténèbres: Potocki et de Maistre en Russie", in Philippe Roger (ed.), *L'Homme des Lumières: de Paris à Pétersbourg*, Naples: Vivarium, 1995, pp. 291–305

Fraisse, Luc, *Potocki ou l'itinéraire d'un initié*, Nîmes: Lacour, 1992, 140 pp.

'Potocki voyageur et romancier: l'influence des voyages *Au Caucase et en Chine* sur *Manuscrit trouvé à Saragosse*', *Revue d'Histoire Littéraire de la France* (Paris), 97: 1 (1997), 32–56

'Les châteaux dans le *Manuscrit trouvé à Saragosse* de Potocki: une entrée symbolique dans les arcanes de la création littéraire', in François-Xavier Cuche (dir.), *La Vie de Château. Architecture, fonctions et représentations des châteaux et des palais du Moyen-Age à nos jours*, Strasbourg: Presses Universitaires de Strasbourg, 1998, pp. 233–51

'Le romanesque et l'intertextualité: piège et assistance mutuels dans *Manuscrit trouvé à Saragosse*', in Jan Herman, Paul Pelckmans and François Rosset (eds.), *Le Manuscrit trouvé à Saragosse et ses intertextes*, Actes du colloque international,

Leuven – Anvers, 30 March–1 April 2000, Louvain and Paris: Peeters, 2001, pp. 33–58

'La circulation des letters dans le *Manuscrit trouvé à Saragosse*', *Europe* (Paris), 863 (March 2001), 153–74

Frantsev, Vladimir A., 'Puszkin i hr. Jan Potocki' [Pushkin and Count Jan Potocki], *Ruch Literacki* (Cracow), 9: 7 (1934), 193–5

Frantsev, Vladimir A., *Poslednoe učenoe putešestvie grafa Jana Potockogo 1805–1806. Iz materialov dla ego biografii* [The Last Scientific Journey of Count Jan Potocki 1805–1806, material for his biography], Prague, 1938, pp. iii–xviii + 28 pp.

Frybes, Stanisław, 'Les recherches polonaises sur le roman de Potocki', *Les Cahiers de Varsovie* (Warsaw), 3 (1974), 125–34

Gengembre, Gérard, 'Manuscrit trouvé à Saragosse', in Jean-Pierre de Beaumarchais and Daniel Couty (eds.), *Dictionnaire des œuvres littéraires de langue française*, Paris: Bordas, 1994, pp. 1198–9

Giaveri, Maria Teresa, 'Le Mille e una Notte di Potocki', *Cahiers d'études maghrébines* (Cologne), 6–7 (1994), 188–92

Goulemot, Jean-Marie, 'Le système des pronoms dans le *Manuscrit trouvé à Saragosse* du comte Jean Potocki', in Guy Serbat (ed.), *E. Benvéniste aujourd'hui*, vol. 1, Paris: Bibliothèque de l'information grammaticale, 1984, pp. 99–104

Grabski, Andrzej Feliks, *Myśl historyczna polskiego Oświecenia* [Historical Thought in the Poland of the Enlightenment], Warsaw: PWN, 1976, pp. 90, 161–2, 277, 327–33

Greń, Zygmunt, 'Jan Potocki. Szkic portretu z *Podróży* i wyobraźni' [Jan Potocki. Sketch of a Portrait Based on the 'Travels' and Imagination], *Twórczość* (Warsaw) 12 (1959), pp. 89–95

Guérin-Castell, Anne, *La place de Manuscrit trouvé à Saragosse dans l'œuvre cinématographique de Wojciech Jerzy Has*, thesis, Université de Paris VIII, 1997, 589 pp.

'Présentation du film *Manuscrit trouvé à Saragosse*', in Jan Herman, Paul Pelckmans and François Rosset (eds.), *Le Manuscrit trouvé à Saragosse et ses intertextes*, Actes du colloque international, Leuven – Anvers, 30 March–1 April 2000, Louvain and Paris: Peeters, 2001, pp. 257–70

'A Film Saved from the Scissors of Censorship', with a bio-filmography of Wojciech Jerzy Has, *Comparative Criticism* 24, Cambridge: Cambridge University Press, 2002, pp. 167–92

Guillamón, Julià, 'Quan els vampirs parlen en català', *Serra d'Or* (Barcelona), 292, Jan. 1984, pp. 21–3

Hafid-Martin, Nicole, *Voyage et connaissance au tournant des Lumières (1780–1820)*, Oxford: Voltaire Foundation, Studies on Voltaire and the Eighteenth Century, 334, 1995, 264 pp.

'Aspects symboliques d'un topos à propos du *Manuscrit trouvé à Saragosse* de Jean Potocki', in Jan Herman and Fernand Hallyn (eds.), *Le Topos du manuscrit trouvé. Hommages à Christian Angelet*, Louvain and Paris: Peeters, 1999, pp. 277–85

'Le sort des juifs marocains à la fin du XVIIIe siècle, d'après le voyageur Jean Potocki', *Transactions of the Tenth International Congress on the Enlightenment*, Dublin, 1999, Oxford: The Voltaire Foundation (to appear)

'Voyage et connaissance', *Europe* (Paris), 863 (March 2001), 48–69

'L'hommage caché de Potocki à François de Rosset dans l'*Histoire de Thibaud de la Jaquière*', in Jan Herman, Paul Pelckmans and François Rosset (eds.), *Le* Manuscrit trouvé à Saragosse *et ses intertextes*, Actes du colloque international, Leuven – Anvers, 30 March–1 April 2000, Louvain and Paris: Peeters, 2001, pp. 131–8

Herling-Grudziński, Gustaw, 'Srebrna kulka' [The Little Silver Ball], *Kultura* (Paris), 1–2 (1966), 204–10 (reprinted in *Dziennik pisany nocą (1980–1983)*, Paris: Instytut Literacki, 1984, pp. 337–44, and in *Godzina cieni. Eseje*, Cracow: Znak, 1991, pp. 172–9)

Herman, Jan, 'Tout est écrit ici-bas: le jeu du hasard et de la nécessité dans le *Manuscrit trouvé à Saragosse*', *Cahiers de l'Association Internationale des Etudes Françaises* (Paris), 51 (1999), 137–54

Herman, Jan, 'La désécriture du livre', *Europe* (Paris), 863 (March 2001), 107–18

'Le *Traité des Sensations de* Potocki', in Jan Herman, Paul Pelckmans and François Rosset (eds.), *Le* Manuscrit trouvé à Saragosse *et ses intertextes*, Actes du colloque international, Leuven and Anvers, 30 March–1 April 2000, Louvain and Paris: Peeters, 2001, pp. 219–29

Hervier, Julien, 'Jean Potocki ou les métamorphoses du picaresque', *De Shakespeare à Michel Butor. Mélanges offerts à Monsieur Charles Dédéyan*, Paris: PUPS, 1985, pp. 43–53

Hoisington, Thomas H., '"Historia Komandora Toralvy" Jana Potockiego i "The Grand Prior of Minorca" Washingtona Irvinga: dwie różne opowieści oparte na tej samej fabule ['The Commander of Toralva' by Jan Potocki and 'The Grand Prior of Minorca' by Washington Irving: two different stories based on the same plot], *Pamiętnik Literacki* (Wrocław), 71: 2 (1980), 113–21

Jastrun, Mieczysław, 'Jan Potocki', *Twórczość* (Warsaw), 24: 11 (1968), 101–12 (reprinted in *Eseje*, Warsaw, 1984, pp. 243–61)

Kemp, Robert, 'Imaginaires', review of *Manuscrit trouvé à Saragosse*, in *Les Nouvelles littéraires* (Paris), 21 Aug. 1958, p. 3

Kirn, Günter von, *Jan Potockis Die Abenteuer in der Sierra Morena. Ein Roman zwischen Aufklärung und Romantik, zwischen Revolution und Restauration*, thesis, University of Hanover, 1982, 298 pp.

Klaproth, Julius von, *Notice sur l'Archipel de Jean Potocki, situé dans la partie septentrionale de la Mer Jaune*, Paris: J.-M. Eberhart, 1820, 8 pp.+illustration

'Préface' and 'Liste des ouvrages du comte Jean Potocki' *Voyage dans les steps* [sic] *d'Astrakhan et du Caucase ... par le comte Jean Potocki*, Paris: Merlin, 1829, vol. 1, pp. iii–xi, xii–xvi

Kostkiewiczowa, Teresa, 'Proza Jana Potockiego' [Jan Potocki's Prose], *Klasycyzm, Sentymentalizm, Rokoko*, Warsaw: PWN, 1975, pp. 393–406

'"Comme une truite parmi les carpes"': Jean Potocki dans le paysage intellectuel des Lumières européennes', *Cahiers de l'Association Internationale des Etudes Françaises* (Paris), 51 (1999), 101–17

Kotwicz, Władysław, *Jan hr. Potocki i jego podróż do Chin* [Count Jan Potocki and his Journey to China], Vilna: Lux, 1935, 113 pp.

Kowzan, Tadeusz, 'La parodie, le grotesque et l'absurde dans les *Parades* de Jean Potocki', *Les Cahiers de Varsovie* (Warsaw), 3 (1974), 231–8

Krakowski, Edouard, *Un témoin de l'Europe des Lumières: le Comte Jean Potocki*, Paris: Gallimard, 1963, 234 pp.+8 pp. illustrations

Krejči, Karel, 'Le roman du comte Jean Potocki, sa génologie et sa généalogie', *Les Cahiers de Varsovie* (Warsaw), 3 (1974), 209–16 (original version: 'Roman Jana hr. Potockého, jeho genologie a genealogie', *Slavia* (Prague), 60: 4 (1971), 554–76)

Krzyżanowski, Julian, 'Dziewica-trup. Z motywów makabrycznych w literaturze polskiej' [The Virgin Corpse. Macabre Motifs in Polish Literature], *Pamiętnik Lubelski* (Lublin), II, 1935, pp. 9–23 (reprinted in *Paralele*, Warsaw: PIW, 1961, pp. 524–39)

Historia literatury polskiej [History of Polish Literature], Warsaw, 1939, pp. 438

Kukulski, Leszek, 'Przedmowa' [Préface] and 'Nota edytorska' [Editorial note] in Jan Potocki, *Rękopis znaleziony w Saragossie*, Warsaw: Czytelnik, 1956, pp. 5–21 and 629–39

'Wstęp' [Introduction], in Jan Potocki, *Podróże*, Warsaw: Czytelnik, 1959, pp. 5–17

'Nachwort', in Jan Potocki, *Die Abenteuer in der Sierra Morena oder Die Handschriften von Saragossa*, Berlin: Aufbau-Verlag, 1962–3, pp. 743–69

'Posłowie' [Afterword], in Jan Potocki, *Rękopis znaleziony w Saragossie*, Warsaw: Czytelnik, 1965, pp. 755–74

'Wstęp' [Introduction], in Jan Potocki, *Parady*, Warsaw: Czytelnik, 1966, pp. 5–16

Lacroix, Paul (pseud. P.-L. Jacob bibliophile), 'Lettre à Monsieur Techener', *Bulletin du bibliophile* (Paris), 1857, pp. 205–7 (reissued under the title 'Les romans de J. Potocki', *Enigmes et découvertes bibliographiques*, Paris: Lainé, 1866, pp. 57–60)

Ladrague, Auguste, 'Petite question de paternité littéraire', *Le Bibliophile belge* (Brussels), 2 (1867), 290–4

Lajarrige, Jean, 'Potocki Jan' in *Dictionnaire encyclopédique de la littérature française*, Paris: Laffont 'Bouquins', 1997, p. 820

Landa, S. S., introduction and afterword to the Russian edition of *The Manuscript Found in Saragossa*, Moscow: 'Hudozestvennaja litteratura', 1971

Liaroutzos, Chantal, '*Le Manuscrit trouvé à Saragosse*', in Arlette Camion et al. (eds.), *Ueber das Fragment*, colloques des Universités d'Orléans et de Siegen, vol. 4, Heidelberg: Winter, 1999, pp. 22–9

Libera, Zdzisław, '*Rękopis znaleziony w Saragossie* na tle polskiej kultury literackiej XVIII wieku' [*The Manuscript Found in Saragossa* in Polish Literary Culture of the Eighteenth Century], *Przegląd Humanistyczny* (Warsaw), 16: 6 (1972), 37–43 (reprinted in *Wiek Oświecony*, Warsaw: PIW, 1986, pp. 203–12)

Lorentowicz, Jan, 'Jan hr. Potocki' [Count Jan Potocki], in Jan Potocki, *Rękopis znaleziony w Saragossie*, Warsaw: S. Orgelbrand 'Biblioteka Muz', 1917, vol. I, pp. i–xv

Łojek, Jerzy, 'Giulietta la bella', *Strusie króla Stasia – Szkice o ludziach i sprawach dawnej Warszawy* [King Stanislas's Ostriches. Sketches on the Men and Affairs of Old Warsaw], Warsaw: PIW, 1961, pp. 69–74

Maclean, Ian, 'Introduction' in Jan Potocki, *The Manuscript Found in Saragossa*, New York: Viking, 1995 (Harmondsworth: Penguin, 1996), pp. xi–xviii

McLendon, Will L., 'A Problem in Plagiarism: Washington Irving and Cousen de Courchamps', *Comparative Literature* (Eugene, OR), 20: 2 (1968), 157–69

McLendon, Will L., 'Le rôle de Charles Nodier dans le plagiat de Courchamps', *Studi Francesi* (Turin), 17 (1973), 293–300

Une ténébreuse carrière sous l'Empire et la Restauration: le comte de Courchamps, Paris: Minard, 1980, pp. 163–73

'Compatibility of the Fantastic and Allegory: Potocki's *Saragossa Manuscript*', in Robert A. Collins and Howard D. Pearce (eds.), *The Scope of the Fantastic-Theory, Technique, Major Authors*, London: Greenwood Press, 1985, pp. 143–50

Madonia, Francesco, 'L'esthétique de la laideur dans le *Manuscrit trouvé à Saragosse*', in Jan Herman, Paul Pelckmans, François Rosset (eds.), *Le* Manuscrit trouvé à Saragosse *et ses intertextes*, Actes du colloque international, Leuven – Anvers, 30 March–1 April 2000, Louvain and Paris: Peeters, 2001, pp. 179–88

Makowiecka, Gabriela, *Po drogach polsko-hiszpańskich* [On Hispanic-Polish Paths], Cracow: Wydawnictwo Literackie, 1984, pp. 190–3

Małecki, Antoni, 'Jan hr. Potocki' [Count Jan Potocki], in *Lechici w świetle historycznej krytyki*, 2nd edn, Lvov, 1907, pp. 100–4

Markiewicz, Zygmunt, 'L'Espagne dans le *Manuscrit trouvé à Saragosse* de Jean Potocki', *Espagne et littérature française. Actes du quatrième congrès national de la Société française de littérature comparée*, Paris: Didier, 1961, pp. 85–97

'Jean Potocki, auteur du *Manuscrit trouvé à Saragosse* et ses liens avec les intellectuels français des Lumières', *Approches des Lumières. Mélanges offerts à Jean Fabre*, Paris: Klincksieck, 1974, pp. 309–18

'Quelques énigmes de la vie de Jean Potocki et celles du *Manuscrit trouvé à Saragosse*', *Les Cahiers de Varsovie* (Warsaw), 3 (1974), 171–81

'L'aspect préromantique du *Manuscrit trouvé à Saragosse* de Jan Potocki. Sa réception par les romantiques polonais', *Revue de littérature comparée* (Paris), 50: 1–2 (1976), 67–75

'Ostatnia miłość Jana Potockiego' [Jan Potocki's Last Love], *Ruch Literacki* (Cracow), 20 (1979), 359–63

Masseau, Didier, 'Potocki, homme des Lumières', in Jan Herman, Paul Pelckmans and François Rosset (eds.), *Le* Manuscrit trouvé à Saragosse *et ses intertextes*, Actes du colloque international, Leuven – Anvers, 30 March–1 April 2000, Louvain and Paris: Peeters, 2001, pp. 1–13

Miège, Jean-Louis, 'Préface' in Jean Potocki, *Voyage dans l'empire du Maroc*, Paris: Maisonneuve et Larose, 1997, pp. 3–15

Miłosz, Czesław, *Histoire de la littérature polonaise*, Paris: Fayard, 1986, pp. 266–9

Moussa, Sarga, 'Le nomadisme chez Potocki: des récits de voyages au *Manuscrit trouvé à Saragosse*', *Revue de littérature comparée* (Paris), 287:3 (1998), 231–53

Neuhaus, Volker, 'Jan Potockis *Handschrift von Saragossa*', *Typen multiperspektivischen Erzählens*, Cologne and Vienna: Böhlau, 1971, pp. 12–21

Nicolas, Claire, 'Tajemnica rodu Gomelezów w *Rękopisie znalezionym w Saragossie*' [The Secret of the Gomelez family in *The Manuscript Found in Saragossa*], *Twórczość* (Warsaw), 6 (1973), 62–80

'Du bon usage de la franc-maçonnerie dans le *Manuscrit trouvé à Saragosse*', *Les Cahiers de Varsovie* (Warsaw), 3 (1974), 273–85

'Correspondants polonais de Madame de Staël', *Cahiers staëliens* (Paris), 25 (1978), 45–54

Orlovskaia, N. K., 'Ian Pototskii i Gmziia', *Trudy Tbilisskoge universiteta. Literaturoredenie* 163 (Tbilisi, 1975), 119–29

Otorowski, Michał 'Klucz do "Rękopisu ..." Jana Potockiego (część I)' [Key to *The Manuscript ... of Jan Potocki* (part one)], *Ars Regia* (Warsaw), 9/10 (1995/1996), 11–35

'*Rękopis znaleziony w Saragossie* jako Księga i gra inicjacyjna' [*The Manuscript Found in Saragossa* as Rite-of-Passage. Book and Game], *Ars Regia* (Warsaw), 13/14 (1998/1999), 49–67

'Rebeka i Velasquez. Koncepcja równowagi w *Rękopisie* Jana Potockiego' [Rebecca and Velasquez. The conception of balance in Jan Potocki's *Manuscript*], *Gnosis* (Warsaw), 12 (2000), 137–44

'Czekając na Mesjasza. Tajemnica Boskiego imienia w *Rękopisie* Jana Potockiego' [Waiting for the Messiah. The Mystery of the Name of God in Jan Potocki's *Manuscript*], *Midrasz* (Warsaw), Feb. 2001, pp. 33–8

Ouasti, Boussif, 'La représentation du paysage marocain dans le voyage du philosophe Jean Potocki à travers le *Voyage dans l'Empire chérifien en 1791*', in *Profil du Maroc. Voyages, images et échanges*, Tétouan, Publications de la Faculté des Lettres et des Sciences Humaines de Tétouan, 2000 (sous presse)

Parvi, Jerzy, 'Le *Manuscrit trouvé à Saragosse* à l'écran. Quelques problèmes de l'adaptation', *Les Cahiers de Varsovie* (Warsaw), 3 (1974), 77–82

Paul, Jean-Marie, 'Le *Manuscrit trouvé à Saragosse* de Jan Potocki: du maniement de l'invraisemblable à la perte du sens', in Suzanne Varga and Jean-Jacques Pollet (eds.), *Traditions fantastiques ibériques et germaniques*, Arras: Artois Presses Université, 1998, pp. 41–58

Pauli, Żegota, 'Wiadomość o życiu i pismach Jana hr. Potockiego' [Note on the Life and Writings of Count Jan Potocki], in Jan Potocki, *Podróz do Turcji i Egiptu*, Cracow: D. E. Friedlein, 1849, pp. i–xxvi

Pelckmans, Paul, 'Les Lumières vues du Maroc', *Europe* (Paris), 863 (March 2001), 72–81

'L'Evangile selon le Juif Errant', in Jan Herman, Paul Pelckmans and François Rosset (eds.), *Le* Manuscrit trouvé à Saragosse *et ses intertextes*, Actes du colloque international, Leuven – Anvers, 30 March–1 April 2000, Louvain and Paris: Peeters, 2001, pp. 107–17

Pietrov, Aleksander, 'Potocki, graf Jan', in *Russkij Biograficheskiij Slovar* [Russian Biographical Dictionary], St Petersburg, 1905, New York: Kraus Reprint Corporation, 1962, vol. xiv, pp. 692–7

Piotrowski, Wojciech, *Horyzonty światopoglądowe* Rękopisu znalezionego w Saragossie [The Horizon of Ideas in *The Manuscript Found in Saragossa*], Słupsk: WSP, 1993, 232 pp.

Preiss, Axel, 'Potocki, comte Jean', in Jean-Pierre de Beaumarchais, Daniel Couty and Alain Rey (eds.), *Dictionnaire des littératures de langue française*, Paris: Bordas, 1984, vol. ii, pp. 1905–6

Quérard, Jean-Marie, *La France littéraire ou Dictionnaire biographique des savants, historiens et gens de lettres de la France, ainsi que des littérateurs étrangers qui ont écrit en français, plus particulièrement pendant les XVIIIe et XIXe siècles*, Paris: Firmin Didot, 1835, vol. vii, pp. 295–6

Les Supercheries littéraires dévoilées. Galerie des auteurs apocryphes, supposés, déguisés, plagiaires et des éditeurs infidèles de la littérature française pendant les quatre derniers siècles, Paris: L'Editeur rue Mazarine, 1847, vol. i, pp. 177–93, 286–7, 290–1

Radrizzani, René, 'Préface', in Jean Potocki, *Manuscrit trouvé à Saragosse*, Paris: José Corti, 1989, pp. vii–xx

Rapacka, Wanda, *Thèmes et structures dans le* Manuscrit trouvé à Saragosse *de Jean Potocki, avec la traduction et la reconstitution du texte*, thesis, Université des Sciences Humaines de Strasbourg, 1984, 610 pp.

Renales, Juan de, 'De argentario a pandesauna (avatares del bondolero antropófago)', *Revista de Filologia Romànica* (Madrid), 8 (1991), 293–301

Reychman, Jan, 'Jan Potocki et l'orientalisme des Lumières', *Les Cahiers de Varsovie* (Warsaw), 3 (1974), 31–4

Romagnosi, Gian Domenico, 'Sul viaggo del conte Potocki ad Astrakan', *Opere*, Florence: Piatti, 1836, vol. XVI, pp. 15–34

Romey, Charles, 'Histoire d'un plagiat – *Le Val Funeste*', *Hommes et choses de divers temps*, Paris: E. Dentu, 1864, pp. 241–68

Roselló Bover, Pere, 'Mercè Rodoreda i *El manuscrit trobat a Saragossa*', *Revista de Catalunya* (Barcelona), new series, 108 (June 1996), 118–32

Rosset, François, 'W muzeum gatunków literackich: Jana Potockiego *Rękopis znaleziony w Saragossie*' [In the Museum of Literary Genres: Jan Potocki's *Manuscript Found in Saragossa*], *Pamiętnik Literacki* (Wrocław), 76: 1 (1985), 47–68

'La cérémonie de narration dans le *Manuscrit trouvé à Saragosse*', *Literary Studies in Poland – Etudes littéraires en Pologne* (Warsaw), 23 (1990), 19–40

Le Théâtre du romanesque: Manuscrit trouvé à Saragosse *entre construction et maçonnerie*, Lausanne: L'Age d'Homme, 1991, 269 pp.

'Le *Manuscrit trouvé à Saragosse* par lui-même', *Ecriture* (Lausanne), 39 (spring 1992), 176–89

'Le fantastique fantastique ou la feinte illusion de Jean Potocki', *Les Cahiers des Paralittératures* (Chaudfontaine), 4 (1992), 157–66

'Révéroni Saint-Cyr, Cazotte, Potocki: trois peurs romanesques', in Jacques Berchtold and Michel Porret (eds.) *La Peur au XVIIIe siècle*, Geneva: Droz, 1994, pp. 165–77

'Labirynt Jana Potockiego' [The Labyrinth of Jan Potocki], *Tygodnik Powszechny* (Cracow), 14 (7 April 1996), 18

'Saragosse ou le siège du lecteur', in Jan Herman et Fernand Hallyn (eds.), *Le Topos du manuscrit trouvé. Hommages à Christion Angelet*, Louvain and Paris: Peeters, 1999, pp. 255–66

'Cherchez l'auteur dans le *Manuscrit trouvé à Saragosse*', *Vives lettres* (Strasbourg), 5, 1998, pp. 39–60

'La géographie du *Manuscrit trouvé à Saragosse*', *Cahiers de l'Association Internationale des Etudes Françaises* (Paris), 51 (1999), 119–36

'Bibliographie de Jean Potocki – 1989–1998', *Cahiers de l'Association Internationale des Etudes Françaises* (Paris), 51 (1999), 169–78

'Ecrire d'ailleurs', *Europe* (Paris), 863 (March 2001), 3–7

'Introduction au *Manuscrit trouvé à Saragosse*', *Europe* (Paris), 863 (March 2001), 84–90

'*Manuscrit trouvé à Saragosse* et protocole intertextuel', in Jan Herman, Paul Pelckmans and François Rosset (eds.), *Le* Manuscrit trouvé à Saragosse *et ses intertextes*, Actes du colloque international, Leuven – Anvers, 30 March–1 April 2000, Louvain and Paris: Peeters, 2001, pp. 15–31

'Quotation and Intertextuality: the Books in *The Manuscript Found in Saragossa*, *Comparative Criticism* 24, Cambridge University Press, 2002, pp. 99–110

Rosset, François and Triaire, Dominique, *De Varsovie à Saragosse: Jean Potocki et son œuvre*, Louvain and Paris: Peeters, 2000, 328 pp.

Rostworowski, Emanuel, 'Debiut polityczny Jana Potockiego w r. 1788' [The Political Beginnings of Jan Potocki in 1788], *Przegląd Historyczny* (Cracow), 47: 4 (1956), 685–711

'Post scriptum do "Debiutu politycznego Jana Potockiego"' [Postscript to 'The Political Beginnings of Jan Potocki'], *Przegląd Historyczny* (Cracow), 48: 2 (1957), 285–8

'Jean Potocki témoin de la crise de l'ancien régime en Europe et en Pologne', *Les Cahiers de Varsovie* (Warsaw), 3 (1974), 15–25

'Dwa pisma polityczne Jana Potockiego z lat 1790 i 1792' [Two Political Pieces by Jan Potocki in the years 1790 and 1792], in *Wiek XVIII. Polska i świat*, Warsaw: PIW, 1974, pp. 85–97

Roudaut, Jean, 'Les demeures dans le roman noir', *Critique* (Paris), 147–8, 1959, pp. 713–36 (reprinted in *Ce qui nous revient*, Paris: Gallimard, 1980, pp. 145–73)

Rudnicka, Jadwiga, 'Opowiadanie w XVIII-wiecznym cyklu *Tysiąc nocy i jedna* w zestawieniu z opowiadaniem w *Poncjanie* i *Rękopisie znalezionym w Saragossie*' [Narrative in the *Thousand and One Nights* of the Eighteenth Century Compared to Narrative in *The Story of the Seven Wise Men* and *The Manuscript Found in Saragossa*], *Przegląd Humanistyczny* (Warsaw), 6 (1967), 109–22

'*Tysiąc nocy i jedna* w Polsce doby oświeceniowej' [*The Thousand and One Nights* in Poland of the Enlightenment], *Przegląd Humanistyczny* (Warsaw), 18: 2 (1974), 97–115

Ruiz, Luc, 'Le paratexte comme lieu de la théorie d'un fantastique de la fin du XVIIIe siècle (Walpole, Cazotte, Sade, Lewis, Potocki)', *Cahiers du CERLI* (Nantes), 7–8 (1997), 39–49

Des romans au second degré. Emergence du fantastique et représentation critique à la fin du XVIIIe siècle, thesis, Université de Paris VII, 2000, 641 pp.

'Don[atien] Belial[phonse François] de Gehenna: Sade chez Potocki', *Europe* (Paris), 863 (March 2001), 139–50

Ryba, Janusz, 'Jana Potockiego tetralogia o szczęściu' [Tetralogy on the Good Fortune of Jan Potocki], *Pamiętnik Literacki* (Wrocław), 71: 2 (1980), 101–2

'Jana Potockiego ekstrawagancje wydawnicze' [The Editorial Extravagances of Jan Potocki], *Studia Bibliologiczne* (Katowice), 1 (1983), 55–73

'Anatomie des voyages du comte Jan Potocki', *Literary Studies in Poland – Etudes littéraires en Pologne* (Warsaw), 22 (1990), 31–55

Między wiarą a libertynizmem. O rozterkach religijnych Jana Potockiego [Between Faith and Libertinism. Jan Potocki's Religious Hesitations], *Acta Universitatis Wratislaviensis* (Wrocław), 1368, Prace Literackie 31, 1991, pp. 201–12

'Osobliwe arcydzieło – *Rękopis znaleziony w Saragossie* Jana Potockiego' [A Strange Masterpiece – *The Manuscript Found in Saragossa*], in Lech Ludorowski (ed.), *Powieść polska XIX wieku. Interpretacje i analizy*, Lublin: Wydawnictwo UMCS, 1992, pp. 29–47

'Czy Jan Potocki jest autorem opowieści o Fatme?' [Is Jan Potocki Author of the story of Fatmé?], in Renarda Ocieczek (ed.), *Szkice o literaturze dawnej i nowszej*, Katowice: Wydawnictwo UŚ, 1992, pp. 107–18

Motywy podróżnicze w twórczości Jana Potockiego [Travel Motifs in the Work of Jan Potocki], Wrocław, Warsaw and Cracow: PAN, 1993, 179 pp.

'Jan Potocki (1761–1815)', in Teresa Kostkiewiczowa and Zygmunt Goliński (eds.), *Pisarze polskiego Oświecenia*, Warsaw: PWN, 1994, vol. 2, pp. 424–50

'Motywy włoskie w *Rękopisie znalezionym w Saragossie* Jana Potockiego' [Italian Motifs in *The Manuscript Found in Saragossa*], in Jan Malicki and Piotr Wilczek (eds.), *Kultura baroku i jej tradycje*, Kolokwia polsko-włoskie, 2, Katowice: Wydawnictwo Śląsk, 1994, pp. 135–45

'*Rękopis znaleziony w Saragossie* Jana Potockiego: od plotki potwarzy ku mistyfikacji' [Jan Potocki's *Manuscript Found in Saragossa*: from slanderous gossip to hoax], in Krzysztof Uniłowski and Cezary K. Kędera (ed.), *VI Konferecja pracowników naukowych i studentów instytutu Nauk o Literaturze Polskiej*, Katowice: FA-art, 1994, pp. 82–8

'Kilka uwag o edytorsko-typograficznym kształcie francuskich dzieł Jana Potockiego' [Some Remarks on the Typographical and Editorial Presentation of the French Editions of Jan Potocki], in Renarda Ocieczek (ed.), *Od baroku ku pozytywizmowi*, Katowice: Wydawnictwo UŚ, 1995, pp. 72–81

'Poszukiwacze prawdy: Blaise Pascal i Jan Potocki' [Truth seekers: Blaise Pascal and Jan Potocki], in *Filologia Polska – Prace historycznoliterackie* (Gdańsk), 17 (1995), 147–58

'"Gry" osobliwe z utworami Jana Potockiego' [Strange 'Games' with the Works of Jan Potocki], *Pamiętnik Literacki* (Wrocław), 86: 2 (1995), 45–57

'Dwaj hrabiowie: Jan Potocki i Edward Raczyński' [Two Counts: Jan Potocki and Edward Raczyński], *Twórczość* (Warsaw), 53: 8 (1997), 110–18

'Stanisław Augusty Poniatowski i jego niesforny poddany – Jan hrabia Potocki' [Stanislas Auguste Poniatowski and his Turbulent Subject, Count Jan Potocki – with a Summary in French], *Wiek Oświecenia* (Warsaw), 15 (1999), 247–55

'Les aventures éditoriales de Jean Potocki', *Europe* (Paris), 863 (March 2001), 10–23

Sermain, Jean-Paul, 'Roman mémoires et conte merveilleux dans le *Manuscrit trouvé à Saragosse*', in Jan Herman, Paul Pelckmans and François Rosset (eds.), *Le Manuscrit trouvé à Saragosse et ses intertextes*, Actes du colloque international, Leuven – Anvers, 30 March–1 April 2000, Louvain and Paris: Peeters, 2001, pp. 139–50

Sicre, Jean-Pierre, 'L'Homme de Nulle Part', in Jean Potocki, *Au Caucase et en Chine*, Paris: Phébus, 1991, pp. 9–18

Siemieński, Lucjan, 'Bogactwo fantazji w romansie. Powieść Jana Potockiego' [Richness of Fantasy in Fiction. Jan Potocki's Novel], in *Kilka rysów z literatury i społeczeństwa*, vol. II, Warsaw: Gebethner & Cie, 1859, pp. 197–228

Sigaux, Gilbert, 'Les *Parades* de Jean Potocki dans la tradition du théâtre de la foire', *Les Cahiers de Varsovie* (Warsaw), 3 (1974), 221–6

Sinko, Tadeusz, 'Einige Quellen und Tendenzen des *Handschrift von Saragossa* von Jan Potocki', *Bulletin international de l'Académie polonaise de Sciences et Lettres, Classe de Philologie* (Cracow), 1 (1919–20), 42–3

Historia religii i filozofii w romansie Jana Potockiego [The History of Religion and of Philosophy in Jan Potocki's Novel], Cracow: PAU, 1920, 90 pp.

Sinko, Zofia, *Powiastka w Oświeceniu stanisławowskim* [The Story in the Time of Stanislas Auguste Poniatowski], Wrocław (etc.): Ossolineum, 1982, pp. 285–96

Skowronek, Jerzy, 'Jan Potocki polityk konserwatywny czy liberalny?', *Przegląd Humanistyczny* (Warsaw), 16: 6 (1972), 17–35 (abridged French version: 'Jean

Potocki, politicien éclairé et conservateur', *Les Cahiers de Varsovie* (Warsaw), 3 (1974), 39–49)

'Podróże oświeceniowe' [Enlightened Journeys], *Prezegląd Humanistyczny* (Warsaw), 27: 1–2 (1983), 168–74

Skrzypek, Marian, 'Między Oświeceniem a ideologią. Jan Potocki i Constantin-François Volney' [Between Enlightenment and Ideology. Jan Potocki and C.-F. Volney], *Przegląd Humanistyczny* (Warsaw), 16: 6 (1972), 1–16 (French version: 'Les sources françaises de la théorie de la religion chez Jean Potocki (Potocki et Volney)', *Les Cahiers de Varsovie* (Warsaw), 3 (1974), 57–70)

'La présence des philosophes français du XVIIIe siècle dans le roman de Potocki', in Jan Herman, Paul Pelckmans and François Rosset (eds.), *Le* Manuscrit trouvé à Saragosse *et ses intertextes*, Actes du colloque international, Leuven – Anvers, 30 March–1 April 2000, Louvain and Paris: Peeters, 2001, pp. 205–18

Smoleński, Władysław, 'Publicyści anonimowi z końca wieku XVIII' [Anonymous Publicists of the End of the Eighteenth Century], *Przegląd Historyczny* (Cracow), 14: 1, 2, 3 (1912), 48–74, 195–214, 317–37

Smolik, Przecław, 'Słowo wstępne' [Introductory Note], Jan Potocki, *Podróż do Turcji i Egiptu w 1784 r.*, Cracow: Towarzystwo Miłośników Książki, 1924, pp. i–viii

Snopek, Jerzy, *Objawienie i Oświecenie. Z dziejów libertynizmu w Polsce* [Revelation and Lumières. History of libertinism in Poland], Wrocław (etc.): Ossolineum, 1986, pp. 139–49

Sobieszczański, Franciszek Maksymilian, 'Jan Potocki', *Encyklopedia powszechna*, Warsaw, 1865, vol. XXI, pp. 434–7

Sobolewska, Anna, 'Czytanie kabały' [Lecture of the Cabal], *Twórczość* (Warsaw), 40: 7 (1984), 62–83

Suematsu, Claire, 'Le récit labyrinthique: avatars et fonctions de l'enchâssement dans le *Manuscrit trouvé à Saragosse* de Jean Potocki', *Bulletin of the College of Ube* (Ube, Japan), 27 (July 1990), 171–85 (reissued in *Etudes de Langue et Littérature Françaises* (Tokyo), 62 (March 1993), 29–41)

Sulerzyska, Teresa, 'Jan Potocki scenografem. O projekcie kostiumu do roli Czyngis-Chana' [Jan Potocki Stage Designer. On costume plans for the role of Gengis-Khan], *Pamiętnik Teatralny* (Warsaw), 38: 3–4 (1988), 407–22

Swiggers, Pierre, 'L'Histoire de (ou: des) Hervas et le savoir encyclopédique', in Jan Herman, Paul Pelckmans, and François Rosset (eds.), *Le* Manuscrit trouvé à Saragosse *et ses intertextes*, Actes du colloque international, Leuven – Anvers, 30 March–1 April 2000, Louvain and Paris: Peeters, 2001, pp. 189–203

Szczepaniec, Józef, 'Wokół Drukarni Wolnej i "Journal Hebdomadaire de la Diète" Jana Potockiego w Warszawie w latach 1788–1792' [Around the Free Press and *Journal Hebdomadaire de la Diète* of Jan Potocki in Warsaw in the Years 1788–1792], *Archiwum Literackie* (Warsaw), vol. 18, Wrocław, 1973, pp. 229–96

'Drukarnia Wolna Jana Potockiego w Warszawie w czasach Sejmu Wielkiego' [Jan Potocki's Free Press at the Time of the Grand Diet], *Sprawozdania Wrocławskiego Towarzystwa Naukowego*, 1987, series A, vol. 42, Wrocław, 1989, pp. 36–8

'Jan Potocki w poezji lat 1788–1789' [Jan Potocki in the Poetry of the Years 1788–1789], *Wiek Oświecenia* (Warsaw), 10 (1994), 51–88

Drukarnia Wolna Jana Potockiego w Warszawie: 1788–1792 [Jan Potocki's Free Press in Warsaw: 1788–1792] Wrocław: UW, 1998, 356 pp + 11 pp. illustrations

Taillade, Nicole, 'La construction du *Manuscrit trouvé à Saragosse* et sa portée', *Annales de l'Université Toulouse-Le Mirail*, 13 (1977–8), 7–36

Tarnowski, Stanisław, 'Romans polski w początku XIX wieku' [The Polish Novel at the Beginning of the Nineteenth Century], *Przegląd Polski* (Cracow), 5 (1871), 171–233 (on Potocki, pp. 222–30)

Taylor-Terlecka, Nina, 'Jan Potocki and his Polish Milieu', *Comparative Criticism* 24, Cambridge: Cambridge University Press, 2002, pp. 55–78

Todorov, Tzvetan, *Introduction à la littérature fantastique*, Paris: Editions du Seuil, 1970, *passim*

Tomassini, Giovanni Battista, 'Introduzione', in Jan Potocki, *Nelle steppe di Astrakan e del Caucaso: 1797–1798*, Milan: Mondadori, 1996, pp. vii–xviii

Tomaszewski, Marek, 'Jan Potocki: voyageur et ethnologue', in Annick Benoit-Dusausoy and Guy Fontaine (dir.), *Histoire de la littérature européenne*, Paris: Hatier, 1992, p. 539

Toporowski, Marian, 'Wstęp' [Introduction], in Jan Potocki, *Rękopis znaleziony w Saragossie*, Warsaw: Czytelnik, 1950, I, pp. 5–16

Trautwein, Wolfgang, *Erlesene Angst: Schauerliteratur im 18. und 19. Jahrhundert, systematischer Aufriss: Untersuchungen zu Bürger, Maturin, Hoffmann, Poe und Maupassant*, Munich and Vienna: C. Hanser, 1980, pp. 21–8

Triaire, Dominique, 'L'histoire selon Jean Potocki', *Romanistische Zeitschrift für Literaturgeschichte* (Heidelberg), 1981, 4, pp. 443–53

Œuvre de Jean Potocki – inventaire, Paris: Champion, 1985, 342 pp.

Introduction and notes to Jean Potocki, *Ecrits politiques*, Paris: Champion, 1987, 335 pp.

'Regarder et comparer ou Jean Potocki en voyage', *Wiek Oświecenia* (Warsaw), 5 (1988), 193–206

'Préface', in Jean Potocki, *Parades – Les Bohémiens d'Andalousie. Théâtre édité par Dominique Triaire*, Arles: Actes Sud, 1989, pp. 7–16

'Les ouvertures narratives dans le *Manuscrit trouvé à Saragosse* de Potocki', in Pierre Rodriguez and Michèle Weil (eds.), *Vers un thesaurus informatisé: topique des ouvertures narratives avant 1800*, Montpellier, Centre d'étude du dix-huitième siècle de Montpellier, Université Paul Valéry, 1990, pp. 397–401

Potocki, Arles: Actes Sud, 1991, 270 pp.

'A l'occasion d'un bicentenaire: le no XXXII du *Journal Hebdomadaire de la Diète*, publié le 21 juin 1789', in Marthe Molinari and Dominique Triaire (eds.), *Parole et révolutions*, Paris: Champion, 1992, pp. 63–75

'Jean Potocki, franc-maçon', *Ars Regia* (Warsaw), 2: 3/4 (4/5) (1993), 203–10 (Polish version: 'Jan Potocki wolnomularz' in same vol. pp. 51–60)

'Potocki et l'indépendance nationale pendant la Grande Diète (1788–1792)', *Wiek Oświecenia* (Warsaw), 8 (1993), 157–67 (an abridged version of this article appeared with the same title in *Studies on Voltaire and the Eighteenth Century* (Oxford), 216 (1983), 408

'Jean Potocki et la Fin d'un Monde', in *Les Fins de siècle dans les littératures européennes*, Warsaw: Université de Varsovie, 1996, pp. 111–17

'Le théâtre de Jean Potocki', *Cahiers de l'Association Internationale des Etudes Françaises* (Paris), 51 (1999), 155–67

'Repères chronologiques', *Europe* (Paris), 863 (March 2001), 188–96

344 Bibliography of Jan Potocki

'Conclusions', in Jan Herman, Paul Pelckmans and François Rosset (eds.), *Le Manuscrit trouvé à Saragosse et ses intertextes*, Actes du colloque international, Leuven – Anvers, 30 March–1 April 2000, Louvain and Paris: Peeters, 2001, pp. 271–78

'The Comic Effect in *The Manuscript Found in Saragossa*', *Comparative Criticism* 24, Cambridge: Cambridge University Press, 2002, pp. 79–98

Turowska-Barowa, Irena, 'Echa orientalne w literaturze stanisławowskiej' [Oriental Echoes in Literature in the Time of Poniatowski], *Prace historycznoliterackie – Księga zbiorowa ku czci Ignacego Chrzanowskiego*, Cracow, 1936, pp. 205–15

Van Gorp, Hendrik, 'Le *Manuscrit trouvé à Saragosse* et le roman gothique' in Jan Herman, Paul Pelckmans and François Rosset (eds.), *Le* Manuscrit trouvé à Saragosse *et ses intertextes*, Actes du colloque international, Leuven – Anvers, 30 March–1 April 2000, Louvain and Paris: Peeters, 2001, pp. 235–45

Vercruysse, Jeroom, 'Le *Manuscrit trouvé à Saragosse* sous le poids des Lumières', *Les Cahiers de Varsovie* (Warsaw), 3 (1974), 247–62

Veronese, Pietro, 'Postfazione', in Jan Potocki, *Viaggio in Turchia, in Egitto e in Marocco*, Rome: Edizioni e/o, 1990, pp. 189–94

Versteeg, Jan, 'Potocki et Cazotte', in Jan Herman, Paul Pelckmans, François Rosset (eds.), *Le* Manuscrit trouvé à Saragosse *et ses intertextes*, Actes du colloque international, Leuven – Anvers, 30 March–1 April 2000, Louvain and Paris: Peeters, 2001, pp. 231–6

Vivó Mànez, Cristina, 'El manuscrit trobat a Saragossa', *La Rella* (Elche), 6 (June 1988), 108–11

Witt, Piotr, 'Talia kart' [The Card Game], *Kultura* (Warsaw), 7 March 1977, p. 13

'Wtajemniczenie według Jana Potockiego' [The Beginning According to Jan Potocki], *Kultura* (Paris), 505 (Oct. 1989), 114–28

Wojciechowski, Tadeusz, *Chrobacja – Rozbiór starożytności słowiańskich* [Chrobacya – Analysis of Slavic Antiquities], Cracow: Kraj, 1873, vol. I, pp. 77–116

Wołoszyński, Ryszard. W., 'Jean Potocki et son essai de synthèse des civilisations occidentale et orientale', *Les Cahiers de Varsovie* (Warsaw), 3 (1974), 291–7

Ziętarska, Jadwiga, 'Relacje Jana Potockiego z Turcji, Egiptu i Maroka na tle piśmiennictwa podróżniczego doby Oświecenia' [Jan Potocki's Account of Turkey, Egypt and Morocco and Travel Writing in the Time of the Enlightenment], *Przegląd Humanistyczny* (Warsaw), 17:1 (1973), 41–59

Żmijewska, Helena, 'Le voyage de Jan Potocki en France et en Angleterre en 1787', *Kwartalnik Neofilologiczny* (Warsaw), 29 (1982), 221–31

Żółtowska, Maria Evelina, *Un précurseur de la littérature fantastique: Jean Potocki et son* Manuscrit trouvé à Saragosse, thesis, Yale University, 1973, 676 pp.

'La genèse du *Manuscrit trouvé à Saragosse* de Jan Potocki', *Les Cahiers de Varsovie* (Warsaw), 3 (1974), 85–99

'Jan Potocki w oczach żony: nidokończony szkic biograficzny' [Jan Potocki as Seen by his Wife: an unfinished biographical sketch], *Wiek Oświecenia* (Warsaw), 3 (1978), 65–70

'Epilog działalności politycznej Jana Potockiego: Artykuły w *Journal hebdomadaire de la Diète* z 1792 r.' [Epilogue to Jan Potocki's Political Action: articles from *Journal hebdomadaire de la Diète* in 1792], *Przegląd Historyczny* (Cracow), 70: 3 (1979), 499–518

'La démocratisation de l'idée de l'honneur dans le *Manuscrit trouvé à Saragosse* de Jean Potocki', *Etudes sur le XVIIIe siècle* (Brussels), 11 (1984), 39–52

'Potocki Jan', *Polski Słownik biograficzny* [Polish Biographical Dictionary], 28/1 (116), Wrocław (etc.): Ossolineum, 1984, pp. 36–42

'Rękopis znaleziony w tezie' [The Manuscript Found in a Dissertation], *Kultura* (Paris), 506 (Nov. 1989), 116–23

'La légende du Juif errant dans le *Manuscrit trouvé à Saragosse*', *Literary Studies in Poland – Etudes Littéraires en Pologne* (Warsaw), 23 (1990), 7–17

'Stosunek Jana Potockiego do insurekcji. Listy Jana Potockiego do Henryka Lubomirskiego z 1794' [Jan Potocki's Standpoint on the Uprising. Letters from Jean Potocki to Henri Lubomirski in 1794], *Wiek Oświecenia* (Warsaw), 10 (1994), 21–41

'Le manuscrit qui n'a pas été trouvé à Saragosse', in Jan Herman and Fernand Hallyn (eds.), *Le Topos du manuscrit trouvé*, Louvain and Paris: Peeters, 1999, pp. 267–76

'Potocki, lecteur des romans de Diderot', *Europe* (Paris), 863 (March 2001), 121–36

'Le dernier Décaméron du *Manuscrit trouvé à Saragosse*', in Jan Herman, Paul Pelckmans and François Rosset (éds.), *Le Manuscrit trouvé à Saragosse et ses intertextes*, Actes du colloque international, Leuven – Anvers, 30 March–1 April 2000, Louvain and Paris: Peeters, 2001, pp. 247–58

Żurowski, Maciej (pseud. Del), 'Francuzi odkrywają *Rękopis znaleziony w Saragossie*' [The French Discover *The Manuscript Found in Saragossa*], *Przegląd Humanistyczny* (Warsaw), 2: 3 (1958), 171–3

'Artyzm i sens *Rękopisu znalezionego w Saragossie* (I)' [Art and Meaning in *The Manuscript Found in Saragossa*], *Przegląd Humanistyczny* (Warsaw), 16: 6 (1972), 45–64

'Le *Manuscrit trouvé à Saragosse* et la technique romanesque du XVIIIe siècle', *Les Cahiers de Varsovie* (Warsaw), 3 (1974), 105–12

Works of fiction

Bradecki, Tadeusz, *Saragossa. Romans sceniczny na motywach życia i powieści Jana Potockiego* [Saragossa. Theatrical Account of the Life and Novel of Jan Potocki], *Dialog* (Warsaw), 1 (1998), 5–35 (script for a play produced at the National Theatre of Warsaw)

Franco, Ernesto, *La carta e il vetro*, in *Vite senza fine*, Milan: Einaudi, 1999, pp. 24–25 (short story)

Gretkowska, Manuela, 'Czy Potocki Jan wampirem byl?' [Was Jan Potocki a Vampire?], *Ex-Libris-Życie Warszawy* (Warsaw), 39 (Nov. 1993), 12–13 (short story)

Jurasz, Tomasz, *Rozkosze nocy, czyli ostatnia podróż Jana hr. Potockiego* [The Pleasures of the Night or Jan Potocki's Last Journey], Warsaw: Iskry, 1997, 219 pp. (novel)

Kremer, Rüdiger, *Der Graswanderer*, radio play produced by Bremen radio in 1980, published in Polish translation by Grzegorz Dlubak under the title *Wędrowiec wśród traw* [The Walker in the Grass] in *Dialog* (Warsaw), 8 (1993), 21–33

Nieva, Francisco, *El Manuscrito encontrado en Zaragoza*, in: *Teatro completo*, vol. 2, s. I., Servicio de Publicaciones de la Junta de Comunidades de Castilla–La Mancha, 1991, pp. 1005–51

Perucho, Joan, *Alhama i el manuscrito trobat a Saragossa*, in *Obres completes*, vol. 2,

Barcelona: edicions 62, 1986, pp. 175–6 [1st edition in *Els balnearis*, Barcelona: ed. Destino] (short story)

NOTE

Thanks are due to Adelaida Martín Valverde for supplying information on works published in Spanish and Catalan.

Comparative Criticism 24, pp. 347–366.   © 2002 Cambridge University Press
Printed in the United Kingdom

Index to *Comparative Criticism* volumes 1–24 (1979–2002)

COMPILED BY KAY McKECHNIE

This index is arranged in four sections:
  I. Articles
  II. Literature and translation
  III. Reviews
  IV. Bibliographies

Index of articles

Essay reviews are indicated by (*) at end of entry.

Index of literature and translation

Note: entries are listed by name of author, with cross-reference from the translator.

Index of reviews

American postmodernism in Germany: a
review of reception, by Douwe
Fokkema, 10. 313–26
Les Avant-gardes littéraires au XXe siècle,
published by the Centre d'Etude des
Avant-gardes littéraires de l'Université
de Bruxelles, dir. Jean Weisgerber,
review by Stephen Bann, 7. 265–78

Bacigalupo, Massimo, *The Formèd Trace: the
Later Poetry of Ezra Pound*, review by
Donald Davie, 6. 315–26
Bacigalupo, Massimo and Giovanni Giudici,
Ezra Pound: Hugh Selwyn Mauberley,
review by Donald Davie, 6. 315–26
Barrell, John, *The Political Theory of Painting
from Reynolds to Hazlitt – 'The Body of
the Public'*, review by Stephen Bann, 10.
255–66
Bassnett, Susan, *Comparative Literature: a
Critical Introduction*, review by Douwe
Fokkema, 20. 315–25
Bayly, C. A., *Empire and Information:
Intelligence Gathering and Social
Communication in India 1780–1870*,
review by Peter Robb, 22. 242–50
Bernstein, Michael André, *The Tale of the
Tribe: Ezra Pound and the Modern Verse
Epic*, review by Donald Davie, 6. 315–26
Bertens, Hans and Douwe Fokkema,
International Postmodernism (ICLA
Comparative History of Literature, vol.
XI), review by Thomas Docherty, 21.
245–53
Black, Edwin, *Rhetorical Criticism: a Study
in Method*, 2nd edition, review by Peter
France, 3. 269–77
Brecht in Hong Kong: the International
Brecht Festival, 1986, review by Elinor
Shaffer and Karl-Heinz Schoeps, 10.
241–53
Büchner, Karl, ed., *Latein und Europa*,
review by Arnaldo Momigliano, 3.
259–68
Bulgakov, Mikhail/Saratov Academic Theatre
of Drama, *The White Guard*, stage
adaptation by Aleksandr Dzekun and
Olga Kharitonova, review by Lesley
Milne, 14. 233–57
Butler, Christopher, *Early Modernism:
Literature, Music and Painting in Europe,
1900–1916*, review by J. J. White, 18.
243–50

Charles, Michel, *Rhétorique de la lecture*,
review by Peter France, 3. 269–77
Chatman, Seymour, *Story and Discourse:
Narrative Structure in Fiction and Film*,
review by Frank Kermode, 2. 291–301
Chen Xiaomei, *Occidentalism: a Theory of
Counter-discourse in Post-Mao China*,
review by Douwe Fokkema, 18. 227–42
Clements, Patricia, *Baudelaire and the English
Tradition*, review by Clive Scott, 10.
267–85
Constantine, David, *Hölderlin*, review by
Mark Ogden, 12, 273–81
Corngold, Stanley, *The Fate of the Self:
German Writers and French Theory*,
review by Mark Ogden, 12. 273–81
Culler, Jonathan, *On Deconstruction: Theory
and Criticism after Structuralism*, review
by Stephen Heath, 9. 281–326
Cunningham, Andrew and Nicholas Jardine,
eds., *Romanticism and the Sciences*,
review by Roy Porter, 13. 273–76

Davie, Donald, *A Gathered Church: the
Literature of Dissenting Interest,
1700–1930*, the Clark Lectures 1976,
review by Elinor Shaffer, 1. 311–16
de Beauvoir, Simone, *The Second Sex*, review
by Nicole Ward Jouve, 9. 327–43
Derrida, Jacques, *The Truth in Painting*,
trans. Geoff Bennington and Ian
McLeod, review by Christopher Norris,
11. 235–51
Detienne, Marcel, *The Gardens of Adonis*,
trans. Janet Lloyd, review by Richard
Gordon, 1. 279–310
Detienne, M., L. Gernet, J.-P. Vernant and
P. Vidal-Naquet, *Myth, Religion and
Society: Structuralist Essays*, ed. R. L
Gordon, review by Riccardo di Donato
(trans. Jesper Svenbro), 5. 333–41
Docherty, Thomas, *After Theory: Post
Modernism/Post Marxism*, review by
Nick Kaye, 14. 217–26
Dyersinck, Hugo, ed., *Internationale
Bibliographie zur Geschichte und Theorie
der Komparatistik*, review by Glyn Tegai
Hughes, 8. 301–6

Eagleton, Terry, *Literary Theory: an
Introduction*, review by Stephen Heath,
9. 281–326
Etiemble, René, *L'Europe chinoise*, vol. I, *De
l'empire romain à Leibnitz*, vol. II, *De la*

363

Index of bibliographies

Annual bibliographies of comparative literature in Britain and Ireland appear in volumes 1–20. After volume 20 the bibliography was compiled on-line on the British Comparative Literature Association website (www.bcla.org) by Duncan Large. In the list that follows, the years covered by the bibliographies are indicated first.

Cumulative bibliographies of comparative literature in Britain and Ireland appear as follows:

Special bibliographies